# Global Governance of Food Production and Consumption

## Issues and Challenges

Peter Oosterveer

*Environmental Policy Group*
*Wageningen University, The Netherlands*

**Edward Elgar**
Cheltenham, UK • Northampton, MA, USA

Published by
Edward Elgar Publishing Limited
Glensanda House
Montpellier Parade
Cheltenham
Glos GL50 1UA
UK

Edward Elgar Publishing, Inc.
William Pratt House
9 Dewey Court
Northampton
Massachusetts 01060
USA

A catalogue record for this book
is available from the British Library

Library of Congress Control Number: 2007920111

ISBN: 978 1 84542 938 6

Printed and bound in Great Britain by MPG Books Ltd, Bodmin, Cornwall

# Contents

# Figures

# Tables

# Boxes

# Glossary

| | |
|---|---|
| BSE | Bovine Spongiform Encephalopathy |
| Bt | Bacillus thuringiensis |
| CAAR | Coastal Alliance for Aquacultural Reform |
| CAP | Common Agricultural Policy (EU) |
| CBD | Convention on Biodiversity |
| CP | Charoen Popkhand |
| EC | European Commission |
| EEZ | Exclusive Economic Zone |
| EFSA | European Food Safety Authority |
| EPA | Environmental Protection Agency (US) |
| EU | European Union |
| FAO | Food and Agriculture Organisation of the United Nations |
| FDA | Food and Drugs Administration (US) |
| FEAP | Federation of European Aquaculture Producers |
| FLO | Fair Trade Labelling Organisation |
| FMD | Foot and Mouth Disease |
| FSA | Food Standards Organisation (UK) |
| GAA | Global Aquaculture Alliance |
| GATT | General Agreement on Tariffs and Trade |
| GDP | Gross Domestic Product |
| GEM | Global Environmental Mechanism |
| GM | Genetically Modified |
| GMO | Genetically Modified Organism |
| GMP | Good Management Practices |
| HACCP | Hazard Accident Critical Control Point |
| ICA | International Coffee Agreement |
| ICO | International Coffee Organisation |
| IFOAM | International Federation of Organic Agriculture Movements |
| IMF | International Monetary Fund |
| IPPC | International Plant Protection Commission |
| ISO | International Standardisation Organisation |
| LCA | Life-Cycle Analysis |
| MAFF | Ministry of Agriculture, Food and Fisheries (UK) |

| MBM | Meat and Bone Meal |
| MEA | Multilateral Environmental Agreement |
| MMPA | Marine Mammal Protection Act |
| MPA | Medroxyprogesterone-acetate |
| MSC | Marine Stewardship Council |
| NGO | Non-Governmental Organisation |
| OCA | Organic Consumers Association (US) |
| OECD | Organisation for Economic Cooperation and Development |
| OIE | Organisation Internationale des Epizootiques |
| PCB | Polychlorinated Biphenyl |
| SPS | Sanitary and Phytosanitary Measures |
| TBT | Technical Barrier to Trade |
| TNC | Transnational Corporation |
| TSE | Transmissible Spongiform Encephalopathy |
| UK | United Kingdom |
| UN | United Nations |
| UNCED | United Nations Conference on Environment and Development |
| UNCTAD | United Nations Conference on Trade and Development |
| US | United States |
| USDA | United States Department of Agriculture |
| vCJD | variant Creutzfeld-Jacobs Disease |
| WCED | World Commission on Environment and Development |
| WFP | World Food Program |
| WHO | World Health Organisation |
| WSSD | World Summit on Sustainable Development |
| WTO | World Trade Organisation |
| WWF | World Wildlife Fund |

# Preface

When I started the research that forms the basis for this book, food producers, consumers and governments in Western Europe were trying to adjust to the BSE crisis, and while I am finishing the research, the world is attempting to understand and deal with bird flu. During the six years between these moments, nearly all countries have been confronted with crises about the safety of food or about the environmental risks in using particular production or processing methods. The subject of this book therefore fits well into the contemporary public and political debates in many developed countries. Concerns about food, particularly its health and environmental impacts, figure almost daily in the media. The objective of this study is to offer a consistent scientific reflection on one of the most challenging questions in contemporary societies: 'how to organise the provisioning of safe food in a sustainable manner'.

This book is based on a PhD thesis, defended at Wageningen University in June 2005. Within this project, several empirical case studies were completed in combination with reflection on different relevant theoretical viewpoints and ongoing academic debates. I would like to express my gratitude to all those who contributed to this research: to Gert Spaargaren, a friend since the early days of studying sociology in Wageningen, and Arthur Mol, whom I got to know and respect during my PhD research working at the Environmental Policy Group of Wageningen University and to all permanent and temporary colleagues from the Environmental Policy Group, who supported my work, provided comments and offered a very pleasant working environment. Thanks also to the many experts, whose names are listed in the annex, who agreed to be interviewed and to answer the sometimes difficult questions that contributed to the empirical foundation of this thesis.

The 'Giddens circle' deserves a special word of thanks. Rien Munters initiated this reading circle in the 1970s to encourage the study of and the reflection on contemporary sociological theory, and the group has survived until this very day. Although its composition has changed over the years, the 'Giddens circle' remained for me a stimulating environment for reflection on the work of modern social theorists. Without the intensive discussions on social theory in this group, I would never have been able to bridge the gap between 1982 and 2000, the years when I was not actively engaged in academic work.

Preparing a publication involves many different tasks. These have been accomplished thanks to the practical support from Corry Rothuizen (who provided general assistance on many occasions), Susan Parren (who corrected the English language in several chapters) and Alexandra Milton, senior editor at Edward Elgar. I would like to express my gratitude to two anonymous reviewers who offered extensive and detailed comments on the first draft of this book.

A special word of thanks goes to my parents, Giel and Bep, for their support over so many years. As is the custom, an acknowledgement concludes with the direct family. Although I did try to limit the social inconveniences of working on this book to a minimum, I know that on occasions they have suffered the consequences. Suzanne, Hanne, Tim, Micheline and Lise, thank you very much for being so considerate during these years. I hope that the future will bring many opportunities to make up for at least some of the missed moments.

# 1. Introduction

Two apples a penny! Two for a penny!
His gaze passed over the glaze apples serried on her stand. Australians they must
be this time of year. Shiny peels: polishes them up with a rag or a handkerchief.
(James Joyce, 2000, *Ulysses*, London, Penguin Books: 192)

'Yes, we have fair trade bananas'
Growing up, I often rode shotgun with my father on grocery runs, which often
included scouring Toronto's supermarkets for the cheapest bananas.
Born before the Depression, my father knew 'the value of a dollar' and delighted
in finding the best buy. ... This was in the good old days, before recycling, before the hole in the ozone layer and before fair trade bananas Now, the most socially conscious Canadian consumers demand to know where what they eat
comes from, how it was grown and whose hands helped to bring it to the table.
... Wholesale, there's a floor price on fair trade bananas, as well as a premium of
$1.75 (U.S.) a crate, which goes toward grass roots social programs, such as edu-
cation, health care and housing, in the banana producing countries. Regular bananas have a bruised background by comparison. ... Fair trade bananas 'with
their social justice flavour' appeal to people who are eager to be good global citizens, not just find a good price. Many fleece-clad Vancouverites fit this bill. ...
And just how much are these customers prepared to pay for the black and white
sticker on their breakfast snack? The current price is $1.55 a pound.
My father would be aghast.
(Austin MacDonald, *The Globe and Mail*, 5 June, 2004)

## INTRODUCTION

The organisation of food production and consumption has changed dramatically over the last 30 years or so as more and more food is transported all
over the globe. However, what are the environmental impacts and health
consequences of such globalised food provisioning? Can the conventional
nation-state-based regulation adequately deal with these environmental and
food safety risks in the changing circumstances? Alternatively, are alternative instruments required to address the previously unknown food risks that
seem to develop at an increasingly faster rate, such as BSE, dioxins and GM
food? Should contemporary consumer worries about their food be considered a concern for psychologists, or does responding to them require drastic

changes in modern society's organisation of its food supply? What would such regulatory tools be and in what ways could different groups in society become involved?

These challenging questions make up the subject matter of this book. It explores ways in which problems associated with the organisation of contemporary food production and consumption (particularly environmental and health) are conceptualised and regulated. Before presenting the central questions to be addressed in this study and the theoretical notions constituting its conceptual framework, this chapter will provide some necessary background information. In the following section, I will elaborate the recent phenomenon of globalisation in food production and consumption. This will be followed by an overview of the environmental and health concerns related to this transition. Then, the challenges these environmental and food safety problems pose to governments, private actors and consumers will be reviewed more in depth. The central questions for this study will be presented in the fifth section and the final section will provide an outline of the remainder of this book and introduce the different chapters.

## GLOBALISATION OF FOOD PRODUCTION AND CONSUMPTION

Many observers consider food to be something special, not just as any other category of commodities. Particularly its organic character makes food special and this is clearly expressed in the 'necessary presence of the "natural" at both the beginning and the end of the systems of food provision – both in agriculture and in palatability' (Fine, 1998: 8). The organic (or biological) nature of food has implications throughout the entire food system in terms of quality, value and risk. 'Food is a liminal substance ... bridging ... nature and culture, the human and the natural, the outside and the inside' (Atkinson, 1983: 11).[1] In the same manner, Beardsworth and Keil (1997) highlight the 'omnivore's paradox', pointing to the fact that all omnivores (including humans) experience the opposing pulls of the inclination to sample novel food items and caution when confronted with novel items, as they may be harmful. Throughout human history this organic character, exemplified in the different agricultural seasons, the natural conditions for food production (soil, climate, and so on) and the physical need of every human being to consume food daily, has created the basis for, sometimes long distance, trade in food. Therefore, food trade has existed since the first agricultural activities although the actual trade practices have altered continuously over the years. Recently the magnitude of international food trade as well as its structure is again undergoing fundamental changes. Over the last decades, the growth in the volume of the world trade in agricultural products (including food) has been impressive, and despite a consistent downward trend in the world market prices for most agricultural commodities the total value of trade has expanded at the same time, except for the most recent years.[2] (See Table 1.1.)

*Table 1.1   World exports in agricultural products (index: 1990 = 100)*

| Agricultural products | 1992 | 1994 | 1996 | 1997 | 1998 | 1999 | 2000 | 2001 |
|---|---|---|---|---|---|---|---|---|
| Volume world production | 103 | 106 | 113 | 116 | 117 | 121 | 122 | 123 |
| Volume world export | 110 | 120 | 130 | 137 | 140 | 141 | 147 | 149 |
| Unit value | 99 | 100 | 112 | 104 | 97 | 93 | 89 | 88 |
| Value world exports | 108 | 119 | 145 | 143 | 136 | 131 | 132 | 131 |

*Source:* WTO (2002), table A1: 167.

The total value of global food exports in 2000 was estimated by the World Trade Organisation (WTO) at 442.3 billion US$, representing 9 per cent of the world's total merchandise trade and 40.7 per cent of the world's exports in primary products (WTO, 2001).[3] Despite these impressive figures and despite the global character of food trade in general, in fact only a very limited number of countries dominate the international trade in food products.[4]

*Table 1.2   Top 15 food exporting and importing countries (2000)*

| Exporters | Value ($bn) | Share in world (%) | Importers | Value ($bn) | Share in world (%) |
|---|---|---|---|---|---|
| USA | 70.87 | 12.7 | USA | 66.69 | 11.0 |
| France | 36.52 | 6.5 | Japan | 62.19 | 10.3 |
| Canada | 34.79 | 6.2 | Germany | 41.54 | 6.9 |
| Netherlands | 34.14 | 6.1 | UK | 32.49 | 5.4 |
| Germany | 27.76 | 5.0 | France | 30.39 | 5.0 |
| Belgium | 19.86 | 3.6 | Italy | 29.39 | 4.9 |
| Spain | 16.88 | 3.0 | Netherlands | 20.90 | 3.5 |
| UK | 16.67 | 3.0 | China | 19.54 | 3.2 |
| China | 16.38 | 2.9 | Belgium | 18.52 | 3.1 |
| Australia | 16.37 | 2.9 | Spain | 16.98 | 2.8 |
| Italy | 16.09 | 2.9 | Canada | 15.27 | 2.5 |
| Brazil | 15.47 | 2.8 | Korea, Rep. | 12.99 | 2.1 |
| Thailand | 13.28 | 2.4 | Hong Kong, China | 11.73 | 1.9 |
| Argentina | 11.97 | 2.2 | Mexico | 11.06 | 1.8 |
| Denmark | 10.94 | 2.0 | Russia | 9.87 | 1.6 |

*Source:* WTO (2001), table IV 7, includes intra-EU trade.

The US, France and a few other (mostly) developed countries are responsible for about 60 per cent of both global food exports and imports. (See Table 1.2.)

Notwithstanding the rapid growth in global food trade, most food still is consumed domestically in the country where it was originally produced, except for a limited number of tropical crops like coffee, cocoa and palm oil. (See Table 1.3.)[5]

*Table 1.3   Approximate share of world production traded across borders*

| Product | Production share traded internationally (%) |
| --- | --- |
| Coffee | 80 |
| Tea | 40 |
| Soybeans | 30 |
| Sugar | 30 |
| Bananas | 20 |
| Wheat | 17 |
| Food grains | 11 |
| Rice | 6 |

*Source:* Einarsson (2000) based on USDA, FAO and World Bank sources.

Some agricultural products are traded globally in large quantities but these exports only represent a small percentage of their total production. Wheat, for example, is the world's largest export crop among the cereals, but only 17 per cent of the global wheat production is exported. The remaining 83 per cent is consumed in the producing countries themselves. The US, Australia and Canada have two-thirds of total exports between them and almost 80 per cent of the exported wheat goes to developing countries. In the case of rice, only 6 per cent of the global production is exported, but interestingly, this trade is not dominated by developed countries but by Thailand, Vietnam and China, and 90 per cent of the rice is imported by other developing countries such as Indonesia, the Philippines, Bangladesh, Iran and Brazil. Today, coffee, a tropical crop that has been traded internationally for a long time, is mainly produced in Brazil, Vietnam and Colombia, while the US and the EU remain the principal importing countries. Trade in soybeans is particularly fascinating because it occupies the middle ground between coffee and cereals, with an export share of around 30 per cent. The US produces well over half of the soybeans exported and Brazil, Argentina and Paraguay almost cover the rest. The EU buys about half of the soybeans traded worldwide while Japan, Korea and Taiwan import the remaining part.[6] Meat is exported in growing quantities, facilitated by global cooling chains which allow long distance trading. Nevertheless, meat exports still represent less than 10 per cent of the total world production. The export is almost completely in the hands of a rather small group of developed countries, split differently according to the particular meat product concerned: beef (US, Canada, EU, Australia, New Zealand, Argentina, Brazil and Uruguay); pork (EU, US and Canada); lamb (Australia and New Zealand), and poultry (US and EU). The larger importing countries are Japan, Russia and China, also varying according to the particular type of meat concerned (Einarsson, 2000: 10–12). Fish is traded heavily as well, reaching to around 33 per cent of the total world fish production in 2000 with a value of US$55.2 billion. Moreover, this trade is still increasing. Thailand was the leading exporter (US$4.4 billion) in 2000, while Japan was the main importer (US$12.8 billion). In terms of volume, only a few fish products dominate the international fisheries trade: shrimp (both cultured and wild), tuna, fishmeal and fish oil. In contrast to most other food products, the prices of fresh and frozen fish have shown a long-term increase in real terms since the Second World War. (See also Chapter 7.)

An interesting observation is that trade in processed foods for the first time outstripped the trade in unprocessed agricultural products in the years 2001–02. This is consistent with a broader trend in world trade – a shift to an increasing share of manufactured products at the expense of primary ones (UNCTAD, 2004). Thus, despite the fact that sometimes only a limited share of the total quantity of food produced is traded globally, this share will most likely rise in the near future, particularly through the rapid growth in the trade of processed food products. Globalisation in all stages of the food supply chain will continue to become a more important trait in the daily lives of producers and consumers (Clay, 2004).

The (relative) quantities of food and food products traded globally are growing, but simultaneously the organisation of international food trade is changing. In particular, the increasingly central role of retailers, global brands and consumers at the expense of local food producers and food processors is remarkable (Lang, 2003). It is no longer very meaningful to approach global food trade as if this only concerns the export of agricultural products from one country to another. Global food trade has become more and more an integrative element of globalised food supply chains whereby raw materials produced by agriculture are used as inputs for the food processing industry and subsequently transported to supermarkets, and whereby national borders have become irrelevant to a large extent. Consumers in Western countries choose food in the supermarkets based on price, quality, quantity and trust.[7] In an average American supermarket, where new products are added every day, they have to make their choices among 12,000 (mostly food) products coming from all over the world (Busch, 1997). Many food products are transformed technically as well as socially and culturally during this process of globalisation. For example, the tortilla, which started as the staple food of the Mayan and Aztec people in Latin America, became a fast food component of the diets of many twenty-first century Americans and Europeans (Lind and Barham, 2004).

Therefore, the quantities of food products that are traded globally are growing. At the same time, the organisation of this trade is changing and these transitions result in global food supply networks. These fundamental changes, taking place over the last decades, have had radical impacts in different domains.

## ENVIRONMENTAL AND FOOD SAFETY IMPACTS OF GLOBALISING FOOD PRODUCTION AND CONSUMPTION

Concerns about environmental, social and human health impacts of food production and consumption seem to have become increasingly important in the everyday lives of consumers, political authorities, NGOs and private corporations in most developed countries. For this reason, these food-related social concerns should be of special interest for social scientists. Although the origin of these concerns may vary, nowadays they are generally closely associated with the process of globalisation. In particular, environmental problems and food safety concerns have contributed to sometimes intensive public debates about the global provisioning of food and are used to justify proposals for radical reforms in food policies and practices.

Very different kinds of environmental problems have raised public concerns during the last 30–40 years repeatedly resulting in changing food production and consumption routines. Some of these concerns are directly related to primary food production itself, such as soil erosion, the widespread use of pesticides and fertilisers, the presence of different pollutants from industry in the natural environment, the declining attractiveness of the countryside, reduction of biodiversity and the unethical treatment of farm animals (Kirchmann and Thorvaldsson, 2000; Horrigan et al., 2002).[8] Other public concerns, such as the large quantities of waste produced and the energy necessary for food transport over long distances (so-called 'food miles'), are more related to distribution and consumption practices (OECD, 2001, 2002).[9] Critical environmental problems are furthermore related to food-processing industries, such as air and water pollution, the large quantities of solid (often organic) waste produced and the considerable amounts of energy used in these industries (Oosterveer, 2004).[10]

Globalising food supply chains are often considered the cause of threats for the safety of the food itself.[11] For example, the growth in international food trade has meant that pathogens that were once confined to a particular geographical region can now travel around the world on aeroplanes in a matter of hours (see the examples of bird flu in Asia in 2004 and 2005, and foot-and-mouth disease in the UK in 2003). In addition, mistakes in the production or processing stages of food may have wide-ranging consequences, like dioxins in chicken (1999) and medroxyprogesterone-acetate (MPA) in pigs (2002). (See Box 2.3 in Chapter 2.) The centralised nature of the contemporary food distribution system thus exposes far greater numbers of people over wider geographical areas to contaminated products than in the past (Woteki et al., 2001), which may result in considerable economic impacts. The discovery of the first case of BSE in the US in 2003, and the following trade restrictions by Japan, resulted for example in an immediate 18 per cent decline in the beef exports from the US to Japan (Leuck et al., 2004). In reaction, food safety issues are used by larger industrial food processors as a tool to increase their market share using means of private governance, thereby shifting responsibilities from the food processing firms to the farmer (Busch, 1997). Global competition between large industrial food processors and food retailers may also reduce the scope for different national food safety politics.[12] Whether the food safety risks resulting from the globalisation in food provisioning actually lead to more casualties remains extremely hard to determine because it proves rather difficult to establish the exact number of victims from contaminated food (Nestle, 2003).[13] Yet, food safety issues seem to have a serious bearing on consumer behaviour and thereby inevitably also on governance arrangements dealing with food production, processing and trade (Frewer, 2004).[14] Increasingly, governments come under pressure to introduce more effective forms of food safety governance.[15] National governments often try to respond to global transformations in food production and consumption with the help of rapid information exchange and strengthened international co-ordination to achieve better control over (potentially) contagious animal diseases and food risks.[16] Despite these attempts to increase governmental control over food supply, the increasing number of food safety incidents and scandals seems only to incite public concerns, which leads to discussions about the necessary regulatory policy change. Opinions differ very much, however, on the content and on the ways in which to establish adequate new regulatory regimes (Tickell and Peck, 1995). The cases of Bovine Spongiform Encephalopathy (BSE), or 'mad cow disease', and genetically modified food are interesting examples of the changing and global character of food risks and these crises and their related policy debates will be analysed in Chapters 4 and 5 respectively.

## GOVERNING ENVIRONMENTAL AND FOOD SAFETY RISKS

Repeatedly, the existing regulatory mechanisms managed by national governments are confronted with public pressure to deal more effectively with the emerging food safety and environmental problems. The conventional nation-state-based regulation of food risks seems no longer able to deal adequately with the newly emerging consumer concerns. Until recently, the recommendations from natural science research seemed to provide an undisputed basis for this conventional, or standard, risk politics, but it looks like public trust in science and experts is diminishing as food risks are evolving within global modernity. Familiar food safety problems, such as *Salmonella* and *E. coli*, seem to increase in frequency and intensify, while new and unknown food safety risks (or concerns), like BSE and genetically modified food, emerge and spread rapidly over the globe. Environmental concerns, such as the use of pesticides in food production, the large number of food miles involved in transport and the threats to animal welfare in modern intensive practices of animal husbandry, all seem to intensify in the context of global food trade and to challenge the existing governmental regulations dealing with food production and consumption. Not only new problems and concerns about food, but also new social actors are exerting pressure on conventional regulatory practices. More and more (groups of) citizens, consumers, producers and retailers are expressing their worries about environmental and food safety risks and take initiatives to intervene actively in the governance of food. The growing consumer demand for organically grown food and fair trade commodities forms a clear indication of the intensification of consumer concerns about food and the willingness from consumers to find practical solutions to their concerns.[17]

The consequence of these changing risks and the involvement of more and different social actors in food governance is a proliferation of different regulatory responses.[18] Traditionally, environmental and food safety regulation was the singular responsibility of nation-state governments, sometimes supplemented with international agreements. National laws and regulations were introduced and implemented in combination with institutions for supervision and control. Globalisation puts this regulatory regime under severe pressure because harmonisation of different national regulations is necessary to facilitate global trade. At the same time, this nation-state-based regulatory response is confronted with different alternative market-based and privately initiated forms of governance dealing with these evolving food risks and consumer concerns in a different manner (Henson and Caswell, 1999). The declining public trust in the standard (natural) science-based risk politics further complicates conventional regulation. The result of these trends is the emergence of several competing regulatory regimes which differ in dimensions such as the scale (local, national, regional, global), the concerns included (health, environment, ethics, and so on), the extent to which they are market- or legal-based, public or privately organised and in what way they involve consumers.

## CENTRAL QUESTION

Innovative food governance arrangements, currently in the making, are meant to supplement or replace existing national governmental regulations addressing food-related environmental and health concerns. However, many aspects of such innovative governance arrangements remain unclear, conceptually as well as empirically. How can governance outside the conventional nation-state be understood within the context of globalisation? In addition, if conventional nation-state-based regulatory practices are no longer capable of adequately dealing with food concerns, should other forms of governance replaced them completely? Alternatively, can they still perform essential roles on the condition that they are supplemented by other regulatory mechanisms? What will be the future roles of scientific arguments, public interest and citizen participation in the decision-making practices developed through different innovative governance arrangements? In addition, can different concerns (environmental, health, ethical and social) be combined in one particular form of governance arrangement and, if so, in what way? How can innovative governance arrangements in food production and consumption deal with the continuous interaction between local and global level dynamics? How would such innovative governance arrangements function in practice, in particular in relation to the conventional nation-state-based arrangements? These are all key questions with regard to the current transitions in governing food, which require further study through empirical and conceptual reflection. *The central objective of this study is therefore to identify innovative governance arrangements in relation to food production, processing and consumption and to review if and in what way they deal with existing, evolving and emerging environmental and consumer health concerns more adequately than the conventional nation-state-based regulatory practices.*

Answering this question requires a combination of theoretical conceptualisation and empirical research. The remainder of this book will therefore be dedicated to the identification of possible responses to this central question and to attempts to increase our comprehension of the related social dynamics that affect many people's everyday lives when they produce, process, sell or consume food.

## OUTLINE

This book can be divided in two parts. The first part, comprising chapters 1, 2, 3 and 4, provides the theoretical and conceptual background for analysing the central question presented above. Social science literature on globalisation, food risks and food consumption is reviewed in Chapter 2 in order to position this study in the wider field of social analysis of food production and consumption and to identify the key challenges facing conventional nation-state-based regulation of food in the changing context of globalising food supply networks. Understanding the dynamics of contemporary food governance and analysing alternative arrangements require the use of new conceptual frameworks. This goal will be pursued in Chapter 3, where I will try to build on recent innovative thinking in social theory. In particular, Manuel Castells' concept of 'the global network society' and John Urry's notion of 'global complexity' seem promising tools to grasp some of this new phenomenon's relevance better. Although this study essentially consists of a search for innovative governance responses, these new responses cannot be understood without recognising the continued role of nation-state-based governmental regulatory practices. Therefore, Chapter 4 will offer background information about existing government-based regulations of food, both at national and international (EU and WTO) levels.

The second part, covering chapters 5–8, will present the results of four case studies. These cases were selected to gather concrete insights into the transition towards new regulatory arrangements and the social dynamics involved. The first case study in Chapter 5 deals with the ways in which BSE (or 'mad cow disease') and the regulatory responses to it have been publicly debated between 1985 and 2000 in the EU and in the US in 2003. The review of public debates will be combined with the changes this particular food crisis has brought in (thinking about as well as practices in) risk politics. The BSE crisis has become a model case of the changing food safety risks in contemporary western societies and often commentators refer to this crisis when discussing newly emerging food risks and the need for innovative forms of (food) risk politics. Chapter 6 reviews the production of genetically modified food (GM food) because, since the mid-1990s, GM food has been at the centre of many public manifestations and intense political debates, as well as a topic of extensive scientific research. The objective of this chapter is to compare the public debate and the official regulation of GM food in the US with the situation in Europe. This comparison will provide particular insights into the tensions between a demand for detailed and specific national government-based food regulations and the need for uniform global arrangements to facilitate international food trade. After these two case studies reviewing different public worries about food and the challenges facing political decision-making in the field of food governance, the next two chapters will identify and examine innovative governance arrangements and practices. Chapter 7 analyses aquaculture because this way of producing fish for an increasing demand on the global market has given rise to serious public concerns about its environmental and health impact. Controversies surrounding modern aquacultural practices are reviewed by looking into salmon raising and shrimp farming with a focus on Thailand. Different initiatives taken by producer organisations and nation-state authorities attempting to deal with these concerns are discussed whereby particular attention is given to the extent to which they involve consumers. The final case study deals with the labelling of food and forms the content of Chapter 8, as labelling seems to have become one of the most attractive tools in the eyes of many NGOs and other private organisations to deal with the social and environmental impacts of globalising food supply. More and more food products are offered to consumers accompanied by information about the production process and production circumstances involved, such as whether the food product has been produced in a more environmentally friendly manner or produced by farmers and agricultural workers under socially acceptable circumstances. Examples of food labels such as the Marine Stewardship Council (MSC) for fish and the Fair Trade label for coffee will be studied in this chapter, and they will be compared with the existing, more conventional regulatory mechanisms.

Chapter 9, finally, resumes the discussion on the central question formulated above and summarises the main findings from the different case studies. This chapter concludes with some reflections about future prospects for governance practices attempting to deal with the environmental and health impacts of food production and consumption in global modernity.

## NOTES

1. The organic character of food is often used to explain developments in the sector. For example, Boyd and Watts (1997) suggest that the specific nature of 'just-in-time' practices in the US broiler industry derives in particular from the organic qualities of the product.
2. The quantity of food exported increased fourfold between 1961 and 1999 from 190 million metric tonnes to 774 million tonnes. By 2000 more than one out of ten food products was exported, representing a total value of US\$ 256 billion (Millstone and Lang, 2003: 60).
3. Among the agricultural products traded globally, the total value of trade in more luxury food products, like fresh fruits and vegetables in particular, has shown a very marked increase over the last years (FAO, statistics database (http://apps.fao.org).
4. At the same time, the persistent problem of hunger in many (particularly African) countries should not be ignored (Gupta, 2004).

5. McMichael (2000) for example claims that roughly 90 per cent of the world's food consumption occurs in the country where it is produced. Sixty per cent of the food is consumed by the rural population that produces it, whereas urbanites largely (90 per cent) depend on the market. Only about one-fifth of the world's almost six billion people actually participate in the cash economy.

6. Recently soybean production and processing is shifting away from mature markets, such as the US, to emerging markets, such as Brazil and Argentina. Since the early 1990s, the US share of world soybean production has declined steadily from about 50 per cent to less than 40 per cent, while Brazil's share increased to 25 per cent and Argentina's to 15 per cent (http://www.foodnavigator.com/news)(accessed 11 December 2003).

7. An example of globalised food chains is the production of concentrated animal feed in Western Europe. The composition of this fodder is based on several general indicators (proteins, energy, and so on) while the exact composition (what products from which country are actually put into the feed) may differ from day to day depending on the availability of different products and their relative prices.

8. The environmental impact of food production should not be approached in a simplistic way, for example IFPRI (2002: 23) observes that 'it is commonly thought that intensification of agricultural production usually leads to environmental degradation. [However], in most developing countries too little intensification is a major cause of natural resource degradation, as desperately poor farmers mine soil fertility and climb the hillsides in an effort to survive. ... Agricultural development, poverty reduction, and environmental sustainability are likely to go hand in hand when agricultural development is broad-based, market-driven, participatory and decentralised, and driven by appropriate technological change that enhances productivity.'

9. Large retailing firms are often held responsible for these environmental problems because of their decisions on packaging food in supermarkets and because they decide to transport food products from all over the globe. Nevertheless, they can also become a potential leverage for changes in agri-food chains. Konefal et al. (2003) observed contradictory tendencies in the food retail sector, where on the one hand concentration tendencies led to a global oligopoly in the sector, while on the other hand increased consumer pressure has resulted in incentives for food retailers to incorporate social and ecological attributes into their production practices.

10. The analysis of the environmental effects of agro-industrialisation by Barrett et al. (2001) goes beyond the consequences generally associated with this process. They conclude that 'vertical co-ordination through contracting or organisational integration permits downstream interests to exert unprecedented influence over farming practices in which they are not directly engaged' (p. 423). This influence may have negative environmental effects, for example, when aesthetic requirements stimulate increases in pesticide use. On the other hand, vertical co-ordination in agro-food chains may also induce environmentally friendly practices in order to get premium prices. The resulting net effect of this influence from agro-industries remains, according to the authors, an issue of empirical verification. Interestingly, larger corporations seem to be more inclined to introduce voluntary compliance than smaller firms do because they are more susceptible to official monitoring and to public scrutiny endangering their brand image.

11. See, for example, 'the pollution of ecosystems, the growth of genetic engineering of food products and the absorption of chemicals into the bodies of producers and consumers of food mean that there are ethical connectivities between actors at one location in the chain and those at other sites' (Leslie and Reimer, 1999: 408).

12. The fact that developing countries are allowed until the year 2015 to phase out methyl bromide use in agriculture contrary to developed countries, which had to achieve this already by 2005, led to serious trade concerns among US farmers. Rodger Wasson, president of the California Strawberry Commission, complains that 'the 50-acre grower in California may be competing with a multinational corporation based in China who gets to use the product 10 years longer' (*Environment News Service*, 23 March 2004).

13. The *Toronto Globe and Mail* reported on 15 October 2002, 'about 20 per cent of the food we eat is contaminated with trace amounts of pesticides, even though most of them have been banned for decades … such as DDT and dieldrin'.
14. However, despite the global character of food safety concerns, consumer trust may differ considerably per country without being directly correlated to food safety problems. For example, in Europe consumers in the UK express high levels of trust in the safety of food although the country has known several serious problems in this domain (Poppe and Kjaernes, 2003).
15. For example during the whole of 2004 the Dutch food safety agency analysed only 140 samples of lettuce and 41 samples of fresh spinach for nitrates, while fulfilling its obligation for the EU (Keuringsdienst van Waren, 2005). These numbers are infinitesimal in comparison to the total quantities of these produces that are traded and consumed annually.
16. See Maxwell and Slater (2003) for an insightful and detailed comparison between 'old' and 'new' food policy.
17. Market analyst Mintel reports a 75 per cent increase in spending in the UK on ethically produced food, rising to £1.75 billion in 2003 (Novis, press report, 23 April 2004).
18. Some observers consider these latest institutional innovations from private firms as aimed at further disciplining producers, suppliers, workers and consumers when agro-food networks become ever more transnationally dispersed. These standards not only define product attributes but also production practices, handling requirements and distribution guidelines (Konefal et al., 2003).

# 2. Current debates on global food governance

## INTRODUCTION

Governing food production and consumption is becoming a complex challenge at the beginning of the twenty-first century compared with the situation in the 1950s because contemporary societies have witnessed several fundamental changes. These transitions are reflected within the social sciences. Societies in this so-called 'second modernity' can no longer be understood with the help of sociological concepts developed during the first, or 'simple', modernity (Beck and Willms, 2004). New concepts are necessary to deal adequately with the drastic social changes that have occurred towards the end of the twentieth century. Simple modernity was predominantly conceptualised as a logic of structures, whereby the concept of 'society' coincided with the boundaries of the nation-state and where society and nature could be clearly distinguished. In this perspective, progress was defined as development based on technical rationality, presuming that broader and deeper knowledge would enable more and more natural and social phenomena to be better controlled by humans. Global modernity has undermined this clear and promising image. In particular, the assumption that further rationalisation in combination with a fully implemented nation-state-based governance system guarantees progressive reduction of risks can no longer be considered valid. The disruption of this 'simple modern' view on the process of modernisation also questions several basic elements in the conceptualisation of food governance. Therefore, understanding contemporary food governance requires conceptual tools that better fit the problems facing the transforming globalising food production and consumption practices, such as the emergence of new food risks and the shifting role of the nation-states in governing international food trade. Elaborating such a much-needed new conceptual model will be the subject of the following chapter. In this chapter, I shall review several of the key changes that constitute the principal challenges that nowadays face the conventional, nation-state-based, or simple modern, governance practices dealing with food production and consumption in the context of global modernity, notably:

- the changing position of the nation-state in the context of globalisation,
- the disappearance of the clear distinction between the public and the private sphere,
- the inadequacy of conventional science-based risk politics in dealing with food risks in global modernity as well as with different other emerging food-related consumer concerns,
- the growing involvement of non-state social actors in food governance, in particular consumers and NGOs.

The next section will first summarise the key characteristics of conventional, nation-state-based practices applied to food governance. In the following four sections the principal societal changes that put pressure on this, until recently undisputed, form of governance are reviewed. The third section examines the process of globalisation because, as the first chapter has already indicated, the rapid transition towards globalised food provisioning puts growing pressure on the existing nation-state-based food governance practices. The fourth section reviews the literature on different forms of governance relevant for identifying possible options for governing global food. New and transforming food risks, the topic of the fifth section, are challenging the existing governance arrangements that seem increasingly unable to deal with them satisfactorily. Understanding the particular and structural traits of food-related risks in global modernity as well as the identification of promising alternative arrangements to govern them more adequately makes the involvement of the social sciences indispensable. Particularly striking are the active roles taken up by other than the conventional actors in governance, in particular the growing involvement of consumers and their organisations (see the sixth section). The different dynamics and challenges confronting governance of food in global modernity, reviewed in this chapter, will be summarised in the concluding section in order to guide the search for innovative governance arrangements, which will be our task in the next chapters.

## CONVENTIONAL FOOD GOVERNANCE

Conventional, or simple modern, governance of food is based essentially on the assignment of strictly separated tasks and responsibilities to government and science. This division of tasks reflects the familiar clear distinction between 'nature' and 'society' and division between public and private responsibilities. Although conventional food governance practices have been further detailed and expanded tremendously over the last 30 years or so, this approach seems nevertheless no longer adequate at the beginning of the twenty-first century.

Food risks have always made up a very sensitive category of risks because food is intimately associated with everyday life and the physical survival of human beings (Fine, 1998). Governing food production and consumption has therefore been part of the responsibilities of nation-state governments in Europe and the US since the early nineteenth century. The first governmental measures at that time formed a response to public unrest about the then common ways of adulterating foodstuffs, like adding water to milk or skimming off the cream. Ever since, concerns about the quality and safety of food have contributed to a growing body of official regulations. The implementation of these regulations in practice was handed over to special governmental institutions (Braithwaite and Drahos, 2000; Atkins and Bowler, 2001; Buuren et al., 2004).[1] Governments in Western countries determined the acceptable composition of foodstuffs as required by law and different local and national authorities were empowered to detect fraud and penalise offenders. In the course of the twentieth century, national legislation as well as specialised inspection agencies expanded dramatically.[2] Regulations were based on a strict separation between public and private responsibilities. The national state was charged with the overall protection of its citizens against potential dangers related to food consumption, while private firms meanwhile competed among themselves on the price and quality of the different food products. Nation-state-based public regulation primarily dealt with the safety of food and acquired its shape generally through mandatory guidelines. Continued scientific and technological progress resulted in a growing governmental capacity to determine food safety and to translate scientific knowledge into concrete regulations. An effect of this development was a tremendous increase in the number and complexity of food laws and guidelines during the 1980s and the 1990s, contrary to the trend towards de-regulation in many other political domains.

Nation-state-based food governance traditionally focussed on the dangers associated with particular food products and applied conventional risk politics to deal with them. Conventional risk politics is guided by actuarial approaches (Bernstein, 1996) and is based on a strict division into three separate phases (Krimsky and Plough, 1988; Stonehouse and Mumford, 1994; FAO/WHO, 1997):

1.  *Risk assessment*: the risk associated with a particular hazard is determined by scientific experts based on independent and objective research. The risk is then characterised through an evaluation of the relationship between dose and effect and on a judgement of the exposure rate.

2. *Risk management*: the information resulting from the previous phase constitutes the input for political institutions that compare different responses to the risk based on 'public cost–public benefit' calculations. Authorities subsequently select the optimal alternative via rational decision-making procedures.

3. *Risk communication*: after the authorities have determined the optimal response to the ascertained risk the public is informed about this decision and if necessary legal and communicative instruments can be used to influence public behaviour in order to reduce the potential impact of the risk.

This conventional risk politics assigns separate roles to different scientific disciplines as well. Natural sciences are supposed to examine the relationships between causes and effects in case of particular hazards and predict the possible health and environmental consequences. Social sciences are charged with guiding decision-making processes and risk-communication strategies as well as with analysing the (potential) distributive impacts in society of the risks and the related policy regulations. Generally, these social sciences are required to follow an objectivist approach, so consequently a central role is given to economics (cost–benefit analysis) and psychology (individual perception) (Renn, 1992; Slovic, 2000).[3]

Until the 1990s, food regulation remained the responsibility of sovereign nation-state governments with the exception of the European Union. It is therefore not surprising that theorising about (inter)national food politics was dominated by approaches that considered national states and individual societies as their main units of analysis (Ostrom, 1990). Global food governance, as well as environmental governance in general, was analysed from the perspective of nation-states, whereby rational actor theories were applied to understand the modus operandi of nation-states at the global level.[4] According to this approach, the lack of well-defined institutions outside the national states forced them to collaborate pragmatically at the transnational level to solve those problems that go beyond individual nation-states. International institutions, or regimes, were established because nation-states were considered rational actors who were pragmatically willing to exchange some of their own legal freedom of action for some influence on the actions of other states (Keohane and Nye, 2002). Several observers even claim that international regimes have an epiphenomenal character, because nation-states are only pursuing their own self-interest through them (Lake, 1999).[5] The need for effective international co-ordination may nevertheless result in the development and implementation of a persistent and well-connected set of rules and regulatory practices prescribing behavioural roles, constraining activities and shaping expectations (Haas et al., 1993). Sometimes such international regimes are institutionalised to deal more effectively with a limited number of concrete transnational (environmental or other) problems. However, this process of institutionalisation is, in political science literature, generally not perceived as changing the role of nation-states in any fundamental way (Young, 1997; Cutler, 2002).[6] For example, Keohane and Nye (2002) claim that the prime democratic legitimacy remains at the domestic level and Karkkainen (2004: 72) states that 'sovereign states are presumed to be the natural locus of decision-making, although their behaviour may be influenced horizontally by inter-sovereign best practice standards, or constrained vertically by supra-sovereign rules and norms'.

These models for analysing, understanding and designing environmental governance and food safety regulations based on sovereign national states and international regimes are increasingly being challenged (Litfin, 1998).[7] In the era of globalisation, nation-states generally maintain their conventional food politics initially but over time more and more alternative mechanisms are introduced to govern environmental and food safety concerns and they involve regional and global governmental institutions as well as private companies.[8] In addition, 'many non-governmental organisations (NGOs), businesses, and communities are playing important roles in the emergence of global environmental governance as we know it' (Speth, 2002: 13). A restricted focus on formal institutions only to judge global food governance therefore fails to grasp the complex and dynamic involvement of these other social actors in the changing international food governance practices. As will be shown in the following sections, the conventional nation-state-based regulation of food production and consumption is less and less able to deal effectively with the complex challenges on food governance emerging in the context of global modernity.

## DIFFERENT VIEWS ON GLOBALISATION

Globalisation is one of the main social changes that explains why conventional nation-state based regulation of food is no longer adequate. Understanding the process of globalisation and its consequences has become the topic of intensive debates within social sciences. Several social scientists regard globalisation essentially as an economic transition in which the needs of global capital are imposing a neo-liberal economic discipline on societies all over the world. In their analysis, large transnational corporations are becoming footloose and imposing their mode of production on a world scale, while their power goes virtually unchallenged. This view is categorised by Held et al. (1999) as 'hyperglobalist', according to which globalisation is considered the near culmination of capitalism. Capitalist production relations are expected to replace all that remained of pre-capitalist modes of production around the globe and to unify the world into one single mode of production and one single global economic system (Robinson, 2001). These views are challenged by 'transformationalists', who consider globalisation to be a much more differentiated phenomenon involving diverse fields of activity and interaction, such as the political, military, economic, cultural, migratory and environmental domains.[9] Transformationalists moreover do not view globalisation as a continuous and inevitable process towards growing global cultural and economic homogeneity.

Hyperglobalist views on the globalisation of food production and consumption focus on the increasing subordination of food-producing regions to global food supply chains in which production relations are controlled by transnational food companies. Agriculture in all countries is considered to be restructuring in response to the demand from transnational agro-food companies for inputs to their manufacturing and distribution agro-food complexes (Friedmann and McMichael, 1989). This capitalist penetration is supposed to go hand in hand with replacing and substituting natural processes with industrial processes, with facilitating the transportation of food products over longer distances, and with creating favourable conditions for the expansion and lengthening of food supply chains (Bonanno et al., 1994).[10] This conceptualisation of the 'hyperglobalisation of food supply' is elaborated further using the 'commodity chain' concept (Friedland et al., 1981; Janvry, 1981; Le Heron, 1993; Friedland, 1994; Murdoch, 2000). This commodity chain concept can be broken down into several theoretical perspectives, such as the 'global commodity chain' (Dicken et al., 2001; Gibbon, 2001), the 'system of provision' (Fine, 1998) and 'commodity circuits' (Leslie and Reimer, 1999).[11]

Changes in the organisation of food production and consumption since the middle of the nineteenth century are described by several hyperglobalists as the succession of three different, but in themselves relatively stable, stages. Each stage is regulated by internal market mechanisms, state interventions and continuous pressure from different social forces. However, the inherent contradictions of capitalist production ultimately and inevitably result in a process of restructuring and in the transition from one stable system of relations of production to another. This means a reorganisation of agricultural production practices and structures as well as fundamental changes in the regions affected. The first of these three stages, periods, or food-regimes (Friedmann and McMichael, 1989; Le Heron, 1993; McKenna et al., 2001), roughly covering the period between 1870 and 1914, was characterised at the global level by colonial trade relationships, that is unequal exchange of agrarian raw materials from the colonies for finished goods from the respective mother countries (Ilbery, 2001).[12] Mixed farming dominated agriculture in these mother countries in Europe.

In the second stage, rapid urbanisation and industrialisation led to a growing spatial separation between food producers and food consumers, a process facilitated by innovations in production technologies, improved storage and faster transport options. Consequently, during this second food regime (fordism) and particularly after 1945, an intensive system of accumulation developed around the mass production of standardised food brands products. Agriculture became dominated by larger-scale and technology-intensive practices, replacing the traditional, extensive ways of farming. The daily menu became increasingly based on the consumption of standardised cheap food products (bought in supermarkets), produced within agro-industrial complexes using grain-fed livestock production and fats/durable foods. A remarkable development in this period was the continuously increasing distance between food production and food consumption, in space as well as in time (Dickens, 1992).

In the transition towards a third food regime (post-fordism) since the 1980s, the global food trade is expanding more rapidly than global food production. At the same time the state is withdrawing from agrarian markets through deregulation and liberalisation. International private corporations, particularly retailers, aim at flexible sourcing of food products from different regions around the globe, changing over time depending on the specific local production circumstances and market demand.[13] While new mass markets for standardised processed foodstuffs are appearing in many developing countries, consumer demand in industrialised countries seems to become increasingly differentiated. This process of differentiation in consumer demand in Western countries makes (the definition of) food quality an essential element in the marketing of food.[14] This so-called 'consumerist- and quality-turn' requires a more flexible organisation of food production, replacing the mass production of the fordist-era. (See Box 2.1 for the case of tropical crops.)

---

## BOX 2.1   THE PRODUCTION AND TRADE OF TROPICAL FOOD CROPS BETWEEN 1930 AND 1990

Between 1930 and 1980, the production of tropical food crops like coffee and cocoa was mostly in the hands of smallholders producing largely undifferentiated crops. The (colonial and) national state played the role of valorising peasant production through credit-based input schemes, extension services, national systems of quality control and pan-territorial pricing. International trade was dominated by a small number of big trading companies based in the US and Europe (Morgan, 1980). Market relations between these transnational corporations (TNCs) and suppliers dominated over forms of direct control. The major mechanism linking suppliers with these international traders took the form of simple, inclusive quality conventions combining price with certain crude physical crop properties chosen with the involvement of producers or their governments. A concrete example of this kind of agreement is that set by the International Coffee Organisation (ICO).

Around the year 1980, this structure began to change, and by 1990 the world of producing and trading tropical food crops was definitely reshaped. The organisation of the producer–trader networks displayed a far greater diversity than before. International producer cartels had collapsed and public intervention and regulation at the national level in developing countries greatly reduced because of the implementation of structural adjustment programmes imposed by the International Monetary Fund (IMF). Private contracts between producers, traders and industrial consumers began to dominate international trade in tropical food crops. Market co-ordination was reduced and therefore secularly falling prices were accompanied by increasing price instability, both in international and in domestic markets. Reduced market predictability was translated into falling margins and increased risks for traders, leading to stronger bargaining positions for processors and retailers. These transitions coincided with a growing differentiation in taste among consumers in importing countries. At the same time, vertical co-ordination by international traders persists and has become even more important, although this is accompanied by a proliferation of more direct forms of co-ordination (contracts, certification, and so on). The simple matrix linking crop quality and price has disappeared. Currently, increasingly commodities are sold in undifferentiated forms as inputs for processing industries, while consumer-driven quality conventions are proliferating at the same time. These conventions distinguish between products based on origin, production process or certain quality characteristics and are privately negotiated. They insist on ex-ante rather than ex-post forms of quality monitoring. This proliferation of quality demands makes monitoring increasingly costly

and buyers of tropical food crops are repeatedly trying to transfer much of these costs to the producers.

*Source*: Gibbon (2001).

Contrary to the conceptual model of successive food regimes developed within this hyperglobalist frame of reference, transformationalists consider globalisation to be a contingent and multidimensional phenomenon involving many different domains. They oppose those views that merge globalisation and the development of global capitalism (Held et al., 1999). Globalisation should be conceptualised, according to them, as a set of (long-term) historical processes replete with contradictions embodying transformations in the spatial organisation of social relations and transactions. These global transformations should be interpreted as the emergence of transcontinental or interregional flows and networks of activity, interaction and power (Giddens, 1990; Castells, 1997).[15] Social relationships are no longer based primarily on local face-to-face interactions but become increasingly disembedded and again re-embedded across time and space. Globalisation does not necessarily result in homogenisation because it may also lead to delocalisation in the production of goods and services (Mol, 2001). Moreover, globalisation may create heterogenisation and hybridisation in different spheres, such as finances (Hoogvelt, 2001), information and communication (Lash and Urry, 1994) or management (Gilmore and Pine, 1999).[16] Even when strong global economic, political and cultural forces operate similarly all over the world, these forces may have different local effects depending on the specific local contexts (McMichael, 1994, 1996). Transformationalists therefore see globalisation of food production and consumption as changes in (agri-food) networks involving different social actors (Lockie and Kitto, 2000; Marsden, 2000; McMichael, 2000). It is through such networks that social actors at diverse and sometimes very distant locations (re-)construct food in different ways and they do this almost on a daily basis (Arce and Marsden, 1993).

Despite their different views on globalisation in general, and on the changing organisation of food production and consumption in particular, both hyperglobalists and transformationalists challenge the central position of the sovereign nation-state. Hyperglobalists stress the growing dominance of private firms in the international organisation of food supply networks. Transformationalists point at flexibility and heterogeneity in recent transitions and at the importance of combining local and global dynamics in conceptualising the process of globalisation and contemporary food provision.

# GLOBAL FOOD GOVERNANCE

As Mol (2001) observed, globalisation processes may indeed have real and significant detrimental environmental side effects. Through globalisation, the governance of environmental and food safety problems therefore seems to enter a fundamentally different phase. While in the past, the problem of international environmental governance could be formulated in terms of the discrepancy between a globally organised ecosystem and a nation-state based system of governance, this seems no longer adequate (Weale, 1992; Young, 1994, 1997).[17] The networks of interdependence between different nation-states are intensifying through increasing trade and communication, the growing numbers of people (refugees as well as tourists) travelling between different countries and through the increasing awareness of common problems, such as climate change and terrorism. These trends reduce the possibilities for nation-states to deal with particular problems autonomously as internal dynamics are to an increasing extent determined by external processes (Held, 2004).[18] Traditional demarcations between domestic and foreign policies and between territorial and non-territorial responsibilities are called into question. Increasingly 'nation-states and national political actors are embedded in broader frameworks of governance and politics, consisting of multiple layers, from local to global, and multiple actors from private firms to non-governmental interest groups' (Mol, 2001: 219). Thus, the standard nation-state-based regulatory model seems ill fitted to deal with the specific challenges facing contemporary food governance. More and more, this conventional model seems to lag behind the growing cross-boundary flows of trade, finance capital, technology and expertise (Griffin, 2003). Consequently, the resulting changes in the interaction patterns between different nation-states and between different state and non-state actors lead to a variety of new kinds of governance arrangements involving diverse social groups at different spatial and sectorial scales. This is generally referred to as 'multi-sector and multi-level governance' (Picciotto, 2002; Held, 2004) or 'network-based governance'.[19]

A thickening web of multilateral agreements, institutions, international regimes, civil society organisations-based schemes and different private forms of governance is emerging, making global governance a significant arena for struggles over wealth, power and knowledge (McGinnis, 1999; Karkkainen, 2004).[20] New arrangements have been proposed to solve governance problems in global modernity and these innovations can be either state- or non-state-based or hybrids between both. Suggested state-based models for global governance mostly imply some form of a global state, copying the example of the traditional nation-state at worldwide level. With regard to food, networks of supranational governance have been estab-

lished, most of which aim at limiting authority to nation-state-based governing bodies (Young, 1997; Paterson, 1999; Griffin, 2003). Examples of such
supranational institutions are the European Food Safety Authority (EFSA)
and the WTO. (See Box 2.2.)

Nevertheless, the presence of such international institutions substantially
limits the sovereignty of individual national states to control global food
trade effectively for other interests, such as environmental or human health
concerns. Nation-states are compelled to adjust to globally agreed upon
regulatory arrangements not necessarily by force 'but because they will be
excluded from global capitalist commodity chains if they do not and, today,
this means "economic marginalisation and ruin"' (Schaeffer, 1995: 266).[21]
However, despite its decreasing power, the public continues to holds the nation-state accountable for dealing adequately with food production and consumption concerns and with food safety crises. Moreover, it seems as
though the nation-states are not only accountable to domestic constituencies
but also more and more to transnational citizenry as well (Haas, 1999). At
the same time, increasingly, food safety and animal welfare concerns are
added to the already existing economic, environmental and social concerns.
The mutual and overlapping influences between environment, trade and security make it less and less feasible to consider them as separate policy domains. Therefore, it becomes increasingly difficult to solve food problems
via specialised international policy regimes.[22] In addition, since no mechanisms exist to deal effectively with conflicts between different regimes, the
various institutions and processes in global modernity remain disarticulated
and fragmented and thus short of success and legitimacy (Keohane, 2002;
Lipschutz and Fogel, 2002).

---

## BOX 2.2   THE WORLD TRADE ORGANISATION AND FOOD REGULATION

The World Trade Organisation (WTO) co-ordinates the regulation of international trade in general and since 1995 the regulation of food trade as well. The WTO is a membership organisation where sovereign nation-states meet to develop common
rules for global trade. These rules are the result of extensive
processes of deliberation between the member-states, whereby
normally decisions are reached without voting but through
unanimous agreement between all members.

In principal, WTO regulations are based on economic considerations, but in the case of food, health concerns are also included. According to the WTO, global food safety regulations

should be based on recommendations from the Codex Alimentarius Commission and should then be translated into global food safety standards. Such agreed-upon global standards define the limits for the presence of specific substances in food products. Regulation of international food trade based on the production process ('non-product-related production and process methods') is not acceptable if it does not change the characteristics of the final product itself. These principles are detailed further in the Technical Barriers to Trade (TBT) and the Sanitary and Phytosanitary (SPS) agreements. (See also Chapters 4 and 8).

This combination of conventional nation-state-based food regulation and international institutions dealing with global food trade seems insufficiently capable of dealing with the problems faced by contemporary food supply chains. Therefore, increasingly such state-based forms of global food governance are supplemented in the international arena by innovative non-state-based practices. Large multinational firms seem to control increasingly larger portions of global food production, processing, trade and even retailing. Many observers claim that the existing international structures, such as the United Nations, are lagging behind this rapid 'process of corporate-led globalisation'. They suggest that only with the help of global, democratic political institutions, whether state- or non-state-based, the global power of TNCs can be controlled (McMichael, 1994, 1996, 2001; Sklair, 1999; Robinson, 2001; Camilleri, 2002).[23] Different social movements are opposing the establishment of 'global regimes of food production and trade' because they claim that food should not be considered an object for economic concern alone, as just an item of consumption, because it also embodies the links between man and nature, including human survival and death, culture and livelihoods (McMichael, 2000: 32). The growing public concerns about the social and environmental impact of food production processes cannot sufficiently be covered by the existing official product-oriented regulations (see chapters 4 and 5 for the concrete examples of BSE and GM food). Building on these concerns among citizens and consumers, social movements exercise public pressure, which can sometimes be highly effective (Dicken et al., 2001; Lang, 2003). The rising efficacy from a multitude of resistance movements contributes to the permanent reformulation of objectives and practices within global food governance arrangements (McMichael, 2001; Speth, 2002). Global civil society is 'constantly active – with ambivalent results – in redirecting global economic processes into less harmful directions' (Mol, 2001: 116) and has become an important political actor engaged 'in global governance by mobilising means of governance that operate independently of the state system' (Wapner, 1997: 81).

Certification and labelling schemes form an interesting example of such non-state-based global food governance arrangements involving social actors, such as NGOs, consumers, farmers, processors and retailers. Since the 1990s, alternative food supply chains, and private certification and labelling schemes have proliferated, as can be observed in the growth of organic labelled food, the certification of fish through the MSC label and HACCP labelling within food supply chains.[24] As these 'non-state and market-driven' instruments are not based on formal governmental decision-making procedures, the allocation of authority and power within them is not always very transparent. Mostly, responsibilities in non-state-based innovative forms of food governance are distributed among producers, retailers, consumers and civil society organisations. Nevertheless, 'they often convey and/or appear to have been accorded some form of legitimate authority' (Hall and Biersteker, 2002: 4) based on public opinion or resulting from effective improvements in the behaviour of market actors. Ecolabels, for example, rely heavily on the moral persuasion of customers and on strategic moves by producers and retailers trying to profit from price premiums, market access or market niches. Such a diffuse basis of authority seems not truly problematic unless different certification and labelling schemes are mutually competing within the same food supply network (Gulbrandsen, 2004).

Despite the growing importance of non-state-based innovative forms of global food governance, the continued importance of the nation-state should not be overlooked. The national state still provides the required stable legal context for this involvement of non-state actors and is regularly interacting with them, which may lead to different forms of hybrid governance. Hybrid forms of governance are blurring different previously clearly distinctive categories, such as the separation between the national and global levels and between public and private approaches to governance (Karkkainen, 2004).[25] 'World politics is being transformed into a "polycentric" or "multinucleated" global political system operating within the same geographical sphere (and/or overlapping spaces)' (Cerny, 1999: 190).[26] This trend might eventually generate some form of globalised functional differentiation with different specialised international institutions, in which civil society associations may fulfil multiple roles (Lipschutz and Fogel, 2002).

The presented transition towards (various forms of) global food governance arrangements is accompanied by a diversification in the regulatory mechanisms and the ascription of changing roles to different social actors. This multitude of mechanisms, roles and actors in global food governance may create several tensions in particular with the conventional ways in which national governments approach food risks.

## QUESTIONING CONVENTIONAL FOOD RISK POLITICS

The conventional ways in which nation-states are dealing with food risks in global modernity is becoming an issue of serious scientific and public debate. Conventional risk politics is particularly criticised for its inability to conceptualise risks as social phenomena (Douglas and Wildavsky, 1983; Perrow, 1984; Adams, 1995).[27] Human risk behaviour cannot be understood by studying the objective features of the risk itself or analysing individual attitudes alone but has to be comprehended as part of wider social practices (family and community relations, institutional decision-making processes, and so on).[28] Social constructivists go even further when they challenge the epistemological assumption underlying conventional risk politics that risks can be defined in an unproblematic and neutral way with the help of scientific knowledge (Hagendijk, 1996).[29] They consider risks as socially constructed through the beliefs, interpretations and rationalities of the various societal actors involved (Wynne, 1996).[30] According to this view, different types of (context-related) rationalities exist, so the actual approach to risk that dominates politics is the result from a constant struggle by all actors to put their particular interpretation of the risk on the public agenda and impose their definition on other actors ('whose reality counts?').[31] Within this perspective, more scientific research alone cannot resolve conflicts about risks, because this struggle involves (at least partly) different (frames or) meanings of risk (Luhmann, 1991, 1997).[32] Therefore, constructivist views claim that our understanding of today's risks and risk politics cannot gain from further elaborated natural sciences or cost–benefit analyses alone. They point to the need for profound social science analysis of the societal dynamics involved in (the definition of) risks and resulting risk politics.

The changing characteristics of risks in globalising modern societies contribute further to the challenges already facing conventional risk politics mentioned above (Beck, 1992, 1996, 1997; Beck and Willms, 2004).[33] Continuous scientific and technological progress may result in new risks, thereby transforming what used to be considered side-effects of progress in science and technology into challenges confronting the basis of society itself (Lash et al., 1996). Contemporary Western societies can be called effectively 'risk societies' (Beck, 1992; Giddens, 1990) because they cannot escape from modern risks. At the same time, the central institutions in contemporary Western societies (modern science and technology and the welfare state) are increasingly incapable of dealing with them in a reassuring manner.[34] Nevertheless, the modern institutions of science and technology remain the prime sources of information for politicians and the public about the potential impacts of these modern risks and the possible responses to them.[35] This dependency is problematic because expert views on specific risks may differ, while revisions of these views have become permanent. This dilemma forces lay people to evaluate and modify their daily behaviour in the light of a continuous flow of information stemming from different (and often disagreeing) scientific experts, as well as from politicians, media and NGOs. Thus, when confronted with risks in modern society, lay people can do little more than choose which (scientific) expert they trust the most (Giddens, 1991; Beck, 1992).[36]

Increasing global interdependencies in the 1990s and the changing position of the nation-state put conventional risk politics under further pressure (Beck, 1999).[37] The impact of globalisation on risks and, consequently, on risk politics should be understood as changes in both the objective and the subjective distribution of risks (Giddens, 1990: 124–5, italics in original):

> Objective distribution of risks:
> 1) *Globalisation of risk* in the sense of *intensity*.
> 2) *Globalisation of risk* in the sense of the *expanding number of contingent events*, which affect everyone, or at least large numbers of people on the planet.
> 3) Risks stemming from the *created environment*, or *socialised nature*: the infusion of human knowledge into the material environment.
> 4) The development of *institutionalised risk environments* affecting the life-chances of millions.
> The subjective perception of perceived risks:
> 1) *Awareness of risk* as *risk*: the 'knowledge gaps' in risks cannot be converted into 'certainties' by religious or magical knowledge.
> 2) The *well-distributed awareness of risk*: many of the dangers we face collectively are known to a wide public.
> 3) *Awareness of the limitations of expertise*: no expert system can be wholly expert in terms of the consequences of the adoption of expert principles.

Conventional nation-state-based conventional risks politics are confronted with both the changing objective distribution of risks in global modernity and their subjective distribution among the public. At the same time, the capacities of nation-states to handle such risks are being eroded. Food is a model case for these changes because its production and consumption used to have a local and natural character when seasons, climate and geographical conditions imposed 'natural' limits on the production and preservation of food items. Today this situation has evolved drastically into a globalised provisioning of food and the use of high-tech processing and conservation methods. Food safety is 'difficult to establish in a context of time-distantiation and time lags, that is, where damage and harm are being produced out of sight, below the surface, for often unknown periods of time and where the symptoms do not necessarily allow for a backwards reconstruction to originating sources and causes' (Adam, 1999: 232). Thus, the stretching of food-supply chains in time and space has transformed the previously local and natural character of food risks because the effects of particular risks may be felt over much larger distances in space as well as in time, while the increased use of technology is even changing the definition of 'natural' itself (Adam, 1999). The human senses are in many cases no longer capable to determine food safety risks adequately and therefore people necessarily have to rely more on science and other forms of institutional knowledge. Globalised food supply chains have an increased potential for health hazards and a decreased potential for tracing their sources because of the mobility of the contamination and the time-space distantiation between cause and effect. (See Box 2.3 for an example.)

---

## BOX 2.3   THE GLOBAL FLOW OF MPA: RISKING HUMAN HEALTH

In July 2002, the growth hormone MPA (medroxyprogesterone-acetate) turned up in waste water produced by a pharmaceutical factory in Ireland owned by the drug-maker Wyeth based in the US. MPA is a growth hormone approved for use in the US, Australia and New Zealand, but banned in the EU where scientists believe it might cause infertility in humans.

Waste water containing MPA was wrongly labelled as unharmful and shipped by Cara Environmental Technology Ltd, an Irish waste recovery company, to the Belgian reprocessing plant Bioland that mixed the waste water into glucose syrup and then sold it to Dutch animal feed makers. These firms processed it further into raw material inputs for cow and pig feed and re-sold it throughout Europe. Shipments of glucose syrup and molasses laced with MPA were traced to at least 74 feed producers. Later, animal feed containing traces of MPA were found on farms in 11 EU countries, whereby the Netherlands, Germany and Belgium were hit hardest. For example, about 2,100 German farms received emergency closure orders preventing them from selling their produce until their animals had been tested for the presence of MPA. Damages for Dutch farmers were estimated to range between 70 and 100 million Euros, mostly for the destruction of up to 55,000 pigs. Belgium's health

food safety agency also found traces of MPA in the materials
Bioland supplied to two soft drinks firms.

*Source*: Reuters News Service, different editions between 15 and 26 July 2002.

Global modernity not only changes the objective characteristics of food
risks, but their subjective traits are evolving as well, accelerating a drive
towards alternative practices of risk politics. Science and technology have
decontextualised the bulk of today's food production and consumption
(Tickell and Peck, 1995).[38] The resulting growing distance in time and
space between food production and consumption precludes the conventional
face-to-face building of trust and makes it indispensable to build trust
through other, impersonal mechanisms such as abstract expert systems.[39]
Moreover, although usually trust in the abstract systems involved in food
provisioning is taken for granted in everyday life, in times of a (food) crisis,
people are compelled to actively re-examine and eventually reconstitute
their trust in a different manner.[40] Trust stemming from abstract systems is
mostly built on scientific expertise, but as already mentioned, public trust in
science has an ambiguous character. In particular, with regard to food,
which affects everyone's life every day, people have to choose what information from which expert they believe. Therefore, on the one hand consumers are conscious of the involvement of abstract expert systems in the
creation of food risks, while they on the other hand remain dependent on information from experts to take their decisions. Uncertainty has become a
central feature of modern everyday food consumption practices.[41] Trust in
the abstract systems seems to have become more a matter of individual
choice and therefore each choice requires adequate justification for not taking the other options. The necessity to regularly review and re-establish
trust marks the end of the expectation that social and natural environments
will be subjected increasingly to rational ordering, and this signals the transition towards 'reflexive' modernisation (Beck, 1992, 1996; Beck et al.,
1994; Beck and Willms, 2004; Giddens, 1990). In the context of reflexive
modernity, social practices have to be re-examined and reshaped continuously in the light of incoming information about (the consequences of) these
very practices (Giddens, 1984, 1990, 1991, 1994; Mol, 2001).[42] Therefore,
consumers confronted with new food risks in the context of global modernity can no longer automatically rely on the conventional nation-state-based
standard regulation of risk (Cardello, 1995).[43] In addition, consumer trust in
food and food regulation can no longer simply be pre-supposed or recon-
structed with the help of science alone (Dagevos, 2002).

New ways of (re-)constituting consumer trust in food are therefore needed and this requires active consumer involvement in setting up alternative mechanisms or in re-establishing trust with the help of conventional mechanisms (Rowe and Frewer, 2000; Rowe et al., 2004). Analysing such innovative ways of constituting consumer trust demands better understanding of consumer practices and transformations in their engagement with food provisioning and its regulation.

## CONSUMERS AND THE CONSUMPTION OF FOOD

Generally, food consumption has been conceived as the fulfilment of a physical need and an economic activity similar to consumption in general. Consequently, none of the social sciences other than economics has paid serious attention to food consumers and in case they did study those, social scientists generally conceptualised consumers as passive, or 'captive', consumers. Recently these views have undergone considerable change and since the 1990s, increasingly food consumers are understood as social actors, actively engaged in essential social practices. These innovative conceptualisations mark the wider changes in understanding consumer behaviour within the context of global modernity.

Ritzer (1996) has expressively described consumers as passive beings. In his McDonaldisation thesis, he considers consumers as caught in the iron cage of mass consumption: multinational corporations produce identical products in the largest possible volumes and they try to sell these products all over the globe, using media and advertisements to impose their brand (Klein, 2000). Bourdieu also underlines the importance of structural variables, notably social class, in understanding consumption behaviour, but he allows somewhat more room for human agency. He regards consumption practices as the result of individual agency (an individual's 'habitus' in combination with his or her (cultural, social, and so on) capital) and the structure (the 'field' in which the individual agents find themselves), whereby both agency and structure may show important variations (Bourdieu, 1979; Warde, 1997; Ritzer, 2001). However, consumption has turned into a significant means for cultural expression and lifestyle in contemporary, (post-)modern societies, and constitutes an issue of considerable psychological and emotional importance. Therefore, consumers today should be considered active social agents (Bauman, 1993, 2000; Warde, 1997).[44] Consumption can thus no longer be seen as the simple fulfilment of existing needs through buying and consuming particular products, but as a collection of evolving social practices whereby people can even display different kinds of consumer behaviour at different times (Gabriel and Lang,

1995).[45] 'Consumption is the result of a series of acts that are located in different sites and actual purchase is often only a small part of these acts' (Jackson and Thrift, 1995: 211). Thus, consumption should be studied as a contextual social practice in which people use products and services as mediating materials to relate to other people (Spaargaren, 2000).

The consumption of food should therefore also be conceptualised as a social activity in which buying food, preparing and eating it is embedded in wider social practices. However, most observers continue to approach food consumption as a social activity structurally subordinate to the production of food (Mennell, 1996; Ritzer, 1996; Allen and Kovach, 2000). Even in more recent agro-commodity studies, 'the consumer emerges only to disappear again into a production-centred framework' (Goodman and DuPuis, 2002: 7; see also Lockie and Kitto, 2000).[46] However, conceptualising food consumption as a social practise means analysing shopping, cooking and consuming food in combination with an understanding of issues like living conditions, cooking preferences and capabilities, family circumstances, relationships between man and wife and eating routines (Dixon, 2002). For example, even though contemporary food consumption practices in Western countries remain largely characterised by daily routines, within them consumers have to make numerous choices (products, cultures and styles) depending on many non-nutritious and non-economic considerations. This way food choice becomes one tool in defining and expressing one's social and cultural identity. 'There is no essential, one-to-one, correspondence between particular commodities and particular identities: the same commodity can have radically different meanings for different individuals and for the same individual over time' (Jackson and Thrift, 1995: 227). The transition towards globalised food production and consumption further increases the everyday options for food consumers in Western countries.[47] Stretching the distance in time and space between the production and consumption locations of food modifies the position of consumers because food supply networks become more complex, involving many more actors and forcing them to make choices among many more options (ibid.).[48] The practices involved in the production and processing of food are also changing as the result of the increased interference of science and technology with nature, which may contribute to consumer convenience but also widens consumers' choice even more. Exotic and previously only seasonally available food items have become common and everyday reality for many consumers (Warde, 1997) while pre-sliced and pre-cooked foods are more and more replacing raw food ingredients (Eberle et al., 2004).

The transition towards global modernity is also changing the ways in which consumers deal with food quality. Food consumption necessarily involves an intimate and complex relationship between man and nature, making food particularly sensitive. Consumers' handling of food quality is socially and culturally broader than the cognitive rationality assumed in scientific expert knowledge and administrative procedures developed to secure the safety of food. Consumer behaviour also includes religious, ethical, social and other considerations. How consumers handle food quality is furthermore characterised by ambivalence – multiple meanings, dilemmas and negotiations whereby people take part in creating and reproducing meaning in daily life by 'attempting to knit together the different experiences and roles of life' (Halkier, 2001: 802). Therefore, stretching the distances in time and space between food production and consumption and intensifying the interference of science and technology with food give rise to new consumer concerns. Although the impact of the different changes on the food products themselves may not always be directly visible to consumers, they do contribute to the already existing ambivalence. According to more and more consumers in contemporary societies, defining food quality has to go beyond simply detecting the objective characteristics of food products and needs to include the (in-)direct environmental, animal welfare and social impacts as well. These widening consumer concerns, combined with the increasing dependency on global dynamics create particular challenges for conventional nation-state-based regulatory practices. As nation-states seem decreasingly able to take action, more and more consumers engage themselves actively in voluntary regulatory practices (Giddens, 1991; Beck, 1992; Bauman, 1993, 2000).

New forms of environmental politics through markets are developing despite the continued presence of stereotypical views considering consumption as an inherently unsustainable social practice (Horrigan et al., 2002) and the difficulties in clearly defining sustainable consumption practices (Spaargaren, 1997, 2000; Beckers et al., 2000; Dagevos, 2004).[49] The concept of 'political consumerism' seems to capture the emerging phenomenon of consumers' engagement adequately (Micheletti, 2003). Although political consumerism may not necessarily fully replace the existing more traditional forms of political participation, it does represent an enlargement of the political repertoire in global modernity. Via political consumerism, critical citizens practice alternative forms of political action (sub-politics, cf. Beck, 1999) by making conscious everyday choices within the market based on non-economic considerations. Following the principle of autonomy, according to which every citizen is allowed to exert a relatively autonomous influence on his or her own living conditions, political consumers may attempt to influence institutional or market practices by the use of their shopping-bag power (Halkier, 1999). Consumer power, then, is used in its constructive and transformative, or political, capacity (Held, 1987). (See Box 2.4 for an example.)

Political consumers may thus engage in politics through buycotts and boycotts, thereby opening up new arenas for politics outside the nation-state (and traditional politics in general) while linking their everyday life with global politics. A critical issue is that unless some form of institutionalisation takes place through NGOs, through labelling and certification schemes or through political institutions, the scattered and unorganised consumer activities remain invisible within the mass-mediated public sphere as well as within the political sphere itself (Halkier, 1999). If such institutionalisation does take place, the structured engagement by citizens through political consumerism can help to rearrange existing practices in food production and consumption and to revise related policies, although the transformative capacity of political consumerism should not be overestimated.

---

### BOX 2.4   POLITICAL CONSUMERISM: ADOPTING CHICKENS

After the bird flu crisis in the Netherlands in early 2003, several environmental NGOs developed an initiative they baptised as 'adopt a chicken' and just after one year, over 25,000 chickens have been adopted.

'Adopt a chicken' wants to show that organic chickens have a much nicer life than other chickens and that organic agriculture is in all respects an optimal agricultural practice which needs a robust impulse. Consumers adopting a chicken pay €29.50 for one year. In return, they get a certificate, access to a webcam to look at their and other chickens at the farm and coupons to collect a box of six eggs at an organic food shop every month. These adoptive consumers were prepared to pay in fact more than twice as much for their eggs in comparison with organic eggs regularly bought in supermarkets. The organisers claim that this campaign has a remarkable impact, much wider than the direct number of 'consumers' adopting a chicken. While the turnover in regular eggs in the Netherlands decreased, the sales of organic eggs in regular supermarkets increased by one-third.

*Source*: http://www.adopteereenkip.nl/

---

So conventional nation-state-based regulatory practices based on 'passive' consumers are being challenged in the context of global modernity. The changing practices in contemporary food production and consumption and the novel roles taken up by consumers can in certain cases result in growing pressure on actors in the agro-food chain forcing them to respond to different and evolving concerns.

## CONCLUSION

Globalisation is transforming the organisation of food production and consumption in a fundamental, although not necessarily homogeneous, manner. This contingent and multidimensional character is embodied in the transforming roles of the nation-state, of science and of the social actors involved. Simply enlarging the state functions into worldwide institutions in order to replace the conventional nation-state will not offer an adequate response to these changes. Food-related consumer concerns are evolving as new technological options emerge and information about social and environmental impacts becomes more available and more easily accessible. Overall, these consumer concerns are related to food production, processing and trading practices as well as to easily detectable properties of the food products themselves. The conventional, simple modernist model of food regulation has become increasingly unable to fulfil its tasks in the context of global modernity. Complex relationships in time and space between the causes and effects of food risks are becoming visible. The concepts applied until now to analyse the practices of food governance seem less and less able to grasp these new dynamics.

Therefore, before reviewing several innovative governance arrangements aimed at dealing more adequately with food production and consumption, first the required conceptual tools will be developed in Chapter 3. These concepts will enable a more profound understanding of the changes taking place in governance practices dealing with globalising food production and consumption.

## NOTES

1. Food regulatory practices already date from the Greeks in classical Athens who nominated an inspector to monitor the quality of wine, but consistent local food-quality regulation really developed during the Middle Ages when cities and different guilds formulated prescriptions and installed food safety examiners.
2. Atkins and Bowler (2001: 215) mention that around 3,800 additives are used in our daily food to make products look more attractive to the senses, to prolong the product's shelf life, and to assist in the manufacturing process. 'About 380 of these additives had officially been approved by the EU by 1987'.

3.  Recent psychological research has concluded, however, that risk is inherently subjective: although dangers are real, there is no such thing as real risk. Risk is based on subjective and assumption-laden psychological models (Slovic, 2000) and individuals respond according to their own perception of risks and not according to officially determined 'objective' definitions of risks. Although there may be some consistent patterns in these individual responses, the aggregation of individual preferences into common denominations proves to be very difficult (Renn, 1992).

4.  A rather unpolished version of this theory is that all actors are opportunistically seeking to manipulate the terms of any relationship to their advantage, abandoning, entrapping or exploiting their partners whenever possible. The actor's cost of opportunistic behaviour by the others is determined by the extent to which he disposes of specific assets demanded by the other parties (Lake, 1999). Keohane approaches the question of international governmental collaboration more subtly as a governance dilemma: although institutions are essential for human life, they are also dangerous because they go against the natural human inclination towards self-regarding actions. 'People require institutional protection both from self-serving elites and from their worst impulses' (Keohane, 2002: 247). However, human actions are never only guided by egoist-rationality, but also 'by expectations of how others will behave and, therefore, by underlying values and beliefs' (ibid.: 257). This rational behaviour becomes translated into international institutions which, from a democratic standpoint, should provide accountability, participation and persuasion and change people's choices partly independent from their calculations about the strategies of other players.

5.  Whether the sovereignty of nation-states is declining (Held, 1995; Held et al., 1999; Castells, 1997) or not (Hoogvelt, 2001) is heavily debated within the social sciences. It seems as though the sovereignty of the nation-state is affected by globalisation without resulting in a complete withering away of the nation-state itself. Nation-states remain the central locus of political debate, but at the same time, their roles are being redefined and transformed in their relationship with global political institutions, structures and actors. The fast increasing number of multilateral agreements limiting the room for manoeuvre for nation-states is the most visible but certainly not the only sign for this process of change.

6.  Studies on private and transnational regimes have paid particular attention to the formation, change and maintenance, as well as to the effectiveness, of political institutions (Schram Stokke, 1997). Treating international institutions or 'regimes' as tools for the reduction of transactions costs is not convincing, according to Sandholz (1999), because there is no competition between countries as there is between firms. Markets in general are social constructs depending for their existence on deep and dense networks of shared understandings and rules. Thus, the social rules that define roles, rights and responsibilities are logically prior to the cost–benefit calculations of specific agents.

7.  Scott (1998) shows the disastrous effects of several nation-state interventions, although they were developed with the best intentions.

8.  Multilateral environmental agreements (MEAs) contribute to the emergence of a relatively independent environmental realm in global politics. Nevertheless, regional institutions like the EU are of greater relevance. These strong political institutions and arrangements, originally intended to further economic integration, increasingly include environmental protection as well (Mol, 2001).

9.  Held also distinguishes a third group of theorists, 'the sceptics', who consider globalisation not a significantly different phenomenon requiring specific theoretical reflection, but their views seem less relevant in the context of food production and consumption.

10. Through the global chains of food production and consumption, not only do economic relationships stretch out over time and space, but also the time and distance between the origins of environmental neglect and the actual environmental consequences in specific localities increase as well (Mol, 2001).

11. Related concepts are 'value-chains' and 'supply chains' (Raikes et al., 2000).

12. The years mentioned here are indicative only, because in general such processes of transition have no fixed moment for start and finish, but also because there are many differences in timing between different parts of the world, particularly in the first two stages.

13. More and more global agro-food networks are being created, mostly under the influence of a few large retailers (Konefal et al., 2003). The flexibility thus created allows for 'Just-in-Time' delivery (Dixon, 2002). One interesting example of these changes is 'relational contracting': contracts that are based on interactive, flexible but stable supply networks. While the day-to-day orders may vary and are understood as flexible, the contracts are valid for a number of years, thus creating stability within the network.

14. In 1998, 11,037 new food products were introduced in supermarkets in the US, compared with fewer than 6,000 annually in the mid-1980s. Since 1990, 116,000 different packaged foods and beverages have been developed, all competing for the limited available space on the supermarket shelves (Nestle, 2002: 25). See also McKenna et al. (2001) for the example of the introduction of (sustainable) integrated fruit production programmes in New Zealand's apple production under the pressure of European consumer demand.

15. McMichael (1996: 38) points at the remarkable fact that 'the reach of economic globalisation itself is so limited in terms of the populations it includes, and yet its impact is so extensive'.

16. Ritzer (1996) claims that a global culture subordinated to global economic interests is being created (McDonaldisation). However, it is unlikely for a global culture to have a uniform character because expressions of global culture are always mingled with other cultural expressions and operate in a specific local cultural context. The cultural dynamics of globalisation should therefore be conceptualised as based on diversity and variety rather than on uniformity and homogeneity. Moreover, these dynamics do not always take the form of a top-down process because local (counter-) cultures can contribute to global culture as well (Mol, 2001; Franklin et al., 2000). Technological innovations greatly contribute to cultural interaction by facilitating exchanges of information and experiences.

17. Weale (1992) also shows how the environment is becoming a separate domain of articulated and institutionalised practices under the conditions and via the processes and dynamics of globalisation. Multilateral environmental agreements, world summits, global environmental NGOs and internationally recognised private labels (ISO 14000) are all examples of these attempts to globalise environmental management practices.

18. Sassen (2002) claims that through partially denationalising what has historically been constructed as national and facilitating the creation of private regimes with powerful transnational corporations, the nation-state is actively engaged in its own evaporation process (see also Tehranian, 2002). Beck and Willms (2004) comment on this thesis when they contend that the absence of a well established global governance system is also a problem for global corporations because they are confronted with the lack of a clear legal framework and are thus open to all kinds of claims from consumers, NGOs and so on.

19. The European Union is often hailed as an innovative example of multilevel governance, 'developing a framework of international institutions while respecting national sovereignty as the bedrock of the international legal order' (Maher, 2002: 113). See Skjaerseth and Wettestod (2002) for further analysis of the EU's environmental policy with the help of the governance and regime concepts.

20. Many authors have introduced the concept of 'governance' to cover the emerging new forms and practices of official and non-official regulation and, although the exact definitions vary, it always involves interactions between public and private actors in some mix of formal and informal practices (Hajer et al., 2004). Government is subsequently conceptualised as a subset of governance acting with legal authority and creating formal obligations (Keohane and Nye, 2002).

21. See McMichael (2000) who claims that transnational food companies reduce the room for autonomous national food regulations via the institutionalisation of a global, WTO-controlled, trade regime. See also Young (2004) for an analysis of the impact of this situation on food security and Paterson (1999) for an overview of the roles of state and corporate actors.

22. Von Moltke (1997) observes that the goals of the economic and environmental regimes overlap without being congruent, creating difficulties in the case of regulating international food trade.

23. More popularised versions of this thesis can be found in Klein (2000) and Hertz (2001).

24. MSC is the abbreviation for Marine Stewardship Council and HACCP stands for Hazard Accident Critical Control Point. (See Chapter 8 for further details.)
25. Such arrangements involve a heterogeneous array of agents, consisting of 'a set of practices for governance that improve co-ordination and create safety valves for political and social pressures' (Keohane and Nye, 2002: 204). They require these arrangements to be 'consistent with the maintenance of nation-states as the fundamental form of political organisation'.
26. In many international arrangements the quasi-judicial capabilities and 'soft legislation' (or soft law), have moved ahead much faster than 'hard legislation' or executive capabilities (Keohane and Nye, 2002).
27. Several corporations and scientists, especially from the US, nevertheless fiercely defend this standard model of risk politics when they criticise the European Union for ignoring for 'protectionist reasons' the conclusions from 'sound science' in the formulation of political measures (NFTC, 2003).
28. The social sciences' analysis of risk often considers risks a separate category of social behaviour and tries to understand it based on general cultural traits (Douglas and Wildavsky, 1983). From this perspective risk behaviour becomes a different category isolated from other social practices. However, it seems rather naïve to equate the way in which (a certain category of) consumers deal with food risks with the way this same group deals with traffic risks.
29. Constructivist approaches can be even further distinguished in moderate and radical versions. Moderate constructivists consider the development and acceptance of scientific knowledge as context-dependent, but accept that reality and knowledge are ultimately two different realms. Radical constructivism does not accept this distinction and regards both scientific knowledge itself and its use (including the distinction between 'facts' and 'context' as such) as the result of social interaction. However, if damage to the environment can only exist by constructed human knowledge, it becomes impossible to qualify different frames of meaning, leaving only taste or mere power (Hogenboom et al., 2000; Macnaghten and Urry, 1998).
30. For example, the lay public's rationality is predominantly 'relational' in character, contrary to the rational-calculative models of science (Szerszynski, 1999).
31. The range of possible social constructs of reality is limited by the need to compromise between self-interest and the obligation to construct a socially meaningful reality (Renn, 1992).
32. Luhmann concludes that each subsystem in society uses its own internal binary code and symbols, making communication between different social subsystems impossible. This severely limits the options for society to deal with risk (Miller, 1994; Arnoldi, 2001). According to Dryzek (1987), a transcending environmental rationality would enable bridging different rationalities in different social sub-systems, although demanding an institutional re-orientation as well. Such an ecological rationality should have a natural science base that can be studied objectively to inform social decision-making processes. Other authors claim that communication between different subsystems, that is between social actors using different frames of meaning, is not excluded by definition (Giddens, 1976; Papadakis, 2002). Signifying frames are not necessarily completely consistent (self-referential) nor inevitably free from outside norms or interests. Each frame of meaning is developed in reference to other frames and mediated by them. Therefore, it must be possible to establish mutual links, thereby solving the hermeneutic problem of how to understand other social realities and practices through one particular frame of meaning. Unfortunately, this observation does not solve the problem of determining the 'truth', as there is no observation without theory and no neutral, objective language. This is particularly problematic for social sciences because they are confronted with a double hermeneutics (Giddens, 1987).
33. See also Perrow (1984) explaining the incidence of accidents as a normal feature when living together with high-risk technologies.
34. During the early 1980s, the national government came under pressure in a number of industrialised countries for its inability and ineffectiveness to regulate and control sources

of ecological deterioration. Global economic, political and cultural processes all contributed to the (perception of) governmental failure to act effectively in protecting its territory from environmental deterioration and made it more difficult for national governments to find legitimacy for their actions (Hogenboom et al., 2000). This challenge was exacerbated through the higher levels of education, better access to information and improving living standards among the general population in these countries resulting in a growing unwillingness by the public to accept (environmental and food safety) risks and to trust scientific and political institutions in managing them.

35. If scientific experts want to engage in political debates and generate consensus, they have to neglect the considerable uncertainties embedded in the layered assumptions of their models. They also have to exclude ethical and moral issues, because 'formal risk assessment is deemed to be a delimited, technical exercise, one where inputs from objective science are seen to be crucial' (Scoones, 2001: 19). Politicians, on the other hand, have to include such ethical and moral issues in many decision-making processes because the public considers them essential (Marsden, 1997).

36. Considerations applied by the public in their choice of experts include the independence of different scientific experts, their own experiences and an assessment of the correspondence between the underlying assumptions applied in scientific research and the daily reality of lay people.

37. For example, Boselie and Buurma (2003) observe that food safety requirements of private buyers of food in Thailand have increased rapidly and often surpass public safety standards.

38. Decontextualisation refers to freedom from context – that is, from time and place – which is considered one of the great achievements of science and industrialisation as the emancipation from the cycles of want and plenty (Adam, 1999).

39. Systems of professional and technical expertise (expert systems) increasingly organise large areas of the material and social environments in which we live today. When these systems are not personalised but stretched over time and space, they can be called 'abstract systems' (Giddens, 1990).

40. Giddens (1990) concludes that trust and risk permeate all aspects of daily life. Pragmatic acceptance can be sustained towards most of the abstract systems that impinge on individuals' lives but by its very nature, such an attitude cannot be carried on all the while and in respect to all areas of activity.

41. See Bauman (2000) on the (potentially) profound consequences at social and individual levels of the increased uncertainty and anxiety in contemporary globalising societies.

42. Within environmental thinking, reflexive modernisation fits in the conceptual frameworks of 'sustainable development' (WCED, 1987; Adams, 1990; Carter, 2001) and ecological modernisation (Mol, 1995; Spaargaren, 1997). Sustainable development does not define an ideal situation but argues that environmental reform involves a process-approach through the interplay between economics and market-actors on the one hand and (organised) citizen-consumers and political institutions seeking to condition them on the other. The concept of sustainable development was made more concrete in Agenda 21 during the UNCED meeting in 1992 (WSSD Plan of Implementation). Evolving thinking about sustainable development has resulted in a continued search for sustainability indicators in different fields. One example of the search is the introduction of the concept of the environmental footprint (Wackernagel and Rees, 1996). See with regard to indicators for sustainable agriculture: Zhen and Routray (2003) and Dragun and Tisdell (1999).

43. This observation points at the challenges facing the nation-state as its capacity to deal with food risks seems diminished and public confidence in its role as caretaker is reduced, while many consumers and non-state actors continue to regard the state as the most appropriate institution to reduce these risks (Grove-White et al., 1997).

44. People have to choose more often from more options that are different and, because they have become disembedded from the protective shield of a habitus, these choices are associated with uncertainty and anxiety. In reaction, people may create 'imagined communities' offering a sense of belonging. The identity of such an imagined community may vary considerably: ethnic, local or temporary 'style groups'. One specific version is the prolif-

eration of 'neo-tribes': 'elective groupings, exhibiting high levels of temporary commitment, whose boundaries are identifiable through the shared lifestyles of members'
(Warde, 1997: 16).

45. See also Mintz (1995: 11) 'all living organisms are faced with an imperious necessity: not
to eat is to die. But beyond this, foods have meanings that transcend their nutritive role.'

46. According to this approach, producers react to changing consumer demands that result
from their increased income and growing awareness about risks. Therefore, consumer
agency is limited to the consumers' capacities to adapt their (economically defined) demand on the food market. Commodity chain analysis and actor-network theories do not
consider consumers as social agents because the first approach disarms consumers and the
second one disarms politics (Goodman and Dupuis, 2002).

47. Our understanding of the consumption of food in modern society confronts conundrums,
apparent contradictions, contrasts and polarities of a kind because of the changes that result from market forces that penetrate social relationships at the level of everyday life.
According to Mintz, 2002: 24) 'it never seems to turn out to be quite as simple as we
might think'.

48. Like any other product, food products also contain hidden geographies and social relations of production that lay embedded within the relations of contemporary consumption
until they are uncovered (traced back and revealed) by experts or other social actors (Appadurai, 1986).

49. Maybe this lack of serious understanding of the relationship between food consumption
and the environment can explain why specific policies on sustainable food consumption
are lacking in many countries despite the inclusion of food consumption in more general
policy plans and particularly in health policies (OECD, 2002).

# 3. Studying the governance of flows of food in the global network society: a conceptual framework

## INTRODUCTION

Food production and consumption is increasingly organised at a global scale (see Chapter 1) as increasing quantities of food, processed into more and more diverse food products, are traded internationally.[1] The physical distance between food producers and consumers is increasing while the (potential) social, environmental and safety effects of global food provisioning are growing as well, with potentially large-scale and sometimes radical impacts. Conventional nation-state-based governance practices can no longer adequately deal with these problems (see Chapter 2). The role of the nation-state is changing as other levels of governance and other social actors such as consumers and NGOs assume new responsibilities. This transition has blurred the traditionally clear distinction between public and private responsibilities and between nation-state structures and international co-ordinating institutions. The permanently present human concern about the safety of food is supplemented today with various environmental, ethical and social considerations, making strict science-based governance arrangements today even more inadequate than in the past. Consequently, innovative governance arrangements and practices are needed to deal with contemporary concerns about food production and consumption to complement and replace the already existing ones. Identifying and analysing such alternative global food governance arrangements, which is the overall objective of this book, requires, however, a more profound understanding of the transformations that food production, consumption, and the related governance practices are undergoing in the context of global modernity. Therefore, before presenting the results of the empirical research (chapters 4 –7), this chapter will review the key concepts that will make the study of these transformations possible.

In the next section, I will analyse the principal changes in the contemporary organisation of food production and consumption, in particular the growing distance between producers and consumers, which is fundamentally altering both social practices of food production and consumption. In order to grasp this transformation, concepts are required that are able to deal with social phenomena going beyond the traditional concept of society as an individually contained nation-state. Therefore, in the third section, several concepts elaborated by the social theorists Castells and Urry will be reviewed to consider their applicability in the context of globalising food production and consumption. These concepts should facilitate a better understanding of the different ways in which time and space are organised in global modernity. The emerging new ways of structuring time and space requires and simultaneously enables innovative governance arrangements and these innovations will be reviewed in the fourth section. The challenges facing these newly emerging global food governance arrangements will be discussed in the fifth section. This chapter concludes with a re-examination of the research questions in this book in light of the new analytical framework presented.

## FOOD PRODUCTION AND CONSUMPTION IN GLOBAL MODERNITY

In pre-modern societies food production was related intimately to food consumption and mostly this was done through self-provisioning whereby people consumed the food they produced themselves. This situation changed radically in the course of the nineteenth century when the industrial revolution resulted in rapid industrialisation and urbanisation. Because of this (first or simple) modernisation process, more people were forced to buy their food, transforming them from producers into consumers (Fernández-Armesto, 2001). Since then, food trade has become an essential and large-scale activity, although food had been traded already long before. Nevertheless, even during this simple modern era of modernisation most food production and consumption remained rather closely linked to specific geographical locations and to particular times or seasons. Since the transition process towards global (or second) modernity in Western societies started in the 1970s, food production has however become increasingly uncoupled from food consumption. For the first time in human history, the specific place and time of the production of food has become more or less irrelevant for the specific place and time of its consumption. Figure 3.1 provides a schematic representation of this transition.

Agricultural seasons are increasingly of less importance in guiding consumer choices in Western countries. Consumers expect to find the same food products all year round on the supermarket shelves, thereby encouraging producers and processors to prolong the seasons and to re-arrange supply chains to make this possible.[2] For example, every day fresh tropical fruits are available in the supermarkets in Western Europe and the US but their origin may be very different. One day avocados may come from Thailand and another day from Ivory Coast, while the average consumer does not notice any difference. In addition, while until recently in the Netherlands fresh green beans could be consumed only in summertime, today they can be bought all year round. In summer, green beans are produced locally, while in spring and autumn they are imported from Spain and in winter flown in from Egypt or Kenya. So today, the availability of fresh green beans in the local Dutch supermarket is no longer an indication that it is summertime in the Netherlands.

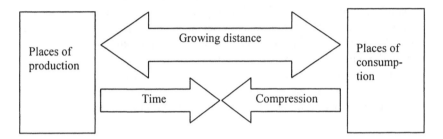

*Figure 3.1    Globalising food*

The uncoupling of time and space is intimately linked to a progressive industrialisation of food (replacing and substituting natural processes with industrial processes), allowing food products to be transported over longer distances at lower costs, facilitated by improved communication and storage and preservation technologies.[3] (See Box 3.1 for an example.)

## BOX 3.1  THE MAKING OF CHOCOLATE

From a luxury beverage in the seventeenth and eighteenth century, chocolate became a solid food with a mass market by the end of the twentieth century. The technology came from continental Europe – from Spain and Italy, where cocoa presses were first mechanised; from Holland where Conrad van Houten created cocoa powder; from Switzerland, where the Caillier and Nestlé families combined in business to make milk chocolate. However, it was the English Quaker manufacturers of cocoa who did most to revolutionise tastes. Fry's marketed the first true chocolate bars in 1847. They were

> made of Van Houten's powder, mixed with sugar and cocoa butter. The new product was particularly suited to mass production and its further transformations over the next 150 years proved infinite.
>
> *Source*: Davidson (1999); Fernández-Armesto (2001).

Extending food supply chains means stretching the relations between food producers and consumers in time and space. Time–space distantiation means linking places, sometimes at large distances, and requiring the synchronisation of time between different actors involved in the food supply chain.[4] Complex, perpetually changing and differentiating agri-food networks are emerging, involving many social actors, displaying a whole variety of social, technical, economic and natural components, and reproduced through numerous contextualised social practices (Giddens, 1979; Marsden, 2000; Murdoch, 2000; Van der Meulen, 2000; Dicken et al., 2001; Goodman, 2004).[5] These actors and practices are connected closely through a continuous flow of food products, information and money. (See Figure 3.2.)

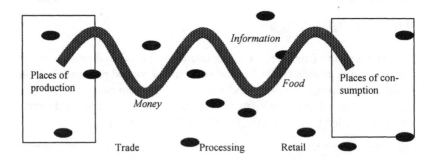

*Figure 3.2    Agri-food flows*

The formation of complex but flexible agri-food networks in global modernity is radically changing not only the social relationships between food producers and consumers but also the linkages between man and nature. Globalisation is stretching the distance in space and time between the consumption of food and the biological processes involved in producing it. Consequently, environmental impacts may occur on a larger scale and at a longer distance both in time and space from the consumer.[6] Moreover, the introduction of technological innovations in agriculture such as genetic modification makes more radical interference with biological processes in plants and animals possible than conventional agricultural technologies do, resulting in different forms of 'socialised nature' (Giddens, 1990). This human interference with 'natural processes' is repeatedly referred to as the main reason for declining consumer trust in the safety of food.

The fundamental social and social-environmental changes in the organisation of food production and consumption make conventional modes of governance increasingly less adequate. Regulating environmental, social, ethical and safety aspects related to food production and consumption requires accommodating the changing global dynamics and the associated radical local impacts as well as their mutual interactions, which evolve over time.[7] Identifying governance arrangements that fit these dynamic processes requires the use of concepts that can better grasp both the stretching of food production and consumption over time and space as well as their local and global impacts.

## FLOWS AND PLACE IN THE GLOBAL NETWORK SOCIETY

According to Urry, understanding the changing organisation of food production and consumption in global modernity remains difficult if the conventional sociological repertoire is used. Sociological concepts often remain based on the idea that a society is essentially the same as an independent nation-state. However, nation-states have moved away from governing a relatively fixed and clear-cut national population resident within a particular territory, constituting a clear and relatively unchanging community. Therefore, societies, interpreted as national states, should no longer be put at the centre of sociological analysis because globalisation has put an end to the possibilities of considering societies as containers that can be analysed in isolation.[8] Castells' interpretation of globalisation as the coming about of the network society and Urry's notion of global complexity may therefore provide the conceptual tools needed to deal with this specific social dynamics.

Global modernity can be understood as the formation of a global network society, organising time and space in different ways from before. The global network society is a new spatial process reintegrating the functional unity of different elements at distant locations made possible by modern transport, information and communication technologies (Castells, 1996). In this process, the traditional material foundations of society are being transformed in a fundamental manner. Until recently, people spent most of their lives in concrete physical places and perceived their space as place-based and a reliable resource to build their identity on, while biological and clock time remained their prime rhythmic organising principles. However, in the global

network society, space and time are organised differently. Connections between people, objects and technologies across multiple and distant times
and spaces may become tightly coupled, complex, enduring and predictable,
as well as more heterogeneous and loose. Such connections spread across
time and space with different reaches, which can be typified through scapes
and flows. Scapes (a generalised notion of 'landscapes' (Leydesdorff,
2002)) are the networks of technologies, organisations, texts and actors that
constitute various interconnected nodes along which flows can be relayed,
reconfiguring time and space. Flows of capital, information, or images, and
so on between physically disjointed positions are created because exchanges
and social interactions are increasingly taking place without face-to-face
contact. When these flows gain some permanence, it becomes possible to
speak about the 'space of flows'.[9] A space of flows may have a largely virtual character, as in the case of informational or financial flows. However, it
may also have specificity that is more material when the flows concern
movements of matter and energy or wastes, and so on, and here the origins,
destinations and the socio-spatial structures of such flows gain importance.
Flows may be organised within and across different societies and travel
along different 'scapes', but they remain unpredictable and lack any final-
ised 'order' because of the very large number of elements which interact
physically and because of the de-materialising transformations over multiple time-spaces. Many effects may be distantiated in time and space from
their origin and encounter positive as well as negative feedback mechanisms, which means that order and chaos are always intertwined. As unpredictable and yet irreversible patterns of path-dependence exist, the linear
metaphor of scales, from micro to macro level, or from the life-world to the
system-world, should be replaced by a metaphor of connections. Such connections are to be viewed as more or less mobile, more or less intense, more
or less social, and more or less 'at a distance'.[10] Iteration, recurrent human
actions, may produce non-equilibrium and non-linearity and, if the parameters alter dramatically, even unintended complex social change may take
place (Urry, 2003). Not only is the spatial dimension of social life changing
in global modernity, but also its time dimension since time and space are no
longer closely bound (Adam, 2000). Biological time that was the prime
rhythmic organising principle during most of human existence changed to
clock time in the industrial age, but now we live in the age of 'timeless
time' (Castells, 1996; Urry, 2000b). In this 'timeless time', the normal sequencing of events starts to disappear. Instantaneous financial transactions
and the integrated electronic communication media are examples of the
mixing of tenses, whereby time seems to have become self-maintaining,
random and incursive, thus breaking down rhythmicity.[11]

The formation of a space of flows with its timeless time may shift the location as well as the institutional structuring of power and this phenomenon is exemplified in the transformations of the state. A nation-state no longer has its traditional meaning as 'a sovereign state, whose hierarchically imposed commands are binding on all parties subject to its jurisdiction, while at the international level decisions are taken by sovereign states acting unilaterally or through formal or informal modes of inter-sovereign co-operation' (Karkkainen, 2004: 76). The 'gardening state' (Bauman 1987) of simple modernity that was chiefly concerned with patterning, regularity, ordering and control is decreasingly able to fully control social processes and can only regulate (the conditions for) mobility. The presence of numerous global flows causes serious difficulties for nation-states no longer in control of the space surrounding them (Urry, 2000b). Any single society finds diverse self-organising networks, fluids and 'policies' seeking to striate its internal space and to transform the space beyond them. National states and international regimes struggle to regulate legal, economic, environmental and social aspects of the de-territorialised and de-centred mobilities of the global network society. According to Castells (1996), the rise of the network society has made economic networks transcend the existing political structures. Thus, in a countervailing fashion, nation-states are transferring selected powers to supranational agencies and institutions such as the European Union (EU) and the World Trade Organisation (WTO).[12] However, despite these initiatives and the presence of exceptional levels of global interdependence, no unified global state has yet replaced the national ones to deal with contemporary transboundary phenomena. The state in the age of globalisation necessarily has to become a network-state, a state made out of a complex web of power-sharing and negotiated decision-making practices involving international, multinational, national, regional, local and non-governmental political institutions and private actors (Castells, 2000).

Yet, although networks and flows change over time, this is not a one-dimensional process of transference of power from local and national levels to global corporate interests but a process with contradictory tendencies of which the outcome is not already known (Mol, 2001). The 'space of flows' with its timeless time and its reduced relevance of physical space may increasingly replace the 'space of places', but most people still live in the space of places with its time discipline, face-to-face interaction and socially determined sequencing. The 'contrasting logic between timelessness, structured by the space of flows, and multiple, subordinated temporalities, associated with the space of places' (Castells, 1996: 468) creates a tension in contemporary society between the global and the local levels. Although most people still perceive their space as place-based on which they can securely build their identity, their world is in reality increasing dominated by the space of flows, forcing them to orient their lives simultaneously to global processes devoid of specific place or time characteristics.

Food forms a typical example of such complex material global flows, travelling along different scapes, expressing de-territorialisation, and de-centred mobilities. Applying the concepts introduced by Castells and Urry will facilitate an analysis of the environmental and social impacts resulting from the growing distance between food production and consumption locations. The need for innovative governance arrangements to address the impacts stemming from this transition can be conceptualised as follows:

1. The growing flows of food become increasingly structured beyond the reach of the conventional regulatory institutions, in particular the nation-state.
2. Next to the conventional nation-state and international governmental bodies, other agencies introduce competing governance arrangements.
3. New concerns about the safety, social and environmental aspects related to food emerge and they demand an active restoring of trust in (the quality of) food.
4. The global character of many challenges related to food flows gives rise to concerns about transparency, participation and democracy in governing them and about equity related to the consequences of decisions made.

## GOVERNING GLOBAL FLOWS OF FOOD

Conceptualising food production and consumption in global modernity as global material flows in a network society allows for a better understanding of both the transformations taking place in the organisation of agri-food networks and the changes confronting both producers and consumers (Beardsworth and Keil, 1997). The organic character of food combined with the current state of technology rules out, at least until now, the option of re-nouncing the space of place altogether as concrete locations for its production and consumption remain essential. It is, therefore, essential to distinguish the ways in which food is integrated in the places of production and consumption from food in the space of flows. This distinction clearly points at the key problems facing contemporary global food governance. (See Figure 3.3 for a schematic representation.)

When attempting to govern food in the global network society, one is confronted with different dynamics occurring at the same time. Difficulties emerge when regulations concentrate on one particular dynamic only. Most conventional ways of governing food were built on the concepts of the space of places, interpreted within the domain of the nation-state (see the previous chapter). Today, the formation of global food supply chains pushes however towards the establishment of some form of food governance into the space of flows.

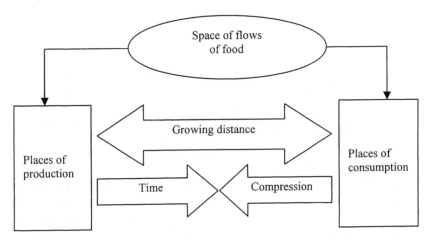

*Figure 3.3    Global flows of food*

## Governing Food in the Space of Places

A frequently suggested response to the difficult challenges facing conventional nation-state-based regulation of food production and consumption today is the creation of locally organised food supply chains. Such local, often community-based, food supply chains 'tend to be place-based, drawing on the unique attributes of a particular bioregion and its population to define and support themselves' (Feenstra, 2002: 100).

This approach opposes the inevitability of a continuous trend towards further globalisation in agro-food production and trade (O'Hara and Stagl, 2001; Halweil, 2002; Green et al., 2003; Hines, 2003). Empirical research has made clear that farmers' practices in Europe remain much more varied than generally expected in thinking about the modernisation process in agriculture (Oostindie et al., 2000; Van der Ploeg et al., 2000a, 2000b; Renting et al., 2003). Furthermore, local diversity should not be considered a relic of the past because it can also be observed in highly specialised farms. These and other studies show that the traditional closed paradigm of simple modernisation is opening up towards a multi-level, multi-actor and multi-faceted nature of rural development. Van der Ploeg et al. (2000a: 399) consider the emergence of new localised food supply chains as 'maybe the most evident example of the reconfiguration of resources and networks in rural development'. A concrete example of the recent appearance of new food supply chains is the recent growth in farmers' markets in the EU and the US. (See Box 3.2.)

---

## BOX 3.2   FARMERS' MARKETS IN THE UK

Since their inception in the 1990s, farmers' markets have captured the imagination of policy makers, media, producers and consumers in several European countries and the US. For example, the number of farmers' markets in the US has grown from nearly 300 in the mid-1970s to more than 3,100 in 2000. Farmers' markets are considered a positive response to some of the problems associated with the conventional food supply system. These alternative food supply chains are based on two guiding principles: firstly that the produce for sale is of a localised origin (in the UK, for example, with a maximum ranging between 30 and 75 km), and secondly that the market vendors themselves should have been involved in the food production process.

The price and quality (freshness) of the food products remain important but are not the only reasons for consumers to buy food at farmers' markets. The local and social embeddedness of the exchange at farmers' markets is essential as well and this is maximised when consumers can relate directly to the actual producers selling their own produce that has been processed only selectively.

*Source*: Hinrichs (2000); Halweil (2002); Kirwan (2004).

---

Referring to the example of these farmers' markets, several observers consider localising food supply chains as the only real alternative to globalisation in food provision. They consider globalised food supply chains as fundamentally incapable of dealing with contemporary consumer concerns about the environmental, health and social impacts of modern practices in food production and consumption. These concerns are often conceptualised as worries about the diminishing quality of modern food, which has become less 'natural', less 'organic' and more 'processed'. The 'natural' character of the products and production methods used in local food supply networks are considered the best guarantee for the health of human beings, farm animals and the eco-system as a whole (Green et al., 2003).[13] Princen (1997: 250/1) argues this as follows:

> Market expansion and factor mobility increase distance on many dimensions, rendering ecologically informed and ethically responsible decisions impossible. Thus sustainable production requires effective feedback from all decisions in a production chain. When distance approaches zero in, say, a household or a self-sufficient community, that feedback is likely to exist. However, as distance increases, feedback diminishes and the need for accountability and governance increases, possibly exponentially.

Thus, according to Princen, de-globalisation through the creation of small-scale local food networks would enable the checks and balances necessary for sustainable resource use as they can function through direct interaction between food producers and consumers. By developing alternative food networks, local producers can guard themselves against incorporation in spatially extensive food supply chains and thereby avoid becoming vulnerable to subordination within these chains in order to serve the interests of their most powerful actors (Watts et al., 2005). (See Figure 3.4.)

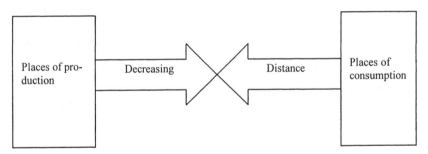

*Figure 3.4   Regulation of food in the space of places*

Active consumer participation is becoming an essential characteristic of the regulation of food in the space of places within modern, localised supply chains. Consumer involvement makes it possible to establish trust in the quality and safety of food based on personalised face-to-face contacts and not only via abstract expert-based systems, as in globalised food supply chains.[14] Becoming involved in the localised food supply chains can furthermore promote a sense of community integration, as networks between like-minded people are strengthened (Watts et al., 2005).

As producers and consumers themselves take up responsibilities in local food supply chains, direct involvement by the nation-state would only unnecessarily interfere with these face-to-face interactions at community level. National governments should therefore protect small-scale farms against global corporate domination and its harmful effects and, in general, support the principles of a localised agro-ecology to ensure food security in combination with the vitality of robust rural economies.

'De-globalising' food production and consumption and creating localised systems of food provisioning may have attractive opportunities for innovative forms of governance, but this model has also been criticised by several scholars on several grounds. Firstly, being physically close does not necessarily result in less market orientation and instrumentalism in the relationships between producers and consumers. As Hinrichs (2000) showed, consumers pay as much attention to freshness and the price of food at local farmers' markets as at any other market and they consider the local provenance of the produce as far less important than conventional considerations among consumers about their food. It is therefore not correct to assume that economic practices that are bounded locally and involve face-to-face interactions will automatically demonstrate all the putative benefits of social embeddedness. This assumption conflates spatial relations with social relations without any justification. Feedback mechanisms necessary for sustainable food production could also be organised in different ways.[15] Secondly, environmental degradation cannot be excluded by definition in small-scale agriculture, as it is not the scale but dimensions such as time, local power structures and specific technical and social practices that determine the environmental sustainability of food production and consumption (Scoones and Toulmin, 1999; Keeley and Scoones, 2003). Moreover, the necessary technical, financial and human resources for dealing with particular environmental problems may even be absent at the local level. In addition, even in small-scale agriculture, those who are responsible for environmental destruction are not necessarily the ones who fall victim to it, in particular when the effects only surface after some time. Thirdly, de-globalisation of food production via locally organised food supply chains would not automatically solve the problems of poverty and environmental degradation in developing countries. Demanding 'self-reliance' in food provision would also deny poor countries the possibility to export agricultural products to rich country markets. This exclusion would only add to the already existing poverty in developing countries and the inequality between the rich and the poor. Kevin Watkins (2002) from Oxfam suggested 'if trade is to work for the poor, we need to challenge the power relations and vested interests that make markets work for the rich. That means putting land redistribution, workers' rights, environmental sustainability and the curtailment of corporate power at the heart of the agenda.'[16] Safeguarding the market access opportunities to the richer countries for the poor in developing countries then could be considered a contribution to sustainability and equality instead of a diminution.

Despite the popularity of locally organised food supply chains as the best response to the challenges facing the governance of food production and consumption today, this option thus has several drawbacks. Such a process of de-globalisation therefore does not necessarily provide the only alternative to conventional nation-state-based forms of food regulation (Evans et al., 2002). In particular, when globalisation is understood as a heterogeneous and complex process, other innovative governance arrangements of global food provision deserve specific attention as they may provide interesting responses as well.

## Governing Food in the Space of Flows

Attempting to organise governance of food in the space of flows requires governance arrangements to be global and abstract, and as much as possible devoid of specific characteristics of place and time – 'place-less and time-less'. Such a form of governance should be based as much as possible on product characteristics alone, because this would mean that if a food product were considered safe at one place, it would also be regarded as safe at another place.[17] (See Figure 3.5.)

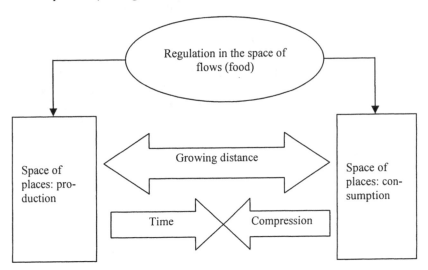

*Figure 3.5   Regulation in the global space of flows of food*

Several regulatory practices have been developed to meet this objective, in particular within the World Trade Organisation (WTO), but also through private initiatives such as ISO and HACCP.

Governing food in the space of flows requires trade regulation at a supra-national level, a domain currently dominated by the WTO. (See Chapter 4 for further details.) WTO-based regulations of food are based essentially on general economic considerations applied to all international trade, but supplemented with health and safety concerns (Josling et al., 2004). Food products that are traded internationally can be checked for the presence of dangerous substances provided this control is justified by sound scientific evidence about the risks involved in the human consumption of these substances. Regulations should therefore be restricted to the composition of the food products themselves and only include the characteristics of the production process if that would potentially have direct effects on the product itself ('product-related production and process methods'). Thus, according to the WTO principles governments should not distinguish between food produced *with* special care for social and environmental impacts and food produced *without* those concerns when the differences between both are not observable in the food product itself.

These official governmental governance arrangements are being supplemented by regulatory instruments initially developed by private firms, for example certification schemes such as ISO 14001 and HACCP. (See Chapter 7 for further details.) ISO 14001 is a certification scheme which has not been developed specifically for food or food products, but is becoming a global standard to assure the environmental performance of food producing companies as well. HACCP (Hazard Analysis of Critical Control Points), introduced as a certification scheme in the late 1960s to support firms in their efforts to reduce food risks, became officially recognised and widely endorsed in the 1980s and the 1990s. Production processes can be certified, and also the final product when all production processes involved have received certification. Although initially developed as a voluntary instrument for private firms, HACCP certification is recognised by different governments as a fulfilment of the legal obligations imposed on private food processing industries to ensure the safety of their food products (Unnevehr and Jensen, 1999).

Next to these official regulations and private certification schemes dealing with governing food in the global space of flows, recently NGO-initiated food labels are also being introduced. Multiple NGO-initiated labelling schemes (organics, MSC, free-range eggs, fair trade, and many others) distinguish food products based on their production process. These alternatives seem attractive to many consumers because they are concerned about different practices involved in producing and trading their food, while these practices cannot be detected easily in the final product itself and require additional information. NGO-initiated labelling schemes are particularly well qualified to respond to this growing need for reliable information about food production practices (Raynolds, 2000). For example, whether fish is produced through sustainable fisheries or not is only detectable for consumers through a label indicating the production circumstances, and therefore several NGOs have developed different initiatives for this purpose. (See Chapters 4 and 7.)

## CHALLENGES IN GOVERNING GLOBAL FLOWS OF FOOD

The attempts by the WTO, private firms and NGOs to introduce or oppose particular regulatory practices can be regarded as different attempts to establish food governance arrangements within the space of flows. They all try to facilitate global food trade and are trying to respond to the challenges identified in the previous chapter, albeit in different ways. The presence of different initiatives in establishing global food governance lead to the following, empirical questions:

1. The globalising of food provisioning has changed the characteristics of food risks. WTO- and government-based regulations rely on scientific expertise as well as private certification schemes like ISO 14001 and HACCP. In order to acquire the necessary consumer trust, private initiatives refer mainly to the scientific but also to the global character of their standards as well as to the independence of the certifying bodies (Unnevehr and Jensen, 1999). However, the ambivalence of consumer confidence in science and technology and the multidimensional and shifting character of their concerns are intensified further in the context of the global risk society where the general weakness of official institutions in creating trust becomes even more distinct. The distance between global regulatory institutions, like the Codex Alimentarius, and consumers is even larger than the communication problems already evident in nation-state-based regulatory institutions, involving specialised ministries and national parliaments. Personalising anonymous institutions and thereby creating trust through some form of direct personal interaction becomes nearly impossible in the context of global food supply chains. The question then becomes whether abstract institutions such as science, the nation-state and international governmental agencies can still create consumer trust in the safety and quality of food? Moreover, if so, in what way can they achieve this objective?

2. Strict food safety norms imposed by the richer food importing countries may create serious difficulties for smaller farmers and food-processing firms in general and for those in developing countries in particular

(Reardon et al., 1999; O'Hara and Stagl, 2001; Otsuki et al., 2001). The necessary infrastructure and technical knowledge needed to fulfil the specific requirements may be lacking in these countries, while the costs of certification may also constitute insurmountable problems. Therefore, often these farmers and food-processing firms in developing countries are forced to refrain from exporting food or to depend on multinational firms for providing the necessary funds and management systems to ensure food safety throughout the chain (Unnevehr and Jensen, 1999). So, in what way do the different approaches to global food governance deal with this problem and prevent global environmental and food safety standards from functioning as unjustified (green) barriers to trade (Neumayer, 2001)? In this regard, it is essential to include the important observation by Castells that within global modernity divisions no longer exist necessarily between the developed and developing countries but involve a mixture of divisions in scales, areas and product characteristics. The most important division in the global network society is, according to Castells, the binary logic of inclusion/exclusion. The global network society is in all instances dominating activities and people who are external to the networks (Castells, 2004).

3. The diverse and evolving character of food-related concerns among consumers and citizens is a daily reality and it is unlikely that these concerns will simply disappear or be fixed through the homogenising tendencies within global modernity. Diversity among the consumer considerations related to food may be the result of different local and national food traditions, of different socio-economic features and of differences in public trust in state institutions (Goodman, 2001; Lang and Heasman, 2004). How do different approaches to global food governance combine in their regulatory instruments the concrete food concerns that are similar at the global level with those evolving concerns that have a more diverse and place-bound character?

4. The regulatory arrangements initiated by NGOs are introduced in a context where nation-state-based and global food governance arrangements already exist. Since these private labelling schemes and other innovative regulatory arrangements will not fully replace state-based regulations, several questions may be asked. How can WTO- and national government-based regulations accommodate the novel responsibilities taken up by non-state actors such as consumers, NGOs and private businesses? How can innovative NGO-based arrangements be democratically controlled, comparable to the conventional nation-state-based regulations? The WTO may even have particular problems in dealing with these non-state initiatives to regulate food because within their decision-making procedures only nation-states can officially participate. Contrary to other

multilateral institutions like the Convention on Biodiversity (CBD), civil society has no recognised formal position within the WTO. A particular question with regard to private certification schemes is also if and how they contribute to real improvements in the environment and in the safety of food, because these schemes generally focus on internal management procedures and do not define clear, objectively verifiable environmental and food safety standards (Krut and Gleckman, 1998).[18] On the other hand, these certification schemes are generally more oriented to consumers than most government-based regulations are.

These questions show the complex issues involved in studying the role of existing, and the introduction of alternative, food governance arrangements in the context of global modernity. Despite their importance, it will not be possible to answer all these questions in this study and the focus will be on the evolving risks and concerns (question 1, to a certain extent) and on the relation between governmental and privately initiated tools of food governance (question 4). In this situation, a particular challenge is to identify food governance arrangements that can bridge the gap between the ways in which time and space are organised in the space of flows of the global network society and those in the local space of places; between the global material flows of food and the specific local context where most food producers and consumers still spend most of their daily lives.

## CONCLUSION

The regulatory practices of simple modernity are no longer able to respond adequately to contemporary consumer concerns with regard to food. In the global network society, complex material flows and networks increasingly escape these conventional regulatory mechanisms as they are still based largely on nation-state arrangements. While several global flows, for example of finances and cars, are becoming more and more 'footloose', this does not apply to food, however. At least for the moment, food is different because of its material (organic) character and its intimate linkages with day-to-day human survival. Therefore, a key question is to what extent food governance arrangements within the space of places alone will be able to solve the environmental and safety problems related to the global flows of food, whether global governance arrangements within the space of flows alone can provide a satisfying answer, or whether a combination of both kinds of arrangements is needed.

Globalisation of complex agri-food networks is based mainly on a space of flows of information, financial resources and material food products, but simultaneously involves specific localised practices of production, processing, trade and consumption. These localised practices have concrete material and social impacts and therefore within agri-food supply chains the organisation of time and space in the space of flows creates a tension with their impacts in the space of place. Governing these chains, in particular with regard to (existing and emerging) environmental and food safety concerns, requires innovative approaches. Solving this tension more adequately means developing practices that combine both forms of organising time and space. Such practices for food governance will have to cover different dimensions, different scales and different actors. Existing nation-state-based regulatory practices may remain useful, but they will necessarily have to be transformed to be able to function within the changing time–space circumstances of the global network society.

Future food governance arrangements dealing with globalising production and consumption will have to acknowledge the reality of the following fundamental transition processes:

1. The conventional role and position of the nation-state is changing and during this process, local, regional and international levels of governance are assuming important responsibilities. Moreover, the strict separation between public and private responsibilities, which traditionally formed the foundation of nation-state-based regulations of food, is dissolving. The (potential) impacts of food production and consumption practices are contingent and they display a multidimensional character and acquire different dimensions, depending on place, time and scale. Consequently, to be able to deal with these impacts, different local, regional and global social networks bringing together different combinations of state and non-state actors will have to be established.

2. The use of science and technology in food production, transport and processing is increasing, enabling more radical human interference with nature. The potential impacts of these modern technological innovations on the natural environment and human health may therefore also be more radical than in the past. Simple modern responses, based on the benevolence of increased involvement of science, are no longer adequate because science is increasingly responsible for the occurrence of negative impacts, while science nevertheless also remains essential in understanding and managing these impacts. This ambivalent role of science in the environmental and safety impact of contemporary globalising food production and consumption has to be taken into account in future governance arrangements.

3. The governance of food can no longer be restricted to the conventional food safety concerns for which the standard risk policy provided the un-

disputed basis for many years. Governing risks in the global risk society cannot be as straightforward as simple modern approaches presuppose because the role of science and technology has changed while various previously unrecognised consumer concerns emerge, related to environmental, health, social, ethical or animal welfare issues involved in food production and consumption.

4. Finally, establishing consumer trust in the quality and safety of food also requires changes. The continuously growing time–space distantiation between food producers and consumers forces traditional face-to-face, or more personalised, ways for establishing trust to give way to more abstract ways based on the involvement of 'expert systems' and different mass media. In the context of reflexive modernity, consumers nowadays have to evaluate and modify their daily routines repeatedly in the light of a continuous stream of, often contradictory, information stemming from different expert systems. This information may originate from scientific specialists, but also from political actors, NGOs and different media. The presence of a plurality of viewpoints, sources and opinions forces consumers to *choose* between different experts, which results in a permanent ambiguity in the trust of consumer in their food (Beck, 1992; Irwin, 2001).

These different transitions make simple, one-dimensional solutions to the global food governance challenge beforehand inadequate. Therefore, the involvement of different social actors in different combinations and roles, consumers/citizens, private firms, NGOs, national governments and international institutions, are needed to create flexible adequate arrangements. The engagement of these different actors may be more passive or more active, incidental or permanent, formal or informal and sometimes operating at large distances through global networks or within the immediate surroundings through social communities. Such flexible arrangements may facilitate (different groups of) consumers to deal with concerns about food that are science-based, ethical or political, and that may even change over time and differ per location. Real understanding of this complex and evolving reality of global food governance requires empirical research, and therefore four different and concrete case studies will improve our understanding of the daily reality governing food in the global network society.

After this analysis of the challenges facing conventional nation-state-based arrangements and reviewing current responses, the central research questions in this book will have to be rephrased as follows:

1. How can the innovative governance arrangements better be understood using the concepts of organising space and time within the global space of flows and in the local space of places?
2. How do these innovative governance arrangements function in comparison with conventional nation-state-based regulations, in particular with regard to the roles of the nation-state, the market parties and the civil society organisations?
3. How do these responses meet the following key challenges for food governance in global modernity?
   a. To allow the participation of different social actors in their development and implementation.
   b. To allow the use of different definitions of food quality.
   c. To enable producers and consumers to choose between different (ways of producing) food with different concerns.
   d. To create trust among consumers in the context of the global space of flows.

## NOTES

1.  Not only is food travelling but people as well. It was estimated that in 1995 about 597 million people crossed international borders, taking with them specific food habits and often demanding to be provided with food fitting in their own culinary traditions while travelling to very distant places (Motarjemi et al., 2001).
2.  As many food products can be found all over the world as well, one may be tempted to see the emergence of a 'global cuisine' (Mennell, 1996).
3.  A distinction should be made between agricultural products as inputs in food processing industries (such as soybeans, maize and different kinds of oils and fats) and products for specialised and differentiated (sometimes niche) markets (such as fresh foods and vegetables).
4.  It is essential to be aware that, for the near future, agri-food networks can probably not become fully disembedded from place and time, like 'footloose' financial networks can (Griswold and Wright, 2004). 'Space and time still constitute the essential context (for the plant's life-cycle)' (Adam, 2000: 134). More than is the case with other products, attempts to *de*-contextualise the production of food remain a paradoxical and contentious issue. Goodman (1999: 18) speaks about 'corporeality: to signify organic, eco-social processes that are intrinsic to agriculture and to food' and Fine (1998: 8) states that 'what does set food apart is the necessary presence of the "natural" at both the beginning and the end of the food systems–both in agriculture and in palatability'. Although food consumption may be less directly linked to specific local material practices than food production, it remains embedded in specific localised culinary cultures. For example, global fast food chains take efforts to adapt their menus to local taste. Therefore, only McDonalds' customers in the Netherlands can buy a McKroket, a special version of the typically Dutch kroket (or meat roll). Moreover, elderly Chinese women transform fast food restaurants into slow food ones as they pass large parts of the day in a McDonalds restaurant in Beijing waiting to pick up their grandchildren from school (Watson, 1997).
5.  Agri-food networks are often associated with actor-network theories (Latour), but here these networks are conceptualised as social structures (recursively organised rules and re-

sources used by knowledgeable and capable actors in the diversity of contexts of daily life) (Giddens, 1979).

6.  The distance between food production and consumption in time and space is, however, not necessarily connected directly with their environmental impact. (See also hereafter.)

7.  It is for example impossible to imagine the introduction of a 'fair trade' label for coffee in 1859, although in this year the Dutch writer Multatuli first published his novel 'Max Havelaar'. Yet the 'Max Havelaar' trademark was only introduced in 1986, so fair trade coffee is probably the result of recently emerging consumer concerns combined with changes in the global coffee market and with the possibilities offered by modern communication technologies.

8.  Urry initially conceptualised the recent changes in Western societies as the transition from organised to disorganised capitalism (Lash and Urry, 1987), but in his more recent work (Urry, 2000a, 2002a) he distances himself from such economy-focussed approach and he starts developing the concept of global complexity.

9.  The space of flows still includes a territorial dimension because it requires a technological infrastructure that operates from certain locations connecting functions and people located in specific places (Castells, 2000). However, these network nodes are much less oriented to the particular geographical characteristics of the location and its surroundings and much more to the interaction with the other nodes in the network.

10. Urry (2002b) claims that social relationships at a distance have not fundamentally changed through globalisation or with new information and communication technologies because social relationships have always involved complex patterns of immediate presence and intermittent absence at a distance. Nevertheless, in my view, globalisation has radicalised the scale and the impact of these patterns.

11. In the economic sphere, this means time–space compression in production and the formation of a flexible workforce, while in the social sphere biological rhythms no longer determine life. In the cultural sphere, temporality becomes undifferentiated (at the same time eternal and ephemeral).

12. EU regulation is gradually replacing nation-state-based regulations in Europe, while the WTO dominates global regulations of international trade. The EU is repeatedly regarded as a model for a new regulatory state (Urry, 2000b) as it is a relatively small structure employing few bureaucrats and controlling a modest budget (apart from the Common Agricultural Policy). As the EU's treaties and directives oblige member-state governments to bring their own legislation in line with the EU's and, in addition, allow individual EU citizens to appeal to the European Court of Justice, the EU can effectively be considered a form of multi-level governance (Hajer et al., 2004).

13. See also the 'Manifesto on the Future of Food', formulated by the International Commission on the Future of Food and Agriculture, which brought together scientists and activists mainly from developed countries but also from India and other developing countries. Their ultimate objective is 'a transition to a more decentralized, democratic and cooperative, non-corporate, small-scale organic farming as practised by traditional farming communities, agroecologists, and indigenous peoples for millennia' (ICFFA, 2003: 4).

14. See for example the *Guide to Eating Locally and Seasonally in the Greater Portland and Vancouver Areas*: 'Food has the potential to weave together the land, people and communities into a fabric of relationships that fosters justice and sustainability. Unfortunately, the food we eat often represents unjust relationships and a degraded Earth. Community food security (defined as all persons in a community having access to fresh, local, culturally appropriate food at all times) is a concept and process that creates healthy relationships around food' (Interfaith Network, 2003).

15. Marsden (2004: 138), for example, claims that 'what marks alternative food chains out from the conventional system is by no means their face-to-face nature necessarily. In some of the more mature quality supply chains we see the development of spatially extended networks, which are selling brands and labels and seriously commodifying their culinary repertoires (e.g. Parmigiano Reggiano Cheese). They are still categorically alternative, however, in that they have done and do re-equate nature, space, socio-technical practices, and quality conventions in ways which make it impossible to replicate these

outside that network. These then are the new ecologically deepened supply chains.' See also Van der Meulen (2000) and Goodman (2004).

16. See for further debates on the interests of agricultural trade for developing countries, UNCTAD (2004).

17. A critical issue then is who determines the safety of food, because despite the presence of global food safety norms they may still offer problems for specific producers and certain countries (Busch et al., 2000). For example, the decision by the EU to allow European consumers to choose between GM and non-GM food requires labelling of all GM food everywhere (see Chapter 6). Another example concerns the harmonisation within the EU of food safety standards on the presence of aflatoxins in dried fruits and nuts. Otsuki et al. (2001) estimated that this policy would have devastating consequences for African farmers exporting these products to the EU. Harmonising aflatoxins levels does facilitate trade within the EU, but African farmers will lose their market share because they cannot comply with these norms. This economic model-based calculation, however, did not fully appreciate the concrete complexities related to international governance and global food trade (Moonen, 2004).

18. The democratic legitimacy of private forms of governance is a critical issue, and although this can be established pragmatically through appreciating the quality of the result, it remains unlikely that this solution will satisfy all concerned. Papadopoulos (2003), however, shows that standard political–administrative decision-making systems are not necessarily more democratic and legitimate than co-operative forms of governance are.

# 4. Governments and the governance of food

## INTRODUCTION

Citizens have looked for a long time (and many are still looking) at their governments to guarantee the safety of their food and to limit the negative social and environmental impacts resulting from its production and trade. However, the process of globalisation has fundamentally changed the role of the nation-state and the context in which it operates. Nevertheless, national governments and international governmental institutes remain important actors in food governance. The empirical case studies on BSE and GM food, presented in the next chapters, will illustrate the various ways in which different governments handle particular food concerns among their citizens. Before presenting these case studies, this chapter will review the roles in food governance played by national governments and international institutions such as the World Trade Organisation (WTO).

## NATION-STATES AND FOOD GOVERNANCE

Over time, national governments have developed elaborate legal frameworks dealing with food safety to protect their citizens against domination of private profit interests by unscrupulous producers and retailers. Laws, official regulations, formal controls and enforcement mechanisms were implemented to ensure that the population got wholesome food of the kind they expected and to protect honest manufacturers from unfair competition (Tansey and Worsley, 1995). To be effective, governments and regulators needed flexibility to keep up with advances in science and to be able to respond to changes within their national society. One recent example of the institutional innovations is the establishment by many governments of Consumer Affairs Departments destined to protect the interests of consumers. However, these Departments remain government departments and therefore they tend to adopt a 'neutral' role balancing between consumer and industry interests. The activities of many of such Consumer Affairs Departments are in practice rigidly limited by legislation determined by pressure of economic interests (Nestle, 2002). Enforcing the actual legal regulations and guidelines on food production and consumption in reality is difficult as well, because it requires the involvement of many different national, regional and local authorities to apply them locally and they all have different assignments and use different regulatory tools.

The recent food crises have put the existing food policy routines under pressure and placed food safety (and how to guarantee this) high on the public and the political agenda. The routinised legal and procedural practices and institutions that took care of food safety independently of the direct experiences, knowledge and consciousness of most citizen-consumers became the subject of society-wide discussion. This public debate also discussed the role of science in food risk politics and the responsibilities of the different social actors involved in food safety, such as national governments, consumers and private enterprises. The globalisation process that is occurring simultaneously complicates the public discussion of food politics even further as the sovereign nation-state no longer seems to be able to determine its internal policy independently from other nation-states, multilateral institutions and international agreements, or from private actors operating at different levels. The impact of globalisation on nation-states and their sovereignty is nevertheless contingent and depends on the issue and the particular domain of regulation concerned. The challenge to respond to these transformations is particularly demanding in the case of food, because food provisioning makes use of both private and shared (water) resources and is linked to global networks, global flows and global commons (biodiversity, climate and energy). The principle of sovereignty may suggest that states have authority and control over their own territories but these territories are part of the global ecosystem and therefore they cannot be isolated in any meaningful way. Ecological interdependence thus scrambles the logic of sovereignty as it relates to environmental issues (Wapner, 1998). Ensuring safe and sustainable food can therefore no longer remain an issue of national governments regulating either production processes or mere national consumer concerns, but becomes part of much broader deliberative processes dealing with the challenge to determine what constitutes *acceptable* food production *and* consumption practices as well as the institutionalisation thereof. Introducing innovative food governance arrangements thus demands the involvement of all relevant social actors, including producers, consumers and governmental authorities.

The logical conclusion that the role of the nation-state in imposing environmental standards in the context of globalisation may be expected to be diminishing overall is not supported by empirical evidence (Jänicke and Klauw, 2004). The nation-state remains an important cornerstone of international affairs, simply because, despite the significant changes that are taking place worldwide, it is still the most complete nexus of relationships that continues to exist within the international order. The nation-state remains to be recognised by many as a vital institution possessing both important symbolic and real authority. As Polanyi (1944) convincingly showed, nation-states play a necessary and essential role in curbing the negative impacts of free markets. Despite the fluid and transforming boundaries between public and private, between public and corporate, and between national and international, the state still fulfils essential tasks. The principal reason is that at the global level there is not yet a functional equivalent comparable to national governments as highly visible, legitimised and competent territorial actors and protectors. In contrast to specialised global institutions, national governments are willing and capable of trying to find compromises between economic and environmental demands. In particular, governments do not react to economic pressure alone but also to the preference of voters, although they remain conscious that 'international trade is a transnational reality and those seeking to promote sustainable development must seek to operate within it' (French, 2002: 139).

Globalisation is not, in addition, stripping every state of its longstanding sovereignty in equal measure, due to differences in power as 'state and non-state actors strive to establish principles of their choosing, using the mechanisms they have at their disposal' (Drahos and Braithwaite, 2001: 124). Moreover, the resulting governmental sovereignty depends on the way globalisation takes place and whether what is being globalised is a national regulatory model that advantages a particular state (ibid.). Globalisation has, for example, created a new policy arena for pioneer countries in environmental policies, where often more advanced countries are rewarded for their innovative arrangements. This tendency is supplemented by interventions from private companies, which are operating at the global level. These private companies prefer uniform standards and as the larger markets (where consumers have more buying power) often demand higher standards, these private standards constitute a driving force towards environmental improvements. Therefore, sometimes there may even be a convergence of interests between innovative multinational corporations and environmental policy-makers.

Nevertheless, in the context of globalisation, the central role of the nation-state can no longer be presupposed and they need to reflect upon their position and the necessity to develop appropriate relations with non-governmental and corporate actors. Often these recent changes have been designated as shifts in governance and the emergence of multi-level, multi-actor governance (Van Tatenhove et al., 2000). These shifts in governance have become the issue of both theoretical and political debates and during these discussions, the (sometimes fundamental) differences have been emphasized between the conventional nation-state-based governmental or policy-making arrangements and the emerging innovative forms of governance. Although the shifts have been described repeatedly in rather general and theoretical terms (Haas and Haas, 1995; Young, 1994, 1997), most empirical evidence remains anecdotal (Peters and Pierre, 1998; Marks et al., 1996). Yet it is unclear whether these shifts in governance are spreading and becoming integrated in a new phase of modernity or whether they remain restricted to a limited number of isolated initiatives (cf. Hogenboom et al., 2000). Food forms an interesting case to study these shifts in governance involving multiple actors at multiple levels because its relevance for daily life makes it a sensitive political issue. New forms of local, national and international, and public and private food governance are discussed, developed and partly implemented, and they include innovations in the roles of the different actors involved as well as new instruments, procedures and institutions. These innovations in governance combine changes at the supply side (for example increased control within the food production and processing chains), at the national level (such as legal initiatives and bureaucratic re-arrangements) and at the level of the EU while they are introduced within the wider frame of the WTO as a guiding global multilateral institution.

## THE EUROPEAN UNION

Since 1992, with the implementation of the Single European Act, the European Union (EU) has created an open European market by removing physical, fiscal and transport barriers to international trade. With a combination of harmonisation (all member states adopt the same standards) and mutual recognition (each member state accepts the standards prevailing in the other member states) the EU has consolidated a single market for food. Nowadays, the EU has gained exclusive competence over trade policy and the European Commission is taking the lead in trade policy-making.

Ensuring the safety of food has become one of the major food policy priorities of the European Union. Before the BSE crisis (see Chapter 5), food safety issues were dealt with at the EU level through the 'comitology' system. This comitology system consisted of committees bringing together scientific and food policy experts from the different member states. Despite the presence of this elaborate system, the BSE crisis did occur, thereby challenging this institutional set-up and pointing at the same time at the lack of transparency in the system (Buonanno et al., 2001). Recent food crises caused by the presence of dioxins in poultry and the impacts of Foot and

Mouth Disease (FMD) have led to the creation or growing awareness of new risks, the introduction of improved detection technologies and to an increased concern among consumers about the safety of their food and the presence of potential risks. Combined with a more general reduction of public trust in the capacity of governmental institutions to protect citizens from unwanted harm, these food crises have repeatedly resulted in unrest and furious debates in the media on the presence of particular food risks and on the effectiveness of existing food safety policies. In these debates, several essential characteristics of the conventional food system were questioned: the modern high-technological and science-guided approach to food production, consumption and the management of potential risks, as well as the relatively strong disconnection (in place) between food producers and consumers.

Although the countries in Western Europe were confronted with these crises and connected debates at different levels of intensity, the large public engagement and political significance prompted governments and other social actors in agri-food networks to act strongly in nearly all countries and in the EU as a whole. In order to restore consumer confidence the European Food Safety Authority (EFSA) was established in 2002. EFSA's two main areas of work are risk assessment and risk communication. Risk management measures and the operation of food control systems are not within EFSA's remit and remain the responsibility of the European Commission (EC) and the different member states. EFSA is responsible for providing independent scientific advice on all aspects related to food safety, the operation of rapid alert systems, communication and dialogue with consumers on food safety and health issues, as well as networking with national agencies and national and international scientific bodies. The institution guarantees the independence and transparency of the scientific advice, which forms the basis of the food safety policy within the EU. This approach is incorporated in the White Paper on Food Safety, presented by the EC in January 2000 (EC, 2000a). The EU intends to establish an integrated food safety policy involving the food supply chain as a whole ('from farm to fork'), and also all member states and all relevant decision-making institutions within the EU.[1]

The ability to take rapid and effective safeguarding measures in response to health emergencies throughout the food chain is an essential element in this new food safety policy of the EU. Throughout the policy document, the consumers are recognised as key stakeholders and their concerns should be taken into account. The basis of the food safety policy remains the conventional risk approach (see Chapter 2) and consists of scientific advice and the evaluation of the available information (risk assessment), regulation and monitoring (risk management), and exchange of the available information between authorities and the general public about the dangers and appropriate behaviour (risk communication). This approach is criticised because of the limited involvement of stakeholders such as farmers and consumers in the assessment of food risks. A particular dispute (in the international governmental arena) regarding the food safety policy of the EU concerns the introduction of the precautionary principle as a regulatory tool. This principle suggests refraining from accepting technological innovations when the potential (longer-term) impact is known insufficiently. The EU intends to use this precautionary principle where appropriate although scientific advice should underpin food safety policy. How to determine the appropriateness of using this precautionary principle in particular instances remains rather vague, as no clear guidelines are available. Competitors on the global food market accuse the EU of introducing this principle not to protect the European consumer, but only for economic interests.

Although the EU intends to respond to food safety problems through a multi-actor and multi-level approach, in practice there remain serious shortcomings in implementing this objective. Consumer confidence in the ultimate EU food safety policy may become undermined if their concerns are insufficiently included and, in particular, the recent food crises in Western Europe have brought home the central idea that incorporating consumer trust has to become standard practice in food policy regimes. But how to include consumer trust in food safety policies, to what extent and in what ways citizen-consumers should be involved in food safety policies and at which level (local, national, European) remain subject to public debates and controversies. The challenge of involving consumers in EU food policies is compounded by the continuous debate between proponents of federalism and those of further integration within the institutional set up of the European Union. As the difficulties resulting from the negative vote on the referenda about the European Constitution in France and the Netherlands in 2005 clearly showed, many citizens are worried about the present (and future) role of the EU. Large groups of European citizens seem to distrust the intention (and the capacity) of EU authorities to defend them against the negative impacts of globalisation. Despite official declarations about the importance of the subsidiarity principle and the intention to guarantee the continued sovereignty of the member states, a permanent trend towards further centralisation seems to take place. The presence of a common market and the necessity to operate effectively in the global political arena appear to constitute a permanent driver for further transfer of responsibilities from member-state governments to the central European level. The growing importance of the global political arena, associated with the process of globalisation, requires more political influence than most (in particular the small) EU member states dispose of.

# FOOD GOVERNANCE IN THE GLOBAL NETWORK SOCIETY

The recent trend towards further globalisation in food provisioning brings new challenges to meet the increasing consumer demands for the quality and safety of food, along with new opportunities for food producers. Capturing the opportunities to export high-value food products thus requires elaborate management systems and close control mechanisms from farm to fork to meet the increasingly stringent food safety standards in consumer markets (Unnevehr, 2001). Until recently, sovereign nation-states formulated the food quality standards which were based on different disparate culturally influenced local considerations. Globalisation, however, makes this option no longer feasible, as global food trade requires worldwide harmonisation of quality and safety standards (Echols, 2001). The conventional approach to food governance increasingly fails to give consumers the comfort they demand. Many consumers consider food a product that should not be treated the same as 'a bar of soap', because 'food is more than nourishment and a great deal more than commerce' (Echols, 2001: 154). Consumers are concerned not only about the food products themselves but also about the production circumstances and about the impacts of the production processes involved.

This unease among consumers becomes even more prominent in the context of globalisation, where national governments can no longer unilaterally impose their environmental and safety regulations on food provisioning. The local practices of food production and consumption are disembedded, but not simply re-embedded at the global level. At different moments and in different contexts, food production and consumption organised in the global space of flows is confronted with the particular dynamics of food production and food consumption practices in the local space of place. Therefore, we need to look into the interactions within and between both levels and in particular into the roles of different social actors therein. (See Figure 4.1.)

Recent attempts to develop food governance arrangements in the context of global food provision can be regrouped in two categories. The first category consists of efforts to strengthen global forms of governance building primarily on the powers and traditions of the nation-state. The second category covers different ways to engage non-state actors in various food governance regimes.

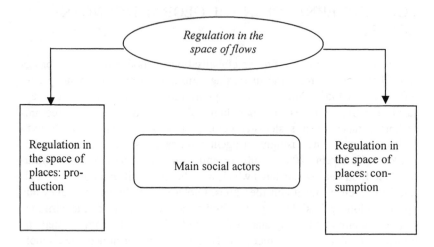

*Figure 4.1    Regulation of global flows of food*

Propositions aimed at strengthening global food governance structures in most cases duplicate the example of the nation-state and generally intend to create some form of global legal authority, although the concrete elaboration of these proposals may take different forms. One concrete model of such a state-based approach to establish global governance arrangements is the attempt to combine multilateral institutions destined to regulate global trade with other institutions focussed on governing global environmental and social problems (Shaw, 2000). Such an arrangement would result in creating specialised global institutions, which could replace the individual sovereign nation-states in dealing with particular global environmental issues, as for example is shown in the International Whaling Committee. This approach is based on the recognition that dealing with certain environmental problems goes beyond the capacities of individual nation-states and thus needs effective supranational institutions. Such institutions should comprise a persistent and connected set of rules and practices, elaborated at the global level, prescribing behavioural roles, constraining activities and shaping expectations (Haas et al., 1993). The objective of these kinds of international regimes is to govern particular environmental concerns in the space of flows under the control of specialised global governance institutions. Other concerns are left to the responsibility of the different individual nation-states, allowing them to apply the appropriate approaches to governance in the space of place. The actual presence of multiple specialised global institutions dealing with different particular concerns, however, makes it rather difficult in certain instances to balance the various interests and concerns because there is no overarching structure able to make and impose decisions in a compulsory manner. Nevertheless, it seems that several observers look at the WTO, charged with the regulation of international trade, to take up this role.[2] Many civil society organisations already criticise the way in which the WTO currently responds to social and environmental concerns in relation to economic interests as is expressed very clearly in the large-scale protests against the WTO, for example in Seattle (1999) and Cancun (2003). The WTO has been criticised for the lack of transparency in its institutional arrangements, the secrecy in its decision-making processes and the overall failure within the organisation to give due weight to broader policy objectives such as equity, human health and environmental protection.

Another approach to build more responsive global food governance regimes starts with the observation that under the present conditions of globalisation, nation-states are embedded in wider governance frameworks. Contemporary politics necessarily involves multiple layers, from local to global and multiple actors, from private firms to non-governmental interest groups (Mol, 2001). Under these circumstances, 'soft' governance instruments such as labels, standards and certification schemes seem to be increasingly preferred to 'hard' instruments such as bans, moratoriums, limits or other legal requirements (Klintman and Boström, 2004). Exemplary cases to apply such flexible governance instruments in global food governance are certification schemes developed by private firms such as HACCP and ISO 14001, particularly focussing on the safety and environmental impacts of food processing (see Chapter 8). If uniform definitions of quality and safety are applied and determined in an objective manner these certification schemes can become a form of global food governance in the space of flows. Such an approach to governance would fit into the science-based global regulation of food trade aimed for by the WTO expressed in its Technical Barriers to Trade (TBT) and the Sanitary and Phytosanitary (SPS) agreements.

## WTO AND GLOBAL FOOD GOVERNANCE

Because of the process of globalisation, economic, social and political networks are transcending traditional political structures more frequently and in more encompassing ways than before. In an attempt to try to countervail the erosion of their powers, nation-states are transferring selected powers to supranational agencies and multilateral institutions, of which the WTO is a prime example. The WTO is responsible for a regulatory framework that increasingly orients the regulatory practices of its member states with regard to international food trade and consequently determines (at least parts of) the context in which different global food governance arrangements operate.

The WTO, established in 1995, is the successor to the GATT (General Agreement on Trade and Tariffs) which was founded in 1945 to co-ordinate international trade and the relevant national regulations. The WTO is a membership organisation of which only national states can become members and today the organisation has 149 member countries, and a further 29 countries are negotiating their future accession.[3] The principal objective of the organisation is to facilitate international trade in support of global welfare. The WTO approach to governing international trade is based on economic principles according to which the reduction of trade barriers is judged the best guarantee for countries to make use of their comparative advantages. The reduction of unnecessary trade barriers and the promotion of free trade will ultimately result in the most optimal allocation of economic resources at the global level.[4] International food trade, which was only included in the responsibilities of the WTO in 1995, forms however an exception because in this case economic considerations are supplemented with the need to secure the safety of the traded food.

According to the WTO, in principle international food safety should be guaranteed with the help of national food safety standards. National standards should be based on the recommendations from the Codex Alimentarius Commission (see below). The recommendations from the Codex are the result of negotiations based on generally accepted scientific evidence and national standards should be harmonised in order to create worldwide food safety standards. This approach to food safety regulation is essentially an attempt to establish global food governance in the space of flows, because it is based on abstract principles, that is not related to specific considerations of place and time. Such global food safety standards define precise limits for the presence of particular substances in food products, but do not prescribe the ways in which these food products should be produced. Governance of global food trade is only acceptable within the WTO framework if it is based on sound scientific evidence and limited to verifiable characteristics of the product itself. Governing international trade based on the characteristics of the processes involved in the production and processing of certain food items is not allowed if these processes do not result in changes in the final food products themselves. When the terminology which is generally used within the WTO is applied, this means that governing international trade on the basis of 'non-product-related process and production methods (ppm)' is not acceptable, but only on the basis of 'product-related ppms' and when it is referred to product properties. Therefore, WTO members are not permitted to distinguish between trade in food produced *with* special care for the social and environmental consequences and food produced *without* this specific attention. This regulatory approach is in principle based on securing and facilitating the global flows of food and not intended to guarantee specific characteristics of the food product in relation to the methods of how or to the places where it is produced or consumed. Following the WTO guidelines, food products can be allowed to be traded anywhere around the globe without any risk, when all necessary information can be observed in the product itself (Potter and Burney, 2002).

These principles are formalised in and supplemented by two separate covenants within the WTO, the Sanitary and Phytosanitary (SPS) agreement supported by the work of the Codex Alimentarius Commission, and the Technical Barriers to Trade (TBT) agreement.

## The Sanitary and Phytosanitary (SPS) Agreement

The SPS agreement was concluded as part of the Agreement on Agriculture within the WTO in 1995 to distinguish between the justified use of trade-restrictive measures for human health and their unjustified use for reasons of protecting national interests. 'The Agreement recognises the governmental and national interests in food safety regulation ("appropriate level of protection"), while significantly abridging sovereignty and rejecting cultural differences as a basis for regulation ("based on scientific principles")' (Echols, 2001: 93).

The SPS agreement permits national governments to develop and implement sanitary and phytosanitary measures even when they affect international trade only as long as these measures are applied for the necessary protection of human or animal health or plant life. Furthermore, these measures have to be based on scientific risk assessment and should not be maintained without sufficient scientific proof. According to the SPS agreement, the conditions for the import of agricultural products should preferably be harmonised in conformity with the guidelines from three international scientific standard-setting bodies: the Codex (FAO/WHO Codex Alimentarius Commission) for guidance on human health, the OIE (International Office of Epizootics) for animal health and the IPPC (International Plant Protection Commission) for plant health. The SPS agreement encourages the mutual acceptance of food safety standards between WTO member states. Countries may only impose higher standards than recommended by these international standard-setting bodies if these standards are applied in a non-discriminatory manner and supported by sound scientific evidence (Mackenzie, 2003).[5] If differences in food safety standards between exporting and importing member states lead to problems, the SPS agreement initially suggests a discussion between the governments of the countries concerned to settle the matter themselves. Only if they fail to resolve the issue

through negotiations, a member state can invoke the existing formal arrangements within the WTO.[6] As one of the few international institutions,
the WTO has established an internal dispute settlement procedure through
which a member state may file a complaint against another member country
with regard to a specific trade-related measure. Through extensive consulta-
tions and designated panels, the WTO attempts to settle such a dispute.[7] If a
member state fails to adapt its rejected laws and regulations after the final
judgement by the different dispute settlement bodies, the WTO remains
nevertheless unable to enforce compliance because the organisation is principally respecting the sovereignty of its member states. However, the WTO
can authorise those countries adversely affected by the presence of unjustified trade barriers to retaliate. In such cases, the organisation permits the
aggrieved member to suspend certain trade concessions to the violating
country, typically by raising tariff rates on the country's exports to such a
level that the damage from the loss in exports is compensated (Kastner and
Powell, 2002).

Several aspects of the SPS agreement are not fully clear yet, but so far
the interpretation of the agreement has obviously been dominated by the intention to facilitate global free trade as much as possible (Charnovitz,
2002a). The recent history of cases brought before the WTO dispute settlement bodies where the SPS agreement was concerned, seems to confirm the
impression that the organisation only accepts the regulation of international
trade when it fits into a global food governance approach based on the space
of flows and that any other measure is considered unjustified and trade restrictive.[8] For example, the way the EU has interpreted and applied the precautionary principle is essentially unacceptable in the views of the WTO
because a WTO member is allowed to call upon this principle only tempo-
rarily when clear scientific evidence for definitive decision-making is lacking. (See for a discussion on the appeal by the EU for the use of this principle in the case of US beef produced with hormones: Princen, 2002, and
Neumayer, 2001.) This way of interpreting the precautionary principle and
the SPS agreement in general in combination with the effects this has had
on consumer health and on the population of developing countries has been
severely criticised (Silverglade, 2000). These critics argue that the SPS
agreement tends to reduce food safety standards to the lowest acceptable international norm instead of developing a consistent level of excellence for
the quality and safety of food. They claim that the SPS agreement can therefore not be regarded as a public health agreement but as a business-oriented
trade arrangement intended to reduce regulatory obstacles and to facilitate
international trade. Furthermore, the SPS agreement is considered inadequate to provide for the necessary special consideration of the needs of developing countries.[9] Finally, in applying the SPS agreement, the WTO relies

extensively on decisions by the Codex to provide an undisputed scientific base, but the proceedings within the Codex itself have repeatedly become political battlegrounds undermining the scientific neutrality demanded for general acceptance of its recommendations.

## The Codex Alimentarius Commission

The Codex Alimentarius Commission has unintentionally become a key player in the governance of global food trade because of the explicit reference to this institute by the WTO in its SPS agreement. The Codex is an international body installed in 1962 by the Food and Agriculture Organisation (FAO) and the World Health Organisation (WHO), both parts of the United Nations structure. The objective of the Codex Alimentarius Commission is to set international health, labelling and other standards for food and thereby to increase food safety and promote fair practices in food trade based on scientifically sound standards (FAO, 1999; Hooker, 2000). By 2003, the Codex had 164 members, all sovereign national states. Decision-making procedures within the organisation are based on consensus achieved through the use of the best available scientific knowledge. Since its foundation, the organisation has produced over 200 standards and 40 codes of practice and guidelines to national food safety regulations, which are applied in many countries on a voluntary basis (Tansey and Worsley, 1995). These Codex guidelines and standards became even more important after the inclusion of agriculture and food into the WTO assignment by 1995 and the formulation of the SPS agreement. The decision to designate a guiding role to the Codex in determining issues of food safety was based on the assumption that this institution would provide neutral, scientific information, as the inclusion of other than scientific considerations in its decision making falls outside its mandate.[10] Thus, for example, 'Codex standards have no direct role in such areas as environmental protection, animal welfare or the protection of endangered species unless such issues directly affect food safety' (Boutrif, 2003: 86). This refusal by the Codex to include other than strict scientific considerations only on food safety is criticised by several observers who comment that food governance should necessarily involve value judgements and economic and social considerations as well. The basic assumption in the Codex that science will ultimately provide undisputed grounds for decision-making about the safety of food is contested as well because public awareness about the presence of uncertainty in science-based policy advice is increasing (Consumer Union, 1998). Finally, it seems that the key role in global food governance given to the Codex by the WTO through its SPS agreement in practice results in the growing politicisation of its internal decision-making process (Motarjemi et al., 2001). Governments and their delegations participating in the different Codex committees become increasingly aware of the potential far-reaching impacts of their decisions and therefore they seem to be more inclined than in the past to consider particular (including non-scientific) interests.

## The Technical Barriers to Trade Agreement

The Technical Barriers to Trade (TBT) agreement covers technical regulations (mandatory provisions), as well as standards (voluntary provisions) and offers general provisions applicable to both. The TBT agreement was already adopted in 1979 within the GATT, to warrant that national product standards and technical regulations would not create unnecessary barriers to international trade. The arrangement covers industrial as well as agricultural products and contains rules with regard to the use of technical regulations for all products.[11] WTO members have agreed to treat imported products not less favourably than 'like products' that are domestically produced.[12] The agreement advises member states to use internationally agreed technical standards and regulations whenever they exist, like the ones developed by the International Standardisation Organisation (ISO).[13] Countries are nevertheless allowed to develop their own national regulations under the condition that they inform the other WTO member states if they expect considerable trade effects or in case the newly introduced technical regulations are essentially different from the existing ones. Member states may apply their own standards and regulations as long as they are based on sufficient scientific evidence and fulfil the criteria of objectivity, non-discrimination and proportionality, and employ two basic principles. First, the 'principle of equivalence', which encourages countries to accept each other's technical regulations which may seem different at first instance, but are similar in essence or 'substantially equivalent'. Secondly, the 'principle of mutual recognition', which stimulates countries to accept the results of each other's assessment procedures and thereby to avoid double testing. The inclusion of these two basic principles has made the TBT agreement into the most relevant regulatory guideline for the development and introduction of eco and other labels for food in the WTO member states. WTO members must ensure that their regulations and standards, including eco labels, are not more trade restrictive than necessary to fulfil a legitimate objective (Appleton, 1999).

Comments on the influence the TBT agreement exerts on the actual global food governance practices focus mainly on the rather narrow interpretation of the possibility for governments to develop food regulations that has been applied by the dispute settlement bodies in conflicts between WTO members (Sheldon, 2002). (See Chapter Six about a complaint lodged at the

WTO by the US and several other countries against the EU with regard to its GM food regulation procedure.) It also remains unclear if and to what extent environmental labelling of a product is, according to the TBT agreement allowed to be based on a life-cycle analysis (LCA) because an LCA explicitly includes the environmental impact of a product during all production stages (Motaal, 1999). Nevertheless, it seems that with regard to eco labelling, generally the TBT agreement is considered more flexible than the SPS agreement. This difference has become clear in the well-known examples of the dolphin–tuna and the asbestos cases when they were disputed under the relevant WTO procedures (Neumayer, 2001).

In combination with the SPS agreement, the TBT agreement forms a key element of the broader WTO framework for the regulation of international food trade intended to create governance arrangements that are oriented towards governance in the space of flows as much as possible.

## CONCLUSION

National governmental regulations still dominate the realm of food safety and to a certain extent the environmental field as well. This chapter has shown that these nation-state-based regulations are supplemented by interventions from several supranational institutions, notably the EU and the WTO. Despite these additions, different observers consider the resulting global food governance arrangements unsatisfactory. These arrangements generally tend to avoid putting limits on the nation-state sovereignty and favour mostly piecemeal responses to particular food crises. In the opinion of these observers, the existing approach to global food governance and its related political practices does not offer sufficient answers to the acute problems of food safety, social equity and environmental protection. To date, the environmental and social impacts of the worldwide economic integration have not been adequately addressed either within the existing international system of regulatory conventions and regimes or by nation-states themselves. 'Global governance is likely to remain inefficient, incapable of shifting resources from the world's wealthy to the world's poor, pro-market, and relatively insensitive to the concerns of labour and the rural poor, despite the progressive role that it recently may have played in promoting liberal democracy' (Murphy, 2000: 789).

Governmental initiatives to introduce more effective global food governance mechanisms remain rather unsuccessful, although some observers suggest that such mechanisms are necessary to respond effectively to both the common elements of national problems and the special demands of transboundary issues and global public goods (Esty and Ivanova, 2002). Narrow, unstructured government-to-government approaches to global food regulation can no longer be sufficient. The existing governmental regulatory arrangements, based on governance in the space of flows, should be supplemented by different forms of private governance initiatives that would allow more room for governance in the space of places. Conceptually, a network-based framework facilitating information exchange, creating space for negotiations and increasing capacity to address important issues could fill the need for the promotion of environmental collective action at the international scale. Practically, it would offer the chance to build a coherent and integrated policymaking and management framework that addresses the challenges of a shared global ecosystem. Consequently, transnational food governance is increasingly the product of private interventions. However, global food governance may rely, at least in part, on market-based arrangements but such food governance tools are limited because markets are considered weak arenas in which to seek political goals. Pressure from activists may have had an impact on the behaviour of particular companies, but to be effective they need to be complemented with regulatory responses by nation-states. The deployment of rules promulgated at the international level remains within the purview and jurisdiction of the state. As implementation of these international regulations is often lacking, pressure is needed and can be exercised through activists using various market mechanisms or through domestic political pressure. For some observers this means that the restoration of politics to global life becomes critical, not because it can create miracles but because it can show us what is missing from a society governed so strongly by market concerns and principles (Lipschutz, 2005).

In this study market-based arrangements are not principally excluded among the options for global food governance. In studying the new approaches to global food governance that are being proposed and/or introduced as responses to the challenges facing contemporary globalizing food provision, this research focuses upon those arrangements that involve non-state actors and especially consumers. This choice resembles the wider academic literature on governance under the headings of multi-actor and multi-level governance. Without underestimating the critical issues of legitimacy, democracy and transparency in all governance arrangements, and the relevance of the continued presence of official regulations, this study mainly intends to take stock of the emerging innovative arrangements and to review their strengths and weaknesses as they may offer more promising perspectives on global food governance than the conventional nation-state-based arrangements. Reviewing these innovative global governance arrangements forms the subject of the remaining chapters in this book.

# NOTES

1. Starting in 2006, the EU has introduced a large, regularly updated body of food regulation to ensure the safety of food in the EU. Food operators, both within the EU and in third countries wishing to export to the EU, have to apply compulsory self-checking programmes and follow the HACCP principles (Food Navigator News at http://www.foodnavigator.com/news, accessed 3 January, 2006).

2. For example, whether the WTO, as a supranational institution, should include environmental and social considerations in their mission or whether these issues should be assigned to other, more specialised supranational institutions is heavily debated (Mol, 2003; Esty and Ivanova, 2002). A critical issue concerns the extent to which global institutions can be representative and accountable to the 'people worldwide' (Griffin, 2003).

3. Data from 11 December 2005. For update see the WTO website: URL http://www.wto.org/index.htm.

4. The WTO claims that the economic case for an open trading system based on multilaterally agreed rules rests largely on commercial common sense. Furthermore, the organisation claims that, supported by empirical evidence, since the existence of the GATT the tariffs on industrial products have fallen steeply and world economic growth averaged about 5 per cent per year. World trade grew even faster, averaging about 8 per cent during the same period (WTO, 2003).

5. The SPS agreement has until now mostly been interpreted restrictively as it is also dominated by the general WTO intention to facilitate global food trade. See for example the dispute between the US and the EU about the use of growth hormones in beef (Cameron, 1999; Echols, 2001; Charnovitz, 2002a, b; Kastner and Pawsey, 2002). Another example is the dispute about the import ban imposed by the United States on tuna imports from Mexico. The US took this decision because fishermen catching tuna were killing dolphins as both species often live in close proximity. A California-based environmental group, Earth Island Institute, sued the US government to enforce the congressional mandate under the US Mammal Protection Act (MMPA) and the federal court ordered the US government to ban the tuna imports from Mexico. The MMPA, enacted in 1972, required the US government to curtail the incidental killing of marine mammals by commercial (US) fishermen. The MMPA also required the Secretary of Commerce to either certify that foreign governments were taking steps to prevent the killing of marine mammals and/or otherwise to prohibit the import of tuna products from offending countries. Mexico argued that its right to sell tuna in the US had been violated and asked the GATT to arrange the matter. In September 1991, the GATT panel concluded that the US was in violation of its obligations because the GATT does not allow trade measures based on production practices. In addition, protection of human or animal life or the conservation of exhaustible natural resources could not justify the US ban (Appleton, 1999).

6. See for further details about these procedures: the WTO website; Vogel (1995); Neumayer (2001).

7. 'Article 3 (2) of the WTO Disputes Agreement states the Dispute Settlement Body is designed to provide security and predictability to multilateral trading, to preserve the rights and obligations of WTO members under the various agreements and to clarify the existing provisions in accordance with public international law' (Anderson, 2002: 11)

8. The way the different panels have interpreted both the SPS and the TBT agreements is contested because many consider the explanation given as too restrictive from an environmental point of view. The WTO did not accept different environmental measures, even when they were clearly not intended to protect particular trade interests (Neumayer, 2001).

9. In general, in developing countries, 'the effectiveness of implementation of SPS requirements is constrained by available funds and technical skills' (Nyangito, 2002: 10). For example, the EU's recent food import requirements force additional costs upon all exporters of fruit and vegetables and therefore some of the smaller producers and outgrowers from developing countries are being deterred from any exporting to the EU (CTA, 2003).

10.  Some consumer groups nevertheless criticise the Codex as being too much under the control of the food industry. At some meetings, more corporations are represented than countries. The National Food Alliance in the UK, for instance, found that out of the 2578 participants in Codex meetings, 660 represented industry interests while only 26 participants represented public interest groups (Tansey and Worsley, 1995).
11.  Technical regulations are particularly important in food trade because 'agricultural exporters may be required to demonstrate that native plant species or human health are not endangered by their products, while simultaneously complying with standards that stipulate everything from ingredients to packaging materials' (Roberts et al., 1999).
12.  WTO members have repeatedly questioned the extent to which the TBT agreement allows for the likeliness of 'products' to be extended to cover the likeliness of 'ppms', that is the degree to which products may be differentiated based on production process criteria that do not clearly affect their final product characteristics (Motaal, 1999).
13.  Appleton (1999) comments on the important problem of the lack of active participation from developing countries in these standard-setting bodies, because this may result in the formulation of standards that are very hard to maintain in lesser developed countries.

# 5. Reinventing risk politics: reflexive modernity and the BSE crisis

In a sense there are no scientists any more, only specialists in different, narrowing branches of science. The lessons of the scientific response to the BSE crisis are that scientists have to do more to acknowledge publicly the fragmented, international nature of their professions, and not let governments get away with glib phrases such as 'our top scientists'.
(James Meek, science correspondent, *The Guardian*, 28 February, 2000)

But meanwhile, being a neo-Luddite seems sane. The 21st-century Luddite feels almost as powerless as the original ones. But we can at least use today's protest of choice, not violence, but economic rebellion. Where possible, boycott.
(Felicity Lawrence, consumer affairs correspondent, *The Guardian*, 28 May, 2001)

## INTRODUCTION

Between 1985 and 2000 Bovine Spongiform Encephalopathy (BSE), or 'mad cow disease', developed from a local UK animal health problem into a globally feared food risk. Especially during the last months of the year 2000, many European countries were confronted with what can be called a real BSE crisis. This chapter will analyse whether this BSE crisis led to the emergence of a new kind of risk policy. In studying the institutional responses to the BSE crisis in the United Kingdom, France, the Netherlands, Germany and the EU as a whole, we will be able to identify the possible presence of different contours of risk politics in an age of reflexive modernity. The analysis of the eventual transition towards innovative practices in risk politics in Europe as an effect of the BSE crisis is given more depth by being compared with the ways in which the US and Japan have dealt with the problem.

In the next section, the concept of 'risk society' is introduced, followed by a brief overview of BSE and its history in the following section. Subsequently, in four different sections the political reactions to the BSE problem are analysed in, respectively, the UK, the Netherlands, France and Germany. In the eighth section the European Union is the focus of attention.

After a comparison between these regulatory responses to BSE in Europe and those in the USA and Japan, some conclusions regarding the eventual emergence of innovative (food) risk politics under the conditions of globalisation and reflexive modernisation are drawn in the final section.

## RISK SOCIETY

The BSE crisis is often quoted as a 'textbook example' of what the German sociologist Ulrich Beck (1999) framed as the new category of risk in the 'risk society'.[1] Contemporary Western society should, according to his view, be conceptualised as a risk society where progress can no longer be equated with ongoing rationalisation and functional differentiation of 'autonomised' spheres of action. According to Beck such instrumental rationalisation has nowadays stopped being the motor of societal development because social transformations are increasingly originating in 'the side effects of technological and scientific development: risks, dangers, individualisation, globalisation' (Beck, 1997: 23). These side effects raise difficult questions about the distribution among different groups in society of the advantages and the disadvantages of technological innovations.

In this new constellation, national governments can no longer continue to use conventional political arrangements in managing risks (Oosterveer, 2002). These 'old' arrangements did not have anything to do with consumers' perceptions, trust or changing social circumstances, but were based on food risks as scientifically and technologically verifiable chances of having adverse effects on human health or on the environment as a result of exposure to a particular 'hazard' (Schierow, 2001). According to Beck, this conventional governance approach to risk can no longer be maintained because: (i) people have become aware of weaknesses in the scientific methods used; (ii) science, technology and politics are increasingly seen as contributors to the production of risks themselves; and (iii) the general public (at least in the richer western countries) are no longer only focussed on fulfilling their direct material needs. Consequently, political institutions in western societies have to develop new policy approaches to deal with risks, which are characterised by insecurity, ambiguity and heterogeneity. Trust has to be created actively among citizens and consumers and can no longer simply be presumed (Beck et al., 1994). For this goal, governments have to adapt their existing risk policy approach and develop a more communicative attitude, focusing on participatory consensus building regarding the definition of the problem, the formulation of policies and introduction of the required policy measures. The more traditional formal governmental policy approaches have showed to be not always fully successful in recreating trust among the general public and as a consequence different forms of 'sub-politics' are emerging: politics outside the existing traditional political institutions (Beck, 1986, 1997; Giddens, 1990; Tacke, 2001).

If BSE is indeed a clear case of this new category of risks characteristic of the risk society, the conventional risk policy instruments and institutions developed during the phase of simple modernity can no longer be expected to deal with it adequately. According to the risk society thesis, new policy models and instruments will have to be introduced to deal with the BSE crisis. If this thesis is correct, we can probably already identify the emergence of such new policy models and political practices dealing with BSE. We could then analyse what these new models and practices look like, and what differences can be found between the conventional forms of risk politics in several European countries. The remainder of the chapter will therefore review the extent to which these hypotheses are correct.

## BSE: A BRIEF HISTORY

In 1985, a cow in the UK died after suffering head tremors, following weight loss and showing lack of co-ordination in her movements. The government asked scientists to study the case and they found evidence of an unknown animal disease, which they named BSE. Several measures were taken to avoid this new disease from spreading to other cows. Initially these measures were implemented by the UK government and later they were supplemented by guidelines from the European Commission. The most important measures that were taken were the obligatory culling of cows showing signs of BSE and the ban on the use of cattle feed containing meat and bone meal (MBM) from slaughtered animals, as MBM containing material from infected cows was considered the main cause for spreading BSE.[2]

For more than ten years, the official government position supported by most scientists was that no risks existed for spreading the disease to human beings. Therefore, 20 March, 1996 came as a shock. On that day the UK Health Secretary had to announce officially that a 'probable link' was established between BSE and a new variant of the Creutzfeldt-Jacob disease (vCJD), thereby creating a new risk for human beings. The first known victim of this disease had died on 21 May, 1995 in the UK. This announcement led to the first BSE crisis, as consumers from all over Europe (and even worldwide) lost confidence in beef and looked for alternatives. There was a sharp drop in the sale of beef, for example 25 per cent in France, although sales generally recovered after several weeks.

Initially the European Union implemented different stringent measures controlling the consumption and export of British beef but these measures were lifted progressively during the following years.[3] However, by autumn 2000 it became clear that the crisis was far from over, as the number of BSE cases continued to grow in other countries than the UK while also (and even more importantly) the number of victims of vCJD increased, mainly in the UK. When in October 2000 infected beef was found on supermarket shelves in France, and in November the first cases of BSE were detected in Spain and Germany, the second BSE crisis led in many countries to even larger drops in the sales of beef than during the first crisis (see Figure 5.1). In December 2000, the European Commission announced a series of drastic measures in an effort to restore consumer confidence.

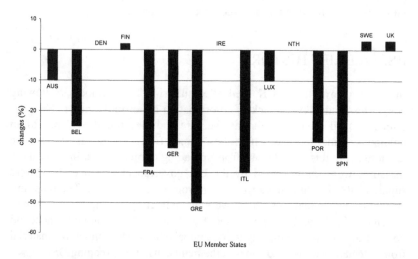

Source: European Union.

*Figure 5.1 Changes in beef consumption (October–November 2000)*

By March 2001, 182,986 cases of BSE were identified in total (see Table 5.1). The height of the European BSE crisis in quantitative terms based on the number of infected cows can be located in the beginning of the 1990s, when most cases were discovered in the UK. During the first quarter of 2001 only a few new cases were detected, despite a substantial growth in the number of cows tested. Figure 5.2 shows the predominant role played by the UK concerning the numbers of BSE cases actually identified. Moreover, by the end of March 2001, there were 99 confirmed or suspected cases of vCJD in the EU, mostly young people. All cases had occurred in the UK

with the exception of France (3) and Ireland (1) (http://europa.eu.int/comm/
food/fs/bse/bse20_en.html).

*Table 5.1    Number of BSE cases per country on 31 March 2001*

| Country | No. of BSE cases |
|---|---|
| UK | 180,967 |
| Germany | 57 |
| Belgium | 27 |
| Denmark | 4 |
| Spain | 38 |
| France | 302 |
| Ireland | 638 |
| Italy | 13 |
| Luxembourg | 1 |
| Netherlands | 14 |
| Portugal | 545 |
| Liechtenstein | 2 |
| Switzerland | 374 |
| Others[a] | 4 |
| Total | 182,986 |

Note: [a] Falkland Islands, Oman (two cases) and Canada.

*Source*: European Union: http://europa.eu.int/comm/food/fs/bse/bse29_fr.pdf

There are no European-wide data available on the numbers of cows slaughtered and destroyed in relation to BSE, but in the UK alone over 4.7 million
cattle were slaughtered for this reason until September 2000 (Phillips, 2000:
par. 9). The European Association of Animal Production estimated the cost
of BSE to the EU member states at more than €90 billion (*Food Navigator*,
22 November, 2004).

Figure 5.2 shows very clearly that the large majority of the BSE-infected
cows were found in the UK although some cases were also detected in other
parts of the world, and particularly in Japan, Canada and the US these discoveries had serious societal and political impacts.

Japan's first case of BSE was announced on 10 September, 2001 and a
second case in November that same year. Until September 2004, the Japanese authorities had confirmed 12 cases. The first discoveries resulted in a
dramatic fall in Japanese beef consumption and in September 2001 retail
beef sales were reported to be down 40–50 per cent. In response, the Japanese government instituted BSE testing of all slaughtered animals and
banned the import, processing and distribution of MBM for all uses. Canada

announced the discovery of its first domestic case of BSE on 20 May, 2003. Importers, such as the US, immediately banned Canadian beef but domestic consumption remained largely unaffected. The US administration announced on 23 December, 2003 that a Holstein dairy cow in Washington State had contracted mad cow disease and in just three days after the discovery, the country lost roughly 90 per cent of its export market (estimated at $3.6 billion in the year 2002).

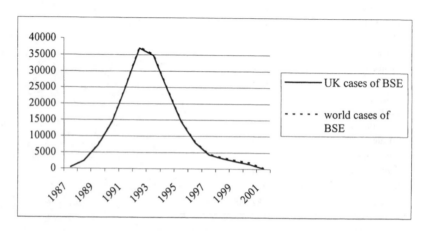

*Figure 5.2   Cases of BSE (1987–2001)*

The dramatic impacts these discoveries of the first cases of BSE had in different countries provide evidence for the disruptive consequences of the occurrence of previously unknown food risks. BSE was initially categorised as a serious disease but restricted to animals, but over time this rather reassuring thought became increasingly undermined by new facts and new scientific information. Over the years, extensive scientific research was done to discover the properties of BSE, the way in which it could be transmitted to other cows and how human beings could acquire vCJD. At this moment, the dominant scientific opinion is that, although the processes causing the initial case of BSE remain unclear, this first case started a chain of transmission spreading the disease to other cows (see Figure 5.3). Leftovers from cows after slaughter were used to feed ruminants, as they provided a rich source of proteins and these rendering practices allowed a resilient strain of scrapie to enter animal feed and to re-emerge into a new form in cattle disease, BSE.[4] Upon inspection, BSE-infected material was found throughout the food chain: in animal feed, in beef and in other products meant for human consumption.

As only a tiny amount of infected material is needed to transmit the disease, just 'the size of a peppercorn' (Phillips, 2000), it spreads very fast, first to other cows and then to humans. Until alternative scientific proof becomes available, this interpretation of the BSE phenomenon and its spread remains the basis for national and international governance arrangements intended to prevent the disease from spreading. However, many years had passed since the first case of BSE before scientists and government agents had developed and accepted these insights. In the meantime, different governments had to respond to a permanently evolving crisis. The following sections analyse how authorities, scientists and citizens in four different European countries and in the European Union as a whole struggled to find an answer to the evolving BSE crisis, while it slowly became clear that the conventional science-based approach to food risk politics had lost much of its uncontroversial position.

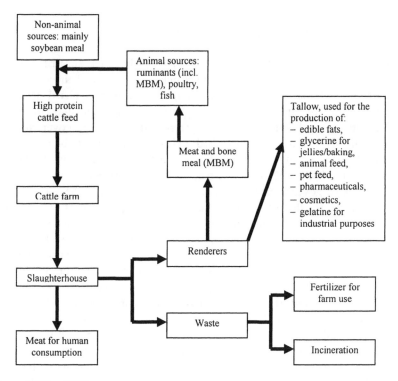

*Source*: Phillips (2000).

*Figure 5.3   Distribution of risk material in the food chain*

# UNITED KINGDOM: FROM SIMPLE TO REFLEXIVE RISK POLITICS

In Britain roast beef is consumed generally at Sunday dinner by the (nuclear) family and this is regarded as an important cultural symbol because it indicates good family life (Urry, 2000b). The risks created by BSE threatened this basic characteristic of British culture and put the government under strong pressure to come up with a rapid solution to solve the problem. The government relied heavily on scientific expertise to develop its strategy for combating BSE, but this reliance on science proved far from easy due to the complexities of the problem (Urry, 2000b; Wynne and Dressel, 2001).

To analyse the BSE policy in the UK, the crisis should be divided into two phases: between 1985 and 1996, when BSE was considered an animal health problem; then from 1996 until 2001 when it became a problem of human health as well.

## 1985–1996: BSE as an Animal Health Problem

When the first case of BSE was identified in the UK in 1986, British scientists were asked to examine this novel phenomenon and their conclusions formed the basis for several official measures. A specialised scientific commission, the Southwood Working Party, was formed to study the possible human health implications. They reported to the UK government in 1989 that the risk of transmitting BSE to humans appeared to be remote and that 'it was most unlikely that BSE would have any implications for human health' (Phillips, 2000: summary par. 4). This Southwood Report remained the basis of governmental policy until 1996 and offered the scientific legitimisation for the official view that no additional measures were needed for the protection of human health. As the independent Phillips report concluded several years later: 'the UK government was preoccupied with preventing an alarmist over-reaction to BSE by the public because they believed that the risk was remote' (Phillips, 2000). Based on the Southwood Working Party report, the British government developed a media campaign of reassurance and tried to settle public unrest, partly by symbolic actions. For instance, at a rural fair in May 1990 the Agricultural Minister John Gummer fed a beef burger to his 4-year-old daughter, dressed in all-white clothes, to show publicly that 'British beef is safe'. Another symbolic action was the decision to forbid the use of risky material from slaughtering beef for human consumption. The Southwood Report had recommended that 'manufacturers of baby food should exclude certain bovine offal' (as quoted in Phillips, 2000: vol. 1, par. 539). This recommendation was considered a precautionary measure of 'extreme prudence' and not one explicitly based on clear scientific evidence. However, when questions were asked in parliament as to why this offal was not banned for human consumption altogether as it was deemed unhealthy for babies, the government had no response. Consequently, the government decided to implement a ban on specified bone offal for *all human* consumption (Phillips, 2000). Although unintended, this measure could in practice have protected the consumers from further exposure to the risk of BSE, but as the measure was considered highly symbolic and mainly intended for public relations objectives, implementing it to the full extent was not seen as essential and therefore remained inadequate.

Overall, the UK government tried to restore public confidence in its food safety policy mainly by relying on scientific advice in the public realm and by taking symbolic measures to show its commitment to the protection of public health and the defence of the agricultural industry. Putting the responsibility in the hands of only one Ministry (for Agriculture), without much communication with other Ministries, is typical for the clear division of tasks in conventional risk politics. Because of this choice, the UK government was unable to respond to the surfacing signs of uncertainty in the recommendations based on scientific research on BSE, so typical for the changing conditions in modern society where science and epistemic communities, risks, uncertainties and complexities mix continuously in new settings (Jasanoff, 1997).

## 1996–2001: BSE as a Risk for Human Health

The situation changed dramatically when the British government was forced to publicly announce the discovery of a new and deadly human disease, a new variant of Creutzfeldt-Jacobs Disease (vCJD), most likely caused by BSE. This radical turn by the UK government made 'consumers feel they had been lied to' (Phillips, 2000) because for more than eight years they had been told that British beef was safe. In reaction to this announcement, consumer trust in beef declined dramatically, as well as trust in science and in the government. In the media and in parliament, the government was accused of unwillingness to take the necessary measures, although they were aware of the risks, because they chose to protect the economic interests of the beef industry.

The discovery of the link between BSE and vCJD sparked a shift in the approach to risk policy within the UK government, from a so-called substantial equivalence to a more precautionary approach. According to the substantial equivalence approach, BSE was considered largely similar to the already extensively studied and much longer existing sheep disease, scrapie.

In addition, because scrapie, as far as is known, did not cross the species boundary to humans, the Southwood Commission in 1989 judged it thus very unlikely that BSE would effectively pose a danger for human health. This judgement proved to be a very costly 'mistake' and backfired very heavily on the government. Due to the changing circumstances in the evolving crisis in the UK, the risk policy approach necessarily had to change towards a much more precautionary one. By 1996, the Ministry of Agriculture declared 'it wishes to protect consumers of bovine products in the UK and elsewhere against any risk, however remote, that BSE may be transmissible to man' (MAFF, 1996). Later on, in 2001, the UK government even explicitly said that 'where there is uncertainty the Government is committed to a proportionate precautionary approach' (HM Government, 2001: 49).

When in 1997 a new Labour government took office in the UK after many years of Conservative rule, they set up an official Commission of Enquiry to study the history of BSE and BSE policy in the UK until 20 March 1996. The Commission had to review the adequacy of past government responses in an attempt to restore public trust in the new government. This 'Phillips Commission' focused in its final report particularly on the lack of communication between different government departments and on the unclear division of responsibilities between scientists and government officials in risk management practices. One of the Commission's recommendations was therefore to clearly separate these responsibilities, without necessarily falling back into naïve positivist science. Scientists should openly communicate their views on the potential dangers of a certain risk to the public and thereby include any doubts they have. On the other hand, the government should retain sufficient in-house capacity to review scientific advice and not simply translate the scientific recommendations they receive into administrative measures and formal regulations. The consequence of this changing risk policy approach will be a more open and more public debate on uncertainties in scientific evidence and thus on the justification of governmental actions (or the lack thereof).

By 2004, the BSE crisis in the UK was considered to be effectively under control, as the number of cows diagnosed with BSE has gone down sharply since 1993 (FSA, 2000) although the number of vCJD cases continued to grow for several years. By early 2004, the British Food Standards Agency found a significant decline in consumer concern over BSE. In their fourth annual food survey, they observed that consumer concern over the safety of raw beef had dropped from 53 per cent in 2000 to 38 per cent in 2003.

It can be concluded that the UK government tried to hold on to the familiar conventional risk policy in its confrontation with a new and unknown food risk (BSE/vCJD). They insisted that first, scientists had to analyse the problem and only then could they act as politicians. However, the undisputed scientific evidence they had hoped for did not come forward and this jeopardised the conventional risk policy approach. As a result, the risk governance practices were necessarily balanced between securing the existing agri-food system and taking public unrest seriously. Symbolic performances and symbolic measures, including lax control of their implementation, were characteristic of this approach to risk policy. When the first people died from vCJD it became clear, however, that the government had misunderstood the changing nature of risk in late modernity. Although efforts were made to maintain a conventional approach to risk politics by stressing the separation between science and politics, more reflexive elements unavoidably emerged in risk politics, for instance in the decision that the public should be informed more openly about diverging scientific views. Increasingly, the view dominates that debating risk policy options should no longer be limited to the inner circle of some scientific experts and government bureaucrats. On the contrary, public debate on scientific uncertainties including dissenting views should become an integrated part of contemporary risk policies.

## THE NETHERLANDS: CONTINUATION OF SIMPLE RISK POLITICS AT LARGE

In the Netherlands, like in most European countries, BSE was for a long time considered a specific UK problem whereby the main risks were thought to be caused by imported cattle and beef from the UK.[5] Official press statements in the period 20 March–30 April, 1996, stressed that the Netherlands was BSE-free and therefore Dutch beef was safe as all the necessary measures had been taken to avoid any risk from imported beef products spreading to consumers (Meere and Sepers, 2000).

Nevertheless a first case of BSE was detected in the Netherlands on 21 March, 1997 and by May 2001 15 cases had been found, while only one case of vCJD has been reported up to 2005. After the first cases of BSE, the Dutch government took several measures, including the forced slaughter and destruction of infected cows and the removal of specific risk material. In reaction to the second BSE crisis, towards the end of the year 2000, all cows slaughtered aged over 30 months were checked for BSE before they were approved for human consumption. This measure made it likely that the number of BSE cases that would be detected would increase. In an effort to prevent this increase leading to a growth in public concern, the government tried to convince the Dutch public that any increase in the number of reported cases should not be interpreted as an indication for enlarged risk, but

– on the contrary – as a sign of diminishing risks. With a big advertising campaign early in 2001, the Dutch government tried to communicate the complicated message: 'More BSE, but still safer food'.

There has not been a clear reaction from the Dutch beef consumers following the BSE crisis, neither in 1996 nor in 2000. The only exception was the last week of March 1996, when the percentage of households buying fresh beef fell from 22.5 per cent to 16 per cent. But by the first week of April this proportion had risen again to 21 per cent (Meere and Sepers, 2000: 16). It seems that the Dutch have more trust in the safety of their food and in government efforts to safeguard it than people in many other countries do (although there are some signals for a decline in this respect).[6] The rather modest reaction by the Dutch consumers may have been caused as well by the actions taken by the Dutch government, which can be considered quicker and more drastic compared to governments in neighbouring countries.

Dutch agriculture has profited much from the EU Common Agricultural Policy (CAP), so the government did try not to endanger the fundamental principles of this policy.[7] However, because of the occurrence of BSE and of the rise in food safety crises in general, criticism of the one-sided economic foundation of CAP seemed to be growing in the Netherlands as well, particularly regarding its negligence of public health, animal welfare and environmental dimensions. The cautious change in the Dutch view on CAP is exemplified by the Dutch resistance to a proposal from the EU commissioner for agriculture, Fischler, in February 2001 to slaughter a large number of cows to avoid a fall in prices after the drop in beef consumption. Supported by public opinion the Dutch Minister of Agriculture declared he did not want to kill healthy animals for economic reasons only, because he considered this 'not ethical'.

The government in the Netherlands tried to handle the BSE crisis as a technical problem: the risk to human health had to be minimised by taking the necessary technical measures. This approach was rather effective in preserving public trust and in controlling the number of BSE cases. It is a typical example of conventional risk politics: the Ministry of Agriculture depoliticised the risk and formulated technical responses to problems defined in technical terms. The continuation of conventional risk politics as such can be explained maybe by the typical Dutch policy style of de-politicising social issues and taking extensive time to look for compromises. However, probably the political choices were supported as well by the fact that – contrary to events in other countries – official statements were not undermined by concrete events while the number of BSE cases remained small as well. Nevertheless, certain exceptions to this conventional risk policy approach can be observed, for example the extensive public information and communication activities undertaken by the government. Furthermore, ultimately, clear scientific evidence did not seem conditional for taking drastic measures; political and economic considerations contributed as much as science to the design of these governmental measures. The BSE crisis itself did not result in changes in Dutch agricultural or risk policies, but it may have contributed – in combination with other food crises – to the emerging debates on food production practices and on the future role of agriculture in the Netherlands.

## FRANCE: FACING THE LIMITATIONS OF SIMPLE RISK POLITICS

France is Europe's most important agricultural country in terms of numbers of people employed in food production, processing and trade and the contribution from agriculture to the national GDP (Gross Domestic Product). The country is also Europe's most important exporter of beef and for a long time it has been the second largest consumer of British beef.

The first French case of BSE was detected in 1991, and by March 2001 the total number stood at 302,[8] while seven cases of vCJD were registered during the same period. The first BSE crisis in France emerged in March 1996, when the relation between BSE and vCJD was announced in the UK. The market for beef imploded and the French authorities decided to ban the import of beef and cattle from the UK. By taking these measures immediately, the French government gave the impression that the crisis was under control. Moreover, they decided to maintain the ban on British beef even after the European Commission lifted the European-wide ban in August 1999. However, a nationwide panic occurred again in October 2000 when BSE-infected meat was discovered at different Carrefour supermarkets.[9] This second French BSE crisis can be regarded as even more profound than the first one. It resulted in a ban of beef in school canteens and in a major drop in the sales of beef. In the second week of this crisis, beef consumption in France dropped by 40 per cent, compared to a 25 per cent drop during the 1996 crisis (Institut de l'élevage, 2000).

The BSE crisis in France can be regarded as both an economic crisis and a crisis of confidence in public administration (Barbier and Joly, 2000).

### BSE as an Economic – But Not Yet Agricultural – Crisis

Seven cases of vCJD have been reported up until now in France. Although the risk of attaining vCJD might thus seem rather limited compared to other food-related diseases, BSE did cause an enormous drop in beef consumption in France. This collective fear had catastrophic consequences for beef producers and for the agro-industry as a whole, but it did not really affect the conventional agricultural production system in the country, for three reasons.

First, French farmers are known for their activism and this is translated into a substantial political influence despite their declining number. Consequently, confronted with the BSE crisis the French governmental authorities tried to combine consumer protection with sustaining the present agricultural production system. Direct support for the French farmers was combined with a large-scale slaughter of cattle (subsidised by the EU) to reduce BSE risks and to support the price of beef. Second, the traditional characteristics of the French food production system (long-standing personal relationships between farmers, food processors and traders) are based on personalised trust, not only within the agri-food chain but also between producers and consumers. It was believed that changing this traditional food production system would only lead to more public unrest and diminishing trust in the quality and safety of French food. Third, different French farmers' unions (Confédération Paysanne, FNSEA, CNJA and FNB) successfully claimed that French farmers are mainly victims of the BSE crisis and do not bear responsibility for it: farmers should be seen as the victims of big enterprises (animal feed producers, and so on) and of unscrupulous politicians. The UK animal feed exports to France were contaminated with BSE while also the local French feed producers (especially the bigger ones) used components that were not BSE-free and as a result French cows were infected outside of farmers' control. Therefore, French farmers considered themselves to be without any blame for causing the BSE crisis and entitled to receive financial support from the government.

Only isolated voices are casting doubt on the continued efforts to preserve the conventional French agricultural production system. For example, the respected French daily newspaper *Le Monde* wrote in an editorial on 17 May, 2001 that the objectives and structures of the Ministry of Agriculture had to change. The objectives of the 'productivistic agricultural production system' (self-sufficiency and producing cheap food) had been laudable in the beginning immediately after the Second World War but had become meaningless in the present practice of producing low quality food ('malbouffe').

## BSE as Crisis of Confidence in French Authorities

Public trust in the French government emerged as a particular problem during the second BSE crisis. This new crisis came on top of preceding food crises and the recent nation-wide scandal of the continued use of HIV-infected blood in French hospitals.[10] French consumers reacted in two different ways to this diminishing confidence in the reliability of the governmental control systems. Higher income consumers switched to better quality products, labelled products and those from organic origin.[11] People from lower socio-economic strata reacted much more aggressively and accused the French government of allowing the BSE crisis to continue while definitive measures to solve it should have been taken at the first signs (Fischler, 2000).

In an evaluative report on the BSE crisis, published in May 2001, the French Senate (Sénat, 2001) studied the question why French cattle were infected with contaminated feed even after the risk was already widely known. They concluded that the Agriculture Ministers in the period from 1994 to 2000 'continuously tried to block or to delay the implementation of precautionary measures'. The main argument brought forward by the French Agricultural Ministry to justify their decision not to act was the 'lack of firm scientific evidence'.[12] It was only in November 2000, when large numbers of consumers showed a total lack of confidence in French beef, that firm action was taken by the government. The French authorities totally prohibited the use of MBM to feed cattle or any other farm animal, increased scientific research and drastically enlarged the number of cows tested in slaughterhouses. From then on, the re-creation of consumer trust in both the government and the domestic food products was considered fundamental in French BSE policy. These efforts to regain consumer trust remained however clearly framed within the boundaries of the traditional agricultural production system.

In conclusion, BSE in France turned out to be the cause of an economic crisis as well as of a crisis of public trust in the national government authorities. Answers to both these crises were found in measures to stabilise the beef market and to reduce the risk for consumers. No fundamental changes in the agricultural system have been considered, as shown for example in the conclusion reached by the French Senate in its report (Sénat, 2001) that organic agriculture cannot be the model for tomorrow's agriculture. In the same report, re-creating consumer trust is regarded as the major task for public authorities, if only to regain legitimacy for themselves. Associating consumer organisations in the elaboration of food security policy is indicated as one of the possible options to achieve this objective and implementing this option would be a rather new phenomenon in French political culture.

As in the UK, it also proved impossible in France to control the BSE crisis by sticking to conventional risk politics alone. The French Ministry of Agriculture initially looked for (national) scientific research to provide reliable information about BSE and to offer appropriate solutions for governmental risk management, but no firm scientific results were produced at the required moment. Nonetheless, forced by increasing public unrest and diminishing consumer demand, the authorities had to take measures in a situation of scientific uncertainty while balancing consumer safety and economic costs. This context of uncertainty and ambiguity did not lead to fundamental public debates on France's agricultural production system. However, some outlines of new reflexive risk politics were beginning to take shape, where in several cases public debate and participatory decision-making processes were considered necessary complements to scientific research in situations of major public risks and uncertainties.

## BSE IN GERMANY: INITIATING REFLEXIVE RISK POLITICS

As in other countries, in Germany too BSE was viewed for a long time as a problem unique to the UK. BSE did not occur in public debates and even in 1997 most German citizens regarded the risk as rather remote and measures taken by the German government as largely sufficient (FAZ, 14 February, 2001). So 24 November 2000 came as a total shock when the first officially German-originated case of BSE was discovered in Schleswig-Holstein. The government reacted immediately and within two weeks measures forbidding the use of all animal meal as animal feed were introduced and enforced. Up to 31 March 2001, a total number of 57 BSE cases had been found in Germany, but not one case of vCJD yet.[13]

German authorities had always claimed that BSE could not occur in Germany and that domestically produced beef was safe, therefore no testing or ban on the use of risk material in human food and animal feed production had to be introduced. BSE was believed to be a British problem and Germany considered BSE similar to scrapie found among sheep. The infection was transferred to cows only because of the changes within the British rendering practices. As Germany did not have many sheep compared to the UK, and as the rendering practices in the country were different, the official position was: 'BSE is not possible in Germany'. This conviction prevented authorities from taking several warnings seriously, such as the warning in January 1999 from four scientists at Kiel University, claiming that internal German infection could not be excluded (*Die Welt*, 08 January, 2001). In a similar vein, the Scientific Steering Committee from the EU concluded in April 2000 that no country, including Germany, could be considered completely safe from BSE, and advised all member states to fully separate risk material during slaughter and destroy it.

## A Crisis in Agricultural Policy

Considering this context, it may not be a surprise that the discovery of a German-originated case of BSE in November 2000 had dramatic political, social and economic effects. First, German consumers panicked and nearly completely stopped buying and consuming meat. Suddenly Germans were seriously concerned about BSE: 73 per cent were convinced that BSE was a serious risk, 54 per cent felt personally threatened, 32 per cent stopped eating beef and 35 per cent reduced their beef consumption (FAZ, 14 February, 2001). Second, both the Minister of Health and the Minister of Agriculture were forced to resign. Third, a broad public debate on the present German agricultural production system and on agricultural politics in general got off the ground. Although triggered by BSE, this debate did not focus on the BSE problem as such, but dealt with the agricultural production practices in general, comparing 'industrial' versus more 'ecological, animal-friendly and sustainable' agriculture. The majority of the population viewed BSE not as an isolated food safety incident, but as just the tip of the iceberg, a sign that many food products were not safe. They demanded guarantees for the safety of their food, in the first place from scientists and the government and in the second place from farmers. Fourth, the discovery of BSE and the following public discussion led to fundamental changes in the objectives of the German agricultural policy. This policy is, however, for a major part EU policy, so the debate did include the need for reforms within the latter institution as well. Consumer protection was widely considered to constitute the necessary new basis for German and Common Agricultural Policy of the EU.[14]

The new programme for food production and for the agricultural policy for Germany proposed by many critics can be summarised as follows: the BSE crisis is the alarm signal for an already existing crisis in the agricultural production system in the country because the practices within this system lead inevitably to the destruction of nature and the environment and to less ethical behaviour towards animals. According to this view, the only real alternative to the present system would be a transparent ecological farming system, based on smallholdings, with an integrated combination of different farming activities and using animal-friendly production methods. Agriculture needs to maintain (or acquire) a regional character and should not become globalised, thus allowing consumers to relate directly with the region of origin of their food. The government should in its agricultural and food policies give even weight to consumer concerns as to producers' interests. This radical programme to reform the existing agricultural policy received broad support among the German public.

German consumers had very mixed opinions about the role of scientists in dealing with the BSE crisis. On the one hand, people demanded rapid and clear answers from the scientific experts, while on the other hand they were confused by the quantity of information they received. At the same time, they felt dissatisfied when these experts used formal scientific language in their answers and did not take the emotions that are present among the public into account. After November 2000, nevertheless large sums of money were spent on research to find quick testing methods for BSE as well as on more fundamental scientific research on the broader phenomenon of Transmissible Spongiform Encephalopathy (TSE) (TAZ, 05 February, 2001).

As a whole, the BSE crisis generated much upheaval in Germany by the end of 2000, but the issue itself almost seemed to disappear behind a wider and more fundamental debate about the future of the agricultural production system in the country. This may be understandable because the German government took all possible measures within two weeks, whereas other countries needed several years in the earlier stages of the crisis.[15] The BSE crisis may have marked the end of conventional agricultural policy, although it remains to be seen whether it also marked the end of conventional agricultural practices as only optimists are expecting organic agriculture to cover much more than 10 – 15 per cent of the German domestic food market in the coming years. Besides the rapid and immediate implementation of regulatory measures already known from other European countries, the main mechanism to recapture consumer trust used by the German government was a political one: the inclusion of consumer protection as a guiding principle for future agricultural policy.

The debate in Germany on the agricultural production system that generated BSE (and other side effects) can be interpreted as a clear example of reflexive risk politics. Surprisingly, there is however very little sign of the presence of ambiguity in formulating an alternative model. The correct model for future agriculture capable of avoiding the risks that result from conventional agriculture seems to be very clearly defined and allows the harmonious integration of farmers', consumers' and environmental interests without any problem. However, integrating these interests will probably not be as self-evident as is expected by the proponents of this alternative model. Only the future will show whether this alternative, but heterogeneous model for food production in Germany will be successful, or whether one of its components will ultimately dominate the others.

# EU AND BSE: A FIRST STEP TOWARDS REFLEXIVE RISK POLITICS

The EU played an important role in the BSE crisis. Agricultural policy in Europe is largely EU policy; the expenditures for this CAP constitute the biggest item on the EU's budget and this repeatedly demands difficult decision-making in the case of budgetary problems. The existence of a common market makes EU involvement necessary when countries want to ban certain imports from other member states. At several moments during the BSE crisis the EU has been actively involved in managing it, and two ways were applied. First, measures were taken at the EU level to prevent the risk from spreading over national borders. Second, the EU brought scientific research together and translated its recommendations into EU-wide policy measures.

Detailed analysis of the EU measures shows a striking gap in activities between 1989 and 1994 (Wynne and Dressel, 2001; Sénat, 2001). This temporal inertia may be explained by the internal strife between different departments within the EU bureaucracy in Brussels and by the role of the scientific committees. These committees continue to play an important role in the EU's decision-making process and the Scientific Veterinary Committee was a very prominent one during the BSE crisis. British scientists dominated this Committee, as well as its BSE subgroup, which seemed to make it rather difficult for the European Commission to take measures between 1989 and 1994 because this would undermine the official denial by the UK authorities of the possibility of any risk for humans caused by BSE.

The EU decision in 1996 to ban the export of British beef led to anti-EU sentiments among British politicians and the British public in general. In an effort to end this ban, the UK brought the case before the European Court of Justice. In their verdict this legal institution concluded that a country should accept that, with uncertainty about the actual presence and the possible effects of risks for human health remaining, governmental institutions are allowed to take protective measures without being forced to wait until the reality and gravity of these risks are fully demonstrated (Sénat, 2001). This signified an enlargement of the precautionary principle to health risks, which until that moment was limited to the field of the environment only.

The second, and nearly EU-wide, BSE crisis in 2000 led to considerable activity by the EU and resulted in several far-reaching decisions that were taken at very short notice. The principal rationale behind these measures was the objective to restore public faith in beef. The deep crisis had led to a large drop in the sales of beef and the EU was obliged to take large quantities of beef off the market to support its price. Until February 2001, the European Commission spent €700 million to buy and destroy or stock superfluous cattle (*Financiële Dagblad*, 13 February, 2001). The EU agricultural commissioner expected to take 1.7 million cows out of the market before the crisis was over. In justifying their policy, the EU authorities combined economic and human health considerations: beef is taken out of the market because consumer demand is lacking and prices are dropping, while the EU no longer allowed untested cows older than 30 months to enter the beef market. This policy nevertheless would run into difficulties because the total budget for CAP remains fixed and to solve the problem the budget had to be increased or the production diminished. Substantial growths in the budget were excluded until 2006 and diminishing the beef production would lead to further falls in farmers' incomes and probably to political problems in countries like France. Therefore, despite the presence of a general agreement among the member states within the EU on the need to take drastic measures, no firm conclusions on market interventions were reached.

David Byrne, EU commissioner for health and consumer protection, declared that comprehensive food safeguards are in place and that BSE is currently only a minimal risk despite scientific uncertainty and consumer unrest (Byrne, 2001). Public communication by the European Commission must make 'known the risks and the protective measures we have introduced to tackle those risks' (European Commission, 2000c). Nevertheless it proved far from easy to communicate these EU measures to the public through European-wide means, because the interference of national policies resulted in particular differences in the regulatory situation per member state. For example, Germany made testing compulsory for cows aged 24 months while the EU regulation was 30 months, and at the same time countries like Finland, Austria and Sweden did not require any testing at all. Maintaining the image of a consistent common BSE policy proved rather difficult in these circumstances. In October 2004, the EC announced that it committed €98 million to tackle BSE. This way the EC intended to implement its commitment to supporting pro-active monitoring, preventive action and disease eradication. Consumer confidence in Europe's beef industry should be boosted to bring more revenue into the sector.

In general, EU measures rely heavily on advice from scientific committees who base their recommendations on clear scientific evidence. This conventional approach to risk politics ran into difficulties because (national) political and economic considerations proved to play a role in the deliberations within these committees and in the decision-making process in the EU as a whole. Science seemed also unable to produce the certainty needed to justify difficult decisions, which involved competing national interests. The evolving BSE crisis itself also continued to produce surprises in scientific terms, repeatedly showing the limited validity of scientific advice. Only later did some significant changes in the food policy approach occur as consumer protection became a separate political objective and politicians accepted the need to take decisions under the circumstances of scientific uncertainty. The EU set up a new independent regulatory agency, the European Food Safety Agency (EFSA), and this institution should apply the tools of risk analysis and the precautionary principle (EC, 2000a). In the same White Paper on Food Safety, the EC also proposed the introduction of a comprehensive integrated approach, including a legal framework, to secure the safety of food by covering all facets of food products from 'farm to table' and through the dissemination of objective information to the consumers (Vincent, 2004). Maybe even more important is the inclusion of the 'precautionary principle' in decision-making procedures on food security, despite the inherent vagueness of this principle for risk politics (Dratwa, 2002).

There are some indications for changes in risk politics within the EU but it remains to be seen whether the common agricultural polity will in effect no longer be dominated by the economic rationale of agricultural production. Some politicians continue to hold on to the idea that the BSE crisis will disappear in the near future because it is 'just a consumer hype'. 'Normal' agricultural politics can then resume like before, except maybe for some minor cosmetic changes.

## GLOBAL SPREAD OF BSE

BSE, which initially seemed a UK problem, later became a European food problem to evolve ultimately into a global health risk. The disease surfaced successively in Japan (2001), Canada (2003) and the US (2003), inciting different policy reactions in these countries. Some of these policy reactions were radical but overall they were not as dramatic as the changes in the risk policy approaches in Europe presented before. Over time, the BSE crisis seemed to lose some of its disruptive character and evolved more into a 'normal' food risk of which the causes and the required policy measures to adequately deal with it were already known.

The normalisation of BSE did however not start in Japan when this country's first case was announced on 10 September, 2001 and was followed by a second case in November that same year. The societal shock resulting from these discoveries led to a dramatic fall in beef consumption as beef sales in the country nearly halved. In response, the Japanese government made BSE testing mandatory for all cattle slaughtered, while purchasing and immediately incinerating all cows that had been slaughtered before this testing requirement was in place (Fox and Hanawa Peterson, 2004). Japan is currently testing every head of cattle destined for human consumption and until September 2004 the authorities had confirmed 12 cases of BSE. The government also implemented a new electronic tagging and traceability system obligatory for all livestock and banned the import, processing and distribution of MBM for all uses. In order to appreciate the radical character of these measures and the swiftness in implementing them, it is important to realise that the consumption of beef in Japan is a recent development, and as the country only has a small domestic cattle industry it depends largely on imports from the US.

Canada announced the discovery of its first domestic case of BSE on 20 May, 2003. An abattoir had rejected the cow already in January the same year because it showed signs of pneumonia. The conclusions of laboratory testing on this case were announced only four months later due to delays caused by a backlog in testing, the ten days to do the test itself in Canada, and the need to confirm the findings by the world BSE reference laboratory at Weybridge in the UK. Surprisingly, in reaction to the announcement to the Canadian public of this BSE case, domestic consumption remained largely unaffected but importers, in particular the US, banned Canadian beef immediately. The loss of export markets was estimated to be over C$500 million per month (Fox and Hanawa Peterson, 2004).[16] This first North American case did result in a public call for drastic changes, particularly regarding animal feeding practices and regulations for testing. However, although some adaptive measures were taken, in reality only minor changes in the currently existing cattle raising practices were effectively implemented. The limited number of confirmed cases and the restrained consumer reactions may probably explain this limited impact.

Only seven months after Canada's discovery of a case of BSE, the authorities in the US announced the first incident of BSE in the country on 23 December, 2003. The infected cow was traced back and found to be imported from Canada. In June 2005, a second US cow already slaughtered in 2004 was retested and found to be infected as well (Nierenberg, 2005). These cases, interestingly, never resulted in fundamental debates on the existing practices in US beef production and consumption or on the regulatory practices in the country.[17] The only visible effect brought about by the detection of BSE was some stepping up of already existing efforts from the US government to ensure the safety of food. The limited impact was probably also due to the US beef industry which seemed to be prepared for the possibility of a BSE outbreak and had invested heavily in calming down potential initial unrest among the American consumers which they obviously did quite successfully. Despite initial fears for dramatic effects on consumer behaviour (as can be witnessed in the initial drastic drop in stock market values for beef processors and fast food restaurant chains immediately after the detection of the first case of BSE), the first identified case of mad cow disease did not visibly affect consumer traffic in the US. Share prices rebounded to the previous levels within two weeks (Reuters, 17 January, 2004). Nevertheless, Ward et al. (2005: 110) concluded based on their empirical research, that 'US consumers, while not necessarily changing their beef buying habits, were subject to some "shock" to their overall perceptions about beef'.

US agriculture and food safety policy was based on the premise that BSE was not really established in the country because it had not been diagnosed until 2003 and even later on, the numbers remained very small. The isolated cases of BSE were considered to be caused by the import of infected cattle from other countries, notably from Canada. The appropriate strategy was therefore to minimise the risks by enforcing import restrictions, particularly on cattle and beef (products) from countries where BSE is known to exist in native cattle. In addition, the authorities prohibited the use of most mammalian proteins in the manufacture of animal feeds given to ruminants, and banned the use of the so-called 'downers' (non-ambulatory animals) from the human food supply (since December 2003).[18] In order to implement this strategy and limit the impact of BSE on US agriculture, the US government spent large amounts of funds.[19] Additional money was needed to test the visibly injured cattle at rendering plants and on farms (about 10 per cent of all cows). Over the years, the number of cows tested for BSE has risen considerably from 5,000 in 2001 to about 130,000 in 2004. The USDA has approved several rapid-screening tests to detect BSE, but these tests proved to be extremely sensitive and could produce false results if the brain samples were prepared improperly. As a result, several positive initial tests for BSE were made public in 2004, but they were cleared after retesting with the use of a more sophisticated and complicated immunohistochemistry test. Cattle industry officials have asked the USDA to reconsider their strategy as these first announcements of inconclusive cases did have dramatic effects on the price of beef. The same cattle industry also opposed the USDA in its intention to develop a national animal identification system that could be used to track cattle from birth to slaughter. Despite strong public support, 'the industry has been cool to the ideas saying it would be difficult to implement and would raise privacy issues' (*Tri-City Herald*, 30 January, 2004). With respect to identification systems for tracking and tracing, the US lagged behind other countries, such as Canada, the EU, Uruguay, Australia and New Zealand (Ward et al., 2005).

The beef industry is one of the most important agricultural activities in the US and the country's total beef production in 2003 was around 36 million cattle slaughtered while the gross farm income from cattle and calf production totalled $44.1 billion in that same year (FSIS, 2004). Beef export, mainly to Asia, had been a lucrative activity for the industry for many years but the US did lose a substantial part of its beef export because of the BSE outbreak. In particular, the closure of the Japanese market for US beef proved damaging. Until 2004, the US had been exporting about 9 per cent of its total beef production, with one-third of that going to Japan. After the detection of BSE in the US, the Japanese import authorities immediately prohibited the entrance of US beef in Japan completely and the market was taken over by beef exporters from Australia and New Zealand. Japanese authorities declared that the US could only resume its beef exports to the country when all cattle were tested and when the USDA confirmed that this testing was being done properly (*Washington Post*, 16 April, 2004).[20] In response, the US authorities claimed that this mandatory testing of all cattle was very costly and even unnecessary because the measures already in place assured the safety of the beef. After many years of tough negotiations, the export of US beef to Japan officially resumed by the end of 2005, but under very strict conditions, which made it rather unlikely that these exports would reach similar levels as before the crisis (*The Japan Times*, 9 December, 2005).

Most remarkable in the ways in which BSE has been dealt with successively in Europe, Japan, Canada and the US is that a food crisis with disruptive impacts after its first appearance in Europe evolved into a rather 'normal' food safety risk in the US, despite the enormous financial impact it still had on the beef industry.

## CONCLUSIONS: BSE BETWEEN CONVENTIONAL AND REFLEXIVE RISK POLITICS

The BSE crisis provides interesting possibilities to analyse the challenges faced by national governmental authorities in dealing with an unknown food risk with potentially dramatic impacts in the context of globalising food provision. 'The importance of the BSE saga does not lie just in its uniqueness or the severity of its consequences' (Van Zwanenberg and Millstone, 2003: 27). BSE is an expression of a crisis of science and governance, where government officials use scientists and their expertise as a political resource. The awareness of this crisis is widely shared and although there is far less agreement about the alternatives, particularly in many European countries and at the level of the EU as a whole, the BSE crisis provoked a wave of structural reforms in food risk politics.

BSE drew wide public attention in all countries where it occurred, but the public and institutional reactions differed per country influenced by particular national circumstances and the different ways in which the events might be linked to other food and public health concerns. While the BSE crisis in the UK can be described to have been initially a problem of animal health and subsequently to include human health concerns as well, it was considered a technical problem in the Netherlands, an economic problem in France and a general problem of agriculture and food production in Germany. Japan mainly took it as a problem of consumer protection, while Canada and the US considered it as a trade concern. Despite these national variations in conceptualising its principal characteristics, BSE has indeed turned into a global food safety concern.[21]

This chapter intended to analyse whether BSE resulted in innovative approaches to risk politics and what would be the principal characteristics of such innovative risk politics. Initially most governments tried to continue their conventional approach to risk politics when confronted with BSE, but many were forced to review their approach as they faced unexpected and unknown dimensions of food risks: scientific uncertainty, widespread public unrest and the problem of balancing public health and economic interests. Despite these new challenges, no radically different approach to risk politics, such as reflexive risk politics, seems to have replaced the conventional approaches yet. Nevertheless, some contours of innovative arrangements can be observed in different degrees in the various countries reviewed and these transformations can be summarised in the following four items.

**Institutionalising Consumer Protection**

Although many politicians claimed during the BSE crisis that 'our food is safer than ever before', all governments intensified their attention to food safety and to consumer protection in particular. They were forced to take action following political and public pressure and many authorities claimed they had put consumer protection at the centre of agricultural and food policies. Government authorities established independent institutions following the example of US Food and Drug Administration (FDA) or broadened the responsibilities of the Agricultural Ministry to include consumer protection. This way the intention to balance public health and economic interests became an explicit dimension of political decisions on food and agriculture. However, the global character of food provisioning complicates these efforts to institutionalise a governance regime that adequately balances different interests and considers consumer protection its prime objective.[22]

**Precautionary Principle**

Especially within the EU, the precautionary principle is being called upon increasingly to guide food risk policy decisions under conditions of scientific uncertainty. This was justified by underlining the obligation for governmental authorities to protect the consumers in their decision-making procedures, while acknowledging the impossibility of guaranteeing zero risk. The precise meaning of the precautionary principle may remain unclear, but probably because of the rather vague denotation of this concept it could become the unifying element in EU politics on issues of food and risk. (See Chapter 6 for further discussion on the use of the precautionary principle.

**Reorienting the Modernisation Process**

Some observers consider the BSE crisis as the consequence of a one-dimensional modernisation process in food production practices, where insufficient attention is paid to the potential side-effects. Some politicians, scientists and NGOs conclude from this that the whole process of agricultural modernisation should be re-oriented and take the protection of its environmental sustenance base explicitly into account at all stages. This reorientation could result in either a process of de-modernisation or one of ecological modernisation. Several other social actors translated their conclusions from the BSE crisis into recommendations for additional regulation without altering their appreciation of the direction in the modernisation of contemporary food provisioning practices in any fundamental manner. They consider consumer protection as an add-on to the conventional approach to food risk politics as they acknowledge the need to include specific supplementary regulations and institutions. Therefore, despite the initial confusion about the future of agriculture after the discovery of BSE, it is not certain this will have a lasting impact on the agricultural production system as a whole, or whether conventional agricultural production practices will resume their course when the BSE crisis is considered to be under control.

**Science and Politics**

Finally, the BSE crisis raised difficult questions about the use of scientific knowledge in relation to political decision-making practices. Being a new problem with limited scientific knowledge available about its causes and remedies, political measures had to be developed in the context of extreme uncertainty about the properties of BSE, its effects and its modes of transmission. From this perspective, BSE can be viewed as an example of a larger category of newly emerging risks. These new kinds of risks in contemporary risk society have three elements in common:

• There can be a big gap between the scientific knowledge produced in laboratories and everyday reality. This may result in serious problems when political measures based on scientific information are applied in concrete social practices. For example, the decision by the UK authorities to avoid risk material from entering in the food supply chain by prohibiting the use of specific designated material as animal feed was scientifically correct. However, this decision was based on testing under laboratory circumstances but slaughterhouse practices are very much different from these circumstances and because the quantity of infected material capable of spreading BSE was much smaller than initially thought, this measure did not prove to be very effective.

- The approach to food risks taken by lay people often differs very much from the one taken by experts. Most experts approach risks in a rather reductionist framework: they try to establish the statistical chances for encountering a specific hazard (Wynne, 1996; Guivant, 2002). But, for example, their message comparing the greater chance of acquiring salmonella poisoning with the much smaller chance of getting vCJD does not seem very convincing to the general public. Lay people's judgement of risks is often not only based on objective scientific calculations, but much more on whether a risk is imposed by distant authorities and whether this risk is reversible or not (Wynne, ibid.). BSE is mostly criticised by lay people because it is the result of intentional changes in food production practices for economic reasons and imposed on consumers, who have no proper means of verifying the safety of their beef.
- Generally, scientific recommendations were formulated by a small group of scientific experts often designated by the government authorities who remain rather sensitive to economic and political considerations. Therefore, at the moment, different politicians underline the need to install a clear separation between scientific research and the decision-making process in politics. Scientific advice should be taken into account in political decisions, but recommendations from scientists should never be simply translated in policy measures. Politicians have to acknowledge their own responsibility in this translation process and they should therefore actively look for divergent scientific viewpoints and not simply accept standard scientific opinions. Public authorities often have to take decisions in the face of incomplete knowledge and uncertainty. This uncertainty and the presence of diverging scientific viewpoints should be recognised and debated in public.

The BSE crisis did have a profound influence on the relationship between politics and science, on the importance of consumer trust in governmental measures guaranteeing the safety of food, and on the ways in which politicians are trying to restore citizens' trust. However, the course of the BSE crisis does not justify the conclusion that an innovative, reflexive approach to risk politics has emerged. However, it remains possible to identify some innovations in food governance in various countries as a response to the shortcomings of the conventional approach to risk politics that appeared during the BSE crisis. This crisis was caused by the process of technological modernisation in food production, but also by the increasingly globalised character of contemporary food provisioning.

## NOTES

1. While Beck used the nuclear accident in Chernobyl (1986) as the main example to show the reality of these new risks, the German (Green Party) Minister for Agriculture in the state of Nordrhein-Westfalen, said that BSE means for agriculture what the nuclear accident in Chernobyl meant for the nuclear industry (FAZ, 11 March, 2001).
2. MBM containing animal proteins was used in cattle feed because:
    a. Increased meat production and lower meat prices during the 1970s had led to an increased availability of cheap meat offal.
    b. Animals digest animal proteins more easily than vegetable proteins.
    c. The use of local inputs would make the EU less dependent on the supply of soybeans from America (Robelin, 2000).
    Furthermore, the use of feed from animal origin was considered an indication for the presence of modern hygienic conditions and for the use of modern economic production practices (recycling) in the 1960s and 1970s. This image changed, however, during the BSE crises and turned into a symbol of the extent to which a cow raised in modern intensive farming in Europe is transformed unnaturally from a grass-eater into a carnivore.
3. These EU measures were considered by many of the leading (conservative) politicians and newspapers in the UK as unjustified and too severe, based more on anti-British sentiments and national interests of other EU member states than on sound scientific arguments (Wynne and Dressel, 2001).
4. Scrapie is a well known and widespread disease among sheep and shows similar characteristics to BSE, but scrapie is not transmissible to humans.
5. The Netherlands is fully integrated in international agro-food supply chains. For example, in 2000 the Dutch meat export grew by 17 per cent to € 11.1 billion and the import by 10.5 per cent to €4.9 billion (*De Volkskrant*, 20 March 2001). Seventy per cent of meat consumed in the Netherlands in 2000 was imported, mainly coming from the neighbouring countries.
6. Consumers seemed to link the risk of BSE to previous food risks like dioxins and salmonella. A poll in December 2000 found that 46 per cent of the households studied did not agree with the proposition that 'our food has never been as safe as today' (*Communicatie*, 2001).
7. For example, the Dutch government was aware of the risks for BSE present in certain German sausages in November 2000 but was not able to act as European regulations only allowed it to take measures by the end of the year 2000. The government referred to the importance of upholding common EU policy practices to justify its non-interference.
8. The number of BSE cases had risen to 923 in the year 2004.
9. 'Affair Carrefour': on 24 October, 2000 a cow was to be slaughtered at a slaughterhouse in Beuzeville, but showed signs of BSE. The cow was tested positive and according to the prevailing regulations 18 other cows from the same herd were supposed to be slaughtered and destroyed as well. However, 11 of them had already been slaughtered on 4 October and thus one tonne of potentially BSE-infected beef was distributed to over 39 supermarkets from the Carrefour retail chain and some other stores. In combination with a television broadcast on young vCJD patients this event created a profound public food scare in France.

10. HIV-infected blood continued to be used for blood transfusion to haemophiliacs in the 1980s, because of a lack of control or bad will from high French authorities. Hundreds of haemophiliacs were infected with AIDS and this scandal was subject to a widely debated legal procedure in 1999.

11. Interestingly previously existing escapes, such as a return to traditional local or regional food products, were not possible as many of these products are no longer available for reasons of food safety. For example, because the listeriosis bacteria can be found on traditional products but not on industrial fabricated food products, many traditional food products are no longer available (Fischler, 2000).

12. France has paid much attention to scientific research to solve insecurities around BSE and related problems. The Comité Dormont, created by the Ministries of Research, Health and Agriculture and composed of 24 scientists, was constituted to give advice to the government on the scientific aspects related to the BSE crisis. Compared to other countries much more was expected from this research in answering important questions to guide policy and ample funding for scientific research was considered a clear indication for the government's commitment to fight the problem. It is very interesting to see the French Senate afterwards criticising this strategy as being an excuse for not acting. France had already started an extensive research programme on prions in 1996, which reached a total expenditure of 70 million Francs in the year 2000 (Minister of Research, 2000). Much more would be invested (140 million Francs) in the following years (Robelin, 2000).

13. This number had risen to 200 cases by September 2002.

14. In January 2001, the new Minister of Agriculture changed its name to the Ministry of Consumer Protection, Food and Agriculture.

15. Other causes for this very rapid shift in agricultural policy objectives are that the German government at that time was based on a coalition of social democrats and greens and these parties do not have the large electoral support from farmers that the Christian Democrats have. Besides, this situation seemed a good opportunity for the Green party to acquire more profile in the coalition government as they were by far the smaller party of the two.

16. 'The U.S. ban on live cattle has been in place since a case of bovine spongiform encephalopathy, or BSE, was discovered in Alberta in May 2003, costing the industry more than $2 billion in lost exports alone' (*The Edmonton Journal*, 9 October, 2004).

17. The only exception, but preceding the actual occurrence of BSE in the US, was the case of Howard Lyman, a former cattle raiser, who appeared on the Oprah Winfrey Show in 1996 to comment on the BSE crisis in the UK. He declared that the modern, factory-style method of churning out millions of tons of meat each year lacks quality controls that could catch and prevent diseases such as mad cow from entering the food system. Modern meat production, Lyman said, is a death machine. In response, Oprah Winfrey vowed 'I will never eat a burger again'. Two weeks later, Lyman and Winfrey were charged with making false and disparaging statements about food. Bumper stickers in Texas blared: 'The Only Mad Cow in Texas is Oprah'. In 1998, a jury decided that Lyman and Winfrey were not liable but a group of livestock owners filed a second suit. The case dragged on for four years. Finally, a US District Court judge laid the matter to rest. Lyman had not said anything knowingly false about the meat industry, the judge determined. 'Every word Howard Lyman said was true', she wrote in her 2002 decision (*Washington Post*, 12 January 2004).

18. Already before the detection of the first case of BSE, observers commented on insufficiency in the existing prevention measures in the country, in particular because of the insufficient and inadequate testing of animals that die on the farm (Fox and Hanawa Peterson, 2004). Animals that die on the farm may be buried or collected for rendering – unlike the situation in Europe where deaths of all animals over 24 months must be notified, the animal tested for BSE, and the carcass collected for incineration. The presence in the US of diseases comparable to BSE, particularly chronic wasting disease in deer and elk which was known since the 1960s, was another cause of concern among some observers fearing an outbreak of BSE in the country.

19. 'Bush wants $441 millions for mad cow, food safety' (*Planet Ark World environmental news,* February 4, 2004).

20.  A Kansas beef producer intended to use recently approved rapid tests to test all its cattle for mad cow disease, so he could resume selling his fat-marbled Angus beef to Japan. In April 2004, the USDA refused this, arguing that these tests were only licensed for surveillance of animal health and the use by this firm would have 'implied a consumer safety aspect that is not scientifically warranted' (*New York Times*, 10 April, 2004). This decision was supported by the beef industry because their spokespersons considered general testing too expensive in comparison to the small number of BSE cases in the US. A '100 per cent testing [is] misleading to consumers because it would create a false impression that untested beef was not safe' (ibid.).

21.  'BSE has been a particularly British disaster. Almost all the victims of vCJD have been in the United Kingdom. Over 170,000 cattle have been diagnosed with BSE here compared with fewer than 1,500 abroad. ... So far, over 4.7 million British cattle have had to be slaughtered, and their carcasses burned or buried as potentially dangerous waste. The livelihood of thousands of farmers and businesses has been damaged' (Phillips, 2000: par. 9). The total costs have been estimated at almost £5 billion.

22.  'Food regulation operates within a highly charged social environment in which policy-making and implementation are shaped by an array of often-conflicting pressures from multiple organised interests, the media, and different sections of the public. The food safety regime is also institutionally highly complex; having a multi-level governance structure that spans national and supra-national policymaking, local authority inspection and enforcement, with major food businesses acting as commercial intermediaries in long international food-supply chains. Relatedly, food safety regulation comprises a patchwork of sub-regimes that are subject to varying pressures, priorities, and ways of working. Consequently, there is considerable scope for divergence and even incoherence in the operationalization of the principle of "putting consumers first" across the food safety regime' (Rothstein, 2005: 523).

# 6. Governing genetically modified food in the global network society

> Genetically modified crops and other biotechnology are safe and their use would dramatically boost food production. ... Yet our partners in Europe are impeding this effort. They have blocked all new bio-crops because of unfounded, unscientific fears.
> (US President Bush at a speech to the graduating class of the US Coast Guard Academy, 22 May, 2003)

> Africa is in danger of becoming the dumping ground for the struggling GM industry and the laboratory for frustrated GM scientists. The proponents of GM technology sell a sweet message of GM crops as the second green revolution and the answer to African hunger, but the reality is quite different. A close look at GM crops and the context under which they are developed makes clear that GM crops have no place in African agriculture.
> (Zachary Makanya in *Seedling Magazine*, published by GRAIN; http://www.grain.org/seedling/?id=294)

## INTRODUCTION

Since the mid-1990s, when Genetically Modified Organisms (GMOs) were effectively introduced in food production, the European public has continuously ranked GM food among the most controversial social issues (Wales and Mythen, 2002).[1] Just recovering from the BSE crisis, Europeans regarded GM food (repeatedly called 'Frankenstein food' in the media) as a new threat to consumer health. In particular, environmental NGOs pointed at the threat to biodiversity formed by this new technology, while organic farmers feared the future of their livelihood when their organic crops would be 'contaminated' with modified genes. Many different social groups in Europe expressed their concerns about this new technological development and tried to put pressure on national and European authorities to introduce regulations that would protect them from the (potential) dangers of GMOs. Therefore, the governance of GM food production and consumption evolved into a serious political problem, initially only in the EU but subsequently at the global level as well. Public debates about the regulation of GM food involve many different social actors each with different views on the potential risks, on the role of science, on the need to facilitate global trade and on the governance arrangements needed to adequately deal with these issues. Thus, the public controversy about the safety of GM food as well as its regulation forms an exemplary case to study the ways in which the governance of food production and consumption in the context of global modernity is challenging conventional nation-state-based arrangements.

As long as food production and consumption was organised locally or regionally, food governance remained local or regional as well, but when food trade became global, global food governance arrangements became indispensable. The production and consumption of GM food constitutes a clear example of the increasingly global organisation of food production and consumption networks at the beginning of the twenty-first century. GM food also clearly shows the complex problems facing food governance in this changing context. The use of GM technology in the production of food is an example of human interference with nature, which becomes increasingly radical over time. Therefore, dealing with different public concerns about human health and the environment demands new forms of governance in the context of the globalised production, processing, trade and consumption of GM food. Governing GM food provides an interesting opportunity to study the possibilities of combining facilitating international food trade while responding to local environmental and food-safety considerations at the same time. Recent history points at the global character of the GM food production and trade and at the active public engagement in the political debates on its regulation. International institutions such as the WTO and the EU, as well as many nation-states, civil society organisations and private firms have become actively involved in the governance of global flows of GM food. Therefore, the question may be posed, what new arrangements in the governance of global flows of GM food are being developed and how can the concepts introduced in Chapter 3 contribute to further understanding the dynamics taking place?

This chapter will review the recent history of the debates and practices on governing GM food in order to identify the ways in which different social actors try to defend their interests and respond to their concerns and how they translate these into innovative governance arrangements. The next section presents some theoretical concepts specifically applied in this case study, building on the conceptual tools already developed in Chapter 3 and supplemented further with the notion of discursive and regulatory networks. With the help of these concepts, the recent history of GM food governance will be described on the basis of the changes that have taken place between 1993 and 2003 in the regulation of GM food in the United States (third section) and in the European Union (fourth section). The increasing involvement of multilateral institutions, such as the WTO and the Convention on

Biodiversity (CBD) as well as the need for China and different countries in southern Africa to develop a specific policy on GM food production and consumption, show that GM food governance has become a global challenge, as I will explain in the fifth section. In the concluding section, I will defend the thesis that the recent history of GM food regulation shows that global governance of GM food cannot be based on product characteristics alone, although it is not yet fully clear in what way characteristics of the production processes can be included in global GM food governance in a satisfactory way.

## CONCEPTUAL TOOLS FOR ANALYSING THE GOVERNANCE OF GLOBAL FLOWS OF GM FOOD AND POTENTIAL RISKS INVOLVED

In the early 1990s, it seemed GM food governance was only a concern for a small number of food and agriculture regulators and agro-food corporations in the United States. However, within less than ten years, the issue of governing GM food has become a global public concern. It is nevertheless remarkable that, although the commercial production of GM food started in the US, it became a public concern mainly in Europe. Particularly in Western Europe during the late 1990s, the media and many environmental NGOs drew wide public attention to these 'Frankenstein foods that threaten our food supply'. At the same time, the European food safety authorities were engaged in a process of redesigning their regulatory approach, which had proved to be inadequate during the BSE and the dioxins crises. Therefore, new governance principles and tools were introduced in the regulation of GM food in the EU, such as the 'precautionary principle' and the 'mandatory labelling of food on the basis of the production processes'. This new approach to governing food within the EU seemed inconsistent with the ongoing trend towards increased liberalisation in the global food trade market, which went together with a continuous pressure to create uniform global standards for food quality and safety. Within this context, several challenges confronting food governance in global modernity, already identified in Chapter 2, become particularly visible. Many consider GM food a typical example of the new kind of food risks facing people living in global modernity. Responding to the diminishing consumer trust in food and particularly in GM food seemed to have become an essential task for all actors involved. In addition, balancing food safety and environmental concerns with economic interests while acknowledging the different tasks and responsibilities of state and non-state actors as well as of multilateral institutions, all require particular attention in the case of GM food.

Comparable to BSE, GM food also bears the classic hallmarks of a manufactured risk as defined by Beck (1992): it is created by humans, has potential catastrophic effects that can be illimitable in time and place and is uninsurable (Wales and Mythen, 2002).[2] The use of GM technology constitutes a more radical interference with nature than previously introduced technological innovations in food production such as the selective breeding techniques introduced to create high yielding plant varieties during the Green Revolution (Atkins and Bowler, 2001). Therefore, although some official bodies hold on to the conventional risk political arrangements to deal with GM food (see Chapter 2), many social actors demand an innovative approach because they claim that this new technology creates new kinds of risk. The example of the failures of conventional science-based risk politics in dealing with BSE is called upon to justify specific innovative governance arrangements to deal with the potential risks involved in GM food. The absence of clear and generally accepted scientific evidence for the presence of risks involved in the production and consumption of GM food should not be used as sufficient argument for the actual absence of risk. As the case of BSE made very clear, conclusive scientific proof for the existence of risks might be lacking, but the disastrous consequences may nevertheless be there. Even with regard to BSE, when some individual scientists did uncover indications for potential risks their conclusions became accepted only much later (see Chapter 5). Providing sufficient scientific evidence for the (potential) environmental and health risks involved in GM food production and consumption may even be more complicated than in the case of BSE. Potential environmental and health consequences of GM food production and consumption might be present but only observable after long-term research. Therefore critics of the use of conventional risk politics in GM food governance demand that regulating the production and the trade of GM-food and preventing possible hazards requires the inclusion of not only the fully scientifically established risks but also the potential ones. Moreover, these critics also point at the importance of not limiting food governance arrangements to the characteristics of the final food product alone but of covering the production practices as well.

Different views on the presence of risks in the production and consumption of GM food and on how to deal with them resulted in the promotion of different governance approaches to their regulation. These different approaches to regulate GM food production and trade can be categorised in three ideal-typical models. Each of these models is based more or less on a coherent discourse about the possible risks involved in GM food production and consumption, about the role of science in dealing with these risks, includes particular key actors and furthermore defines specific guidelines for concrete governance arrangements of GM food (see Table 6.1 for a summary). The first model is based essentially on the intention to facilitate global food trade, the second on the goal to prevent environmental and food safety risks and the third model tries to create an ideal combination of these two approaches.

Facilitating global trade in GM food requires some kind of global governance arrangement to facilitate the reduction of nation-state-based protective and supportive regulatory regimes. Such global governance of GM food would necessarily aim at 'governance in the space of flows', requiring generally applicable science-based principles to establish standards and regulations. Consequently, within this approach, the safety of GM food should be assured by defining particular requirements with regard to the food products themselves and not by referring to the production processes that underlie them. The WTO is an important driving force within this model because this organisation is oriented towards GM food governance in the space of flows. Therefore, a separate regulation for GM food is only acceptable according to the WTO principles, defined in the SPS agreement if GM food posed concrete dangers for human, animal or plant life and health (see Chapter 4). In addition, the presence of such dangers should have been confirmed by sufficient scientific evidence while the regulation itself should be based on a formal risk assessment procedure. Such flow-based governance arrangement is justified by the aim to facilitate global trade and to reduce the presence of unjustified trade barriers, but the consequences of such a strict product-based approach to GM food governance received critical comments from different positions.

Growing concerns about the potential health and environmental impacts of GM food create a driving force to develop a food governance arrangement that would effectively prevent these risks. Consumption of food as such is already delicate (Fine, 1998; Keil and Beardsworth, 1996), but the unknown effects of GM food make its consumption even more sensitive. In addition, the production of GM food might endanger the production of organic food and threaten biodiversity through the spread of genes to wild relatives of agricultural crops. Because of these worries, particular governance arrangements are proposed that are able to deal with the specific characteristics of the food production and consumption practices involved and thus explicitly include the production process in its regulations. Innovative governance arrangements, such as regional food supply chains and organic food producers attempting to re-establish direct links between producers and consumers of food, could offer such an adequate alternative. In so doing, they facilitate the re-constitution of trust on the basis of face-to-face interaction and the inclusion of environmental and animal welfare as well as human health considerations in their understanding. As European consumer trust in GM food remains minimal, these alternative, regional food supply chains and organic food producers would probably not produce food with the use of GMOs. Furthermore, to enable the continued existence of non-GM food producers, alternative food supply chains could enforce strict guidelines to guarantee that GMOs will not intrude in the fields of these non-GM food producers or in their markets. Achieving this objective requires additional forms of food governance organised within the space of place. Environmental NGOs and organic farmers' organisations are the most important driving forces behind this model for governing GM food. Such a model of governance in the space of place would effectively exclude the production and trade of GM food in many regions.

The third model attempts to combine governance in the space of flows with governance in the space of place, and tries to facilitate global food trade while protecting consumer and environmental interests at the same time. These objectives could be achieved with the help of certain national government-based governance instruments, such as regulations in the form of duties, taxes or other charges and through mandatory labelling of GM food products, rather than through import bans, export certificates or other forms of trade restrictions. Labelling of GM food would allow consumers to choose between GM and non-GM food and thereby to influence producers' decisions in an indirect manner. One consequence of offering consumers the opportunity to choose is that farmers, processors and retailers have to preserve the identity (GM or not-GM) of their products throughout the supply chain. Eventually this could result in the establishment of separate chains for GM and non-GM food. The EU and the Biosafety Protocol of the Convention on Biodiversity (CBD) can be considered the driving forces behind this model.

As Table 6.1 shows, contesting the governance approach to GM food regulation is not only based on competing views from different social interest groups on a well defined unequivocal problem characterised by determinate risks, but entails a complex and continuous struggle over the definition of the problem itself and about the objectives of food governance in general (Hajer, 1995). The public debates and political struggles involved have resulted in the formation of different networks of actors each reproducing particular discourses about GM food. In these discourses, distinct views on the potential dangers involved in the production and consumption of GM food are combined with specific opinions about the required regulatory practices while these views are given permanence through 'discursive and regulatory networks' (Toke and Marsh, 2003; Newell, 2001).

*Table 6.1  Models and GM food governance*

| Regulatory models | Risks in GM-food | Role of science | Key actors | GM-food governance |
|---|---|---|---|---|
| Governance in the space of flows | There are no particular risks involved in GM food as such; not using GM technology would lead to insufficient food production on the longer term. | Science provides the information to base decision-making practices on. | US government, WTO. | No specific regulation needed because GM food is not fundamentally different from conventional food products. |
| Governance in the space of place | GM food production may create dangers for biodiversity; consumption of GM food may result in acute health risks and have disastrous consequences in the long term. | Science is the reason for the existence of GM food and cannot be trusted to provide the security needed for its regulation but can only offer information about possible risks. | Regional food supply chains, organic farmers, NGOs, some European governments. | No GM food because the potential risks are too large. Establish direct producer–consumer links, protect the environment, and sustain biodiversity. |
| Combining governance in the space of place and governance in the space of flows | The long-term effects of GM food production and consumption are unknown, but today there is no clear proof for the absence of risks; applying the precautionary principle means protecting other forms of food production, allowing consumers a choice and only accepting GM food if there are clear advantages in their use. | Science should provide information about risks and benefits and inform the public debate and policy makers. | EU, NGOs, some European governments. | Labelling of GM food to allow consumers a choice and guarantee the continued production of non-GM food; facilitate food trade while protecting the environment and guarantee food safety. |

These discursive and regulatory networks may display shifting composi-
tions in terms of the actual members and topics discussed, but they have acquired some form of permanence. The three main models for GM food governance, presented above, are developed and promoted in public and political debates by different discursive and regulatory networks, composed of
both state and non-state actors. The state actors include certain national
governments as well as different intergovernmental and multilateral institutions, while the non-state actors comprise various (groups of) scientists,
NGOs and numerous groups of food producers and consumers. Many different arguments on the advantages and the risks related to GM food production and consumption are promoted within these networks. (See Appendix 1 for a summarised overview of the principal arguments used in these
debates by the proponents and opponents of GM food.) Most of these discursive and regulatory networks have become global networks, linking social actors from very different regions and different backgrounds and this
globalisation of the networks results in a permanent exchange of arguments,
experiences, strategies and viewpoints.

Analysing the historical process of GM food regulatory practices in the
US and in the EU provides an interesting opportunity for reviewing the different ways in which these discursive and regulatory networks have promoted various options for food governance.

## INCREASING GM FOOD PRODUCTION AND ITS REGULATION IN THE US

GMOs, for which the basic technology was discovered in the 1970s, were
further developed in the next decade, and as a result the first genetically
modified agricultural crops could be planted for commercial purposes in the
mid-1990s. Since then the area for growing GM crops increased very rapidly from an estimated 1.7 million hectares in 1996 to 90.0 million hectares
in 2005. (See Table 6.2.)

Currently, GM crops are produced in 21 different countries, although
more than 85 per cent of the area is still located in just three of them: US,
Canada and Argentina. Soybeans make up the main GM crop (60 per cent
of the total area of GM crops) and 51 per cent of the total global soybean
production is nowadays based on the use of GMOs (Weaver, 2003). Herbicide tolerance remains the dominating transgenic trait present in soybeans,
corn and cotton, and accounts for 71 per cent of the global area planted with
GM crops (James, 2005).[3]

The area of GM crops in Europe is infinitesimal compared to the US,
Canada, or Argentina as only Portugal, France and Spain include very lim-

ited areas of Bt maize with limited growth over the years contrary to many non-EU countries. In the year 2005, about 53,000 hectares of Bt maize were grown commercially in Spain. (See Table 6.3.)

*Table 6.2   GM crops worldwide*

| Year | Global area of GM crops (million hectares) |
|------|--------------------------------------------|
| 1996 | 1.7 |
| 1997 | 11.0 |
| 1998 | 27.8 |
| 1999 | 39.9 |
| 2000 | 44.2 |
| 2001 | 52.6 |
| 2002 | 58.7 |
| 2003 | 67.7 |
| 2004 | 81.0 |
| 2005 | 90.0 |

*Source*: James (2005).

*Table 6.3   European area (hectares) under Bt maize*

| Country | 1998 | 1999 | 2000 | 2005 |
|---------|------|------|------|------|
| France | 2,000 | 1,000 | – | 500 |
| Spain | 20,000 | 10,000 | 30,000 | 53,000 |
| Portugal | – | 1,000 | 1,000 | 780 |
| Germany | – | – | – | 400 |
| Czech Republic | – | – | – | 300 |

*Source*: European Commission (2000b); GMO-Compass (2006) for 2005.

When the first GM food crop, the Flavr Savr tomato, was commercially introduced in the US in 1994, the authorities were necessarily obliged to define an appropriate regulatory framework to deal with it. The US authorities chose to base their regulation on the assumption that specific testing and regulation (for example through product labelling) was not needed because GM food could be considered as safe as conventional food. Their regulatory framework was therefore built on the so-called *'substantial equivalence'* approach, which was developed by the Organisation for Economic Cooperation and Development (OECD) and essentially considered the existing, 'conventional' food products as a benchmark against which to assess the safety of the new, genetically modified products. 'If a new food or food component is found to be substantially equivalent (compositionally similar) to an existing food or food component, it can be treated in the same manner with respect to food safety' (OECD, 1993: 16). Therefore, because a transgenic crop differs from an unmodified crop only in the particular trait coded for by the transgene and can be considered 'substantially equivalent' in all other respects, merely this trait needs measuring (Clark and Lehman, 2001).[4] Only in exceptional cases when clear evidence for food safety risks exists is specific additional regulation required. This way, the US regulation of GM food can be viewed as governance in the space of flows because it is not based on the production process (that is, the use of GMOs) but only on product characteristics to the extent they may pose a specific health risk for consumers. This regulatory approach only accepts 'sound scientific evidence' as acceptable input for decision-making on GM food and excludes other elements of governance in the space of places, such as (potential) long-term local environmental consequences, certain ethical principles, the protection of local food culture and agricultural traditions or specific consumer concerns. Based on the absence of generally accepted scientific proof for the presence of particular risks involved in the use of GM technology, the US authorities decided that genetic modification itself should not be seen as risky and its use would therefore not require mandatory labelling (Princen, 2002).

The debate on GM food governance in the US was dominated by federal governmental institutions such as the Food and Drug Administration (FDA), US Department on Agriculture (USDA) and the Environmental Protection Agency (EPA), a limited number of private biotechnology firms (Monsanto, Novartis, Aventis, and so on) and a few farmers' organisations. They built their regulatory approach on optimism about progress in the natural sciences and related technological innovations and on the conviction that society would profit more from GM technology if governments would interfere as little as possible and avoid the introduction of specific legislation. According to the governance approach developed within this discursive and regulatory network, the guidelines for GM food should be science-based and intimately product-related, thus severely restricting the role of the public in decision-making on food risks.[5] The only widely presented viewpoint opposing the way GM food regulation was implemented in the US was built around the Organic Consumer Association (OCA), but only after the European public opinion had been expressed vividly and the US GM food regulation was already fully implemented. The OCA's discourse centres on the promotion of 'natural foods' produced without the use of GMOs, hormones or any other 'unnatural' substance. The organisation considers the promotion of 'natural foods' necessary to fight the 'gene giants' (large biotech firms) who treat food, just like any other commodity, as an opportunity for making profit. Governance in the space of places therefore forms the basis of OCA's regulatory approach and the organisation ultimately only accepts organic agriculture as sufficient guarantee for the safety of food. So far, this alternative discursive and regulatory network has remained quite marginal in the political discussions and unable to influence GM food regulation in the US in any substantial manner.

After the US had developed its 'substantial equivalence' approach in regulating GM food, the EU created its own regulation, which differs in several essential aspects from the US example (see the following section). Because of the deviant EU regulation of GM food, US food exports to Europe dropped substantially as official approvals of certain GM food products by the EU authorities were absent while others got delayed. For example, the US share in EU maize imports fell from 86 per cent in 1995 to 12 per cent in 1999, which was calculated to represent a loss of US$200 million in 1998 alone. The US soybeans exports to Europe also dropped from 9.85 million tonnes to 6.75 million tonnes between 1995 and 1999, while Brazilian (then still considered non-GM) soybean exports soared from 2.99m tonnes in 1996 to 6.87m tonnes in 1999 (Vidal, 2001).[6] In reaction to this substantial loss in exports and the resulting financial damages, the US filed a complaint at the WTO against the EU (see fifth section).

US policy on GM food has been nation-state-based but because of its limitation to product characteristics alone, this approach provided an acceptable basis for the governance for international trade in GM food as well. Politics in the US was founded on a conventional approach to food risks, although the particular character of GM food did require the introduction of the new principle of 'substantial equivalence' to deal with the complexities of this revolutionary form of human interference with nature. Surprisingly, the policy debate in the US remained restricted to a small group of societal actors, whereby the driving discursive and regulatory network mainly comprised officials from USDA and specialists from different biotechnology firms as well as some scientists.

## THE HISTORY OF GM FOOD REGULATION IN EUROPE

The EU's regulatory regime on GM food has not been a copy of the US regulation but was developed independently in reaction to public controversies in the European continent about the possible risks involved in the production and consumption of GM food. In the middle of the 1990s, European NGOs framed GM food as a food safety problem threatening consumer health, while at the same time the food safety authorities in the EU were redesigning their overall regulatory approach. The BSE crisis had proven the inadequacy of the existing European Union's food safety politics and forced a fundamental review (see Chapter 5). The framing of GM food by the NGOs, putting this issue in alignment with the previous food safety crises on BSE and dioxins, built on existing public worries about food safety and thereby opened up a window of opportunity for successfully contesting GM food regulation in the European political arena (Hajer, 1995; Hannigan, 1995). Any review of the evolution of GM food regulation in the EU therefore has to include civil society organisations and cannot be limited to review the roles of official regulatory agencies alone. The history of this debate on governing GM food in the EU can be divided into three periods. The first period covers the years between 1990 and 1996, when GM food transformed from an interesting technological innovation into a highly controversial public concern. This was followed between 1996 and 2001 by a period where social movements and private economic actors enforced the establishment of a 'de facto' moratorium effectively blocking the production and import of GM food in the EU. Finally, during the third period from 2001 to 2003, the EU attempted to develop an innovative regulatory approach that would be acceptable within the EU as well as for the other relevant countries and global institutions.

**1990–96: GM Food Gets Regulated**

Initially the authorities in the EU, notably the EU Directorate-General for Industry and Research and Development as well as the biotech industries in Europe, considered biotechnology, including GM food, an interesting opportunity for the promotion of high-tech industry. Several EU member states had already developed their own national regulations in the late 1980s to deal with this technological innovation. This however resulted in disparity, in content as well as in effect, between the regulations in the different member-states as these different regulations created unequal conditions for competition between firms. Moreover, the differences between these national regulations did create barriers to trade and increasingly this was considered unacceptable in the EU's transition process towards a common market. In reaction, the European Commission felt obliged to look for ways to harmonise the different national regulations on GM-food, but this task was interestingly not assigned to the Directorate-General for Industry and Research and Development, but to the Directorate-General for the Environment.[7] This process of creating a common regulation resulted in Council Directive 90/220 issued to govern the deliberate release of GM-food into the environment through both field-testing and marketing to the public.[8] This directive imposed uniform environmental standards on the production of GM food and facilitating food trade throughout the EU and, thus, this regulation can be considered as largely based on the concept of governance in the space of flows. Risk assessment procedures had to be performed by the member states themselves and subsequently forwarded to the other EU members, who could then eventually oppose the conclusions from these assessments. In line with this procedure, the EU licensed Monsanto's Roundup Ready soybean in 1996 and Ciba-Geigy Bt maize in 1997, and consequently in 1998 some 20,000 hectares of GM maize were grown in Spain and about 1,000 hectares in France (Princen, 2002). Nevertheless, the Directive 90/220 already referred to the precautionary principle as its main regulatory approach, while the criteria to be used for the environmental risk assessment remained rather vague. In this context, it was possible for different EU member states to interpret the regulatory arrangements contained in this directive in accordance with their own preferences, and thereby they introduced several elements of an approach to governance in the space of places (Barling, 2000). Therefore, despite the presence of a common EU policy for regulating the production of GM food, the latitude offered by the directives in combination with the public debates in several member states put this uniform basis under pressure already before it was implemented fully.

### 1996–2001: GM Food Becomes a Public Concern

The commercial introduction of GM food in Europe by Monsanto importing maize from the US in the mid-1990s led to widespread public unrest and, the existence of a communal EU policy on GMO notwithstanding, to unilateral initiatives by individual member states. The principles for GM food regulation incorporated in Directive 90/220 came under pressure, because Austria and Luxembourg did not allow the production of GM crops while Denmark, France and the Netherlands developed national measures to segregate GM food offering consumers a choice between GM and non-GM food. These different national decisions in the implementation of Directive 90/220 led to a 'race to the top' whereby different EU member states competed among themselves by issuing standards that claimed to be more adequate in safeguarding public health and the natural environment. The unilateral initiatives taken by the member states influenced in their turn GM food regulation for the EU as a whole. Issuing and implementing a particular law or regulation by an EU member-state that differs from the regulatory regime in the other member states, invariably places this inequality on the agenda of the Union as a whole. It was for this reason that around 1997 the growing tensions between the official requirement for maintaining a single market regulation and the reality of different national regulations implemented in the member states created a political pressure towards the elaboration of a new and more appropriate GM food governance framework in Europe. Under the pressure of different national governments, particularly those from France, Denmark, Italy, Greece and Luxembourg, the EU was in 1998 compelled to decide to momentarily interrupt the approval processes of new GM crops in order to harmonise different opinions and to review the existing regulations. This way the EU materially established a 'de facto' moratorium (Sand, 2001).[9] By the end of 1998, the EU had already formally approved the cultivation of 14 GM crop varieties: maize (4), rapeseed (4), carnation (3), chicory (1), soybean (1) and tobacco (1). At the same time, the EU had 19 applications for approval of GM crop varieties pending: maize (7), oilseed rape (5), sugar beet (2), cotton (2), fodder beet (1), soybean (1) and potato (1) (JRC, 2003).[10] The European authorities decided to review the approval procedures prescribed in Directive 90/220 with the intention of looking for ways to reduce potential environmental and health risks involved in the production and consumption of GM food.

While the EU institutions were preparing new regulations, different non-state actors took various initiatives to establish some form of GM food governance based much more on governance in the space of places. Public trust in the regulatory agencies had been undermined in Europe by the consecutive food scandals in the mid-1990s (Joly, 2000). In their efforts to find new ways to regain consumer trust in the safety of their food, supermarket chains felt compelled to respond explicitly to the public concerns surrounding GM food. Private involvement in GM food governance started in the United Kingdom in 1996, when the American Soybean Association, Monsanto and the US trade association declared that the full segregation of GM soybeans from conventional soybeans, as requested by several British retailers, would be impossible (Margaronis, 1999). These firms and associations described British food retailers as 'backward Europeans, who should just accept what is right for their consumers' (McGarity and Hansen, 2001: 55). However, in the mid-1990s public fears about the safety of GM food rose particularly high in the UK because of the BSE crisis occurring at the same time (Toke and Marsh, 2003).[11] The environmental NGO Friends of the Earth then requested the public in the UK to write letters to supermarkets, urging them not to stock foods containing GM ingredients. In reaction, Tesco, the UK's leading supermarket, declared in February 1999 that it would become the first supermarket to label all GM soybean derivatives and not just proteins. Marks & Spencer banned GM food from its own-brand products altogether and labelled 100–50 products that could contain 'a minimal trace of GM ingredients'. The UK frozen food retailer, Iceland, responded to the consumer unrest surfacing in 1998 by leading a search to find non-GM sources of soybeans for the production of their own-brand food items. In addition, since October 1998, Asda supermarkets asked suppliers to exclude GM food from their own-brand products where possible, and in February 1999, McDonalds and Burger King declared they would be sourcing non-GM food in the UK, while KFC would be labelling GM products. Most UK food retailers removed GM products from their home brands, refused to purchase from potentially GM-contaminated US sources and turned to GM-free sources instead.[12] Major food processors, under pressure from these retailers, followed suit, as did some restaurants and catering groups.

*Table 6.4   Overview of private GM food labelling by retailers*

| Retail food chain | Target market | Non-GM product coverage |
| --- | --- | --- |
| Carrefour | France | Own label food products |
| Delhaize | Belgium | All products |
| Edeka retail association | Germany, Czech Rep., Denmark, France, Poland | All products |
| Effelunga | Italy | All products |
| Iceland Group | UK | Own label products (as well as artificial colours/flavours) |
| Marks & Spencer | UK | Own label goods (<0.1% tolerance level) |
| Migros | Switzerland | All products |
| Northern Foods | UK | All products, except derivatives |
| Park N'Shop | Hong Kong | Own label products |
| Sainsbury's | UK | All products |
| Somerfield | UK | All products |
| Superquinn | Ireland | All products |
| Tesco | UK | All products; encouraging the use of non-GM feed for meat production |
| UK Co-op | UK | Eggs to be produced from chickens fed on a GM-free diet |
| Waitrose | UK | Own label products |
| Walmart (Asda) | UK | Own label products |
| Whole Foods Mkt. Inc. | US (Texas) | All products |
| Wild Oats Mkts. Inc. | US (Colorado | All products |
| Woolworth | South Africa | Will seek alternatives to GM products, or label |

*Source:* Phillips and Foster (2000: 13).

Given that several European food processors have integrated their operations on a continental basis, it became nearly impossible to produce non-GM food products for the UK and food that potentially contained GMOs for the rest of Europe so many food processing and trading firms decided to avoid GMOs in all of their food products (Phillips and Foster, 2000).[13] (See Table 6.4 for an overview of the different firms engaged in private regulation.) Interestingly, biotech companies themselves also showed support for these private labelling initiatives; for example, Novartis decided in 1997 to label all its genetically modified products to give consumers a choice. In 1998, Monsanto also declared its support for labelling genetically modified foods in Europe, but on the condition that labelling would be 'science based' (Bhatia and Powell, 2000).[14]

Interestingly, between 1995 and 2000, while the official EU regulatory approach seemed to be bogged down, a fully elaborated system of market-led private governance was emerging under pressure from the European public.[15] This process was facilitated by the merging of small-scale food firms into large-scale retailing, processing and catering corporations, and by improvements in detection technology for GM proteins. This innovative form of governance, which combines governance in the space of places with governance in the space of flows, started with local consumers' and citizens' concerns and was implemented further by private companies who took these measures probably not only for ethical or environmental reasons but on commercial grounds as well (Phillips and Foster, 2000; Toke and Marsh, 2003).[16]

### 2001–03: EU Attempts to Combine Governance in the Space of Flows with Governance in the Space of Places

The emerging privately initiated governance arrangements combined with the inability to implement existing official regulation created a growing pressure on the EU institutions to review its regulatory arrangement. The European Commission therefore took steps to adapt the Directive 90/220 and thereby to harmonise different national regulations among the member states anew and end the 'de facto' moratorium. This process, aimed at bridging opposing viewpoints among the member states, can be regarded as an attempt to combine governance in the space of flows with governance in the space of places. This regulatory process resulted in the new Directive 2001/18, which did not prohibit the production and commercialisation of GM food as such, but attempted to give consumers a choice and to protect organic and conventional farmers.[17] The procedures in this directive were based on a case-by-case approach using a process of notification and consent between the member states and requiring the presence of satisfying, science-based risk analyses and risk assessments underpinning the decision-making process. Member states are allowed to diverge from the formal decisions taken at the EU level only if there are possible hazards which are specific to the local conditions in their countries (Sand, 2001).[18] Despite the elaborate requirements and the restrictive character of these regulations with regard to the production and trade of GM food, the EC essentially still considered the technology itself a positive contribution towards the necessary increase in food production and to technological progress in general. Thus official regulations within the EU should 'not unnecessarily hinder the potential of technological innovation' (EC first proposal for amendments COM (89) 85). The Directive 2001/18 required the labelling of GM food but the European Council was able to establish the exact details of the procedural guidelines for labelling only in July 2003.[19] The EU currently demands the labelling of all food containing GM ingredients above a threshold of 0.9 per cent as well as of all food produced from GMOs irrespective of whether there is DNA or protein of GM origin in the final product itself. This labelling procedure allows the traceability of GMOs 'at all stages in the production and marketing chain, providing a robust safeguard system' (EU press release IP/03/1056).

Besides its intention to allow consumers a choice between GM and non-GM food, the EC also looked for guarantees to secure opportunities in the future for farmers to grow organic or conventional crops alongside other growing GM crops. In order to make such a 'co-existence' possible, the different EU member states were requested to elaborate and implement the necessary concrete regulatory measures based on the directive, which used rather general terms.[20] This approach was chosen because of the large variations between the different countries with regard to their production circumstances and natural environments as well as the differences in the proportion of organic agriculture compared to conventional farming. These differences effectively exclude a uniform regulation for the EU as a whole. The most difficult issue with regard to the regulation of co-existence is that genes (including genes containing GMOs) may be transmitted to other crops of the same species and to wild relatives (Tolstrup et al., 2003). The magnitude of genes transmission depends on crop characteristics, the size of the cultivated area and on inter-field distances.[21] Therefore regulating the co-existence of growing GM crops, conventional agriculture and organic farming requires detailed regulation by the different individual EU member states.[22] The European Commission states that 'no form of agriculture should be excluded in the EU' (EC, 2003b), obliging all national governments to develop regulations to allow the production of GM crops. This second element of governance in the space of places within the broader framework of governance in the space of flows also fits into the intention of the EU to allow consumers a choice between GM and non-GM food. Such a choice is only possible if non-GM food as well as GM crops can be produced at the same time without obstructing each other.

The formulation of Directive 2001/18, including the elaboration of the labelling requirements and the co-existence guidelines, signify the intention by the EU to end the 'de facto' moratorium on GM food production and trade. Between December 1998 and March 2003, no new GM varieties had been approved and so besides the already approved 14 varieties based on Directive 90/220, a further 19 applications for GM crop varieties remained pending. Since 2003, the EU has approved six GM maize varieties and one GM rapeseed variety. In at least four of these cases, the meetings neither in the Standing committee nor in the Ministerial committee reached a qualified majority and the authorisation was granted only after intervention by the EC. The practice of implementing the Directive 2001/18 shows that the different positions within the EU have not yet been sufficiently harmonised to create unanimity about the regulation of GM food among the member states. The repeated interventions by the EC however prevented a continuation of the 'de-facto' moratorium, which became increasingly under attack from food exporting firms, other governments and international institutions.

This brief overview of the history of GM food policy making in the EU focussed on the transition process from a conventional approach to food governance in 1993 to a more innovative governance arrangement in 2003. Initially, EU regulation intended to support a promising technological innovation and applied conventional science-based risk assessment to deal with eventual hazards. During the second half of the 1990s, this approach was abandoned and policies evolved into a search for a governance arrangement that would allow the inclusion of other concerns than the conventional science-based risk considerations. At the same time, the first introductions of GM food products in the European supermarkets coincided with a dramatic rise in consumer worries about the safety of their food and growing suspicions among the general public about the capacity (and willingness) of official authorities to protect their interests. Consequently, consumer protection in particular became a guiding element in the elaboration of new EU governance arrangements whereby authorities attempted to regain consumer trust in the safety of food (Princen, 2002). This transition shows the struggle to combine the intention to facilitate food trade with the need to protect human health and the natural environment, thus to combine governance in the space of flows with governance in the space of places. Several elements played a key role in this evolution and they deserve a more extensive review, in particular the changing approach to food risk and the innovative tools of labelling and co-existence.

Increasingly the European authorities seemed to consider the requirement within conventional risk politics to base the regulation of risks only on 'sound scientific evidence' (as in the US) in the case of GM food as problematic. The possible risks involved in the production and consumption of

GM food are considered fundamentally different from the conventional food risks because they are the result of radically new science-based interference with nature. Consequently, information provided by the same (or other) scientists is needed to offer politicians the required guidance about the possible risks involved in the production and consumption of GM food and to create the basis for official regulation. This forced dependency on scientists to build a framework regulating the potential impacts of hybrids between nature and technology is causing ambiguity in public trust of a science-based politics on GM food. Moreover, risk assessment of GM food involves a wide range of scientific uncertainties both in terms of potential effects to be covered and the time lags involved in observing these effects.[23] This ambiguity in public trust and the presence of these uncertainties has led to a continuous debate on the conclusions of scientific research and their translation into official regulations. Consequently, no scientific committee seems to be able, thus far, to end the dispute on GM food production and consumption on scientific grounds alone (Scoones, 2001; Rowell, 2003).[24] These complexities highlight the reality of food risks in global modernity (see also Chapter 2). The actual presence of GM food requires some form of decision-making in a situation where full and reliable scientific proof about risks is lacking and whereby the potential negative effects may be large-scale and possibly disruptive. The EC therefore concluded over the years that political decisions cannot be based on science alone: 'a (political) decision must be science-based, but is essentially a political or a societal value judgement to be taken by the responsible regulatory authorities' (Dratwa, 2002: 204).[25] This changing view on the role of science as sufficient input for regulations allows the EU authorities to refer to the precautionary principle in their decision-making process.[26] Over time, the precautionary principle has evolved into a basic element in the EU approach to governing GM food production and consumption because this principle makes it possible to acknowledge the complexity and uncertainty of policy-making in this case and to adopt a long-term, holistic and inclusive perspective on environmental protection (Mayer and Stirling, 2002).[27] Despite its evolution into a basic component of the EU's GM food regulation the application of the precautionary principle in food governance practices remains nevertheless rather ill defined.[28]

Labelling of food products containing GM-ingredients has become a central, although still highly controversial, tool for the implementation of the EU policy on GM food. Clear labelling of food would give consumers the opportunity to choose between products containing GMOs and those without them. This measure is justified by referring to the widespread concerns among consumers about the risks involved in GM food production and consumption. Moreover, the labelling of GM food would not block global food trade completely, but only offer consumers the opportunity to make their individual choice.[29] Together these individual choices may nevertheless indirectly influence production practices as the cumulative demand for non-GM food may stimulate the production of food without GMOs. Opponents of GM food labelling state, however, that systematic labelling of food is unnecessary if a product is considered safe according to the existing regulations. Only a GM food product that is significantly different from its conventional counterparts and may have serious consequences for particular consumer categories should be labelled (Caswell, 2000).[30] Mandatory labelling of GM food products would otherwise only confuse consumers, hamper the smooth functioning of global food trade and involve unnecessary high costs for the food industry, because they will be obliged to segregate GM and non-GM crops throughout the food supply chain. Others criticise GM food labelling for completely different reasons, when they state that labelling results in the individualisation and privatisation of risk politics while this should remain a communal and societal responsibility. The labelling of food products would furthermore put the focus on health concerns and ethical issues and exclude considering the potential environmental impacts in decision making because these can be dealt with only through collective measures.

The intention to secure the co-existence of organic and conventional farming when GM food is produced is another innovative element introduced in the current EU regulation. Particular guidelines are needed because in the comparatively small-scale European agriculture non-GM food production would rapidly disappear if GM food production were allowed without any further restrictions. However, in practice regulating co-existence seems rather complicated because genes will always travel to some extent and thus transmit their genetic properties to other crops of the same species (Tolstrup et al., 2003). A recent scenario study commissioned by the European Commission showed that introducing GM crops in the European Union would definitely lead to problems for organic and conventional farming if they want to remain GM-free. Bock et al. conclude, for example, based on their study that a limit of 0.1 per cent for the contamination of GMOs would be extremely difficult to meet. Even 'when considering the 0.3% (production of seed) and 1% (food-feed production) thresholds, co-existence of GM- and non-GM-crops in a region (with 10% or 50% GMO share) might technically be possible but economically difficult because of the costs and complexities of changes associated' (Bock et al., 2002: vi). Some NGOs, like Friends of the Earth, also criticise the refusal by the European authorities to secure co-existence through communal EU-wide guidelines and instead leave this regulation to the national governments of the member states. This choice may lead to confusion throughout Europe and a failure to secure the interests of non-GM food production in particular countries (Friends of the Earth, 2003).

Interestingly these new regulatory tools introduced within the EU aim at combining governance in the space of flows and governance in the space of places. This choice allows global trade in food to continue while the labelling of GM food makes it possible for consumers to choose based on their own considerations, and the co-existence regulations will enable the continued and simultaneous presence of diverging practices of producing food. This innovative governance approach seems particularly adequate to respond to food safety and ethical concerns among consumers but is less able to include environmental considerations. Possibly, the reason for this bias can be found in the limits set by the international obligations for governmental regulations of food and trade to which the EU has to adhere (see the next section).

The transitions in the governance approach to GM food occurring within the EU presented above, the associated struggles as well as the temporary regulatory deadlock in this process, can be explained by the presence of two different discursive and regulatory networks. The first is built around the EC, some member-state governments (UK, Spain and the Netherlands), private firms and different natural scientists and economic experts. According to the discourse within this network, GM food technology should be considered essentially as an important contribution towards technological and economic progress and its further development should therefore be facilitated by EU politics. Any regulation of GM food should be based on scientific information and aim as much as possible towards governance in the space of flows in order not to unnecessarily obstruct its production and international trade. Nevertheless, consumers should be offered the opportunity to choose non-GM food, and this requires the establishment of GM labelling schemes and thus some form of governance in the space of place. The main actors in the second discursive and regulatory network are environmental NGOs and consumer organisations, the European Parliament, different environmental scientists, some governments (Austria, Luxembourg and Germany) and some retailing corporations. Their discourse is based on the conviction that GM food may involve serious environmental and human health risks while GM food production is not even needed because Europe is already producing more food than it consumes. GM food governance should therefore be oriented towards the avoidance of potential risks in particular by protecting producers of non-GM food (organic farming but also regional and traditional food producers) and food consumers. The use of strict guidelines for the production, processing and distribution of GM food, guaranteeing the future of non-GM food producers, can offer the required safeguards and assure consumers they will not be confronted unintentionally and uninformed with GM food. This regulation is in principle based on governance in the space of places, allowing the production and trade of GM food only under very strict conditions. The balance between these two different discourses has been changing over the years as shown before in the historical overview of GM food regulation in the EU. The second discursive and regulatory network has clearly gained in influence since 1990, but remains an uneasy coalition between social actors who support regulatory tools to stop the production and trade in GM food altogether, and others who do accept the production and consumption of GM food as such albeit under specific conditions. Upcoming discussions in the EU about the conditions under which GM food production should be allowed, particularly with regard to the national co-existence guidelines, may eventually lead to a split in this network.

The discussions on the EU governance approach to GM food are not concluded definitively yet because the EU decision-making process can no longer be considered just an internal affair but should be approached as a global issue as well. Whether the EU will actually be able to hold on to the regulatory arrangement it approved in 2003 depends, therefore, not only on internal dynamics within the EU but to a large extent also on the position taken by the WTO and other large-scale food producing and consuming countries.

## GLOBALISING GM FOOD GOVERNANCE

At the WTO, in May 2003, the US filed a complaint against the EU for its GM food policy.[31] So eventually, the discussions on GM food governance had evolved from a limited regulatory challenge for the administrators in the US, via a public debate in the EU into a global food governance concern. The global character of the public debate is shown clearly in the involvement of two important multilateral institutions, the WTO and the Convention on Biodiversity (CBD), in the discussions on the governance of GM food production and trade. The complex challenges facing China and different southern African states in dealing with GM food further underline its global character.

### The World Trade Organisation (WTO)

Until 2003, the involvement of the WTO in debates on GM food governance had mostly been indirect because only its general principles and agreements played a role as part of the background against which different countries developed their internal regulation of GM food production and trade. The complaint lodged at the WTO in May 2003 by the US and several other countries against GM food regulations in the EU, however, forced the WTO to become engaged more actively with this issue. The US complained that its trade interests were harmed unjustly by the EU's GM food policy because of the absence of sufficient scientific evidence for the eventual risks involved in the production and consumption of GM food and that this deficiency makes the 'de facto' moratorium existing within the EU illegal and a threat to the full development of a promising technology (USTR, 2003). The European Commission replied that the European regulation is clear, transparent and non-discriminatory and that the temporary stop in the approval of new GM food crops was necessary to complete a regulatory regime that would adequately address the challenges posed by the technology of genetic modification.[32] Reaching the final decision on this complaint through the WTO Dispute Settlement Bodies will probably take several years if this case follows the example of other disputes within the WTO (compare the beef hormones case which took from 1989 to 1998 before a final decision was reached (Charnovitz, 2002b)). The first step in this process was the ruling by the WTO dispute panel on 10 May, 2006. The content of the report remained confidential and was released only to the parties to the dispute.[33] Nevertheless, it became known publicly that the ruling said that the EU had indeed applied a general 'de facto' moratorium on approvals of biotech products between June 1999 and August 2003, which resulted in a failure to complete individual procedures without undue delay, thereby violating the SPS agreement of the WTO. The ruling also found that national bans on the marketing and import of EU-approved biotech products by individual EU member states were WTO-incompliant (CIEL, 2006). In reaction, the EU declared it did not have to change its regulation because the six-year moratorium ended in 2004 (BRIDGES, *Trade BioRes*, 2006).

The dispute between the US and the EU was brought before a WTO panel because the European regulation was considered as violating the general WTO principles and agreements. These principles seek to promote trade and to reduce unjustified trade restrictions by its member states and abolish or prevent regulations that constitute arbitrary or unjustifiable discrimination against other member states, thus promoting governance in the space of flows (see Chapter 4 for further details). Two WTO agreements are considered especially relevant for GM food regulation: the Agreement on Sanitary and Phytosanitary Measures (SPS) and the Technical Barriers to Trade (TBT) Agreement.

According to the SPS agreement, the members of the WTO are allowed to develop and implement sanitary and phytosanitary measures affecting international trade as long as these measures are only applied for the necessary protection of human or animal health or plant life and based on sufficient scientific evidence. The SPS agreement encourages the mutual acceptance of food safety standards between member states, building on the guidelines agreed upon within the Codex Alimentarius. Therefore, the EU would need concrete scientific evidence if they decided to impose standards for GM food production and consumption deviating from those functioning in the US where they had already undergone a risk assessment process. The labelling of GM food as required by the EU could be considered an unjustified trade barrier as defined in the TBT agreement as well (Sheldon, 2002). In accordance with the TBT agreement, WTO members must ensure that technical regulations, voluntary standards and conformity assessment procedures are based upon product characteristics and not more trade restrictive than necessary to fulfil a legitimate objective while they use relevant international standards whenever they exist. Official labelling requirements should thus be science-based and follow principles of objectivity, non-discrimination and proportionality.

When WTO member states have the impression that other members are not fulfilling their obligations laid down in these agreements, they are entitled to file a complaint at the WTO, which then will be dealt with through the dispute settlement procedures. When direct negotiations between member states concerned have failed, a special dispute settlement panel will be installed to deal with this particular complaint. The way both the SPS and the TBT agreements have been interpreted so far by the different dispute settlement panels is contested, as several observers considered their reading of these agreements too restrictive.[34] Most rulings from the dispute settlement bodies insisted on governance in the space of flows as the only acceptable approach to regulate international trade. Measures based on other considerations than trade and conventional science-based risk politics, such as environmental concerns, were not acceptable even when it was obvious these measures were not intended to protect particular national trade interests (Neumayer, 2001).[35] The US regulation on GM food seems to fit fully into this requirement, but at the moment, it remains doubtful whether the EU regulation will ultimately be considered to fit as well. During the extensive procedures taking place during the dispute settlement procedure on GM food regulation, the opinions expressed by the Codex Alimentarius will probably play an important role.

The Codex Alimentarius Commission (see Chapter 4 for further details) includes a designated committee charged with labelling of food and setting standards for food safety that are enforceable within the WTO. This committee has repeatedly discussed the labelling of GM food, but has so far failed to formulate a recommendation acceptable for all members. Countries supporting mandatory labelling of all GM food (EU, India and most other Asian countries) oppose countries that accept labelling only for specific product characteristics such as safety, composition, intended use and nutrition (US, Canada, Australia, New Zealand, Peru and Brazil) (Bhatia and Powell, 2000). Interestingly, these two opposing groups of countries bridge the divide that traditionally exists between the developed and the developing countries. Whether these particular alliances will be permanent ones remains uncertain, however, as each individual country may have its own particular reasons for the current position it has taken in the case of labelling GM food. Their considerations may vary from national trade interests to consumer protection or farmers' interests. The discussion within the Codex on the labelling of GM food so far gives the impression of the making of a stalemate, because consumer perceptions differ widely between the different countries while the distribution of costs and benefits among them also varies a lot in relation to the diverse labelling options (Kalaitzandonakes and Phillips, 2000).

Consequently, the Codex has not yet produced the clear guidelines on the regulation of GM food demanded by the WTO.[36] This situation also makes clear that the original intention from the WTO to ask international specialised organisations like the Codex to develop undisputed guidelines for the regulation of food trade based on scientific evidence has not materialised. On the contrary, it seems that shifting the politically sensitive debate about food regulation from the internal WTO structures to a 'neutral' and science-based organisation like the Codex has resulted in the politicisation of the debates within the organisation and not in a smooth process of formulating science-based recommendations.

### The Biosafety Protocol of the Convention on Biodiversity (CBD)

The Biosafety Protocol developed under the auspices of the 1992 Convention on Biodiversity (CBD) has also had an impact on the discussions about the regulation of international trade in GM food products. However, the exact relationship between the CBD and the other international institutions remains not yet very well defined, which makes determining the ultimate impact of the Biosafety Protocol in practice unsure.[37] This Protocol intends to establish an adequate level of protection for biodiversity when living modified organisms resulting from modern biotechnology are transferred, handled and used.[38] Central in the governance approach developed in the Biosafety Protocol is 'advanced informed agreement', that is the exporter is obliged to notify the competent authorities in the importing country about the export of living modified organisms beforehand. This advanced informed agreement (also known as prior informed consent) has to follow certain detailed guidelines and does allow the importer to accept (eventually under certain conditions) or prohibit the import of these organisms. An importing country is allowed to have its own regulatory framework for the import of living modified organisms if such domestic regulations are consistent with the objective of the Protocol. This way the CBD permits the inclusion of environmental concerns in the regulation of GMO trade, as long as such regulation 'does not constitute a means of arbitrary or unjustifiable discrimination or a disguised restriction on international trade' (Neumayer, 2001: 145). This approach to govern trade in GMOs leaves much more room for governance in the space of places while still facilitating global flows of agricultural products in comparison to the approach taken within the WTO.

A particular difference in this respect is that the Biosafety Protocol, contrary to the WTO, does accept the precautionary principle as a possible justification for particular regulatory measures. Suspicion of a contamination, which possibly can result from the import of particular living modified organisms, is considered sufficient argument for halting trade under the Biosafety Protocol's approach. Such measures may be inconsistent with the existing WTO obligations but the relationship between the Biosafety Protocol and the WTO is not clarified completely yet. On the one hand, the Protocol declares that it will 'not alter rights and obligations under any existing agreement', while on the other hand 'this Protocol is not subordinate to other international agreements' (Anderson, 2002: 24). Therefore, if and in what manner the Biosafety Protocol will effectively influence GM food regulation in different countries depends on the further elaboration and interpretation of its provisions in the coming years as well as on its relative weight compared to the WTO. An important weakness of the Biosafety Protocol in comparison with the WTO is the absence of a satisfactory dispute settlement procedure or another way to enforce its decisions.

Therefore, the WTO supports an approach to the regulation of GM food production and consumption that is essentially some form of governance in the space of flows because of its overriding objective to facilitate global food trade. The approach chosen in the Biosafety Protocol, on the other hand, accepts that governance in the space of places is a relevant objective, because this would allow the possibility of taking care of consumer concerns, securing the interests of non-GM food producers and protecting biodiversity when necessary.[39] As both the WTO and the Biosafety Protocol approach the regulation of GM food production and consumption from their own respective discourse, it seems that at this moment no easy consensus about the way to establish harmonised global regulation for GM food can be reached.

## GM Food Regulation in China

In the absence of an accepted global regulation of GM food and under the conditions of a continued spread of GM technology and its products throughout the world, different countries are forced to develop their own national GM food regulation. The following two examples of China and Southern Africa may show the complex challenges facing governments of these different countries in their efforts to govern the production and consumption of GM food in practice.

China is developing the largest plant biotechnology capacity outside of North America but the only GM crop widely grown on a commercial basis so far is insect-resistant genetically modified cotton. Between 1997 and 2000, 45 GM plant applications for field trials were approved, 65 for environmental release and 31 for commercialisation, and these numbers represent more than double those of the GM products released in the US (Newell, 2003: 3). The rapid development of China's capacity in the field of GM technology was the result of an active governmental engagement with general scientific research on biotechnology. However, the approval process has slowed down significantly since 2000, and probably this situation is due, at least partly, to changes in the international market for GM products and particularly the growing consumer concerns in the EU (Baumüller, 2003). In reaction to these changes, in 2001 China developed very detailed regulations for the safety assessment, import and labelling of GM food. This development can be considered a transition from a conventional product-based approach towards a more process-based regulation (governance in the space of place) suggesting China is approaching a precautionary position akin to the European stance. GM food regulation in China is developing in interaction with the country's new obligations as a recent member of the WTO and as a member of the CBD, but has to accommodate the interests of private foreign biotech firms and foreign governments with domestic biotech interests and consumer concerns as well.[40] Interestingly, the debates and protests in Europe have provided civil society groups in China, such as Greenpeace China, some leverage on government decisions (Newell, 2003). Therefore, even in China GM food regulation is not a simple process of domesticating foreign regulations and international obligations, but the result of a complex process of translating international debates and discussions on GM food production and consumption into the particular national context. GM food regulation in China has not acquired its definitive shape yet, but the recent decisions by the authorities regarding this regulation cannot be understood without reference to global trade interests and to public debates in Europe and in other countries. Even here, the space of flows is interfering with the space of place and consequently the economic opening up of China means it is becoming more integrated in different global networks and is being influenced by global economic and political debates as well, despite the country's economic power and particular political system.

**GM Food Regulation in Southern Africa**

A second example showing the global character of GM food governance is the food aid provided to Southern Africa in the year 2002. In 2002, nearly 13 million people were facing starvation in different countries in Southern Africa (Malawi, Angola, Zambia and Zimbabwe) as the consequence of drought and the impacts of crop failure. The UN World Food Programme (WFP) provided food aid to the hunger stricken countries to resolve this problem. An important portion of the maize sent as food aid to the region was donated by the US and consisted (partly) of GM maize.[41] At the time this maize was distributed in these countries the relevant national and local authorities were kept in the dark, but when the Zambian government authorities were informed about the possible presence of GM maize, they decided not to allow the UN WFP to continue feeding the 130,000 Angolan and Congolese refugees on its soil with genetically modified maize. Zambian authorities justified this decision by pointing at their concerns about the potential health risks involved for the refugees and the possible environmental consequences if local farmers were to use GM maize as seed. Zambia also feared that the planted GM maize would contaminate domestic grain fed to the livestock in the country, which is mostly destined for export to the European markets. The risk of contamination with GM maize could eventually result in a refusal by European consumers to buy high-quality Zambian meat and this would ultimately lead to a serious financial backlash for the country. For this reason, Zambia also refused to accept milled maize, which could not be used for planting, but still for feeding livestock. Two other countries in Southern Africa, Malawi and Zimbabwe, also expressed concerns over the presence of GM products in the food aid delivered, but these countries eventually did accept milled GM grain (Reuters, 12 September 2002).

Despite some differences between their respective decisions in the end, the Southern African government authorities and numerous developmental and environmental NGOs expressed general concerns about the way 'GM-food aid is being forced on countries in Africa facing starvation' (Peoples Earth Decade, 2003). The WFP responded to this criticism by claiming that there is not yet an international agreement in force with regard to food aid that deals specifically with food containing GMOs. Nevertheless, the standard UN policy is that the decision with regard to the acceptance of GM commodities as part of the organisation's food aid transactions also rests with the recipient countries in Southern Africa. In general, all WFP-donated food should meet the food safety standards from both the donor and recipient countries as well as comply with all applicable international standards, guidelines and recommendations (WFP, 2002). This policy is in line with the Biosafety Protocol of the CBD, stressing the importance of getting prior informed consent from a country before sending in food containing GMOs rather than imposing them on an individual country.

The absence of clear global guidelines or at least fully elaborated national systems of GM food governance within Africa has resulted in confusion and difficult political and ethical problems. A delicate dilemma is whether governments or NGOs can refuse to distribute food that is actually available to nourish hungry refugees for the sole reason that this food was produced with GMOs. So far only four countries in Africa – Egypt, Nigeria, South Africa and Zimbabwe – possess extensive biosafety policies. Even so, these countries encounter problems because their GM food regulations require much larger capacities for monitoring, testing, risk assessment, regulation and control than they presently possess. For example, there has been no assessment of the ecological impact of GM crops already released in Zimbabwe, Egypt and South Africa although this is legally required (Mongelard and Warnock, 2002). In other countries, such as Zambia, attempts to formulate a clear policy on GM food never materialised because these efforts were thwarted repeatedly by a lack of funding, scientific expertise and political will. However, in a globalised economy, such a regulation is an obvious necessity, not a luxury, which is proven clearly by the problems and confusion resulting from the food aid containing GM maize in Southern Africa in 2002.

## CONCLUSIONS AND DISCUSSION

Governing GM food has evolved, between 1990 and 2003, from a technical problem for a small group of bureaucrats in the US into a theme for global public debate involving many different dimensions. Over the last 15 years, countries became increasingly less capable of developing their own national regulations autonomously. Every government today has to take into account its international obligations contained in different multilateral agreements and is influenced by regulatory and discursive networks promoting different regulatory options. For example, China was forced to take public debates in Europe into account when developing its internal domestic regulation and the insecurity about the potential health effects of consuming GM food has placed a traditionally undisputed practice of delivering food aid to hungry people in Africa at the centre of worldwide political debates. This evolution has been driven in particular by consumer concerns in Europe about the safety of consuming GM food products and by national and international NGOs pointing at the potential environmental risks of growing these crops. So, today, the governance arrangements relevant for GM food involve nation-states, multilateral agencies and non-state actors and covers environmental, health, economic, ethical and social considerations.

The introduction and spread of GM food is a clear example of the problems facing food risk politics in global modernity. GM technology is blurring the traditionally clear separation between nature and culture (or technology) of the past and is confusing the distinctive roles of science and non-science in decision-making. The distance in place between the action of planting GM crops on the one hand and the potential impacts of eating GM food on the other may be very large, while the time gap between action and impact may also be big. In addition, if negative environmental or health effects of GM food production and consumption may only be observed after many years, it may already be too late to repair the damage. Thus GM food governance has to take place in the context of basic uncertainty because of the absence of firm scientific evidence about the longer-term effects of the use of GMOs, the difficulties in balancing economic versus environmental and health considerations and the potential positive contributions of this technology to the future provisioning of food, particularly under difficult circumstances. Moreover, the example of GM food governance also shows that dealing with food risks in global modernity no longer remains an assignment for scientific experts and civil servants alone, but that consumers, producers and civil society organisations are becoming involved as well.

Globalisation has resulted in continued pressure towards facilitating global food trade supported by regulations based on product characteristics alone, thus pushing towards the regulation of trade in the space of flows. With regard to GM food, governance in the space of flows would require global and general standards for the safety of specific traits in GM food products, based on clear scientific procedures. Food products that fulfil these requirements should generally be considered safe and be allowed to be traded worldwide without any additional restrictions by national governments or other agencies. Regulating the processes involved in the production of GM food as such is considered unnecessary because scientific research has not yet offered clear evidence that this may be risky. Numerous groups of food producers and consumers, however, oppose these views and want to introduce other elements into the regulation of GM food production and consumption. Consumers, especially in Europe, have become concerned about the safety of their food in general and about the possible environmental and social consequences of GM food production in particular, while producers are demanding more respect for their specific local natural, economic and social circumstances. Therefore, according to the opinion of these NGOs, GM food governance needs to pay much more attention to the way in which food is produced and to include social, food safety and environmental considerations. If these concerns are translated adequately into governance arrangements, they contribute to a form of governance in the space of places of food production and consumption.

Both regulatory models, governance in the space of flows and governance in the space of place, are supported by different discursive and regulatory networks bringing together shifting coalitions of state and non-state actors. Interestingly in the case of GM food, they operate globally as the examples of China and Southern Africa have made very clear. The identity of each of these networks is based on a more or less coherent discourse about the possible presence of risks in GM food production and consumption, about the role of science and technology in dealing with these risks, the importance of international food trade and, consequently, about the appropriate form of governance. The discursive and regulatory network promoting the governance in the space of flows dominates the regulatory practice in the US, while networks promoting governance in the space of place largely influence the debates within the EU. A third network, composed of different environmental NGOs and farmers' organisations, is proposing a definitive ban on the use of GMO technology in food production. The power of this third regulatory and discursive network seems, so far, to be limited to protest actions, such as the destruction of GM field trials and influencing public opinion and political debates, in particular the debates in the European Parliament.[42] Despite the presence of this third network, the first two discursive and regulatory networks dominate the global debate on GM food governance. Whether this debate will result in one common global governance arrangement or in several different national regulations is difficult to predict. However, the analysis of the different networks and debates as presented in this chapter has shown that it is rather unlikely that a science-based approach to regulating GM food, developed completely within the space of flows, will ultimately become dominant in the future. Future GM food governance arrangements will probably have to include different consumer concerns and to consider potential environmental consequences, thus somehow combining governance in the space of flows with governance in the space of place. Shifting coalitions within and between the global regulatory and discursive networks presented in this chapter may play a decisive role in this process.[43]

## NOTES

1.  The terminology used in the debate is often confusing and would deserve a separate study in itself. I use the following concept in this chapter: genetically modified organisms (GMOs) are those organisms produced from genetic engineering techniques that allow the transfer of functional genes from one organism to another, including from one species to another. I will focus my analysis on genetically modified (GM) food, which cover foods and food ingredients consisting of or containing GMOs, or produced from such organisms (European Commission, 2000b).
2.  GM is a credence attribute of food, which means that it is impossible to judge from the appearance of a particular food product, or just by eating it, whether it is produced with GMOs or without. The presence of GMOs can only be established firmly with the help of specialised technologies or through reliable information about the production practices involved.
3.  Herbicide tolerance where certain crops are made resistant to a specific herbicide allows for the use of that pesticide without risking the destruction of the crop itself. The other main GM technology used is insect resistance where the plant is producing the insecticide itself.
4.  These tests are not carried out by the US Food and Drug Administration (FDA) itself but by the applying company while the FDA only controls whether these tests have been conducted properly and no unacceptable risks were revealed (Princen, 2002). This practice is criticised because it would depend too much on information provided by the producers and does not allow the incorporation of justified consumer worries. The concept of substantial equivalence as such is criticised as well because of the absence of clearly defined criteria; for example, how much equivalence is necessary and what are the assurances that the remaining but not tested differences will not be harmful. More in general, critics demand whether a food can be dissected in independent parts for testing or whether it should be considered, holistically, as interdependent elements constituting a living organism.
5.  The limited public involvement in political debates on GM food regulation in the US remains largely unexplained when compared to the situation in Europe. Several observers point at the general lack of public sensitivity among the US population in matters of food production processes, the interests of large private corporations and scientists in the promotion of GM technology and the general policy style in the US, which is oriented to limit governmental interference in the market and in the daily life of US citizens.
6.  The importance of the use of GM technology to explain these changes in soybean exports is however disputed because many observers attribute the declining US soybean export more to price competition from Argentina and Brazil than to the presence of GM traits. In any case, the US soybean growers intending to export to the EU market mostly made sure that the varieties they planted were approved by the EU (Princen, 2002).
7.  The European Commission's first attempt to promote biotechnology in the 1980s, by uniting the relevant industrial actors under the guidance of the DG for Research and Development, was unwieldy and collapsed in 1991 because the structure set up to co-ordinate this activity (the Concerted Unit for Biotechnology in Europe, CUBE) lacked executive capacity. Meanwhile, the Biotechnology Steering Committee had already established the Biotechnology Regulation Inter-service Committee (BRIC) in 1985 and the framework for the regulation of biotechnology submitted to the Council of Ministers in 1986 was produced mainly by the DG on the Environment working through BRIC. The Council of Ministers then assigned the lead role in developing further legislation to the Environment DG. In the European parliament, the Environment Committee thus became the principal committee charged with developing the legislation: the final legislative decision was passed to the Council of Environment Ministers. Furthermore, as national environmental agencies eventually became the effective management institutions, these arrangements did suggest an environment protection-centred rather than an industry-dominated approach (Barling, 2000).

8.  This directive was supplemented by two others, adopted in 1990 as well: 90/219/EEC on the contained use of genetically modified microorganisms and 90/679/EEC on the protection of workers exposed to biological risks (Lunel, 1995). According to the general EU procedures, these directives have to be translated into national regulation by all member states, whereas EU regulations are a form of material law directly applicable throughout the Union.

9.  Until 1998, the EC has issued only 14 positive decisions and 13 of them were approved only with a qualified majority following the internal dispute resolution procedure. The 14th case, a new variant of Bt maize, created further controversies because the committee had been unable to reach the required qualified majority. After consulting three different scientific committees, the EC decided positively, but their decision was subsequently criticised by the European Parliament. The European Parliament stated that the EC had ignored the opposition from the majority of the member states and even scientific evidence about the dangers involved in producing and consuming Bt maize. In reaction, several member states (Austria and Luxembourg) decided to ban Bt maize, while France, the country that had originally introduced the application, now required labelling of the final product (Rosso Grossman and Endres, 2000). Although these EU member states thereby formally violated communitarian regulation they were not punished, so a 'de facto' moratorium was in fact installed.

10. In addition, the EU had also, under the same directive, approved three different vaccines and one test kit to detect antibiotic residues in milk, all applying GM technology, bringing the total number of approvals up to 18 GM food products (or 16 because two approvals concerned further uses of the same product). See for further updates: http://europa.eu.int/comm/food/food/biotechnology/authorisation/list_author_gmo_en.pdf.

11. Two wildlife protection organisations in the UK (English Nature and the RSPB) also expressed concerns about the potential negative effects of GM crops on wildlife. Eventually, the government agreed in October 1998 to conduct a series of research trials (Farm Scale Evaluations) to test the impact of the GM crops on wildlife using the precautionary principle fully (Toke, 2002).

12. For example, the Sainsbury and Safeway supermarket chains in the UK successfully launched a tomato paste made from GM tomatoes in 1996. By the end of the decade, they had to withdraw the product due to failing sales (Barling, 2000).

13. Similar resistance also developed in other EU countries although often combined with country-specific concerns. The French were concerned about the presence of GMOs in food but also about the threat to the country's high quality regional products and the local French food traditions as well as to the independence of small farmers. In Austria the threat GM food production would pose to organic farming got included as an additional reason for opposing GM food production.

14. Monsanto required such labelling to be based on the actual presence of GMOs in a specific food product, which should be established objectively and verifiably through the use of scientific evidence.

15. For example, in the Netherlands public concerns were expressed via NGOs and public opinion polls. In reaction, the Dutch government organised a public debate on GMOs and food under the responsibility of an independent commission entitled 'Eten & Genen' (Eating & Genes). The objective was to involve the 'common' citizen and the 'average' consumer in the public debate on GMOs and food and not only the very vocal environmental activists. Forced by limits in time (one year) and money (around €5m), the commission had intensive discussions with a restricted group of 150 individuals considered representative for all Dutch citizens. In addition, (networks of) private associations and schools were invited to discuss the issue internally while the wider public was involved via the media (including a website) and public hearings. Finally, two representative surveys were realised to monitor the opinions of the Dutch public in general. This process showed that the majority of the Dutch public did not support the use of GMOs for food production. Interestingly the commission also found that proponents and opponents of GMOs did not change their position after extensive debates and information exchange, they only defended their original opinions with more elaborate arguments. This result un-

dermines the rather widespread view that the European public opposes GM food mainly because it is not sufficiently informed about the pros and cons of this modern technology.

16. People can also make use of different consumer guides to orient their shopping behaviour, such as the 'Self-defense guide for consumers' from the US Organic Consumer Association (Cummins and Lilliston, 2000), which is very critical of GM food and the 'Consumer's guide to GM food' from Alan McHughen (2000) which is basically defending GM food.

17. The original 90/220 directive demanded scientific information about the following elements (Mayer and Stirling, 2002):
    • the GMO – the recipient and donor organism, the vector and the GMO,
    • potential for gene flow,
    • conditions of release and the receiving environment when in use,
    • assessment of potential health effects including toxicity and allergenity,
    • interactions between the GMOs and the environment.
    The revised version 2001/18 also required:
    • assessment of indirect effects on biodiversity as a result of changes to agricultural practice,
    • consideration of indirect effects arising from changes in management practice,
    • provisions for post-release monitoring and traceability.
    In addition, authorisation is only given for a period of ten years and 'member states may take into consideration ethical aspects' (Princen, 2002: 220). The European Commission furthermore established threshold-labelling requirements for maize, soybeans, additives and flavourings in January 2000, in the Commission Regulation 49/2000 and the Commission Regulation 50/2000 (Rosso Grossman and Endres, 2000).

18. In practice, the member states remain central in many concrete decision-making procedures. It is the member state that makes a decision on field trials, following the EU Directive 90/220 (and since 17 October, 2002 the Directive 2001/18/EC) and informs the Commission, which thereupon informs the other member states. Also concerning the marketing of a GM food product, the application is filed at the relevant agency in the member state that also remains responsible for the procedures while following the EU directives, although other member states have the opportunity to raise objections prior to approval. If objections are raised by one or more member states, which has been general practice until now, a dispute resolution procedure follows (Rosso Grossman and Endres, 2000). This procedure may result in a lengthy process whereby important roles are given to the EU committees of scientific experts, but whereby little transparency is provided towards the public or even to the applying firm.

19. These are the regulation on GM food and feed (Regulation 1829/2003) and the regulation on the traceability and labelling of GMOs and on the traceability of food and feed products produced from GMOs (Regulation 1830/2003).

20. After discussions with the European Parliament, the European Commission amended Directive 2001/18/EC and inserted a new article (Article 26a) which stipulates that 'Member States may take appropriate measures to avoid the unintended presence of GMOs in other products' (European Commission Press Release, MEMO/04/16; 28 January 2004).

21. The most important routes of transmission are via seed, pollen, straw, volunteer seed left in the soil, sowing and harvesting machines, transport equipment and storage facilities.

22. In this regard, Austria requested to consider the whole country a GM-free zone to protect its organic farmers, but the EC did not accept this measure.

23. The media image of scientific research on GM food is generally simplified because it builds on the metaphor of the (bio)chemical engineer working in a laboratory with precision and control over the transfer of genetic traits to plants for the interest of mankind. Complex plant genetic traits may, however, have multiple genetic bases and insertion of new genes may have major ramifications for that plant's biological functioning (Scoones, 2001). In addition, if peer-reviewed scientific articles are considered sound science then both the proponents and the opponents to GM food have extensive scientific arguments to justify their position. See Clark and Lehman (2001) for references to different scientific articles substantiating this claim.

24. The high economic, political and scientific stakes involved complicate these decision-making processes even further (Scoones, 2001; Rowell, 2003).
25. One alternative solution could be to shift the role of science from a substantive role ('science knows and informs the politicians and the public') to a procedural role ('science contributes to public debate about potential outcomes, based on a two-way dialogue'). See for a concrete example on such a shift the public debate on GM food in the UK (AEBC, 2003).
26. The EU puts the precautionary principle in the centre of its human health and environmental policies. See, for example, the 'Communication from the Commission on the precautionary principle' (EC, 2000b). In this document, a distinction is made between reliance on the precautionary principle and the search for zero risk, which is rarely to be found in reality. The EC defines the precautionary principle as a useful tool for risk management, but it should not justify arbitrary decision-making. According to the precautionary principle, scientific research can clarify many potential effects of a new technology but when important areas of uncertainty or indeterminacy remain, regulatory agencies can decide not to take chances and ban this new technology. In the case of a new category of risks in global modernity, such as GM food, ignorance cannot be removed completely and immediately with the help of science, and therefore the regulation of risks should include multi-criteria analysis, scenario studies and participatory deliberative approval processes, as well as the potential inclusion of the precautionary principle (Scoones, 2001).
27. See Löfstedt et al. (2002) and Lehmann (2002) for an historical overview of the use of the concept.
28. As well as for its vagueness, the precautionary principle is also criticised because it would block progress in society as all innovations inevitably involve unknown risks and therefore the costs of applying the precautionary principle should be included in the decision-making process as well. Proponents of the precautionary principle feel that a cost–benefit analysis is never fully possible because there is too much uncertainty about eventual positive and negative outcomes, particularly in the longer term. This debate is also related to the choice between type 1 and type 2 errors as the guiding principles in decision-making. Type 1 error means that if a risk assessment is too cautious it will conclude that a technology is unsafe although it is safe in reality. Type 2 error means that if a risk assessment is not cautious enough it will conclude that a technology is safe although it really is unsafe. See Giampietro (2002), Lehmann (2002), Löfstedt et al. (2002), and Van der Belt (2003a, b), for further discussions on the use of the precautionary principle in the regulation of GMOs.
29. The labelling of GM food is in practice however less straightforward than initially thought because defining standards, specifying the certification process and determining the content of the label all involve complex choices by regulators and private companies. For example, the exact location and wording of the label has to be defined, such as the degree of certainty the label conveys (for example 'does contain', 'may contain' or 'does not contain'). Despite these comments, there is clear evidence for overwhelming public support within Europe for the labelling of GM food (Klintman, 2002; Shaw, 2003).
30. For example the introduction by Pioneer Hybrid International of a Brazil nut protein into a soybean. The Brazil nut protein could cause an allergic reaction in persons sensitive to nuts, who consume these soybeans and derived products. In reaction, Pioneer voluntarily withdrew the crop (Echols, 2001).
31. This complaint (DS 291) was followed by a similar complaint from Canada (DS 292) and the next day by Argentina (DS 293). Interestingly, while Egypt initially supported the US in its complaint, it withdrew its support just a few days later.
32. The EC does not accept the other argument used by the US to justify the introduction of GM food of promoting the interests of developing countries to reduce hunger, because 'it is the legitimate right of developing countries' governments to fix their own level of protection' (EC, 2003a).
33. The report, which could be appealed, is scheduled to be released to the public within six weeks after the panel's final ruling on 10 May, 2006, although some sources have suggested that this might not happen before September 2006.

34. The restrictive interpretation of the texts of the treaty and the agreements by the dispute settlement bodies in the WTO is not the only critique observers express on this procedure. In particular, the lack of transparency in the deliberations and the exclusion of non-state actors in the dispute settlement process also receive many comments. In the case of the US's complaint about the EU's regulation of GM food an exception has been made on this limited access as the dispute panel has accepted several so-called 'amicus curae' briefs from NGOs and concerned scientists (see: http://www.lancs.ac.uk/fss/ieppp/wtoamicus/).

35. See, for example, Anderson (2002: 11) 'article 3 (2) of the WTO Disputes Agreement states the Dispute Settlement Body is designed to provide security and predictability to multilateral trading, to preserve the rights and obligations of WTO members under the various agreements and to clarify the existing provisions in accordance with public international law'.

36. Nevertheless, during their 2003 meeting the Codex has approved three risk analysis standards for food derived from biotechnology. Interestingly these standards include references to the tracing of products and food labelling as a risk management tool. Although the exact definition of the terms seems not yet commonly agreed upon, it is considered a breakthrough vindicating at least partially the EU's insistence on labelling and traceability systems (BRIDGES BioRes, 11 July 2003).

37. The CBD only entered into force on 11 September, 2003 and its concrete role in practice is not yet clear, particularly whether the CBD or the WTO should take precedence in the regulation of GM food. This lack of clarity is further obscured by the fact that the EU has signed and ratified the Biosafety protocol contrary to the US, which has not even signed it.

38. A 'living modified organism' is defined as any living organism that possesses a novel combination of genetic material obtained through the use of modern biotechnology; and 'living organism' as any biological entity capable of transferring or replicating genetic material, including sterile organisms, viruses and viroids. A living modified organism may be considered a sub-category of GMOs in general because the term only covers those organisms that are living and have the capacity to regenerate.

39. In its reaction to the US complaint filed at the WTO, the EU explicitly refers to the CBD to claim international acceptance for its regulatory approach, in particular to justify a separate regulation for GM food because it might contain specific risks.

40. With regard to international rule making China's position remains flexible. For example in the WTO, China may work together with other developing countries in opposing more restrictive patenting provisions, but at other moments with food exporting countries like Australia to promote the liberalisation of the world markets for agricultural products (Newell, 2003).

41. For example, the WFP gave US$51 million as a loan to Zambia to allow the private sector to import maize from the USA.

42. A remarkable activity has been the commissioning of research by Greenpeace at the scientific institute Plant Research International of Wageningen University and Research: 'Crops of Uncertain Nature? Controversies and knowledge gaps concerning genetically modified crops' by Visser et al. (2000), Wageningen, PRI report 12.

43. Future regulations may, however, also be influenced by new emerging food safety crises comparable to the way in which the evolving BSE-crisis has had dramatic impacts on European discussions on GM-food in 1998/1999.

# 7. Turning blue into green?

> While the idea that wild harvest fisheries are approaching limits is not a new one, people have generally failed to see aquaculture as the next logical step. Part of the problem is that while terrestrial-based livestock production has taken hundreds of years to convert over from small-scale subsistence production to today's large-scale operations, aquaculture operations have been trying to make the switch from wild harvest to large-scale farmed production in a matter of decades. Aquaculturalists have also been trying to accomplish this task at a time when all large-scale livestock operations have come under increasing scrutiny related to issues such as antibiotics use, production of nonnative species, use of genetically modified organisms, animal rights, and waste disposal.
> (Harvey, 2003, LDP-AQS-18: 1)

> Towards the end of the 20th century the 'farming' of salmon developed into a big business, with various results, some good and some undesirable. Farmed salmon can be marketed cheaply, and the supply has become so plentiful that there seems to be a risk of repetition of the situation which existed in some places in medieval times, when (to take one well-worn example) apprentices in the north of England stipulated that their free meals should not include salmon more than three times a week.
> (Davidson, 1999: 685)

## INTRODUCTION

Consumer demand for fish, especially in the richer countries, is growing, but capture fisheries can no longer provide the necessary supplies for this demand because of the well-known problem of depleting stocks caused by overfishing and environmental degradation. Consequently, fish production through aquaculture (or fish farming) is growing very rapidly and is becoming the fastest growing food-producing sector worldwide. At the same time, aquaculture is accused of causing serious environmental problems and health risks, such as the destruction of mangroves and the intensive use of chemical substances, which pollutes water, soil and the final product. The growth of aquaculture gives rise to several challenging questions. Is fish farming the latest form of bio-industry, producing food in an industrialised manner at the expense of animal welfare, the environment and human health? Alternatively, can fish farming become an important provider of food for the world's growing population in a sustainable manner now that traditional capture fisheries are approaching their limits? These intensely debated questions will be reviewed in this chapter by analysing the recent evolutions in fish farming and the related changes in regulatory practices.

This chapter will start with an introduction on the particular theoretical concepts needed to analyse the current regulatory practices in aquaculture. The remainder of this chapter then consists of two parts, whereby the first, more descriptive, part comprises sections with overviews of the recent developments in global fish production and consumption, aquaculture in general, salmon raising and shrimp farming (particularly in Thailand). The second part of this chapter looks into recent attempts to respond to the particular challenges facing the governance of aquaculture, starting with political and scientific debates on governing fisheries in general, then two key discourses on aquaculture are identified that guide initiatives by governments and the private sector, and by civil society. This chapter concludes with a final section reconsidering the main arguments in the current debates on governing the environmental and health impact of aquaculture with particular reference to the discourses and practices of environmental NGOs.

## AQUACULTURE AND GOVERNANCE

Aquaculture is associated with many different environmental and food safety impacts and because of their ambiguous and complex character, these problems must be systematised before they can be acted upon constructively (Ward et al., 2004). Rapid technological and economic developments in aquaculture in combination with the growing demand for the products from fish farming, in particular for salmon and shrimp, lead to serious challenges for the governance of their (potential) environmental and food safety consequences. Because the fish produced by fish farms has become traded globally, the governance of aquaculture requires arrangements that fit into this context of global food governance. Thus aquaculture and the trade in its products form a clear example of globalisation of contemporary food production and consumption practices, for which governance can no longer be organised through conventional nation-state-based regulatory arrangements only. Developing adequate innovative governance mechanisms requires the participation of different state and non-state actors, thus governments, producers, traders, consumers and NGOs all play a role in the debates on governance of aquaculture and in the resulting practices.

Modern aquaculture constitutes a new step in human interference with nature, through the controlled production of fish and fish products, comparable to the transition from hunting and gathering to husbandry in agriculture. Traditional capture fisheries can be considered as essentially still based on a clear separation between the ecosystems allowing the growth of fish under 'natural' conditions on the one hand and the human activities catching part of the surplus of the fish stock on the other. However, when too much fish is caught or if the natural eco-system is destroyed by environmental pollution, serious problems emerge. This clear principle in the management of wild fish stocks where humanity is allowed to harvest only the surplus produced by natural ecosystems disappears with the introduction of modern aquaculture because this activity is based on active human interference with processes that were traditionally considered natural. The unclear boundary between nature and culture in aquaculture complicates referring to simple modern technological improvement to solve problems in fish farming as it also becomes increasingly difficult to fall back on the image of 'nature' or 'natural dynamics' to find possible solutions to these problems. Dealing with environmental and food safety concerns in the case of aquaculture, thus requires interventions that are better adapted to this much more complex context, conscious of its possible 'side-effects' (see Chapter 2). Innovative forms of risk governance are necessary, also because of the global character of aquaculture, whereby both the regions of production and the areas of consumption are spread all over the world.[1]

Establishing innovative governance arrangements to deal with the environmental consequences of fish production practices requires inventive and reflexive thinking about the concept of sustainable aquaculture and about possible ways to achieve this ideal in practice. Different social actors are trying to frame environmental policy guidelines for aquaculture based on their particular understanding of the existing environmental problems and the possible causes. These different social actors have developed various narratives on the problems within aquaculture, on the causes of these problems and on the ways in which to regulate them. These discourses do not only help to define the problem, but they also create a social and moral order and facilitate the establishment of regulatory and discursive networks. NGOs seem particularly involved in the process of conceptualising discourses on aquaculture and creating regulatory and discursive networks. Environmental NGOs repeatedly challenge existing governmental regulations and they are becoming an important driving force for the development and introduction of innovative governance arrangements. Understanding their different strategies and activities requires conceptualising their discourse as 'a specific ensemble of ideas, concepts, and categorisations that are produced, reproduced and transformed in a particular set of practices and through which meaning is given to physical and social realities' (Hajer, 1995: 44). Environmental NGOs attempt to create new public spaces, and to understand these attempts it is fundamental to put these social movements and their discourses in the context of socio-political, economic and environmental developments (Eyerman and Jamison, 1991). Environmental NGOs concerned about the negative effects of aquaculture are confronted with the dilemma of how to combine reducing the negative environmental impacts from an expanding fish farming sector without at the same time increasing the pressure from intensive capture fisheries on the endangered fish stocks at open sea. Essential for understanding the discourse of environmental NGOs on the future role of aquaculture is their argumentative struggle with other social actors, such as governments, fish farmers, consumers and so on. In this debate, NGOs try to influence the ways in which these other actors define the problem and, in some cases, they are able to establish common regulatory and discursive networks (Hajer, 1995; Howarth, 2000).

Thus aquacultural fish production constitutes a definite challenge for global food governance since this globalised way of food production and consumption is a source of new kinds of risks and engages many different social actors each with their own discourse about the way forward to create sustainable fish farming. These different social actors formulate different answers to some of the following fundamental questions about aquaculture. To what extent is it possible to introduce a form of governance in the space of flows in combination with the governance in the space of places? Can a form of global food governance be developed that does not lead to the creation of additional, green barriers to international trade, as aquaculture is considered an important source of export income for developing countries? How can the various economic, environmental, food safety, ethical and social concerns be combined in consistent global food governance arrangements on aquaculture?

## TRENDS IN GLOBAL FISHERIES

Fish makes up the main source of animal protein for millions of people and it currently provides employment for some 35 million people.[2] Production of fish is still growing but this is made possible only by fish farming because this forms the single sector where production is substantially increasing. Aquaculture is even growing more rapidly than all other ways of producing meat.[3] (See Table 7.1.)

The real prices of fresh and frozen fish and fish products have increased since the Second World War, in contrast to most other food products. Therefore, it is probably not the price but the taste or the growing health concerns among consumers in Western countries that have led to the shift in consumption from beef and pork to fish (and to a lesser extent to poultry as well) (Brown et al., 2003).

*Table 7.1   Annual growth in world animal protein production by source, 1990–2001*

| Source | 1990 (million tonnes) | 2001 (million tonnes) | Annual growth (%) |
|---|---|---|---|
| Beef | 53 | 57 | 1 |
| Pork | 70 | 92 | 3 |
| Mutton | 10 | 11 | 1 |
| Poultry | 41 | 69 | 4 |
| Eggs | 38 | 56 | 4 |
| Marine fish capture | 86 | 95 | 1 |
| Aquacultural output | 13 | 36 | 10 |

*Source*: Brown et al. (2003: 47).

Whereas in 1950 the global fish harvest was estimated to be around 21 million tonnes, this had risen to 100 million tonnes in 1990 and to 129 million tonnes in 2001 (see Table 7.2).

*Table 7.2   World fisheries production and utilisation (million tonnes)*

| | | 1996 | 1997 | 1998 | 1999 | 2000 | 2001 |
|---|---|---|---|---|---|---|---|
| Production | Total capture | 93.5 | 93.9 | 87.3 | 93.2 | 94.8 | 91.3 |
| | Total aquaculture | 26.7 | 28.6 | 30.5 | 33.4 | 35.6 | 37.5 |
| Total world fisheries | | 120.2 | 122.5 | 117.8 | 126.6 | 130.4 | 128.8 |
| Utilisation | Human consumption | 88.0 | 90.8 | 92.4 | 94.4 | 96.7 | 99.4 |
| | Non-food uses | 32.2 | 31.7 | 25.1 | 32.2 | 33.7 | 29.4 |

*Source*: FAO (2002) Table 1.

By that same year, capture fisheries accounted for 59 per cent and aquaculture for 41 per cent of the total fish harvest. However, these figures are generally not considered fully reliable as they are highly influenced by production figures from China (see Table 7.3) while several studies have suggested that Chinese statistics may overestimate the real production in the country (FAO, 2002). In any case, worldwide aquaculture production has increased at an average compounded rate of 9.2 per cent per year since 1970 and this sector now accounts for about 25 per cent of the total employment in fisheries (ibid.). Production from fish farming has doubled between 1989 and 1998 with an average annual increase of 15 per cent (ibid.).

Aquaculture production increased from 2.6 million tonnes in 1970 to 35.6 million tonnes in 2000 (Anderson et al., 2003a). An overview of the main producing countries is presented in Table 7.3.

*Table 7.3   Fish production through aquaculture (1998)*

| Country | Production (million tonnes) | Value (billion US$) |
|---|---|---|
| China | 20.8 | 21.7 |
| India | 2.0 | 2.2 |
| Japan | 0.8 | 3.1 |
| Indonesia | 0.7 | 2.1 |
| Bangladesh | 0.6 | 1.5 |
| Thailand | 0.6 | 1.8 |
| Vietnam | 0.5 | 1.3 |
| USA | 0.4 | 0.8 |
| Other | 4.5 | 12.5 |
| Total | 30.9 | 47.0 |

*Source*: FAO (2000).

Global fish trade amounted to US$55.2 billion in 2000, equal to about 33 per cent of the total fish production having witnessed an increase of some 52 per cent between 1990 and 2000 (Anderson, 2003a).[4] Also, in relative terms, global fish trade is gaining importance since a growing percentage of fish production is entering global trade and by 2001 over 38 per cent of the world's fishery production was traded internationally (FAO, 2004a). Developing countries provide some 50 per cent of the global fisheries exports through which they earned US$11 billion in 1993 (Stone, 2002).[5] Currently China is the leading fish exporting country in value terms, a position the country just recently took over from Thailand (FAO, 2004a). Japan is the main fish and fish products importing country (US$15.8 billion), whereas the EU is the largest market for fish products. Interestingly, despite the enormous variation in fish species the international fisheries trade is dominated by only a few fish products, especially shrimp (both cultured and wild), tuna, fish meal and fish oil.

Consumption of fish is growing especially in richer countries like Japan, the USA and Europe where per capita seafood consumption is already considerably higher than in most developing countries. Despite their lower consumption rate, fish nevertheless constitutes an essential source of animal protein for poor people living in developing countries. Fish supplies approximately 6 per cent of the world's protein requirements (16 per cent of total animal protein) and provides micronutrients, minerals and essential fatty acids to many people in low-income food deficit countries (Allison, 2001). The overall average per capita fish consumption at the global level increased from about nine kilograms per year in 1970 to 16 kilograms in 1997 (ranging between 7.8 kg/capita in least developed countries and 27.8 kg/capita in developed countries). The growing world population, the increased presence of fresh and frozen fish at affordable prices and the changes in consumer attitudes ('consuming fish is healthy and prevents overweight and coronary problems'), as well as more traditional cultural traits and geographical characteristics are important driving factors behind the growing consumption of fish (Trondsen et al., 2004).[6] As shown in Table 7.4, average annual fish consumption differs considerably between different regions in the world, while differences between individual countries are even larger: people in Mongolia consume virtually no fish at all, while people in Japan (66 kg) and in Iceland (91 kg) consume much more than the global average of 14 kg per capita.

*Table 7.4   Summary statistics of annual per capita fish consumption by region (in kg)*

| Region[a] | Mean | Standard deviation | Minimum | Maximum |
| --- | --- | --- | --- | --- |
| Africa | 10 | 10 | 0 | 45 |
| Asia | 18 | 19 | 0 | 66 |
| Middle East | 10 | 8 | 1 | 29 |
| West | 16 | 17 | 1 | 91 |
| World | 14 | 15 | 0 | 91 |

*Note*: [a] Countries are divided as follows in these four groups: West (Europe, N/S America, Australia and New Zealand), (East) Asia, Africa (sub-Sahara) and Middle East (West Asia and North Africa).

*Source*: York and Gossard (2004: 296)

The growing demand for fish, in combination with the increase in fish trade and coupled with the technological developments in fish handling, preservation and distribution, is contributing to the creation of new, often spatially extended, commodity chains linking the practices of fish production and of fish consumption.[7] These trends have led to continuously growing captures, putting certain fish stocks at risk because of over-fishing (Hutchings and Reynolds, 2004).[8] Currently at least 70 per cent of the world's important fish stocks are considered in urgent need of stricter management and control, while Myers and Worm (2003: 280) even estimate 'that large predatory fish biomass today is only about 10% of pre-industrial levels'. Besides over-fishing, other factors also contribute to a worsening environmental situation in many seas and oceans around the world. Ground trawling in the North Atlantic is destroying ecosystems at the bottom of the sea, while the use of dynamite and cyanide for fishing is poisoning large areas in the Indo-Pacific Ocean. In addition, chemicals, oil spills and other pollutants discharged by households, industries, the shipping trade and agriculture are contaminating certain parts of the seas and oceans, particularly the coastal zones of indus-trialised countries (Constanza et al., 1999).[9] Currently, consumers, particu-larly those living in Western countries, are more and more concerned about these environmental effects of capture fisheries and about the health risks involved in fish consumption (particularly the presence of heavy metals (mercury, copper, cadmium, molybdenum, chromium) and other chemical substances (dioxins, PCBs) which accumulate throughout the aquatic food chain). Despite these problems and concerns, the projected demand 'for food fish could be as high as 121 million tonnes by the year 2010. This is some 22 million tonnes more than the volumes that were available for con-sumption in 1999/2000' (Wijkstrom, 2003: 464). If fish captures remain at the current levels, which should be considered the most optimistic prognosis according to experts, fish farming or aquaculture has to provide the neces-sary additional supply by that time.

## AQUACULTURE

The FAO (2002) defined aquaculture as 'the farming of aquatic organisms including fish, molluscs, crustaceans and aquatic plants with some sort of intervention in the rearing process to enhance production'. According to this definition, aquaculture covers a broad spectrum of different fish-producing practices in various environmental and social settings. These practices in-clude land-based closed water-recycle systems, open water fish cages, poly-culture in rice paddies, ponds, small-scale aquaculture in drains of urban ar-eas, and so on.[10] More than 220 different species of finfish and shellfish are currently raised in different aquacultural production systems (Naylor et al., 2000; Tacon and Forster, 2003). Worldwide, the majority of the production from aquaculture comes from freshwater sources (58 per cent in 1999), fol-lowed by mariculture (aquaculture at sea) with 36 per cent and brackish wa-ters six per cent (IFPRI, 2003).[11] Fish production from aquaculture grew particularly fast during the 1980s (from 4.7 million tonnes in 1980 to 13.1 million tonnes in 1990), but this trend continued during the 1990s (to 35.6 million tonnes in 2000) (Anderson et al., 2003a) and will most likely be sus-tained in the near future (Eijk, 2001).

Traditionally aquaculture was low labour- and capital-intensive, but the introduction of modern techniques, which started in the early 1970s with salmon farming, has led over the years to certain labour- and capital-intensive practices resulting from the continued search for a reduction of costs, optimisation of size, improved management, vertical integration and technical advancements.[12] The largest production areas are located in China, where farmers are still producing by rather traditional means considerable quantities of low-valued species such as carp, often in aquaculture systems mixed with agricultural activities. Over the recent years, the most spectacular growth can however be found in the production of high-valued species destined for the international market, an activity taking place in different developing and developed countries. Today, over three-quarters of the salmon and two-thirds of the shrimp entering international trade are produced through aquaculture (Anderson et al., 2003b). Nevertheless, the initial expectation that simple modernisation of aquaculture through further intensification and technological development would result in a virtually unlimited source of fish has not materialised, as this growth was accompanied by different important negative environmental and socio-economic side effects.[13]

### The Principal Environmental Impacts from Aquaculture

Modern intensive aquaculture is repeatedly criticised for its environmental damage. The main problems are the impact of shrimp farming on mangrove forests and other coastal zones and the use of wild fish to feed farmed fish, which puts a high pressure on existing fisheries resources. In addition, critics also point at water pollution through the discharge of water from ponds and net pens and the introduction through aquaculture of exotic fish species threatening biodiversity (see Pillay, 1992; Matthews et al., 2002; Goldberg et al., 2001 for further details).[14] For instance, it is estimated that an average of between 2 to 5 kilograms of wild fish are necessary to raise just one kilogram of farmed species (Gardiner, 2002).[15] This so-called 'fish-trap' means that aquaculture ultimately runs into its own limits and therefore cannot be considered a sustainable solution for food supply under the circumstances of depleting fish stocks (Naylor et al., 2000). An alternative for the use of original fishmeal through adding proteins of plant and animal origin to smaller quantities of processed fish inputs remains at the moment still problematic because of the limited availability of the correct proteins and because of palatability problems (New and Wijkström, 2002). The continuous demand for wild fish to feed farmed fish creating a global market for fishmeal as well as the introduction of exotic species are examples of global environmental impacts from aquaculture, while other environmental threats have a local character.[16]

### The Main Food Safety Concerns in Aquaculture

The principal food safety risks involved in aquaculture are associated with the unintended and uncontrolled ingestion of antibiotics by the consumers of the final product and the indirect effects of growing antibiotic resistance in bacteria that are pathogenic to humans (Benbrook, 2002; FAO, 2002).[17] Antibiotics are applied in aquaculture to stimulate growth and to prevent diseases from spreading rapidly, which concerns in particular viral and bacterial diseases that have a high probability in aquaculture.[18] Generally, these antibiotics are administered through commercially available medicated feeds, but during outbreaks of disease farmers may also use other routes, which have not always been applied responsibly and may lead to a number of risky situations for consumer health.[19] Besides antibiotics, products from aquaculture may also contain risks for human consumption comparable to those from wild fish, such as their possible contamination with mercury and cadmium and other trace metals as well as with presence of organochlorines, salmonella and algal toxins (dioxins and PCBs) in the final product.[20] A particular consumer worry was caused by the discovery of BSE among cows, showing the complex and risky relationships between feeding and food production and processing practices, and these relationships might have an impact on fish farming as well. Currently, the invention and potential use of genetically modified fish receives particularly anxious reactions from consumers and environmentalists.[21]

Although accompanied by these different (potentially) serious environmental and health risks, aquaculture is becoming rapidly an important and globalised practice of food production. Conventional, nation-state-based regulatory approaches for dealing with these concerns seem insufficiently able to adequately respond to them as will be shown with the help of the following two concrete cases: salmon raising and shrimp farming.

## THE CASE OF SALMON

Wild salmon caught by numerous individual fishermen dominated the world market until the 1980s. The natural variations in salmon stocks made these fishermen dependent on biological dynamics whereby years of large harvests led to lower prices and years of low harvests resulted in higher prices.[22] Thus, variations in catches were offset, at least partially, by the variations in unit value and, overall, salmon remained an expensive food product. However, since 1980, when farmed salmon amounted to only 1 per cent of the world's salmon production, this situation changed rapidly. The practice of producing salmon through aquaculture expanded very fast, and by 1991 the output of farmed salmon already exceeded the entire wild stock harvest of salmon in the United States.[23] In 1992, farm-raised salmon accounted for 32 per cent of the world's production and by 2002 over 60 per cent. The growth in aquaculture output in Northern Europe and North and South America also meant an increase in the share of salmon in the overall global trade in fish, reaching 8 per cent in 2001 (FAO, 2004a).[24] Worldwide, the production of farmed salmon grew from 527,000 tonnes in 1995 to 989,000 tonnes in 1999 while international trade increased from virtually zero to about 1 million tonnes (2001) in less than two decades. The species traded today are mainly Atlantic salmon and, to a lesser extent, Pacific salmon, which accounted for 88 and 10 per cent of the production in 2001 respectively (see Tables 7.5 and 7.6).

*Table 7.5 World production of Atlantic salmon by country, 1992–2000 (1,000 tonnes)*

| Country | 1992 | | 2000 (estimate) | | % change |
|---------|------|------|------|------|------|
| | 1,000 tonnes | (%) | 1,000 tonnes | (%) | |
| Norway | 141 | 54.1 | 422 | 50.1 | 213.5 |
| United Kingdom | 36 | 13.8 | 122 | 13.8 | 238.9 |
| Chile | 24 | 9.2 | 152 | 17.2 | 533.3 |
| Canada | 17 | 6.5 | 68 | 7.7 | 300.0 |
| Faroe Islands | 17 | 6.5 | 41 | 4.7 | 141.0 |
| United States | 10 | 3.8 | 23 | 2.6 | 130.0 |
| Ireland | 10 | 3.8 | 20 | 2.3 | 100.0 |
| Australia | 3 | 1.1 | 11 | 1.2 | 266.7 |
| Iceland | 3 | 1.1 | 3 | 0.3 | 0.0 |
| Total | 261 | 100.0 | 882 | 100.0 | 237.9 |

*Source*: Phyne and Mansilla (2003: 113).

The bulk of salmon production is concentrated in Norway, Chile and Scotland, but the consumption of salmon is global whereby Japan continues to be the largest importer by far, followed by the EU and the US. Farm-raised salmon is mainly sold fresh or chilled, while wild-caught salmons are sold canned or smoked as well.

The production of salmon worldwide grew very fast with the spread of fish farming technologies but was not combined with a similar growth in consumer demand, so this quantitative growth led to lower prices and falling profits. 'On average, between 1990 and 2000, the price for salmon dropped by 60 per cent from US$10.00/kg to US$3.50/kg' (Anderson et al., 2003b: 63) turning salmon from an expensive product into a relatively mid-priced one in international seafood markets (FAO, 2002). This price squeeze contributed to increased intensity in the search for technical improvements aimed at reducing the costs of salmon farming, so for example direct production costs in Norway declined from US$5.52/kg in 1985 to US$1.97/kg in 1999 (Anderson, 2003b: 153).

*Table 7.6   World production of Pacific salmon by country, 1992–2000*

| Country | 1992 | | 2000 (estimate) | | % change |
|---|---|---|---|---|---|
| | 1,000 tonnes | (%) | 1,000 tonnes | (%) | |
| Japan | 24 | 38.7 | 10 | 9.0 | -58.3 |
| Chile | 23 | 37.1 | 84 | 75.7 | 265.2 |
| Canada | 12 | 19.4 | 10 | 9.0 | -16.7 |
| New Zealand | 3 | 4.8 | 7 | 6.3 | 133.3 |
| Total | 62 | 100.0 | 111 | 100.0 | 79.0 |

*Source*: Phyne and Mansilla (2003: 113).

Farmed salmon originate in hatcheries where eggs are hatched and finger-lings subsequently raised in land-based tanks nearby. Once fingerlings become smolts, they are put in smolt-rearing facilities in fresh-water cages. After a period of 12–18 months, the smolts are shipped (sometimes by helicopter) to seawater cages and bred for another period of 12–18 months. Salmon, a carnivorous fish, is fed a diet consisting primarily of fishmeal typically made from anchovies, herring, or the remnants of the fish processing industry.[25] Whereas salmon's pink-coloured flesh in the wild comes from eating krill and other small crustaceans, farm-raised salmons are fed colour additives (astaxanthin or canthaxanthin) routinely to get the same effect.[26] When full-grown, salmon are harvested and further processed according to the different standards of the principal consumer markets (Phyne and Mansilla, 2003).

Many observers consider salmon farming as the cause of several environmental problems. First, the practice may pose serious risks to wild salmon stocks because every year hundreds of thousands of farmed salmons escape from net pens creating an (uncertain) impact on their wild relatives. These escapes are caused by storms, predator attacks (primarily seals), human error and vandalism (Goode and Whoriskey, 2003). In Norway, the escaped farmed salmon seem increasingly to displace wild Atlantic salmon and currently makes up for about 30 per cent of all salmon in Norwegian rivers, thereby outnumbering the resident salmon in many inland streams (Aerni, 2001: 18).[27] Other environmental problems concern the waste produced in the offshore pens where large quantities of salmon are concentrated, the spread of epidemics, particularly of sea lice and infectious salmon anaemia in combination with the regular use of pesticides and antibiotics to combat the outbreaks of infections and diseases (Brown et al., 2003; Goode and Whoriskey, 2003).[28] The presence of dioxins and PCBs in farmed salmon may reach critical levels for human consumption as they regularly accumulate in fish that are placed higher in the food chain. Hites et al. (2004) even claim that farmed salmon has significantly higher contaminant burdens than wild salmon, which potentially may even offset the beneficial effects of fish consumption.[29]

The environmental and food safety problems related to salmon farming mentioned above have resulted in several attempts to find solutions for them. Most suggestions contained proposals for policy measures focussing on spatial planning and environmental protection. For example: the Canadian province of British Columbia imposed a ban on building new fish farms in 1995 and only lifted this ban in 2002 when additional environmental regulations for fish escapes and waste disposal were reviewed and implemented. Other measures were taken within the salmon supply chain itself, for example the multinational Nutreco, which claimed it had already stopped adding antibiotics in Norwegian salmon raising in 1995, had doubled the nets protecting the pens to prevent salmon from escaping and decided to replace dangerous colour additives in the salmon feed by less dangerous ones. Until now, specific international regulations for farming salmon are still lacking, although incidentally certain general guidelines developed for existing fisheries agreements have been applied. In this regard the North Atlantic Salmon Conservation Organisation (NASCO), established in 1982, constitutes an exception because this organisation has initiated the formulation of specific guidelines for salmon farming.[30]

Despite the introduction of several environmental and food safety protection measures, salmon farming still provokes a lot of criticism from NGOs. One example of this is the opinion expressed by the British Soil Association, a leading NGO in organic agriculture, which considers intensive salmon farming the 'modern equivalent of battery chicken production'.[31] Against such criticism, proponents of farmed salmon defend their practice by claiming that the salmon-farming industry provides 'food safety and quality and economic benefits to the regions in which the farms operate' (Infante, 2003: 11). Furthermore, many arguments used by the critics are being challenged by those involved in the industry in different ways. For example, salmon producers in Norway contend that the environmental impact of salmon excrements on the Norwegian fjords is exaggerated. They also claim that the problem of fishmeal is incorrectly stated because the species processed in it, such as anchovies, are not as interesting for human consumption as salmon are and therefore the salmon farmers are producing added value through aquaculture.[32] These comments from different social actors show that salmon farming remains a controversial issue.

# THE CASE OF SHRIMP[33]

Shrimp currently account for 20 per cent of the total value of internationally traded fishery products and constitute the most important fish commodity in value terms, while nearly 80 per cent of the world's total shrimp production enters the global market (Goss et al., 2000: 522). In the year 2000, world shrimp production reached 4.2 million tonnes, of which some 1.2 million tonnes (or 28 per cent) originated from aquaculture, compared to about 5 per cent in the early 1980s (EJF, 2003b: 6). Worldwide shrimp farming represents a total value of US$6.9 billion at the farm gate and US$50–60 billion at the point of retail. Most shrimp produced are black tiger shrimp (Penaeus monodon), a warm, brackish water species. Its production requires substantial quantities of water, so the farms are mostly located alongside rivers, estuaries and coastal areas in tropical regions. Shrimp production is a very volatile activity because shrimp are a very vulnerable organism and their production is more subject to negative impacts from weather and disease than most other forms of aquaculture.[34] Intensive shrimp farming began during the 1980s in Taiwan and then spread to about 50 different countries in Southeast Asia and Latin America whereby the leading producers in the year 2000 were China, India, Thailand and Indonesia (see Table 7.7).[35]

Thailand has become the largest exporter by far, exporting some 90 per cent of its total production (EJF, 2003a: 6).[36] The US remains the most important shrimp importer with steadily increasing volumes and values in the period between 2000 and 2002 and the country is nowadays importing 88 per cent of its total consumption.[37] Japan's shrimp imports and consumption remained more or less unchanged since 1998 (FAO, 2004a).

Many developing countries are promoting shrimp farming to earn export income thereby giving the industry a very dynamic character. Shrimp production and consumption is transforming more and more into a global material flow of food, largely unregulated, and virtually unhindered by trade barriers or distorting subsidies. Shrimp production and consumption has changed from 'a relatively specific capture-to-market basis to global production to a world consumption system' (Skladany and Harris, 1995: 182). Consequently, 'the ability of the nation-state to manage these contradictions effectively is simply overwhelmed by the international scope of the industry's fluid structure' (ibid: 185).

*Table 7.7  Annual shrimp production per major producing country (1,000 tonnes)*

| Country | 1991 | 1995 | 2000 |
|---|---|---|---|
| China | 564.1 | 665.6 | 1,241.9 |
| India | 300.5 | 406.1 | 405.7 |
| Thailand | 289.9 | 389.3 | 398.5 |
| Indonesia | 296.8 | 334.7 | 398.4 |
| USA | 148.5 | 140.5 | 153.0 |
| Vietnam | 81.3 | 138.1 | 151.1 |
| Canada | 44.7 | 63.1 | 130.6 |
| Malaysia | 104.7 | 99.6 | 111.9 |
| Mexico | 70.6 | 85.9 | 95.1 |
| Greenland | 73.1 | 81.9 | 81.5 |
| Philippines | 84.9 | 127.5 | 79.4 |
| Norway | 49.0 | 39.3 | 66.2 |
| Bangladesh | 19.6 | 34.0 | 58.2 |
| Brazil | 42.3 | 43.0 | 56.6 |
| Ecuador | 118.8 | 112.1 | 51.4 |
| Rep. of Korea | 55.8 | 42.5 | 37.2 |
| Others | 532.7 | 594.5 | 651.7 |
| Total | 2,877.3 | 3,397.4 | 4,168.4 |

*Source*: FAO (2002).

Like most other aquacultural practices, shrimp farming is also repeatedly criticised for being the cause of some serious environmental problems. The environmental impacts of shrimp aquaculture can be distinguished in those impacts resulting from the pond construction and those related to the operation of these ponds. Shrimp pond construction is particularly sensitive because it often involves clearing mangrove forests that protect coastlines and serve as nurseries for local aquatic species.[38] The construction of ponds may also contribute to the degradation of other important habitats, such as salt marshes and freshwater wetlands, and can be the cause of serious conflicts over rights to land and over access to natural resources when originally multiple-user, open-access natural resources are converted into single-user, single-owned production resources. In some cases, particularly in India and Bangladesh, conversion led to the forced displacement of tens of thousands of poor people causing increased poverty, landlessness and reduced food security (Maybin and Bundell, 1996; EJF, 2003a). In addition, shrimp pond operation itself may affect the environment as well in different ways (Kaosa-ard and Wijukprasert, 2000). An important environmental problem is chemical pollution, because in order to prevent and to treat diseases, often large quantities of chemicals are applied.[39] Moreover, shrimp feed contains high quantities of fishmeal, comparable to salmon feed, thereby further increasing the already high pressure on oceanic fish stocks (Brown et al., 2003). The way this feed is handed out may furthermore result in eutrophication of the surface water and pollution of the pond bottom.[40] Finally, the discharge of the water and pond bottom sludge may also affect the surrounding ecosystems through salinisation of soils, and surface water pollution from the spread of used pesticides, bleaches and antibiotics.[41] The actual environmental impact of this discharge of water and pond sludge depends on specific factors such as the way in which the production is organised, the technical capacities of the shrimp farm operators, the degree of pollution of the sludge and the presence (and actual use) of water treatment facilities.[42]

Thailand provides an interesting case for better understanding the specific dynamics involved in shrimp aquaculture production and trade. Thailand has the optimal climate for shrimp farming and in addition possesses a well-developed infrastructure and a coastline of about 2,600 kilometres. Therefore, it may not be considered a surprise that the country has become the largest shrimp-exporting nation in the world, acquiring about 18 per cent of the global market for frozen shrimp during the last decade. Thai shrimp trade has become global as Table 7.8 makes clear.

Unlike many other countries, the overall majority of shrimp farms in Thailand has always been small-sized family-based enterprises, providing self-employment to many thousands of producers. About 80 per cent of the shrimp farms are smaller than 1.5 ha, while 18 per cent range between 1.5 and 2.5 ha and only about 2 per cent of the farms are larger than ten hectares (Rosenberry, 1997).[43] Aquaculture has increased the overall wealth of the coastal communities but has caused inequities between different social categories in these communities as well (Lebel et al., 2002). Currently, however, there seems to be a trend emerging towards the creation of more vertical integration and consolidation and the shrimp industry in Thailand is evolving towards a more fully integrated industry (ibid.).[44] Vital to this process of change were the influx of capital and experiences from Taiwan, as well as the introduction and growth of low salinity culture techniques because they increased the opportunities for land-based systems that were introduced by the 1,000 hatcheries (small-scale, backyard operations in Thailand) and spread by the Charoen Popkhand (CP) Group (Goss et al., 2000).[45]

*Table 7.8   Thai frozen shrimp exports in 2001*

| Country | Quantity (tonnes) | Amount (million €) |
|---|---|---|
| United States | 66,990 | 576.4 |
| Japan | 24,837 | 247.0 |
| Canada | 5,758 | 47.6 |
| Singapore | 6,610 | 45.1 |
| Taiwan | 6,308 | 37.3 |
| Australia | 3,638 | 29.8 |
| Republic of Korea | 4,121 | 26.9 |
| China | 3,412 | 22.3 |
| Hong Kong | 2,610 | 20.6 |
| United Kingdom | 1,587 | 12.7 |
| France | 1,553 | 10.5 |
| Germany | 1,242 | 10.0 |
| Italy | 876 | 3.4 |
| New Zealand | 337 | 2.4 |
| Others | 5,031 | 35.6 |
| Total | 134,910 | 1,127.6 |

*Source:* www.foodmarketexchange.com.

Commercialisation of shrimp on the global market has become highly complex involving traders, processors and retailers from all over the world, as well as supermarkets, hypermarkets and convenience stores.[46] Central wholesale markets in Thailand – Mahachai near Bangkok and Nakhon-Si-Tammarat – play a crucial role in serving the processing industries all over the world. In this global market, shrimp prices may vary considerably, depending understandably on shifts in demand, but mainly on the market destinations and the quantity and quality of shrimp being on offer. Thailand's dependency on global markets makes the country rather vulnerable to changes (in the economic situation as well as in the import regulations in force) in Japan, the US and the EU.[47] Despite this vulnerability, the opportunities for high and quick returns on investments continue to make the shrimp aquaculture industry a very attractive activity for many farmers and investors.

Thailand's booming shrimp industry is, however, also responsible for some serious environmental problems. Shrimp farming has contributed to the rapid reduction of the mangrove area along the coast which halved between 1961 (364,000 ha) and 1993 (168,700 ha) (Huitric et al., 2002: 445; see also Barbier et al., 2002).[48] As exact data are lacking, it remains problematic to establish with certainty the specific contribution from shrimp farming to the destruction of the mangrove cover in the coastal zones of

Thailand. The fact is that this damage could have been caused by several other trends as well, including urbanisation, growth in and movement of human settlements, tourism and related infrastructure construction, and salt-water farming.[49] Nevertheless this demand for land from shrimp farms exists because even today, while the total area in use for shrimp farming is no longer expanding, farmers regularly have to find new locations because the lifespan of an intensive shrimp farm on a particular location is estimated to be between five and ten years. Once a shrimp farm is closed down, the polluted soils left behind in combination with the other environmental damages make conversion to new productive activities quite difficult. The second environmental problem is the annual dumping of, mostly untreated, 100–500 metric tonnes of sediment per ha, containing faecal matter, uneaten food and inorganic fertiliser, which threatens the production capacity of agricultural areas and the functioning of natural ecosystems.[50] The introduction of semi-closed inland shrimp farming systems will not solve these environmental problems because the presence of saline water, despite its low percentage of salt, continues to form a serious threat to the soils and the freshwater systems of inland Thailand. In these rural areas shrimp farming is competing with rice production for the limitedly available fresh water supply, because shrimp farming is very responsive to water pollution, while the productivity of rice is very sensitive to the presence of salt in irrigation water.

In response to these environmental concerns, the Thai Department of Fisheries had begun to tighten its regulatory policies already in 1991 (Kaosa-ard and Wijukprasert 2000).[51] In the end, these measures proved to be ineffective, principally because of non-compliance by a majority of the shrimp farmers. Furthermore, the authority to monitor and enforce compliance at the farm level remained scattered among several government agencies, each operating under a different legal mandate and using different regulatory approaches (Flaherty et al., 1999).[52] Repeatedly attempts to create stricter environmental legislation or to enforce the actual implementation of existing rules or decrees effectively were obstructed by protests from the industry (Lebel et al., 2002). For example, enforcing the ban on inland shrimp farming except for brackish and estuarine areas, imposed by the Thai government in July 1998, is still quite problematic. Currently different models of self-regulation by the shrimp sector in Thailand are suggested and supported by state authorities.[53] One suggestion for future regulation is the distribution among shrimp farmers of tradable permits for the production of shrimp based on the carrying capacity of the water resource system. Whether such a regulatory arrangement will be successful critically depends on the presence and functioning of a strict monitoring system to secure adherence to the prescriptions included in such permits. An alternative would be to adapt shrimp farming practices gradually to the local environmental and institutional settings in a participatory way, which would result in large variations among the appropriate trajectories and require flexible government support. 'In some favourable locations this will imply de-intensifying production, whereas in many other places, the solution will be finding alternatives to growing and eating shrimp' (Lebel et al., 2002: 321; see also Huitric et al., 2002). A third alternative approach to the regulation of shrimp farming is to continue the search for technological innovations which allow more fully controlled production practices, as for example can be witnessed among shrimp farmers who adopt closed water management systems which tend to have higher survival rates than open system farms (Duraiappah et al., 2000).[54]

Therefore, intensive shrimp farming has spread rapidly over the globe since the 1970s primarily forced by a high consumer demand in developed markets, thereby transforming the shrimp production chain into a global material and informational flow. This transition is a clear example of a trend that becomes increasingly visible in many more fish production practices through aquaculture. The flow character of aquaculture is exemplified by the global character of shrimp production and consumption, and by the successive relocations of shrimp farming throughout different parts of the world (particularly Asia and Latin America) following a boom and bust sequential trend in exploitation. In particular the sometimes disastrous local environmental effects force shrimp farmers repeatedly to move to new locations. Thus, the environmental problems in the locations of shrimp production are linked, at least indirectly, to Western consumption practices through the international trade relations sometimes controlled by transnational corporations or national governments and sometimes functioning more or less without central controlling agencies. Furthermore, repeatedly the practices of relocation, intensification and further technological innovation seem to move ahead of the development of adequate nation-state-based environmental governance measures.

## GOVERNING FISH

The rapid growth in the production and global trade of fish and fish products produced from aquaculture has had several negative impacts on the environment and on human health while currently several attempts are being made to reduce these consequences. However, governing aquaculture is confronted with the extraordinary problem of its overlap with capture fisheries, because the distinction between both practices can be clearly established at the place of production but not at the place of consumption. Unless

it is clearly labelled, consumers are unable to distinguish the shrimp produced through aquaculture from that produced through capture fisheries.
Aquaculture has become part of the dynamic of global flows of food and is
confronted regularly with numerous competing interests in various particular local, natural and socio-economic contexts. At the same time different
governmental institutions are involved at various levels of governance.
Within this global flow of food, fish produced from aquaculture becomes
mixed together with fish from capture fisheries. Therefore, contemporary
initiatives to govern aquaculture are influenced immediately by the different
recent efforts to establish adequate practices for the governance of capture
fisheries. Before discussing the different initiatives taken in the realm of
governing aquaculture, I will therefore first review the transformations that
have taken place in the governance of capture fisheries.

Historically, the world's fish stocks have constituted an open access resource without strong legal institutions to control and manage the fisheries
involved in using this resource. In particular, the very limited possibilities
for monitoring and regulating capture fisheries on the high seas excluded effective control of the species and quantities of the fish captured by the large
numbers of small and larger fishermen (Dommen, 1999; Jackson et al.,
2001). The obvious ecological and economic effects of overfishing, however, intensified an already existing pressure to install regulations that are
more effective. Capture fisheries should be regulated to protect the remaining fish stocks. This pressure resulted (in Western countries) in the introduction of command-and-control-based management systems, whereby
fishermen were ordered to remain in the harbour until the designated fish
stock attained the optimum level defined by scientists, after which the quotas based on the sustainable yield for this stock would be distributed among
the fishermen (Roughgarden, 1998).[55] Despite the use of these modern science-based and state-controlled fisheries management practices, fish stocks
continue to decline, so two alternative solutions are suggested to stop this
process: on the one hand, the imposition of a strictly controlled, integrated,
ecosystems-based management system; and on the other hand, the individualisation and privatisation of fishing rights.[56] Integrated ecosystem management 'requires an explicit consideration of multiple objectives not only
for the production of commodity species but also for the protection of species that provide ecosystem services' (Hanna, 1999: 282). An integrated
management system has to provide for the environmental needs of the ecosystems as well as for the economic, social and cultural needs of the fisher-
ies-dependent communities. This model of governing capture fisheries requires the development and the use of tight control measures to monitor the
behaviour of both fishermen and ecosystems. Several authors consider privatisation of fishing resources a better response to the problem of over fish-

ing because private ownership rights will provide more security for fishermen, and allow them to plan and invest and improve the possibilities for consistent production and marketing management (Anderson, 2003b). Bailly and Willmann (2001: 96) claim that 'legislation on integrated coastal area management (is required), defining rights and limitations to various types of activities, recognising basic individual rights would help private and public promoters of aquaculture development to plan their activity in more secure and informed circumstances'. However, in practice, such a privatisation approach would be confronted with the complicated challenge of identifying the owners of fishing resources with certitude and determining the precise definition of their fishing rights (do they concern an area, a fish stock, a catchment or an ecosystem?).[57]

Meanwhile, more and more international, sometimes even global, governance arrangements are replacing the traditional national institutions destined to manage the country's fishing resources. These international arrangements did not solve all problems as even 'the "enclosure of the oceans", codified in the 1982, Convention on the Law of the Sea, with the establishment of exclusive economic zones (EEZ) out to 200 miles from the baseline, did not eliminate the high-seas fisheries management challenge' (Schram Stokke, 2000: 206). Currently, there are over 100 multilateral, regional and bilateral treaties to supplement the general trends in international ocean law as codified in the Law of the Sea, as well as a huge variety of national laws and practices. There are 14 UN agencies and 19 International Governmental Organisations with management of the oceans as part of their responsibilities (Allison, 2001; see also Appendix 2, for a summary of the most important instruments used for international fisheries governance). While the number of international legal arrangements and regulatory institutions involved in capture fisheries' management is growing, more and more 'soft' governance instruments are being introduced at the same time. In this regard, the Code of Conduct plays an important role for Responsible Fisheries, elaborated by the FAO in 1994/5 based on the relevant existing rules of international law. This Code of Conduct has offered policy guidance for many national and international legal regimes and is supposed to be applied on a voluntary basis. In addition, the Kyoto declaration (1995) provides orientation for national governments as it identified a critical link between food security and the need to ensure the future sustainability of fisheries because fishing contributes substantially to the income, wealth and access to food of many people (Hanna, 1999). Other kinds of innovative governance arrangements are the NGO-based certification schemes, such as MSC (see Chapter 7), introduced in different Western countries aiming at producing more fish in a sustainable manner and providing credible information about production practices to consumers. In addition to these innovative governance arrangements, official and private technical regulations such as food safety measures, labelling requirements and quality standards are increasingly replacing tariffs and different quantitative restrictions in food trade. According to the FAO (2004b), an integrated agro-food supply chain approach is required, recognising that the responsibility for the provision of food that is safe, healthy and nutritious is shared along the entire food chain – by all involved in the production, processing, trade and consumption of food. All actors involved in fish production, processing and trade have to be aware that fish can be contaminated from the moment of capture until it is eaten, due to the growth of pathogenic micro-organisms that form part of the normal flora of the fish or to cross- or re-contamination or faulty handling and processing. This common understanding in the chain has contributed to the adoption of private and official means to secure traceability, thus allowing the identification of fish products back to their origin throughout the chain, and the implementation of HACCP-based monitoring and control systems in all stages of the fish chain.[58]

These innovative governance arrangements, developed and introduced during the last decades to govern capture fisheries, have also had an immediate impact on aquaculture, because fish farming overlaps largely with capture fisheries and because their production contributes to the operation of globalised fish supply networks. Existing nation-state-based legal and private-initiated governance arrangements are creating a tangled web. Although difficulties remain in the area of enforcing these governance arrangements, other forces in society are pressuring global and regional markets to implement practices that are more sustainable, environmentally as well as socially (Van Houtte, 2001). Conventional, official command-and-control measures remain essential to outlaw specific unsustainable practices but they seem unable to promote continued improvements in the production and processing practices or to accommodate supranational dynamics. Therefore, besides the conventional nation-state-based regulations of fish production and trade, other forms of governance are being introduced, such as international trade and environmental protection agreements, labelling and certification schemes, best management practices and codes of conduct. The recently initiated governance arrangements have been developed under particular circumstances at different levels and often applied in some form of public–private arrangement.[59]

## DEFINING SUSTAINABLE AQUACULTURE

Governing capture fisheries is nowadays taken up by several state and non-state agencies, but governing the many, often unexpected, environmental, social and food safety impacts of aquaculture requires specific measures. Distinctive discourses about aquaculture exist and they are determining the challenges faced by the existing governance arrangements and constituting the driving forces towards the introduction of more innovative ones. Establishing sustainable aquaculture as part of global food supply chains requires not only a straightforward definition of the necessary production practices and the required identity preservation assurances throughout the chain, but also in-depth understanding of the social processes involved.[60] Therefore, in governing global flows of food it cannot be the end product alone that is used to define what counts as quality and as relevant environmental, social and health concerns, because the meaning of 'quality' and the content of these concerns is assembled within the structuration process of the material flow itself. 'Quality differences influence the geography of supply and demand, which not only affects the prospects for the existing industry, but also gives rise to industries in new places and to new trade patterns' (Mansfield, 2003b: 13). Therefore, the discourses not only help to define the problems linked to aquaculture and their governance, but also to create a social and moral order determining the possible solutions to these problems and furthermore to establish discursive and regulatory networks involving different social actors aimed at implementing these solutions.

In the different discourses or story lines about sustainable aquaculture, two ideal types of 'sustainable aquaculture' seem to emerge. On the one hand, there are observers who regard sustainable aquaculture as only possible when it is based on the traditional practice of land-based fish farming, and on the other hand there are others who look for modern, technologically improved and closed fish-farming systems as a possible future base for sustainable aquaculture. The first model, based on traditional practices, builds on 'extensive and balanced "polyculture": an integrated fish farming practice adopted over 4000 years ago in China and over 1500 years ago in Hawaii. Polyculture techniques mix fed species, herbivorous species and extractive species in a more balanced ecosystem-approach aquaculture' (Frankic and Hershner, 2003: 518).[61] This model has proven its sustainability over centuries in everyday practices and if herbivorous species are given a central place and aquacultural activities are further integrated with agriculture this model becomes even more sustainable (Weber, 2003). The main advantages of integrated practices that mimic ecosystem processes and functions and are more in tune with their natural environments are seen to be their capacity to make a more sustainable, and potentially more efficient, use of marine resources and the fact that in some areas such integrated marine/coastal and terrestrial food production systems are already in place. In contrast to intensive monocultures, in particular of salmon or shrimp, such ecocyclic practices should appropriate smaller ecological footprints. 'Such ecologically adapted practices need to be linked to institutional designs protecting them from policies and economic driving forces that undermine the capacity of ecosystems to sustain seafood production' (Folke et al., 1998: S70).

The other ideal type of sustainable aquaculture aims at further technological development towards the realisation of closed intensive aquaculture systems (Rosenberry, 2003). Technological innovations oriented towards improved food conversion through selective breeding could contribute to the reduction of the current environmental burden.[62] Another potentially interesting innovation is the introduction of re-circulation systems aiming at optimal use of water through re-use while filtering off superfluous feed and other organic waste or separating them through sedimentation.[63] Where a traditional pond system requires 2,000–20,000 litres of water to produce one kilogram of fish, such a new re-circulation system would require only 10–30 litres (Eijk, 2001).

Currently neither of the two ideal types presented above are common practice in most of the commercially oriented aquaculture systems. On the contrary, it even seems that the usage of traditional, integrated fish farming systems is diminishing because the expanded market possibilities put pressure on many producers to introduce the more intensive specialised monoculture fish production systems. Combining several aquatic species, each with their own specific ecological niche and market demand, into a closely controlled aquaculture operation might lower the environmental impact and optimise the use of nutrients. This alternative would, however, at the same time increase the overall complexity of the system, in particular because of the differences in production scales and the various management requirements required to raise the different species and because the marketing opportunities for the different products may be very different as well (STT, 2003).[64] On the other hand, the costs involved in setting up the alternative solution of intensive systems for the re-circulation of water are in most cases still prohibitively high while the technique itself also still encounters problems. Thus, for the near future this option might only be interesting for fish farmers in the richer countries raising the more expensive species such as turbot (Anderson, 2003b).[65]

## OFFICIAL AND PRIVATELY INITIATED FORMS OF GOVERNANCE IN AQUACULTURE

Both ideal types have been guiding different regulatory approaches introduced to deal with the environmental and food safety impacts of modern aquaculture. Although often these regulations were developed within the wider framework of governing fisheries, in general there are several specific options introduced for aquaculture. It seems aquaculture can be controlled more easily as its production activities are generally more localised and more controllable than for capture fisheries.

As mentioned before, the FAO Code of Conduct for Responsible Fisheries is a central point of reference for defining sustainable fisheries and for developing adequate governance practices for aquaculture as well.[66] Article 9 of this Code of Conduct deals with aquaculture in particular and identifies different potential environmental risks resulting from this activity. The approach to determine sustainable options in this Code is based primarily on the ideal type of modern, technology-intensive aquaculture, although some restrictions are added to prevent naïve technological optimism. The introduction of non-indigenous species threatening biodiversity and balance in the present ecosystem is considered especially risky. The need for a safe disposal of waste and a safe, effective and minimal use of therapeutants, hormones, drugs, antibiotics and other chemical inputs, is acknowledged as well. In addition, according to the same Code of Conduct, overall food safety should be ensured and additional techniques to protect endangered species developed. In order to achieve these objectives, national governments should create legal frameworks and co-operate with other governments to install international governmental agreements to govern the transboundary effects of aquacultural practices. By doing so the Code of Conduct, although initially (and formally still) having only a voluntary status, provides policy direction for (inter)national legal regimes and becomes binding at global, regional and national levels.[67] Nevertheless, the concrete implementation of this FAO Code of Conduct for Responsible Fisheries in practice remains rather limited.[68] (See Tacon and Forster (2003) for a general overview of the different governmental regulations; Read and Fernandes (2003) for a summary of EU regulations.) Some governments nevertheless do regulate the stock intensity, control the introduction of exotic organisms and have well-elaborated regulations for the location of fish farms, sometimes requiring environmental impact assessments and waste treatment facilities to be installed (Pillay, 1992).[69]

For regulations to be effective they often demand clearly defined legal ownership rights to land and water resources but sometimes these legal rights are absent, especially in developing countries (Bailly and Willmann, 2001; Anderson, 2003b). Nowadays, aquaculture has spread over many different developing countries and there generally standardised technology packages are applied and standardised products produced. At the same time, very few developing countries have adopted policies specifically developed for aquaculture, because of their limited institutional capacities and because of the problems they face in fitting in local regulatory requirements with the trend towards governance in the space of flows which is becoming critical in global modernity.[70] Consequently, despite the presence of only a limited number of national governmental regulations for aquaculture, growing concerns about the environmental and social problems resulting from these practices have forced different (groups of) producers, trading companies, governments and consumers to reflect on ways to establish environmentally improved practices (Pillay, 1992). These efforts have resulted in the introduction and implementation of different voluntary governance arrangements.[71] Most initiatives are building on the controlled application of the results from continuing technological progress.

In general, these private forms of governance can be differentiated between codes of practice on the one hand and certification (and labelling) schemes on the other. The introduction of different private codes of practice clearly shows that the governance of aquaculture is departing from conventional nation-state-based regulations. A first example of such private codes is the Code of Practice for Responsible Aquaculture developed by the Global Aquaculture Alliance (GAA). The GAA is an industry-based aquaculture organisation bringing together mainly fish processors and traders from different parts of the world, and the association plays a central role in promoting voluntary regulations for fish producers. In part, their code of practice is based on the FAO Code for Responsible Fisheries, introduced above.[72] After reviewing shrimp farming practices, the GAA concluded there are no particular risks involved in this activity as such because shrimp farming is profitable, environmentally sound and socially beneficial, provided the farms are operated while applying good management and business practices.[73] Nevertheless, the GAA points out, as with any young and rapidly growing industry mistakes can be made, but if these errors have negative environmental and social impacts they 'have invariably resulted from poor planning or poor management by shrimp farmers and government agencies rather than as a routine consequence of shrimp farming' (GAA, 2001).[74] Most criticism on shrimp farming from environmental NGOs is therefore not justified. Consumers should be informed better about the real shrimp production practices and then they will express their appreciation for the interactions between shrimp farming and the environment. GAA promotes their Code of Practice as the exemplary framework for environmentally sound and socially responsible shrimp farming.[75] The standards and guidelines included in this Code cover on-site inspections and controls but are not intended to establish some form of certification and labelling of seafood at the retail level aiming at direct involvement by consumers (Roheim, 2003).[76] On the contrary, so far the project mainly gives the impression of a strategic attempt to offset NGO and consumer comments on aquaculture.

The Federation of European Aquaculture Producers (FEAP), the umbrella organisation of national aquaculture producer associations in Europe, has developed its own Code of Conduct as well. The FEAP's Code is also based mainly on the existing (FAO) guidelines for aquaculture and not intended to be prescriptive. The Code is developed 'to motivate and assist the development of the principles of best practices' (FEAP, undated: 2). To achieve this objective, the Code of Conduct offers rather general guidelines inviting fish farmers to respect existing laws and to avoid environmental problems as much as possible through effective self-governance. Finally, the Code suggests fish farmers should develop more specific guidelines for each species that is used in aquaculture. According to FEAP, future technological developments probably will provide the necessary contribution towards applying more sustainable and more efficient fish farming practices.[77] A notable exception to the rather vague wording applied in the FEAP Code is their explicit refusal to accept genetically modified fish. The introduction and use of different codes of conduct, such as those initiated by GAA and FEAP, might contribute to improving practices in aquaculture, but their effectiveness is seriously hampered by the vague formulation of their guidelines as well as by their lack of transparency to consumers and other interested third parties.

Another interesting example of privately initiated governance arrangements for aquaculture are the 'Holmenkollen guidelines for sustainable development', formulated in 1994 and adopted in 1998, elaborated by a group of scientists, authorities, producers and NGOs.[78] These guidelines are based on the conviction that modern aquaculture carries the potential of becoming an important provider of food if the principles of sustainable development are applied, notably using the precautionary principle and the principle of human equity.[79] Technological innovations are expected to be able to reduce or prevent environmental problems such as the threat to biodiversity from the introduction of exotic species or GM fish and the risks involved in the use of chemo-therapeutants or hormones. To be successful in developing sustainable aquaculture, priority should be given to 'integrated, polyculture-based fish farming for omnivorous or herbivorous species' and to the development of other sources for animal feed than fish proteins and fish lipids. National governments should ensure the development of such modern integrated systems of fish farming through the introduction of laws and other regulations, while producers should provide the consumers with information about the concrete practices applied in fish production. An important driving force behind the eventual implementation of such guidelines in practice is that the initiators think that ultimately all parties concerned have a common interest in clean water, a healthy environment, abundant wild stocks and economic prosperity. An open dialogue between all parties supported by sound and objective scientific knowledge should therefore result in governance standards that can be enforced officially by national governments (Goode and Whoriskey, 2003).

Widely used environmental and food safety certification schemes (see Chapter 8 for further information), such as ISO 14001 and HACCP, are also applied within aquaculture. ISO 14001 combines compliance to environmental regulations and response to stakeholder concerns, because firms are required to develop an environmental policy and to set targets and objectives for the performance of their environmental management (Frankic and Hershner, 2003). ISO 14001 can also contribute to establishing a 'green chain' certification from production to disposal, but a weak point remains here that the scheme does not prescribe specific environmental performance levels. HACCP constitutes a management system developed to prevent food risks, whereby process control is emphasised and monitoring concentrates on those points in the production process which are critical to the safety of the final product. Immediate and specific action has to be taken if these critical limits are violated. HACCP is especially relevant and used at the processing stages of seafood.[80] Nevertheless, the primary producer's role remains essential as well because he should 'provide the processor with information concerning chemical contaminants and aquaculture drugs so that the processor can comply with this in his plan' (Miget, 2004: 4).

Organic labelling of products from aquaculture might also contribute to the more sustainable use of natural resources (Bailly and Willmann, 2001), but so far no internationally accepted guidelines exist for organic aquaculture production. Organic fish did exist in the EU, but since August 2000, wild-caught fish cannot officially be labelled organic due to changed EU regulations, which prohibit any food product caught in the wild from being called organic.[81] Also during the recent public process of defining general criteria for organics in the US, the participants concluded that wild fish may be regarded as 'natural' but should not be considered organic because the production process is not fully controlled by humans (Mansfield, 2003a, 2004; Vos, 2000). However, 'farmed fish have the potential to be classified with other types of farms, based on the possibility of control of both the setting in and process by which the organism is grown' (Mansfield, 2004: 227). According to Bailly and Willmann (2001: 99) a number of specifications laid down for organic food production in agriculture would be readily applicable to aquaculture, but 'the adaptation of current international standards for organic food to fish and shellfish from aquaculture is likely to require significant changes in production methods and processes, especially for semi-intensive and intensive aquaculture systems'. Organic labelling of products from aquaculture might offer, nevertheless, interesting marketing opportunities for small producers if they were to receive institutional and organisational support. However, the organic food movement in the US denies the possibility of applying the same criteria on both terrestrial and aquatic animals (fish) and therefore, according to their opinion, farmed fish can never be considered organio (Mansfield, 2003a, 2004).

The absence of well-implemented national governmental regulations for aquaculture constitutes a driving force towards the introduction of private initiatives of governance. Developing and implementing global institutional arrangements generally applicable in the various fish production and distribution networks seems rather complicated because of the large dissimilarities between countries and the fish farming techniques applied. Still, 'in spite of several existing standards in use, the European fish industry sector considers that new standards should be developed on an international level, established by official standard bodies or agreements with industry as voluntary guide models and controlled by third independent party' (Pérez-Villarreal and Aboitiz, 2003: 55). In actual practice, not many of these initiatives have been implemented effectively, nor do they seem to respond adequately to the various problems facing the governance of fish farming in the context of global modernity. In particular, the obvious reticence within many of these initiatives to create more transparency towards consumers is problematic while the lack of precision in defining (the conditions for) safe and sustainable fish farming is also challenging.

## CIVIL SOCIETY INITIATIVES TO GOVERN AQUACULTURE

The (potential) negative social, environmental and food safety impacts of aquaculture combined with the absence of adequate governance arrangements have drawn the attention of different NGOs. In attempting to address the complex problems surrounding aquaculture these NGOs face the dilemma of having to choose between either a complete rejection of modern aquaculture because of its negative consequences and a cautious support for initiatives aimed at improving existing practices. Improving aquaculture might contribute to ensure the income of workers and small (fish) farmers and guarantee the supply of fish for a growing consumer demand in a sustainable manner. Supporting this process would mean that NGOs basically have to solve the problem of combining governance in the space of flows with governance in the space of places, by determining how global fish trade should be organised while managing the local environmental impact and the food safety risks at the same time. Many NGOs are struggling with this complex challenge and therefore it may not come as a surprise that they identify different, sometimes even opposing, solutions.

In particular, the disastrous social effects of shrimp farming in many developing countries have drawn the attention of international NGOs, such as the Environmental Justice Foundation, Greenpeace and Christian Aid (Maybin and Bundell, 1996; Greenpeace, 1997; Barnhizer, 2001).[82] In their discourse, the negative environmental consequences of shrimp farming tend to merge completely with its devastating social impact upon the local populations, whose livelihoods are destroyed. They claim, for example, that 'domestic and foreign investors with few or no ties to local communities exploit the (coastal) areas and undermine the base of natural productivity on which the traditional residents depend. This industrial shrimp aquaculture (produces) a high value cash crop to feed rich consumers in United States, Europe and Japan' (EJF, 2003b: 26). Furthermore, these NGOs argue that industrial shrimp farming requires large quantities of fish to feed the shrimp. These facilities also cause the destruction of mangroves or other coastal wetlands, which are in use as agricultural lands, thereby forcing the displacement of thousands of people and endangering their food security. Other environmental problems such as the pollution of surface water with pesticides and antibiotics may create acute human health risks, especially when this pollution is worsening the quality of their drinking water.[83] Reducing these negative consequences of shrimp farming in developing countries requires, according to these NGOs, a fundamental reorientation towards organic and diversified systems of aquaculture adapted to the local context, a reduction in the use of fish products as feed inputs and a willingness among consumers to pay a much higher price for their shrimp in the shop. Achieving this solution should start with the recognition that local communities have the right to actively participate in all transition processes towards less intensive and more sustainable shrimp farming.

Further intensifying the existing technologies in aquaculture is not considered a solution for the problems mentioned, because this would only focus on solving the shrimp industry's internal problems and not the problems caused by this industry for the local populations. Western consumers should therefore boycott shrimp that are produced through asocial and environmentally destructive practices. Several NGOs consider such a boycott an essential support for a transition towards small-scale and extensive shrimp farming under the control of local people – including traditional rotational systems – in combination with the improved protection of wild shrimp and fish stocks using sustainable fishing methods.[84] International donors and Western governments should apply sustainability criteria in the allocation of funds for development aid when supporting shrimp farming in developing countries. This demand is formulated, for example, in the Choluteca declaration (Accion Ecologica, 1996b) as 'a global moratorium on any further expansion of shrimp aquaculture in coastal areas until the criteria for sustainable shrimp aquaculture are put into practice'.[85] Shrimp importing firms in Western countries should also engage themselves actively in organising sustainable trade (Roberts and Robins, 2000).

Other environmental NGOs, such as the International Union for the Conservation of Nature – Marine and Coastal Programme (IUCN–MCP), advocate the creation of marine reserves. Such reserves would promote, influence and catalyse the sustainable use and equitable sharing of marine biodiversity resources as well as protect the existing ecosystems (Tsamenyi and McIlgorm, 1999).[86] These environmental NGOs concentrate on organising governance in the space of place by defining sustainable shrimp farming as essentially based on the ideal type of traditional and integrated practices under the control of local populations. Consumers should pressurise governments and private firms to promote these sustainable practices while they reduce their own shrimp consumption at the same time (Brownstein et al., 2003). Problematic in this approach supported by many developmental and environmental NGOs is their failure to recognise the global character of shrimp production and trade. Mostly, the alternative governance arrangements they propose are based on a locally developed definition of sustainable shrimp farming demanding nation-state intervention to ensure its implementation. Such arrangements have serious difficulties in incorporating the globalised and fluid character of shrimp supply networks. It seems problematic for many NGOs to identify innovative governance arrangements in the space of flows, fitting in a globalised food supply chain. Such governance instruments are nevertheless necessary in the actual context of the globalised shrimp production and consumption. In this situation, the possibilities for large shifts in the location of the production areas are growing fast while the already seriously limited capacity of national governments to effectively control local production practices seems to decline only further.

Whereas environmental and developmental NGOs have more or less comparable opinions about the way to solve the problems of shrimp farming in developing countries, they have more diverging views with regard to salmon raising. Environmental NGOs like WWF (especially their Norwegian branch), Friends of the Earth Scotland, Coastal Alliance for Aquacultural Reform (CAAR) and the David Suzuki Foundation, all seem to agree on the presence of devastating environmental risks that result from intensive salmon farming. The main environmental risks they identify are water pollution through the discharge of organic waste, which creates eutrophication and the spread of antibiotics, chemicals and metals (particularly copper). Furthermore, marine biodiversity is considered to be threatened by the use of fishmeal, the spread of sea lice, the escape of farmed salmon and the killing of salmon predators. CAAR adds several human health risks to this overview because intensive farming further proliferates diseases that already occur naturally, involves dangerous levels of PCBs and dioxins, adds colouring additives to produce pink salmon and uses antibiotics.[87] The David Suzuki Foundation points at the dangers from salmon farming for the livelihoods of local fishermen catching wild salmon because the market price for salmon is falling due to the growing production of farmed salmon.[88] In contrast to the broad consensus regarding the environmental problems of salmon fish farming, these NGOs do not agree on possible so- lutions to deal with these problems. WWF does not make a particular choice about the future of salmon farming and only underlines the need for addi- tional research to achieve sustainable practices (WWF, 2003). Friends of the Earth Scotland plead for organic salmon farming, more diversification and land-based containment.[89] The David Suzuki Foundation does not even see any realistic possibility for a more sustainable salmon aquaculture and con- siders safeguarding the traditional, local wild salmon fishing as the only sustainable alternative. Most NGOs, however, do agree on the need for ac- tive engagement by national governments to control salmon farming and to enforce sustainable production. Friends of the Earth Scotland, for example, asks for a national governmental policy to reduce stocking densities, to re- locate or remove farms and to label farmed fish to allow consumers a choice. WWF proposes the development of 'a code of conduct for responsi- ble aquaculture', which should in the longer term be supplemented with an environmental certification scheme for farmed fish products. The CAAR suggests a social and environmental regulation of salmon farming by na- tional governments, and until then consumers should refuse to eat farmed salmon, which therefore would have to be labelled in the shops. Finally, ac- cording to the David Suzuki Foundation, national governments should en- force environmental protection and no longer promote salmon farming.

Interestingly, apart from the code of conduct suggested by WWF, no NGO is demanding global governance arrangements but calls upon con- sumers to put pressure on their national governments to take the necessary measures, looking for ways to re-establish conventional nation-state-based governance arrangements in the space of place. For a long time, NGOs' en- gagement with aquaculture seemed to have remained concentrated on pro- duction practices and it is only very recently that some organisations are taking consumers seriously.

An interesting and innovative attempt to bring in consumers in the global food governance debates is 'consumer guides'. Different guides are avail- able and they essentially aim at reducing the environmental impact of fish farming (and fisheries in general) by active consumer engagement. For ex- ample, the Audubon Society explains in its guide: 'consumer demand has driven some fish populations to their lowest levels ever. But you can be part of the solution. You can choose seafoods from healthy, thriving fisheries'.[90]

The Seafood Choices Alliance claims that: 'government regulation of the fishing industry has failed to protect the resource. (But) over time, we believe that the choice made in the open market place will influence the seafood industry and government regulators in favour of better conservation of ocean resources'.[91] These guides can be considered a form of sub politics (see Chapter 3) introduced to promote more sustainable fish production in general (not limited to aquaculture). Wallet guides developed by NGOs are rather simple tools intended to help consumers and restaurant chefs to choose between different fish species based on their relative environmental impact. Although the specific form varies, these guides all differentiate between the fish species common at the local markets that can be bought without problems and those that should not be bought for environmental reasons. The guides themselves often lack details about the criteria used to rank the different species, but sometimes these details can be found through web-based systems providing regularly updated background information. The Audubon Society seafood wallet card, for example, provides an overview of the 30 most popular species and puts them in a ranking order according to their environmental impact.[92] On their website, it becomes clear that the Audubon Society uses several criteria to rank the different species on their card: the abundance of the species (threatened/endangered or not), the fishing methods and the management arrangements. The Monterey Bay Aquarium has produced the 'West Coast seafood guide', which is updated at least twice a year, using the motto: 'You have the power. Your consumer choices make a difference'.[93] The pocket seafood selector from Environmental Defense distinguishes two categories: 'best fish' (21 species) versus 'worst fish' (18 species), both presented in alphabetical order.[94] Other examples of consumer guides are those developed by the NGOs Conscious Choice and Seafood Choices Alliance in the US, the North Sea Foundation (Stichting Noordzee) in the Netherlands and the Marine Conservation Society (MCS) and the Blue Ocean Institute in the UK.

Although these guides are prepared for use at specific regional consumer markets and for a limited period, reference to specific local production circumstances even with regard to farmed fish remains exceptional. Fish is categorised according to general (categories of) species and not to where and how they were actually captured or raised. Fish produced through aquaculture is in these consumer guides listed among other fish species captured in the wild without further explanation. Shrimp are, for example, categorised in the red and no further differentiation is made between farmed shrimp and wild-captured/trapped. The consumer guide recently introduced by the North Sea Foundation in the Netherlands does not make a difference between farmed or caught species either. Nevertheless, this guide forms an exception because in the case of salmon a distinction is made between

MSC-labelled Alaskan salmon which is considered green, Norwegian-farmed salmon which is orange-red and Scottish salmon which is red, while Chilean-farmed salmon is considered to be even further in the red: 'do not buy for the moment, choose an alternative'.[95]

Despite this absence of specific differentiation between farmed and wild-caught fish, in general mussels and clams are ranked among the most environmentally friendly species because they filter feed plankton from the water, do not require wild fish for nourishment and their production does not cause habitat disruption. On the other hand, salmon and shrimp are considered rather problematic in most guides and consumers are recommended not to buy them.[96] Even in the exceptional cases where the criteria for judging the environmental impact of aquaculture are mentioned explicitly, they remain rather general. See, for example, the Monterey Bay Aquarium, Seafood Watch, West Coast Seafood Guide claiming that most farmed salmon 'are raised in net pens, like cattle in a feed lot, use captured fish for feed and pollute the environment through discharging waste and chemicals and putting human health at risk through the spread of PCBs and dioxins'.[97] The same guide considers shrimp farming as the (potential) cause of damage in the coastal zones of developing countries and of social problems resulting from the conflicts between different groups of land users and the declining employment opportunities in these areas.[98] Incidentally, some NGOs suggest alternatives for particular farmed fish products, for example the Monterey Bay Aquarium advises consumers to substitute farmed salmon by arctic char, rainbow trout or wild salmon. They also suggest replacing imported farmed shrimp with wild shrimp or US-farmed shrimp raised under environmentally friendly circumstances. In general, NGOs point at models of raising fish inland, using closed recirculation systems to filter waste water, as the best way forward to improve the environmental performance of aquaculture. According to these organisations, farmed fish can only be considered a supplement and not a replacement for wild seafood because aquatic technology can never provide the variety found at sea and cannot become sustainable because fish farming remains dependent on the sea for its inputs. Limiting fish farming to raising filter feeders (mussels and so on) and plant-eating fish (Tilapia) is considered by many NGOs as the only sustainable option.

Certification of environmentally friendly fishing practices constitutes a more complex innovative tool as it includes governance in the space of flows as well as in the space of place. One example of such a voluntary eco-label for fisheries is the Marine Stewardship Council (MSC) label. Initiated by the World Wildlife Fund (WWF) and Unilever, the MSC label is designed to contribute to the establishment of a global system of sustainable fisheries that offers powerful economic incentives for well-managed sustainable fisheries and stops the catastrophic decline in the world's fish stocks by harnessing consumer power (Constance and Bonanno, 2000). The MSC label conveys to the consumer otherwise unobservable information concerning the fish product's environmental impact. This way, the label allows consumers to buy seafood products that are captured in a sustainable manner thereby creating market signals and incentives to resource managers to offer more sustainable fish products. Market research has shown that consumers are prepared to choose sustainably produced fish products provided the price difference with conventional products is not too large (Roheim and Donath, 2003).[99] So far, the MSC label has not been applied to fish farming but only to certain capture fisheries. (See Chapter 8 for further details on the MSC label.)

The focus on consumers as a driving force for enhancement of sustainable fisheries makes consumer guides and environmental labelling of fish an interesting innovation by including governance in the space of flows. However, the categorisation using only fish species without further details about the production practices applied makes the governance tool rather blunt. Such consumer guides may raise consumer awareness, but without well-performing governance in the production areas in the space of place by national governments in combination with global trade arrangements, they will most likely remain inadequate. Without satisfactory global governance arrangements, the continued growth in fish consumption may even result in endangering aquatic species that are not yet endangered.

## CONCLUSIONS

The global character of the linkages between the production, trade and consumption of fish and fish products, in combination with the large variety in species as well as in the production practices used, makes governance of aquaculture rather complicated. These complications are becoming even more difficult through the overlap of aquaculture with wild-capture fisheries. The considerable environmental problems caused by aquaculture mostly have a localised character, but this actual location is constantly moving due to natural limitations to fish farming and marketing opportunities. Food safety risks nowadays have a global character almost by definition, as fish trade has become a global affair. Dealing with these problems in aquaculture is even further complicated because of the existence of opposing views on the future of fish farming. On the one hand, optimism is expressed about the potential of technological innovations towards better controlled (semi-) closed systems (de-localised production practices) while others, on the other hand, expect sustainability to come only from traditional integrated fish-farming systems mimicking ecosystems (localised production practices).

Until now, introducing governance arrangements in the space of flows has not been attempted very often in the case of aquaculture or for that matter in the case of fish production and consumption in general. Regulation has been left to the different parties operating on the global fish market. 'Trade has become a driving force in the global fishing enterprise, influencing the species of fish targeted and farmed, the intensity of fishing pressure, and, in many cases, the incentives for fishing either sustainably or destructively' (Kura et al., 2004: ix). The only exception concerns the global product-based regulations dealing with the presence of antibiotics and other potentially harmful substances in fish that is organised worldwide although no global agreement exists yet.

The focus has mostly been on introducing governance arrangements in the space of place: reducing the environmental impact of fish farming either by preventing it or by strictly controlling it at the local level. Many, very different, social actors have been involved in the search towards determining sustainable local practices in aquaculture. The result of this involvement is a plethora of governance arrangements based on the space of places alone, demanding national governments to intervene in the interest of the environment and the local population. However, national government arrangements will probably not be able to respond effectively to this call for controlling aquaculture as this supply chain of fish production and consumption has acquired the character of a global flow. Aquaculture activities are moving around the world and linked into global food supply networks. Direct control of fish farming through government-based regulations would therefore require worldwide arrangements as well as the willingness and capability from all national governments to implement such arrangements in the same manner. The complexities of fish farming, including the variations in technologies used and the different definitions of sustainability, as well as the overlap with wild-capture fisheries make it rather unlikely that such global government-based arrangements will become reality. An additional and fundamental problem in this respect is constituted by the consequences of the nation-state-based regulation of localised environmental impacts for the globalised trade, which fall outside the control of the same government. Producer guidelines and codes of practice, such as those suggested by FAO, GAA and FEAP, might provide incentives to producers to improve their environmental performance and thereby supplement governmental regulation. However, these guidelines remain restricted to governing local practices in aquaculture and are disconnected from global trade practices. This way such codes may constitute an interesting step forward towards creating governance arrangements in the space of flows but they still need to be supplemented with other forms of governance.

Interesting alternatives to the conventional government-based arrangements are consumer guides introduced by NGOs and certification schemes developed by private firms, as they constitute a form of governance in the space of flows. Both innovative governance tools are oriented towards active consumer involvement with the intention of pressurising governmental institutions, fishermen and farmers and traders/retailers indirectly to produce fish in a more sustainable manner. Necessarily, consumer guides are bound to place and time because they offer information to consumers for specific regional or national markets and have to be adapted regularly over time to reflect the changes in the environmental conditions of different fisheries and fish farming activities. These consumer guides also provide rather general information, focussing on fish species and offer very little concrete information about production practices, except for incidental references to 'farmed' fish. Consequently, consumer guides still seem to aim primarily at national governments thereby also contributing to establish governance in the space of places. Certification schemes, on the other hand, are linked to specific production practices and local producers, and as certified products they can be marketed globally so this aspect can be considered a governance arrangement in the space of flows. Linking certified fish consumption practices at the global level with environmentally improved production practices at the local level might constitute an interesting driver towards the spread of more environmentally healthy forms of fish farming.[100]

## NOTES

1.  A particular problem is that particular risks involved in aquaculture sometimes coincide with those occurring in capture fisheries and vice versa, particularly at the level of trade and consumption because in these practices fish is rarely separated based on the production process involved.
2.  Nearly 95 per cent of the people depending for their livelihood on fisheries live in developing countries (Aerni, 2001: 5).
3.  The variations in growth rates can probably in part also be explained by the differences between various animals with regard to their efficiency in converting grains into proteins. For cattle in feedlots, it takes roughly seven kilograms of grain to produce a one-kilogram gain in live weight. For pork, the figure is close to four kilograms per kilogram of weight gain, for poultry it is just over two, while herbivorous species of farmed fish, such as carp, tilapia and catfish, need less than two kilograms.
4.  Different new preservation techniques have made this possible. Besides the traditionally practiced techniques of drying, salting and smoking, in the early nineteenth century canning was added and cooling in the second half of the nineteenth century, followed in the beginning of the twentieth century by freezing (Anderson, 2003a).
5.  'Net export revenues from fish exports earned by developing countries reached US$17.7 billion in 2001' (FAO, 2004a: 1). This is nearly twice the earnings from the second major

crop, which is coffee. For low-income food deficit countries alone, net revenues earned from exporting fish were estimated at $7.5 billion.

6.  See Pillay (1992). Nevertheless, consumer research has shown that 'although seafood is very widely acknowledged as the healthy option compared to other proteins, there are varying levels of understanding and knowledge about detailed health properties' (Gross, 2003: 411). In addition, Western consumers prefer carnivore fish to herbivore (York and Gossard, 2004) while their rising income encourages 'away-from-home food expenditures and provides the discretionary income needed for purchases of higher valued prepared food products' (Harvey, 2003: 2). At the same time in Asian countries 'it appears that economic development spurs Asians to eat considerably more fish compared to other cultural regions' (York and Gossard, 2004: 300).

7.  For example, 'some roe herring harvested in Alaska is exported to China where the roe is extracted, processed and exported to Japan. The carcass is retained and utilised in China' (Anderson and Martínez-Garmendia, 2003: 45). The processing of fish into surimi (an intermediate product of fish protein concentrate developed in Japan) provides another example of the industrialisation of fish. Despite this trend towards increasing industrialisation (rationalisation and vertical integration) of the capture fisheries' industry, artisanal fishing and intermediary markets still exist in both developed and developing countries.

8.  'The gross tonnage in the world's fishing fleet grew by 91 per cent between 1970 and 1992' (Hanna, 1999: 277), and the availability of subsidies for vessel construction and operation is seen as the main cause for this growth. The difficult situation of many fish stocks is further aggravated through the large by-catch in commercial fisheries and the poor post-harvest facilities in many developing countries. An estimated total of 27 million ton of fish is discarded annually from commercial fisheries, representing an average of 20 per cent of the total catch (Garcia and Willmann, 1999).

9.  The environmental impact of fish processing has not been the object of intensive research with the exception that different studies have underlined that the waste produced by fish processing plants is characterised by 'their high organic load (protein and fat); thus their dumping to aquatic receptors involves large oxygen consumption' (River et al., 1998: 218).

10. Aquaculture may range from small-scale owner-operated fishponds to large-scale corporate fish farms (Pillay, 1992).

11. The main species of fresh water fish (and their most important producing countries) are: carp (8.7 million tonnes produced in China), tilapia (0.7 million tonnes produced in different parts of the world), eel (0.13 million tonnes produced in Japan), and trout (0.13 million tonnes produced in Norway, Chile, and Scotland); and for salt water fish (products): shrimp (4.3 million tonnes mainly produced in Thailand, China, and Vietnam), salmon (1.0 million tonnes produced in Norway, UK, and Chile), sea-perch and sea-bream (0.12 million tonnes produced in Italy, Greece, Spain and France), and turbot (0.04 million tonnes produced in Spain and France) (Luiten, undated).

12. Growing opposition to coastal fish farms led to the recent innovation in aquaculture of 'open ocean aquaculture', which is fish farming in the exclusive economic zone at sea (3–200 miles off the coast), also allowing culturing species such as halibut and cod. This way some of the risks of current aquacultural systems are reduced or avoided, such as the risk of eutrophication, because the intensity will be lower. On the other hand, open ocean aquaculture is privatising part of the ocean on behalf of corporate fish farms and may lead to growing risks of fish escapes, transference of disease to wild fish, discharge of sewage and unsustainable use of marine resources (Belton et al., 2004).

13. Interestingly, 'aquaculture, which was once considered an environmentally sound practice because of its traditional polyculture and integrated systems of farming based on optimum utilisation of farm resources, including farm wastes, is now counted among potential polluters of the aquatic environment and the cause of degradation of wetland areas' (Pillay, 1992: vii). However, as 'much of the present-day opposition to development is caused by lack of correct information' (Pillay, 2001: 7), the author suggests that most of the problems resulting from this opposition can be solved by providing this correct information to the public.

14. See for example, 'the critics portray fish farming as an alarming environmental and health hazard, not a potential source of food for the world's rich and poor alike. But they glide quickly over the fact that modern aquaculture is at an early stage of development. ... New technologies, new breeds and newly domesticated species of fish offer great hope for the future' (*Economist*, 9 August, 2003: 19), and Harvey (2003: 1): 'while terrestrial-based livestock production has taken hundreds of years to convert over from small-scale subsistence production to today's large-scale operations, aquaculture operations have been trying to make the switch from wild harvest to large-scale farmed production in a matter of decades.'

15. The continuous rising average trophic level of fish raised in aquaculture for Western consumer markets is a worrying trend because the production of these species requires more wild fish for feeding (Goldberg et al., 2001).

16. Many observers ascertain a correlation between the local environmental impacts of aquaculture and the intensity and scale of production, in particular when large numbers are concentrated in protected areas with insufficient water exchange (Pillay, 1992; Folke et al., 1998; Tacon and Forster, 2003). However, fish farmers also have to maintain a minimum water quality level to keep their activity productive and prevent massive damage. The exact minimum standards for water quality, particularly with respect to temperature and salinity, depend on the species cultivated. Further requirements are optimum levels for dissolved oxygen, pH, carbon dioxide, ammonia, nitrites, nitrates, hydrogen sulphide, pesticides and turbidity (Pillay, 1992).

17. In line with growing interest in animal welfare in general, the welfare of fish is also drawing increasing attention, although this is related to the specific species concerned. Several aspects may be of concern in aquaculture, depending on the species involved and the particular techniques used: the density of the fish in the pond, the feeding, transporting and fish killing practices as well as the ways in which   different diseases are treated (Eijk, 2001).

18. Pillay (1992: 68) reports concentrations of 430 grams of antibiotics per tonne of fish produced. He also observes that 'because of its broad spectrum of activity, chloramphenicol is favoured in mollusc, shrimp and prawn hatcheries'. In Norway, the overall amount of antibiotics used in salmon aquaculture declined from 48,000 kg in 1987 to 680 kg in 1998, while salmon production grew dramatically. This decline in volume of antibiotics may however partly be nullified by the use of more potent antibiotics (Weber, 2003).

19. Since 1994, the EU completely forbids the presence of antibiotics such as chloramphenicol and nitrofurans in fish, but in practice the detection limit with the accepted testing instruments was 5 ppb (part per billion) so exporting countries considered this limit as the 'de facto' standard. However with the introduction of new testing technologies the detection limit was reduced to 0.05 ppb and when the EU applied these tests, the forbidden presence of chloramphenicol was detected in shrimp coming from China and nitrofurans in shrimp from Thailand. After these findings, the EU decided to test all shrimp imports coming from Thailand, Vietnam and Myanmar. The Vietnamese vice-minister of fisheries called this EU policy of 'zero-tolerance' for antibiotic residues in shrimp unrealistic, and an unjustified technical barrier to trade that was intended to obstruct food exports from Asian countries. He claimed that nowadays antibiotics are generally present in the majority of water streams all over the world due to past use, thus a zero-tolerance threshold would be untenable. In addition, the accepted level for the presence of antibiotics depended in practice on the actual technology used for analysis, so it would be better to establish a maximum residue limit instead of a complete ban. Nevertheless, Thai shrimp farmers bought testing equipment themselves to make sure that their exports would no longer be rejected by the EU which remains a lucrative market for them (http://www.shrimpnews.com/Chloramphenicol.html, accessed 4 November, 2003; http://www.nfi.org/index.php?a=issues&b=International%20Trade&x=1571, accessed 7 November, 2003).

20. New and Wijkström (2002) claim there is no compelling evidence that farmed fish contains in general higher dioxin residues than wild fish. Nevertheless, the dioxin levels in fish vary according to the origin of the fish and their diet. Consequently, fish products

from a European origin (including those from aquaculture) contain much higher levels of dioxins than those originating from Chile or Peru.

21.  During the BSE crisis (see Chapter 5), questions were raised by concerned consumers and politicians whether mammalian Transmissible Spongiform Encephalopathy (TSE) agents could establish themselves in fish and spread through intra-species and intra-order recycling via feed and whether adaptation from fish species to such agents could occur. The Scientific Steering Committee of the European Commission concluded that no scientific evidence existed for the presence of such a risk. However, since theoretically a certain risk might nevertheless exist, they advised that potentially TSE-infected feed should not be fed to other fish and that sourcing of fish by-products should not be performed from fish that had been exposed to potentially infected feed (European Commission, 2003). Another potential risk, the introduction of GM fish, is the subject of hot debates mainly caused by the fear that transgenic fish would escape to surrounding stocks of the same species. So far, genetic transformation of fish has only been performed in laboratories and a few outside trials, but no commercial introductions have been performed. The only exception remains 'glowfish', which was produced in the US for ornamental purposes in 2003. See Bartley and Hallerman (1995) and Maclean and Laight (2000).

22.  See Jenkins (2003) for a case study on the Atlantic salmon and its decline in the state of Maine. This study shows that already more than a century ago attempts were made to increase the number of salmon through active human intervention.

23.  Salmon aquaculture itself originated in 1857 in Canada, but large-scale forms of raising salmon have only existed since the 1960s when fenced fjords in Norway became used for production purposes.

24.  Norway is still the leading farmed salmon producer by virtue of its advanced technology, nutrition and farm management, quality stocks, disease control, appropriate natural environment and supportive regulations (Anderson et al., 2003b). On the other hand, when pen-raised salmon farming extended all around the world in the 1980s, Alaska placed a permanent moratorium on this technology 'because of environmental concerns and, more importantly, the risk of negative economic impacts on the (existing) Alaskan salmon industry' (ibid.: 64).

25.  In the rapidly changing global salmon industry just a few multinational companies account for a growing share of the production and very often these industries have close ties with the feed industry (Nutreco, Ewos/Cermaq and Ecofeed). For example, Nutreco, the world's biggest farmed salmon producer since 2000, accounts for 16–20 per cent of the global farmed salmon production and approximately 40 per cent of the world's salmon feed (Gilbertsen, 2003).

26.  In order to inform consumers about the presence of colour additives in farmed salmon, three major grocery chains in the US have decided to use labels or signs. This was probably done under the pressure of lawsuits accusing these companies of misleading consumers (www.just-food.com: dd. 2 May, 2003).

27.  WWF claimed that in 2002 more than 630,000 farmed salmon had escaped in Norway alone – more than the total number of the already-endangered wild Atlantic salmon spawning in its rivers (Reuters, 12 August, 2003). Research has shown, however, that escaped farmed fish were only 16 per cent as productive as wild fish when spawning in the wild, thereby reducing the longer-term impact of their escape from the pens (Goode and Whoriskey, 2003).

28.  Such diseases may have devastating consequences, for example an outbreak of salmon anaemia in June 2003 required the slaughtering of 28,000 salmon to prevent the disease from spreading further (*Just-Food News*, 01 July, 2003).

29.  Different food safety authorities in Europe were quick to respond to this article published in *Science* magazine, stating that the observed levels remained clearly within the internationally recognised safety limits and that consumers should therefore not be worried when they consume fish as part of a well-balanced menu. See: the Dutch VWA (press release 13 January 2004), the UK Food Standards Agency (9 January) and French AFSSA (9 January). A fish feed processing organisation even claimed that 'in many cases, farmed

salmon is safer than wild because you can't monitor what the fish are eating in the open environment' (Reuters, 12 January, 2004).

30. NASCO has recognised the threats involved in salmon aquaculture and elaborated protocols (1994) prohibiting non-native strains while calling for the establishment of exclusion zones around wild rivers, but these protocols are not binding (Goode and Whoriskey, 2003).

31. The public opinion about salmon farming in the UK was highly influenced by the ITV documentary shown on television on 7 January, 2001, entitled 'The Price of Salmon', showing several images of farmed salmon damaged by sea lice.

32. In the future, salmon may (at least partly) be fed with vegetarian feed ingredients: soybeans and linseed oil (Andries Kamstra from the Dutch fisheries research institute: RIVO in the Dutch daily newspaper De Volkskrant, 29 April, 2003).

33. This section only uses the term shrimp, although in some countries a distinction is made between 'shrimp' and 'prawns', but as this distinction differs per country, the more generic term shrimp is preferred here.

34. 'For example, the growth of shrimp aquaculture was slowed down considerably (but did not stop) in the late 1990s by diseases such as 'white spot' (Asia, Ecuador and the US) and 'Taura Syndrome' (Ecuador), which took their toll on nascent aquaculture producers' (Anderson et al., 2003a: 27).

35. See Skladany and Harris (1995) for a brief overview of the history of the shrimp industry.

36. Thailand's well-established value-added industry contributes to its image as a reliable source in comparison with many other shrimp-exporting countries, which have a much more volatile organisation of shrimp production.

37. American shrimp producers were contemplating anti-dumping actions against Thai shrimp producers because they claimed that Thai shrimp was sold in the US market at 57 per cent below the actual production costs, causing economic loss for US shrimp producers. The Thai producers, however, point to their high expertise and a more suitable environment resulting in very low production costs (*Bangkok Post*, 10 January, 2004).

38. Mangrove forests support a high diversity of marine and terrestrial life through food web interactions and they act as refuges and nursery grounds for many species of fish, shellfish and crustaceans of ecological importance and of commercial value or essential for the subsistence of fishermen (EJF, 2003a).

39. For example, in 1995 around US$100 million was spent on chemicals for use in shrimp farming in Thailand alone. See Gräslund and Bengtsson (2001) for a detailed overview of the chemical substances used in shrimp farming in Asia and their potential effects on the environment and human health.

40. In some regions, shrimp fries are collected as a resource base for shrimp farming and this activity is accompanied by a large (sometimes 100-fold) by-catch of other fries that are decanted, often dead. However, recently improvements in culturing seed in artificial hatcheries are being made and in particular applied in Thailand.

41. The requirement of certain shrimp species for brackish water means that, over time, salts penetrate the water table, while water exchange practices associated with more intensive shrimp farms typically involve pumping in fresh water from surrounding rivers or groundwater supplies and subsequently pumping out wastewater from the ponds into canals, rivers and near-shore waters.

42. The collapse of shrimp farming in Taiwan and the abandoning of shrimp farms in Thailand, Indonesia and Japan, after only a few years of operation, is 'largely the result of overcrowding and degradation of the local environment through spreading of diseases, acidification of soils, and pollution of water' (Folke et al., 1998: S67).

43. The smaller family-owned and managed shrimp farms are generally considered more productive than the larger ones because their feed conversion rate is lower (that is, they require less feed for growing shrimp) than for the larger farms (ASCC News Q 3/1992/Issue No 11; ASCC News Q 4/1994/Issue No 20).

44. The industries associated with shrimp farms include: the shrimp feed industry; the capture and supply of wild broodstock by fishermen; hatchery production of nauplii and shrimp seed; nursery operations; pond water quality and shrimp disease testing (laboratory ser-

vices); manufacture and sale of shrimp farm equipment (for example paddlewheels and water pumps); live and pellet feed processing; cold storage plant construction; and shrimp processing and exporting.

45. CP owns feed and feed input production facilities (fishmeal, flour mills), provides laboratory services to growers, has an export trade company, processing factories, hatcheries and corporate farms, and plays a major role in research and development (Lebel et al., 2002).

46. Shrimp processing industries in Thailand were employing some 60,000 workers during the mid-1990s (Thailand Department of Fisheries) and the industry remains particularly labour intensive, where young women work for long hours for low pay (Goss et al., 2000).

47. Consumers in these high-income countries demand convenience in their food habits and they are concerned with quality, ask for food that is varied and interesting, nutritious and healthy, and increasingly want their food to be produced in environmentally and socially ethical ways. See, for an interesting case, the import prohibition by the United States of certain shrimp and shrimp products in the 1990s, which was brought before a dispute panel of the WTO by several Asian countries, the so-called 'shrimp-turtle' or TED case (Shahin, 1999; Charnovitz, 2002b). This prohibition was based, at least in part, on concerns among US consumers and citizens about the large numbers of sea turtles killed by fishermen while they captured shrimp at open sea.

48. Huitric et al. (2002) note that in Thailand landownership and landholding rights are considered the most important ones among the private property rights and they are a constitutional right. The legal strength of these land rights has complicated the introduction and enforcement of regulations that affect them in any negative manner. This seems to contradict the opinion of many scientific observers that individual property rights constitute the best guarantee for the sustainable management of natural resources.

49. For example, very large variations were found between different studies in Thailand estimating the impact of the growth in shrimp farming areas on the total reduction of mangrove forests with these estimates varying between 12.5 per cent and 64 per cent (Kaosaard and Wijukprasert, 2000).

50. Sediments also contain chemicals that had been used to control shrimp diseases as well as aquatic vegetation and other nuisance organisms whereby the presence of antibiotics in the pond sludge is particularly worrying. Most farmers use oxytetracycline prophylactically to prevent outbreaks of disease by distributing medicated feed of which over 95 per cent is not assimilated by the shrimp (Flaherty et al., 1999: 2052).

51. The total production area was limited to a maximum of 80,000 hectares and all shrimp farms larger than eight hectares should be registered and allocate at least 10 per cent of their total area for a treatment pond. The BOD from water discharged from shrimp farms should not exceed 10 mg/l and sediments should not be disposed of in public areas.

52. These regulations had limited effectiveness also because authorities continued to subsidise shrimp development and lifted the ban on logging mangrove areas at the same time.

53. The HACCP team of the Thai Department of Fisheries has developed a generic model for HACCP certification of aquaculture shrimp production and processing and adherence to these guidelines will allow shrimp farms to be HACCP labelled, which is a condition for all food exports to the EU and US. This HACCP model monitors especially the food safety risks, such as hygiene and the use of pesticides and antibiotics.

54. An advertisement claims that zero-exchange ponds produce ten times more shrimp than semi-intensive ponds and forty times more shrimp than extensive ponds. These closed production systems are also supposed to have almost no environmental impact (http://www.shrimpnews.com/NewTechnology.html accessed 4 November, 2003). A disadvantage of such systems is the higher financial and labour investments required.

55. Until that time, regulatory regimes were guided by the doctrine of the freedom of the seas and the inexhaustibility of the ocean fisheries (Allison, 2001).

56. Government measures to limit fishing activity contain state-regulated licence limitations, total allowable catches, closed seasons, closed areas and a host of technical measures related to the dimensions and design of the fishing gear. This form of management places

considerable demands on financial and human resources and government expenditures vary between 2 and 70 per cent (with an average of 6 per cent) of the landed value of the catch in OECD countries (Allison, 2001).

57. Therefore, Hanna (1999: 279) concludes, 'the promotion of effective governance does not depend on a particular property rights regime but rather on an institutional environment that promotes these basic functions.'

58. The costs of compliance with sanitary and phytosanitary requirements faced by developing countries when accessing developed country markets can be very high; in certain cases prohibitively so (Henson et al., 2000). A Code of Practice for the Products of Aquaculture is proposed by the Codex Alimentarius and this Code incorporates, since 1997, HACCP as well to ensure the safety of fish for human consumption. This Code of Conduct and the associated regulations were largely developed in joint co-operation with the fishing industry (Read and Fernandes, 2003).

59. Labelling, generally on a voluntary base, but sometimes also mandatory, has predominately been a European phenomenon (Roheim, 2003).

60. The EU is developing 'tracefish', a voluntary labelling scheme to trace the history, the application of different techniques and the production location of fish, relating the final product to its origin and its processing history. Tracefish aims at introducing a systematic scheme applying modern information technology to allow traceability for the fish industry throughout the chain both for wild capture fisheries and for aquaculture (Denton, 2003). The scheme's focus is on food safety risks which they hope to reduce through increased transparency. The required information can be divided into three categories: (1) the basic traceability information, (2) specific (legally required) information, and (3) commercially desirable information. The system does not look for perfect traceability (allowing a particular retail product to be traceable back to a single farm), but takes a pragmatic approach (allowing traceability back to a finite number of farms).

61. China has developed a fish polyculture where silver carp and bighead carp are filter feeders, feeding on phytoplankton and zooplankton, respectively. The grass carp feeds largely on vegetation, while the common carp is a bottom feeder, living on detritus that settles to the bottom. Most of China's aquaculture is integrated with agriculture, enabling farmers to use agricultural wastes, such a pig manure, to fertilise ponds, thus stimulating the growth of plankton (Frankic and Hershner, 2003).

62. Replacing fishmeal and fish oil with alternatives that do not depend on the limited resources of the sea would be essential for sustainable aquaculture, as well as reduced seed collection from the wild through setting up hatcheries.

63. Completely closed systems requiring only water supply to fill the system and replace evaporation can be especially attractive for hatcheries and other more small-scale activities within the larger aquacultural systems (Pillay, 1992).

64. For more concrete examples see STT (2003).

65. Onshore production can minimise problems that plague marine aquaculture operations, such as coastal habitat destruction and excessive nutrient pollution, which can cause algae blooms. It also reduces the risk of introducing non-native species through escapes and spreading the diseases that fish in high-density confinement are prone to (Brown et al., 2003).

66. The FAO Code of Conduct for Responsible Fisheries, adopted in 1995, was expanded in 1997 to include aquaculture (Read and Fernandes, 2003). The Kyoto declaration (1997) provides additional pressure to reduce fishing capacity, to strengthen the scientific basis for multispecies and ecosystem management, to reduce incidental catch and to strengthen institutional co-ordination (Hanna, 1999). 'With respect to the respective duties of (developing countries) government and aquaculturalists (formulated in legal institutional frameworks) to ensure that aquaculture is sustainable, it was noted that roles tend to be formulated in an indicative manner rather than in an imperative manner. The latter is more common in developed countries' (Van Houtte, 2001: 106).

67. An example is the so-called Oslo agreement signed in 1994 by seven member states of the North Atlantic Salmon Conservation Organisation (NASCO): the 'Convention for the Conservation of Salmon in the North Atlantic Ocean to minimise impacts from salmon

aquaculture on the wild salmon stocks' through well-considered siting of salmon aquaculture operations and by avoiding the spread of diseases and parasites and the escapes of farmed salmon endangering wild populations. The signatories agreed to provide annual reports about the measures taken.

68. Most national governmental regulations for aquaculture are still based on a traditional command-and-control approach: banning aquaculture at certain locations, defining maximum permissible concentrations, handing out licences, and so on.

69. Specific taxation of the environmental impact from aquaculture is generally turned down because of the problems for implementing such measures, the effects on competitiveness and the risk of creating disincentives to innovation (Bailly and Willmann, 2001).

70. WWF has suggested the installation of fish-farm-free zones and marine protected areas around coastlines in developing countries to protect vulnerable species and their environment.

71. For example, the code of conduct developed by the Federation of European Aquaculture Producers (FEAP) (see: http://www.feap.info) and the international environmental standard of ISO 14001 (Frankic and Hershner, 2003). So far no international criteria exist for organic labelling of aquacultural products (Bailly and Willmann, 2001).

72. See http://www.gaalliance.org (accessed 7 November 2003).

73. For example, Ocean Boy Farms in Florida, USA, claims that shrimp may be produced on a large scale without polluting the environment. Their inland shrimp farm uses another fish, the tilapia, to mop up the shrimps' waste. These land-based, integrated farming techniques are promising minimal environmental costs (*Economist*, 9 August, 2003).

74. See http://www.gaalliance.org/revi16.html (accessed 11 April, 2002).

75. The code of practice for shrimp farming covers nine topics: mangroves, site evaluation, pond design and construction, feeds and feed use, shrimp health management, use of therapeutic agents and other chemicals, general pond operations, effluents and solid wastes, and community and employee relations. Although the GAA Board of Directors at first intended this code to become a certification system allowing eligible products to display an ecolabel, they decided in the end that this would be too costly, complex and prone to liability cases. The Code therefore remained a voluntary and educational program: 'intended to serve as guidelines for parties wanting to develop more specific national or regional codes of practice or for formulating systems of best management practices for use on specific shrimp farms' (http://www.gaalliance.org/revi16.html (accessed 11 April, 2002)).

76. The standards contain specific prescriptions with regard to community issues (property rights and regulatory compliance, community relations and worker safety and employee relations), environmental issues (mangrove conservation, effluent and sediment management, soil/water conservation, post-larvae sources and storage and disposal of farm supplies) and food safety (drug and chemical management, microbial sanitation and for harvest and transport), while traceability is also required ('Aquaculture facility certification, Guidelines for Standards' at http://www.aquaculturecertification.org (accessed 13 April, 2004)).

77. In its magazine 'Aquamedia' FEAP claims that the history of mankind has shown a progressively more efficient use of all natural resources employed in the provision of food, but that the production and use of fish lags behind in its basic methodology. Nevertheless, fish farming can ultimately contribute to fill this gap provided the activity is performed sustainably, the life-cycle is mastered, the growing process controlled, the environment respected and the final product marketed successfully. See: http://www.aquamedia.org/environment/sustainability/default_en.asp (accessed 2 April, 2004).

78. See for details: http://www.ntva.no/rapport/aqua/report.htm (accessed 21 April, 2004).

79. The principle of human equity refers to obligation to secure the rights of indigenous people and the access of poor people to fish for food and income and to prevent aquaculture from causing social problems.

80. In 1997, the Codex Alimentarius Commission designated HACCP as the accepted method to ensure the safety of fish for human health.

81. See www.graigfarm.co.uk/fishorg.htm (accessed 30 March, 2004).

82. To substantiate these comments most NGOs refer less frequently to the situation in Thailand and more to India and Bangladesh. 'Most Bangladeshi NGOs would like shrimp cultivation to cease, due to its severe environmental and social impacts, although some think it has a potential to be beneficial, provided it is carried out in a way that takes into account the environment and local needs' (Roberts and Robins, 2000: 55).

83. Some NGOs, like Greenpeace, add the use of genetically modified organisms in aquaculture and the introduction of exotic/alien species to the list of environmental dangers.

84. Greenpeace (1997) argues for a global moratorium on new shrimp farms that fail to comply with sustainability criteria.

85. See Accion Ecologica (1996a, b); URL: http://www.earthsummitwatch.org/shrimp/positions/pov2a.html (accessed 6 November, 2003); URL: http://www.earthsummitwatch.org/shrimp/positions/pov3.html (accessed 6 November, 2003); URL: http://www.earthsummitwatch.org/shrimp/positions/isanetguayaquil.html (accessed 6 November, 2003), and ISA Net (1998).

86. The IUCN also maintains the global IUCN Red List, which identifies the plants and animals (including fish) that are threatened most, serves as a tool to set priorities for conservation action and provides baseline information for monitoring.

87. Fishmeal-fed farmed salmon have higher levels of PCBs because wild salmon tend to eat lower on the marine food chain and consume more krill and shrimp.

88. See: http://www.davidsuzuki.org (accessed 13 April, 2004).

89. See: Friends of the Earth Scotland (2001), 'Salmon farming – The one that got away'; URL: http://www.foe-scotland.org.uk/nation/fish_report_summary.html (accessed 13 April, 2004).

90. Audubon, 2002; URL: www.audubon.org/campaign/lo (accessed 21 October, 2003). See also the Monterey Bay Aquarium, Seafood Watch, West Coast Seafood Guide, Fall/Winter 2003.

91. URL: www.seafoodchoices.com/whoweare (accessed 16 April, 2004).

92. See: Audubon, 2002; URL: www.audubon.org/campaign/lo (accessed 28 October, 2003).

93. Monterey Bay Aquarium, Seafood Watch, West Coast Seafood Guide, Fall/Winter 2003.

94. Environmental Defense, pocket seafood selector, updated 8 December, 2002; URL: www.environmentaldefense.org/sustainablefishing (accessed 28 October, 2003). The organisation states that 'because of the variations in production practices for some types of fish, our list is limited to only those fish for which harvesting or farming practices are predominantly environmentally sound or unsound'.

95. See: http://www.goedevis.nl/visgids/beoordeling.html. Interestingly, the organisation explicitly decided not to include animal welfare as one of the selection criteria because of the lack of reliable information, or food miles, because they claim that the environmental effect of transport depends mainly on the particular means chosen and not on the distance alone.

96. See: Blue Ocean Institute, 'Guide to Ocean Friendly Seafood' at website: http://www.blueoceaninstitute.org/seafood (accessed 31 May, 2004).

97. URL: http://www.mbayaq.org/cr/cr_seafoodwatch/sfw_ac.asp (accessed 28 October, 2003).

98. Rather general views on aquaculture are sometimes presented in these consumer guides. For example 'thousands of fish concentrated in one area produce tons of faeces, polluting the water. Diseases can spread from fish in the crowded pens to wild fish. Antibiotics and other drugs used to control those diseases leak out into the environment, creating drug-resistant disease organisms. And if farmed fish escape their pens, they can take over habitat from wild fish in the area. ... In Thailand, Ecuador and many other tropical nations, coastal forests of mangroves once sheltered wild fish and shrimp, which local people caught to feed their families. Mangroves also filter water and protect the coast against storm waves. Many mangrove forests have been cut down and replaced with shrimp farms that supply shrimp to Europe, Japan and America. After a few years, waste products build up in the farm ponds and the farmers have to move on. The local people are left with no shrimp farms – and no mangrove forests' (URL: www.mbayaq.org/cr/cr_seafoodwatch/sfw_ac.asp accessed 28 October, 2003). See also: Hammond et al.

(2002); URL: www.seafoodchoices.com/whoweare (accessed 16 April, 2004); URL: http://ww.mscuk.org/action/gfginfo.htm and URL: http://www.mcsuk.org/action/gfgtop25.htm (accessed 13 April, 2004). The dangers of genetic engineering are explicitly used to criticise fish farming, see URL: www.consciouschoice.com/food/consumerseafoodguide1401.html (accessed 28 October, 2003).

99. The Pacific Coast Federation of Fishermen's Associations makes the suggestion to extend the existing MSC labelling criteria and include social criteria to develop it into a Fair Trade label for fish (*Fishermen's News* of March, 2003).

100. One danger may be the creation of dual markets through the introduction of labels like MSC or ISO 14000 and thus of two different fishing practices, particularly in developing countries with sustainably managed export-oriented fisheries clearly separated from fisheries supplying domestic markets with no environmental control at all (Allison, 2001).

# 8. Environmental governance of global food flows: labelling as new arrangements?

> Many grocery packages today include 'eco-labels' that make attractive claims. Grocery shelves are bulging with food labelled 'natural', 'free-range', and 'sustainable'. But much of this label is just spin.
> (Miller, Matthew L., 2004, 'Good label manners. Not all "eco-labels" are created equal', *Grist Magazine,* 16 March 2004)

> From the activist perspective, market differentiation through sustainability seems a grand strategy. It comes with a catch, though. Neither consumers nor retailers are willing to cover the extra costs associated with making the transition into sustainability. Instead, the tab is being pressed on to farmers.
> (Fox, Tom, 2000, 'Supermarket squeeze', *Tomorrow Magazine,* **10** (5): 22)

## INTRODUCTION

Every day consumers in Europe, the US and many other parts of the world find more food products with special labels in their supermarkets. Some of these labels claim particular health characteristics of the food item concerned while other labels refer to animal friendly or organic production practices. Moreover, other labels indicate that special attention has been paid to the social and economic circumstances of the farmers and workers.

These food labels, particularly those drawing attention to the social and environmental consequences of particular food production practices, are relatively new but their numbers have grown rapidly in recent years (Oosterveer, 2006). Different private companies, NGOs and consumer organisations have initiated or supported food-labelling schemes, because they consider this instrument an attractive means to relate to consumer concerns. In reaction, several commentators have claimed that labels only confuse the customer, are not based on any real improvement in the food production practices referred to and only represent a form of 'corporate green wash'.[1] The presence of these opposing views makes it interesting to take a closer look at food labels and to ask whether private-initiated food labelling and certification schemes form a promising innovative response to the challenges facing contemporary global food governance.

This chapter will start in the next section with a recapitulation of the problems of food governance in global modernity for which labels and certificates claim to be an adequate response. Based on this more theoretical review, two different NGO-initiated labelling initiatives will be reviewed, starting with the Fair Trade label for coffee and followed by the Marine Stewardship Council (MSC) label for fish. These different certification and labelling schemes combined constitute the basis for a discussion in the final section of this chapter on the question to what extent these food labels respond to the challenges for global food governance identified in Chapter 2.

## LABELLING OF FOOD IN THE GLOBAL NETWORK SOCIETY

Nation-state-based regulation of food is facing its limits because global institutions such as the WTO (see Chapter 4) and private companies exercise more and more control over ways of governing food production, processing and trade. At the same time, consumer concerns about the environmental, social and safety impacts associated with food intensify, and therefore tools are needed to adequately manage the quality and safety of food as well as control the impact of the production and trade practices involved. In order to be effective such governance instruments necessarily have to fit into the ways in which food production and consumption are organised within the global network society.

The production and consumption of food structured in the global space of flows is at different moments and in different contexts confronted with the specific dynamics of food production and food consumption in the local space of places. Food governance approached from this perspective consists of multiple layers, from local to global, and involves multiple actors, from private firms to non-governmental interest groups (Mol, 2001). Under these circumstances, 'soft' instruments such as labels, standards and certification schemes seem to be increasingly preferred to 'hard' instruments such as bans, moratoriums, limits or other legal requirements (Klintman and Boström, 2004). Such private firm and NGO-based labelling initiatives do not function in a vacuum but always in the context of global provisioning of food and nation-state-based governmental regulations. However, whereas conventional regulations involve national governments establishing standards and policing performance and remain hierarchical and at arm's length, private forms of governance involve NGOs and firms in standard setting and monitoring roles and establish networks at multiple levels engaging with multiple actors throughout the supply chain. Transnational institutions and the affiliated global standards have become both a cause of disagreement in international trade disputes and a focus of corporate and environmental or social-justice movement attention. It seems a shift is taking place in the establishment of global standards from *relational* (generated and adjudged from within networks) to *notional* standards (defined outside of networks by specialised committees, non-negotiable and verified by external inspections). This trend results in a transition from diversity in standards to convergence where some NGOs even seem to have the intention of establishing global uniform standard and certification schemes covering different production process-related concerns about social, environmental and labour impacts, as for example through the SASA initiative for agriculture.[2]

Many international corporations have introduced internal standards to act as benchmarking criteria against which different business practices, or the performance of different plants located in different countries, can be compared (Thompson, 2005). Such private firm-initiated certification schemes mostly are intended to establish a global and uniform regulation within the global space of flows and thereby to facilitate supply chain management. The result of these efforts has tended towards a proliferation of standards unique to a certain firm or sector. This 'internal' orientation of most private firm-initiated labels and their 'objective' and 'uniform' character means that they essentially hope to get consumer trust based on trust in the firm itself. Intra-firm harmonisation therefore does not yield uniform global food standards but a highly contingent mix of component sub standards of various origins (Mutersbaugh, 2005).

NGO-initiated, or NGO-supported, schemes are much more directly oriented to the creation of global food labels (Freidberg, 2004). Such labels are more flexible and willing to engage in complex and intensive debates involving different and evolving consumer concerns, divergent claims and ideologically diverse positions. In addition, generally NGO-based initiatives are better integrated in networks that stretch from the global to the local (Kleinwächter, 2003).[3] NGO-initiated food labels that provide more information than just the characteristics of the final product are particularly interesting because they may preserve the identity of a food product throughout the food supply chain and contain information about the origin and the environmental and/or socio-economic impacts involved in producing the final product. The reliability and transparency of these labels is supposedly assured through the condition that certification and monitoring is done by independent and officially accredited third party organisations and that transparent, explicit and verifiable criteria are used (Roth and Zambon, 2001; Gallastegui, 2002; Goodland, 2002). It is not necessary for these

NGO initiatives to represent the *mass* public to be attractive, but they should be able to convince the media and retailers alike that they speak to and for a *critical* public. 'Critical in the two senses of the term: that is, the public that are both critical *of* the retailers' sourcing practices and, as consumers, critical *to* their sales' (Freidberg, 2004, 528). NGOs are taking on activities that were previously the sole purview of national governments and international regulatory bodies. Civil society participants are working to fill holes in the conventional government regulation while they transform the nature of the currently existing governance arrangements in doing so. These innovative labelling and certification schemes involve new forms of collaboration, new roles for nongovernmental organizations, new responsibilities of firms, and new responses from local and national government authorities (O'Rourke, 2003).

Private firm-initiated food labelling and certification schemes such as HACCP and ISO 14001 operate and relate to global governance arrangements in the space of flows alone while NGO-initiated labelling schemes, like MSC and Fair Trade, aim at combining different consumer concerns and at (re-) establishing consumer trust.

## ISO AND HACCP AS PRIVATE INITIATED GOVERNANCE TOOLS

The internationally familiar certification schemes ISO 14001 and HACCP constitute two tools for the governance of food production and consumption, essentially relying on markets and market-based strategies intended to govern within the space of flows.

ISO 14001 is a general standard for measuring the environmental performance of industrial activities, not limited to food production, developed by the International Organisation for Standardisation (ISO). A growing number of private companies, particularly large internally operating corporations, is adopting this standard.[4] ISO 14001, formally adopted in 1996, was developed as a global standard in line with the ISO's overall objective to introduce technical standards worldwide to facilitate international trade. The intention of this scheme is to offer support to industries and public institutions for choices in their organisational and process management activities with the intention of guaranteeing the necessary environmental quality (Krut and Gleckman, 1998).[5] Certifying firms according to the ISO 14001 standards falls under the responsibility of independent private agents who are accredited by the national standardisation boards that are members of the ISO. The acquisition of ISO 14001 certification by numerous firms worldwide has turned this label into an internationally recognised indicator for good environmental performance. Certified firms are more and more requiring their suppliers to be ISO 14001 certified as well, thereby securing the environmental performance of the supply chain as a whole (Boudouropoulos and Arvanitoyannis, 1999). The WTO recognises ISO standards as being compatible with its regulatory requirements for global trade while many governments even consider certification with ISO 14001 as sufficient proof for fulfilling the legal obligations for the environmental performance of an industry. ISO standards often are considered weaker than other environmental standards, particularly those developed by NGOs (INNI, 2002). Nevertheless, ISO 14001 will in the future most likely become even more important in international business, environmental policy and global trade. The main reason for this increasing dominance of ISO 14001 is that the future use of ISO 14001 will most likely follow the current success of the ISO 9000 certificate. Additionally, the contemporary trend where national governments are forfeiting much of their traditional regulatory role to the private sector itself is creating an ISO-friendly environment. Finally, food traders are increasingly becoming reliant on international, easily verifiable codes for quality assurance. Although not specifically intended for food, ISO 14001 nevertheless represents the environmental element in a tri-partite assurance scheme together with ISO 9000 assuring the quality and HACCP the safety of the final food product (Wall et al., 2001).

HACCP (Hazard Analysis of Critical Control Points) was introduced in the late 1960s by private firms with the intention of reducing food risks through a voluntary approach. This certification scheme functions in a manner comparable to the more familiar ISO practices. Over the years, particularly in the 1980s and the 1990s, HACCP has become increasingly recognised and widely endorsed as a tool for eliminating identified food hazards or at least for reducing them to an acceptable level (Walker et al., 2003).[6] A food production process can be HACCP-certified separately, but a food product itself can only be HACCP certified if all production processes involved have received certification as well.[7] For this reason, many retailers, especially in Western countries, demand their suppliers to acquire HACCP certification as well and thereby to allow control of food safety throughout the whole supply chain. HACCP certification is organised via independent certifying agencies accredited by national boards. The growing use of HACCP as a food safety standard in international trade led the Codex Alimentarius Commission to adopt general guidelines (1993) and to incorporate HACCP into its food hygiene codes (1995), however the organisation did not provide detailed guidance on its implementation (Hathaway, 1995). Although initially developed as a voluntary tool for private firms to reduce food risks, nowadays implementing HACCP certification is recognised by the US and several European governments as the fulfilment of these firms' legal obligation to control food safety in a systematic manner (Segerson, 1999; Unnevehr and Jensen, 1999).[8]

The evolution of these private certification initiatives, ISO 14001 and HACCP, into worldwide standards corresponds with the broader development towards facilitating global food trade supported by the WTO through the promotion of governance arrangements that fit better into governance in the space of flows.[9] Critical commentators point at the difficulties in establishing consumer trust through these certification schemes, at the position of small producers and processors in developing countries and at the lack of evidence for a real reduction in the environmental impact of certified food processing firms.

Private certification schemes such as ISO 14001 and HACCP rely mainly on scientific procedures and their standards have a global character, while their certifying bodies are fully independent, contrary to many governmental and intra-firm standards (Unnevehr and Jensen, 1999). It is however rather debatable whether the use of private schemes will suffice to convince consumers in the context of the global risk society (see Chapter 2). One may particularly doubt whether a uniform global food safety regime that is limited to science and technology and that excludes local and cultural differences as well as the diversity among consumer concerns can ever be successful (Echols, 2001). In addition, firms do not always communicate their ISO and HACCP certifications to the consumers by labelling their food products, which makes these procedures more management tools than instruments towards establishing consumer trust. Nevertheless, private firms sometimes use their HACCP certificate to offer the general public visible evidence for their active engagement in the prevention of food hazards.[10]

Establishing global food safety norms on the basis of scientific evidence only may result in serious social and economic consequences for firms, who have difficulties in complying with them (Moonen, 2004; O'Hara and Stagl, 2001; Otsuki et al., 2001). For example, the HACCP certification scheme seems to have been developed from the perspective of large-scale food processing companies, which makes its effective utilisation in small businesses, in developing as well as in developed countries, a considerable challenge (Taylor, 2001; Walker et al., 2003). The necessary infrastructure and technical knowledge to fulfil certain requirements may sometimes be lacking in these firms while the costs of certification may also constitute insurmountable problems.[11] Therefore, these food-processing firms are forced either to refrain from exporting food or to become dependent on multinational firms to support the implementation of HACCP certification in their facilities. Sometimes multinational enterprises are willing to provide the necessary funds and control systems to their local suppliers because of their intention to ensure safety throughout the food supply chain (Unnevehr and Jensen, 1999).

A particular weakness of ISO 14001 as well as of HACCP certification is their focus on internal management procedures without defining clear environmental or safety standards for production processes and food products.[12] Thus, certification in itself does not reveal much about the actual environmental and food safety performance of a firm except for the confirmation that a company is fulfilling its legal obligations in these fields (Ammenberg et al., 2001).[13]

These examples of privately initiated food governance arrangements are essentially oriented towards governance in the global space of flows and intended to assure the general safety and quality of food products. Consequently, they may be confronted with specific environmental and socio-economic problems at the space of place of production and consumption. In order to respond to these potential problems additional governance arrangements are needed. Such arrangements should be capable of including consumer concerns beyond the observable traits of the food product itself. Possibly, one response to this challenge may be found in food labels intending to combine governance in the space of flows with governance in the space of place of production and consumption. Interesting attempts to create such innovative global food governance tools are the Fair Trade label for coffee and the Marine Stewardship Council (MSC) label for fish.

## FAIR TRADE COFFEE; INCLUDING THE ENVIRONMENTAL AND SOCIAL CONSEQUENCES OF GLOBAL TRADE

Around 125 million people in over 50 developing countries grow coffee, mainly organised within peasant households on farms of less than ten hectares. Coffee has been internationally traded for several centuries and is currently integrated into global chains and networks, linking producers in countries like Brazil, Colombia and (since a few years also) Vietnam with consumers in Europe, the USA and Japan.

Between the 1930s and the 1980s, national states played a vital role in promoting the production of coffee through credit-based input schemes, widespread extension services, national systems of quality control and pan-territorial pricing. International trade was dominated by a small number of large trading companies based in the USA and Europe. Simple quality conventions combining price with certain crude physical crop-properties formed the major mechanism linking suppliers with these international traders. Through the active involvement of producer-countries' governments, a worldwide regulation of the international coffee trade became established formally through the International Coffee Agreement (ICA).[14] The character of this global arrangement for coffee trade started to change, however, during the 1990s. That time, the producer cartel collapsed while government support to coffee producers in developing countries was reduced considerably through the implementation of structural adjustment programmes. Until today, despite several attempts, no promising innovative forms of government-based global coffee trade arrangement replacing ICA have been identified or implemented.[15] The institutional framework of the international coffee market is moving away from a formal and relatively stable system dominated by the producers towards a system that is more informal, inherently unstable and buyer dominated (Ponte, 2001). The disappearance of formally institutionalised global governance arrangements as well as of the simple quality–price matrix reinforced the already existing asymmetrical distribution of power within the coffee supply chain. Coffee producers in developing countries saw their position weaken while three other global residues of power (importers, roasters and retailers) strengthened their position (Fitter and Kaplinsky, 2001).[16] Therefore, the coffee price for producers, which had shown a declining trend before, fell dramatically in the recent decades resulting in the lowest coffee price in real terms on the world market for 100 years.[17] In the early 1990s, coffee producing countries earned around US$10–12 billion while the value of coffee sold by retailers was about US$30 billion. By 2002, the value of retail sales exceeded US$70 billion but the coffee producing countries received only US$5.5 billion (Osorio, 2002).

International coffee trade has developed by now into a complex and very dynamic global flow, in which private contracts between producers, traders, roasters and retailers dominate. The producer–trader networks involved display a great diversity and, in combination with a growing differentiation of consumer tastes, make the simple matrix that linked the quality of the crop with the price disappear. Complex standards measuring the quality of the coffee are proliferating because the degree of differentiation in coffee blends and prices has grown significantly over the last years.[18] Contemporary quality standards for coffee have more voluntary and less mandatory features while they also pay more attention to production and processing methods and less to objectively verifiable product attributes than 20 years ago (Ponte, 2002). A reason for this growth in interest in production and processing methods is that while coffee farming had little environmental impact in the past, recent efforts to increase productivity seem to lead to a considerable increase in pollution and a loss of biodiversity. Latin America, especially, has witnessed a shift from traditional shade-grown production to 'sun' coffee or 'mono-culture shade' coffee (UNCTAD and IISD, 2003). This process of intensifying coffee production required an increased use of pesticides, fungicides and fertilisers and resulted in a reduction of biodiversity, especially with regard to the number of different bird species. The impact of coffee production on biodiversity is particularly sensitive because often coffee is grown in areas of high biodiversity importance and high vulnerability (ibid.). Furthermore, the introduction of intensive monocultural coffee production systems meant aggravating the already existing soil erosion and deforestation problems. This transformation of the international coffee trade into a complex and dynamic global flow of food coincided with several social and environmental problems at the local level, but made governance at the places of production more difficult. Forced by limited financial resources and under pressure from the IMF to refrain from direct interference with production and trade, governments in developing countries were less able than in the past to play an active role in the organisation and regulation of the international coffee trade.

These consequences of the construction of the global coffee chain formed the driving force behind the creation of a fair trade label for coffee.[19] In 1973, the first fair traded coffee produced in Guatemala was exported to the Netherlands and during a period of over 30 years fair trade coffee has become a substantial part of the global coffee sector. In 2000, the fair trade coffee sector included nearly 200 coffee co-operatives representing 675,000 farmers, more than 70 traders and around 350 coffee companies. At that time, 64,100 tonnes of fair traded coffee, with a retail value of $393 million (still only around 1 per cent of the global coffee production), was sold mainly to consumers in Europe.[20] North American fair trade coffee sales in 2000 amounted to only 10,400 tonnes with a retail value of $64.4 million, but this market is growing rapidly (Ponte, 2002: 24).

The production and trade standards for fair trade coffee are defined by the Fairtrade Labelling Organisation (FLO) and include social, economic and environmental criteria (FLO, 2003).[21] (See Box 8.1 for these criteria.)

---

## BOX 8.1  FAIRTRADE CRITERIA FOR COFFEE

To be able to label coffee with the Fairtrade mark the coffee buyer or roaster must pay a licensing fee and meet the following two criteria while accepting external control on compliance with them. First, to purchase all green coffee directly from producer organisations listed in the International Fairtrade Coffee Producers' register and give them long-term (1-10 year) contracts. Second, to fix the purchasing price in accordance with the standard conditions of trade set by the fair trade organisation, including:

- A minimum price for the coffee and a premium of 5 cents per pound of coffee (15 cents per pound organic coffee) if the world market prices are higher than the minimum prices set,
- The roaster or buyer must facilitate access to crop finance for producers at the beginning of the harvest, under Fairtrade conditions, at regular international interest rates, for up to 60 per cent of the value of the contracted coffee, until the coffee has been shipped.

To be listed on the International Fairtrade Coffee producers' register, coffee producing organisations must meet several criteria, including:

- The organisation is independent and democratically controlled by its members, the majority of whom are small scale coffee producers,
- The organisation is open to new members and no form of discrimination is practised,
- The organisation is committed to improving the quality of their coffee, to diversification of the production to reduce dependency on a singular crop, support social development, apply sustainable production techniques, which respect ecosystems, use natural resources sustainably and minimise the use of chemical inputs.

*Source*: Robins and Roberts (1998).

FLO aims at establishing an international coffee trade system based on fair conditions for the farmers and workers in the disadvantaged regions of the Third World.[22] Organised farmers in developing countries are guaranteed a minimum price for their coffee, independent of the world market price while direct and long-term partnerships are built between the producer organisations and the importers, thereby providing a reliable basis for financial, technical and organisational support.[23] Roasters and retailers buying coffee from the small farmers' organisations registered with FLO, also have to fulfil specific requirements before this coffee can be labelled as fair trade and sold in conventional shops or through alternative trade channels.

The consumer price for fair trade coffee is comparatively higher than the price of conventional coffee and the difference makes it possible to cover the additional social and environmental costs (http://www.maxhavelaar.nl). Initially, the criteria for fair trade coffee only covered social and economic elements but later on environmental considerations were included as well. The conditions for the environmental performance of coffee producers remain on purpose rather vague in order not to exclude small farmers who have difficulties in following strict environmental guidelines. Fair trade coffee standards now require integrated crop management and specific guarantees for shade-grown production (Abbott et al., 1999; Blowfield, 1999).[24] Many European consumers, however, value more strict environmental performance and consequently a substantial part of fair trade coffee (36 per cent of the total in 2000) is labelled following organic standards at the same time.

The fair trade label is a voluntary, private label and thus developed independently of national and international governmental authorities. For example, although the European Commission did express its sympathy for this initiative, the European Union is unable to support fair trade organisations directly. The EU's obligations within the WTO do not seem to permit support to fair trade other than subsidising promotion campaigns.[25] Therefore, fair trade coffee remains a private labelling initiative operating within the existing major global supply chains. Contrary to some other alternative trade initiatives, fair trade does not necessarily aim at establishing a completely separate supply chain linking producers and consumers. Thus, on the one hand, fair trade coffee remains part of the global flow of coffee including the existing trade regulations while the initiative on the other hand builds new social relationships between the coffee producers and consumers beyond their economic relationship of buyer and seller. The strategy underlying the construction of these new social relationships is to provide certain categories of coffee with a specific meaning for the consumers (with regard to ecology, solidarity, fairness, and so on) (Renard, 1999). Fair trade coffee builds on domestic and civic norms, values and mentalities around trust and global responsibility. The label was introduced because consumers in Western countries were concerned about the downward pressure on farmers' incomes in developing countries resulting from conventional coffee trade and about the harmful consequences of modern coffee production techniques for the environment. Consumers buying fair trade coffee are provided with 'personal relationships with farmers (through images, publicity, and educational materials), trust and security in socially-responsible value claims and the elusive feel good factor' (Raynolds, 2002: 415). The special character of this relationship is underlined by the central role played by NGOs in controlling the fair trade label because they are supposed to act in the interests of the farmers in developing countries contrary to private companies seeking profit only. This way, otherwise identical products in impersonal markets become distinguishable, inviting consumers to consider the differences in their purchasing decisions.[26]

Coffee production practices are also changing in the fair trade coffee supply chain because market transactions, although still guided by commercial norms and practices, now are influenced clearly by other arrangements as well. On the one hand, quality standards are monitored inflexibly and rigorously for fair trade coffee, while delivery schedules and purchasing contracts remain based on conventional industrial standards.[27] However, on the other hand, fair trade prices are based on the notion of 'a fair return', covering the production costs supplemented with a social premium for development purposes. Social and cultural objectives are thus included in the organisation of global trade together with the existing economic objectives. The FLO requirement that the coffee producers are collectively organised is intended to strengthen the traditionally existing civic norms, values and conventions. These coffee producers' organisations are provided with technical expertise and market information via the fair trade networks, which may support their position on conventional markets as well. A stronger position on this conventional coffee market is particularly important because, although producer groups may be fair trade certified, this does not guarantee selling all their coffee under fair trade conditions because consumer demand remains insufficient compared to the total supply of fair trade coffee. For example, in Central America on average only 15–20 per cent of the coffee produced by registered co-operatives is sold under fair trade conditions and the remaining 80–85 per cent still has to be sold through the conventional trading channels (Roozen and Van der Hoff, 2001).[28]

In brief, fair trade coffee exemplifies the possibilities of a global food governance arrangement that links social and (to a lesser extent) environmental dynamics at the places of production with those at the places of consumption without dissolving global flows. Labelling coffee based on social and environmental criteria by an NGO proves to be an innovative way to organise coffee production and to relate this way of producing coffee to consumer without disregarding the governance in the space of flows. The label offers an interesting hybrid arrangement with participation from civil actors, private firms and governmental and multilateral institutions while including social and environmental considerations into the governance of global trade next to economic considerations. Another interesting aspect of this arrangement is the active participation of the producers (and to a lesser extent of the consumers) in translating general principles of sustainable food production and trade to specific local contexts. A drawback of fair trade labelling concerns the costs involved, because calling in certifying agencies to execute the certification process requires a substantial financial contribution. Even when foreign NGOs cover these costs, the process of certification still demands a large investment in time, which may also create a problem for food producers in developing countries. The weakest point in the fair trade labelling initiative remains, however, its limited direct effect because fair trade coffee only accounts for just 1 per cent of the global coffee trade.

Therefore, in order to stimulate global coffee trade that effectively includes environmental and social considerations and has a larger impact, several social, political and economic actors discuss different future options. The various considerations and governance options can be summarised in three viewpoints, using the theoretical framework elaborated in Chapter 3. According to the first viewpoint, fair trade coffee should be considered as just an additional niche market next to other ones already existing in a highly differentiated consumer market. This approach would not result in any alternative form of governance in the space of places, but instead limit regulation to the conventional coffee network itself, to governance in the space of flows, as is shown in Figure 8.1.

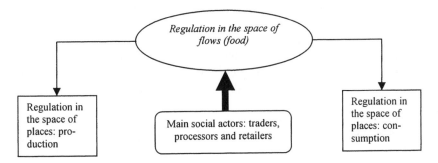

*Figure 8.1   Regulation of coffee in the global market*

According to this approach, the inclusion of global governance arrangements should be very limited, because regulating the (potential) social and environmental consequences of producing and trading coffee should remain the responsibility of the nation-states, and the market parties involved.

The second viewpoint perceives fair trade coffee as fundamentally different from the other existing niches in the global coffee market because the label is based on values of solidarity, ecology and fairness linking southern producers with northern consumers – contrary to conventional relationships dominated by market-based exchanges. According to this view, fair trade coffee tries to find a compromise between ethical principles and the market practices and thereby partly escapes the logic of markets although still functioning to a certain extent within the conventional coffee trade networks (Whatmore and Thorne, 1997; Renard, 1999; Raynolds, 2002).[29] This view is visualised in Figure 8.2, where global food governance is dominated by environmental and social interests at the places of production and consumption, while arrangements in the space of flows remain subordinated to these interests.

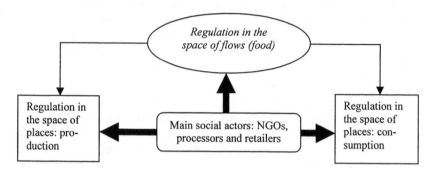

*Figure 8.2     Fair trade-based regulation of the global coffee market*

This view has the advantage of creating an alternative network between the coffee-producers and consumers, but the disadvantage of remaining limited to a rather small portion of the global coffee market. The fair trade NGOs are the central actors supporting this view on the future governance of fair trade coffee.

The third view considers fair trade as an indication of the need for a drastic reorganisation of the international coffee market as a whole, an objective that could be achieved in two different ways. The first strategy would be to include fair trade principles in the existing WTO regulations to achieve global and lasting social and environmental improvements. This suggestion stems from the observation that only a global institution managing the international coffee market can really solve the social and environmental problems (Oxfam, 2002b).[30] Whether such a global government-like approach would possess the necessary flexibility to maintain the global flow of coffee, while facilitating social and environmental governance arrangements and practices at the local level, remains debatable. The second strategy to create fundamental changes in the global coffee market, visualised in Figure 8.3, brings environmental and social interests into the governance arrangements in the space of flows itself through the participation of private actors together with state actors.

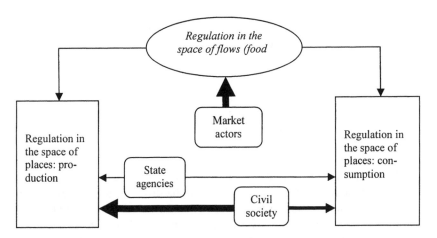

*Figure 8.3    Global trade regulation of coffee*

This way, the existing economic networks are combined with civil societal and governmental networks creating complex linkages within the space of flows and connecting products and prices with communication and the participation of all stakeholders. The combined efforts of national governments, multilateral institutions such as WTO and UNCTAD, private firms and NGOs (or civil society in general) would result in a dynamic form of global governance of the coffee networks which includes different ways of active consumer involvement. Concretely this would require the labelling of all internationally traded coffee to provide consumers with reliable information about the production and trade circumstances involved. Such a label would enable consumers, through their shopping behaviour, to influence indirectly the way in which their coffee is produced. In combination with adequate governmental regulations in the space of places, of production as well as of consumption, this approach would encompass a much larger part of global coffee trade than the existing fair trade initiative.

Several observers claim that this way of combining governance in the space of flows with governance in the space of places is most promising when trying to integrate more fully environmental and social considerations in the regulation of global coffee trade. This arrangement of governing global coffee trade would apply not only formal legal arrangements and private labelling schemes, but also achieve direct collaboration between the different social actors involved.[31]

## MARINE STEWARDSHIP COUNCIL (MSC): GLOBAL ENVIRONMENTAL GOVERNANCE

As already explained in the previous chapter, fish has become, in relative terms, the most worldwide traded food product. Due to a substantial growth in the global marine fish production, from 20 million tonnes in 1950 to over 130 million tonnes in 2001, the global fish stocks are declining because of overfishing. Nowadays, there is nearly universal consensus about the existence of this problem.

The environmental problems caused by overfishing can be divided into the depletion of fish stocks, the reduction of biodiversity and the destruction of natural habitats. Today, some 70 per cent of the world's commercial fisheries are considered fully or over-exploited and only 4 per cent are regarded as under-exploited.[32] Such overfishing is reducing existing fish stocks, and in the end this will inevitably result in lower catches. The levels of by-catch (non-target fish catch) have also reached threatening levels (some 29 million tonnes worldwide), contributing to a further loss of biodiversity. Pollution through processing activities at sea and habitat degradation through trawling and the use of prohibited fishing methods (for example the use of cyanide or dynamite) add to these already existing environmental worries about overfishing. The problems threatening marine fisheries are aggravated by public and industrial waste discharge, tourism, and offshore oil and gas exploitation. The destruction of coastal zones, wetlands and mangrove areas by the growing aquacultural activities is furthermore impairing the role of these areas as natural spawning grounds and nurseries for the necessary replenishment of marine stocks (Garcia et al., 1999). Overfishing results in lower catches and revenues, a process that weakens in particular the position of the approximately ten million small-scale fishermen, who fish for subsistence and provision of the local markets in developing countries. As the competition from often foreign-based commercial fishing vessels is increasing, the number of conflicts between the small-scale (artisanal) fishermen and industrial fishing companies catching large quantities of the already depleting fish stocks is growing as well. These large fishing companies seem to bear little responsibility for the continued sustainability of local fish stocks because they can move easily from one fishing area to another. At the same time, however, their behaviour may lead to the destruction of local fisheries where fish stocks are depleted further and the food security of coastal populations seriously undermined.

In combination, these different trends lead to an increasing pressure on the remaining natural resources and a growing demand for governance interventions to safeguard the remaining fishing resources for the future. Scientists and politicians worldwide conclude that improved fisheries' management to conserve marine biodiversity is becoming essential.[33] As fish trade is globalised, and as both fish stocks and fishing boats move easily across national borders and in international waters, such sustainable fisheries' management necessarily has to be organised globally.[34] Global fisheries' governance has to combine environmental considerations with social as well as economic interests because fish is the primary source of proteins for 950 million people and catching them offers employment to more than 35 million people (Garcia and Willmann, 1999). Regulating global fisheries is, however, rather complicated because fish is an open access resource. 'Fishing grounds are unrestricted "commons" areas and the ownership of a fish is not allocated until the moment of its capture' (Stone, 2002: 290). This particular characteristic of fisheries is the main reason why governing them has remained very limited for a long time. Until the establishment of the 200-mile exclusive economic zones in 1977, oceans formed a common pool resource where everyone had equal fishing rights.[35] However, even after the creation of these exclusive economic zones, the problems of overfishing and the conflicts regarding access to certain fish stocks remained. Multilateral governance seemed indispensable and initially different, FAO-sponsored, international commissions were installed, charged with managing a specific species (for example the International Whaling Commission) or a specific area (Peterson, 1993). Global fisheries' governance started effectively with the creation of the UN Convention on the Law of the Sea (1982), but to date this convention has been implemented only to a very limited extent. (See Appendix 2 for further details.) The 1992 UN Conference on Environment and Development underlined the need to create more effective fisheries' and coastal areas' management regimes. In reaction, the FAO (voluntary) Code of Conduct for Responsible Fisheries (1995) and the UN Fish Stocks Agreement (1995) formulated several guidelines for the protection of existing fish stocks by national governments.[36] However, despite the presence of these different initiatives for global governance of fisheries, their effects remain rather modest because some governments do not seem very committed to implementing and monitoring these suggested guidelines in practice while several other governments lack the capacity to do so. An additional problem is the limited participation from NGOs and other stakeholders in these arrangements (Peterson, 1993).[37] Furthermore, fisheries' issues have remained relatively low on the governments' agendas in general and have attracted little attention from others than those directly involved.[38] Therefore, fish has evolved into a globally traded food product (a global flow of food), without systematic global governance arrangements. However, because this global flow is unsustainable, as is agreed upon almost unanimously, an adequate arrangement for globally governing the production and

trade of fish is urgently needed. In response to this challenge, different suggestions are made, including the systematic labelling of fish.

Some analysts, however, consider the abolition of all fishery subsidies as
the only real solution to the problem of overfishing. During the 2002 Conference on Environment and Development in Johannesburg, fishery subsidies and non-tariff trade barriers were identified as the main causes for depleting fish stocks.[39] 'Subsidies to fishing encourage inefficient producers to
remain in the market and this results in depletion of fisheries' (Gowdy and
Walton, 2003: 7). Equally, during the WTO meeting in Doha in 2001, several members pleaded for the reduction of fisheries' subsidies to spread the
economic and environmental benefits among its members.[40] Other governments, in particular the Japanese, are opposing this thesis as they claim that
inadequate fisheries' management is a more important cause of overfishing
than subsidies.[41] In addition, not all subsidies should be considered as necessarily leading to the same pernicious consequences. Beneficial subsidies
should be distinguished from the trade-distorting ones when they protect the
fish stocks and support the livelihoods of the fishing communities (Dommen, 1999). Reducing the fishery subsidies in the absence of a consistent
global and local governance arrangement of fish production and trade will
most likely only strengthen the global flow character of international fish
trade and not necessarily reduce the negative social and environmental consequences involved.

The creation of the Marine Stewardship Council (MSC) can be regarded
as an interesting attempt towards improving global fisheries management
through more directly linking fish production with fish trade. Unilever and
WWF took the initiative to establish the MSC in 1997, based on the assumption that all actors involved in catching and trading fish in a specific
area will ultimately have a shared interest in guaranteeing the future of their
fishery and thus in developing a common and coherent sustainable management plan. WWF considered improving the sustainability of fisheries by
using a specific label as an interesting opportunity for supporting sustainable development in general and reinforcing other already existing certification schemes in particular.[42] Unilever realised that the future of its commercial fishing activities would be jeopardised in the near future if the threat
from overfishing were not reversed. Initiated by these two global non-state
actors, since 1999 the MSC has evolved into an independent, global non-
profit organisation responsible for the labelling of sustainable fisheries using its own (MSC) label.[43] The objective of the MSC initiative is to bring
environmental, commercial and social interests together by establishing sustainable fisheries.[44] The organisation acknowledges that, although the transition to creating more responsible and sustainable fisheries may initially
lead to a period of reduced catches, a well-elaborated management plan will

ultimately result in the growth of the fish stocks and therefore in better and sustainable yields. The MSC initiative tries to achieve this transition by harnessing 'consumer purchasing power to generate change and promote environmentally responsible stewardship of the world's most important renewable food source' (MSC website).

In order to reward environmentally responsible fishery management and fishing practices, a product label is developed based on general standards for sustainable fisheries. Until August 2004, ten fisheries received the MSC label, of which four were in the UK and the other six in the US, New Zealand, Australia, Mexico, South Africa and Scotland. Fifteen others were undergoing the certifying process: US (6), Australia (2), UK (2), Chile and Canada (2), EU/Norway and Sweden. Finally, another group of 30 fisheries remained in different phases of the certification procedure. Certifying a particular fish stock is a complicated process because of the many interests and the different interpretations of sustainable fisheries that need combining. Some of these difficulties are shown clearly in the example of the New Zealand Hoki (See Box 8. 2).[45]

---

## BOX 8.2   AN EXAMPLE OF THE COMPLICA-
##           TIONS INVOLVED IN MSC LABELLING:
##           THE HOKI CASE

The New Zealand Hoki is a fishery labelled by the MSC-labelling organisation as a sustainable fishery in 2001 and Unilever is selling the fish produced from it as fish fingers (Iglo). From 2005 onwards, Unilever intended to sell only MSC-labelled fish but this aim could only be realised if sufficient certified fish were available (Deere, 1999). As the New Zealand Hoki represents a major global fish stock its labelling is considered crucial. Granting the MSC label to the Hoki fishery has nevertheless been heavily criticised by the New Zealand Royal Forest and Bird Protection Society. Their main objection concerned the killing of seals and albatross by the Hoki fishery. Interestingly enough, although invited to do so, this NGO refused to participate in the certification process itself but criticised the result afterwards. The MSC-labelling organisation replied to this criticism that the labelling was conditional and that several corrective actions will have to be taken by the actors involved in the fishery to retain its certification in the future. In addition, the MSC-labelling organisation claimed that without certification, many of the issues brought up by the New

---

Zealand Royal Forest and Bird Protection Society would remain unresolved. The MSC-labelling organisation thus concluded that the label is not developed to confirm that a fishery is already sustainably managed; but that the actors involved in the fishery are engaged in taking a series of corrective actions towards sustainability that would not have been taken otherwise.

*Source*: Seaweb (2001).

In order to become labelled, fisheries have to introduce specific management arrangements based on the following three general MSC principles. First, a fishery must organise itself in such a way that it does not lead to overfishing or to depletion of the exploited fish population. Second, a fishing operation should allow for the maintenance of the structure, productivity, function and diversity of the ecosystem on which the fishery depends. Finally, a fishery should be subject to an effective management system that respects local, national and international laws and standards while incorporating institutional and operational frameworks that lead to a responsible and sustainable use of the resource. Guided by a certifying agent, who is accredited by the MSC-labelling organisation, these general principles are translated into a concrete and detailed management plan for this specific fishery. In this plan, all actors involved in the fishery agree on the quantity, the way and the timing of catching fish, as well as on the implementation of certain accompanying measures to protect the fish stock. All relevant stakeholders have to participate in the process in order to achieve public and consumer trust in the label. Therefore, for example, certifying agents have agreed to establish contacts with the environmental NGOs concerned and actively request their participation in the process. The MSC-labelling organisation considers support from these environmental NGOs vital 'if our programme is to offer industry the credibility they expect' (MSC, 2002: 1).[46] A notable feature in the labelling process is that governments do not occupy a special position in the certification process and are considered an ordinary participant next to many others. National governments take up the same position as the fishermen or the retailers, underlining the private character of the label. Consumers are more indirectly involved, as the MSC label allows consumers to buy fish caught with care for the environment and the reliability of the label is guaranteed by an independent and private organisation. The MSC-labelling organisation is preparing future public campaigns to inform consumers about the reduced environmental impact of labelled fish products and to encourage retailers to sell fish products that come from sustainably managed and MSC-labelled fisheries. Communication with the general public remains rather limited, as, until now, the market for MSC-labelled fish remains largely restricted to exclusive restaurants and retailers and has not yet entered the mass markets of fish consumers. Entering mass markets for fish consumption, using mass media, would require the availability of larger quantities of certified fish and therefore the certification of more fisheries than is currently the case.

The MSC label is strictly environmental and does not include social or economic criteria because the organisation considers that otherwise labelling, particularly in developing countries, would become too complicated. Inclusion of criteria that demand a higher social and economic performance than required by the prevailing national legislation would bring labelled fisheries into an even more unfavourable position compared with non-labelled fisheries. Even without including such social and economic criteria, MSC labelling has already proved to be very difficult for fisheries in developing countries because the available information about the fish stocks and the fishing practices in these countries is mostly insufficient for the development of a sustainable management plan. In addition, the absence of local expertise forces many developing countries to call on expensive foreign certifying agencies. Therefore, although in theory the MSC label could be a strong incentive to implement environmental improvements for developing countries too, in practice these countries can fulfil the necessary conditions only with great difficulty.[47]

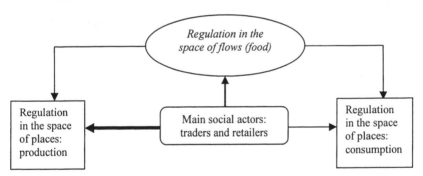

*Figure 8.4   Regulation of fish in the global space of flows*

Therefore, the MSC label can be considered a concrete alternative to the seemingly dominant discourse in institutions like the WTO, where thinking about global governance of fisheries remains limited to a plea for ending fishing subsidies by national governments. When, according to this dominant view, access to fishing resources would be arranged through private instead of through public ownership, sustainability in fisheries would definitely increase (Edwards, 2003). This way of dealing with the global problem of declining fish stocks would leave the governance of particular fishing practices and of global trade in fish as much as possible to the market and the market actors concerned (see Figure 8.4).

The MSC label offers an alternative to this dominant view by introducing a governance arrangement that actively engages all actors concerned in the production of fish. As mentioned before, the formal role of nation-states and governmental institutions in the certification process for the MSC label remains limited, but in practice these authorities generally take up more tasks. National governments have an official obligation to protect the fish stocks within their exclusive economic zones and to co-operate with other governments in the management of shared fish stocks on the high seas (Deere, 1999). In addition, in the practice of the MSC labelling process, only governmental institutions can deliver the necessary scientific data that form the basis for fisheries' management plans, while in some cases governments even finance the MSC certification process itself. Nevertheless, the MSC label can be interpreted as an interesting attempt to introduce an environmental governance arrangement within the local space of place (the fishery) in combination with governance in the global space of flows. The MSC label has its explicit focus on reducing the environmental risks involved in catching fish without ignoring the importance of providing food for the global food market. The fishermen, processors and traders are actively involved in translating the general criteria of the label into concrete guidelines that fit into the local context. Currently, consumer involvement in the MSC label remains limited because the MSC-labelling organisation suggests that first a substantial growth in the production of sustainably labelled fish is necessary before it can become worthwhile to approach consumers on a broader scale. (Figure 8.5 visualises these particular characteristics of the MSC label.)

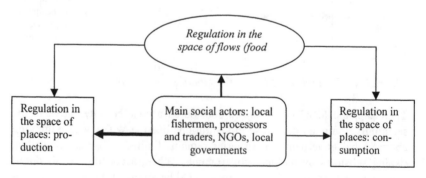

*Figure 8.5   Regulation of fish using the MSC label*

Some commentators criticise the MSC label for its lack of attention to social concerns and for its limited effectiveness in improving the environmental performance of fisheries beyond the few certified ones. A label for sustainable fisheries that would combine social considerations with the existing environmental ones might encourage more active consumer involvement. Such an alternative arrangement could include not only the exclusive, already more sustainable, fisheries but also the still less sustainable, yet improving, fisheries. Building on the example of the fair trade coffee label, a more inclusive certification scheme could be developed such as the fair trade fish label suggested by the Pacific Coast Federation of Fishermen's Associations (Grader et al., 2003). Including the experiences from different labels in an integrated manner is visualised in Figure 8.6.

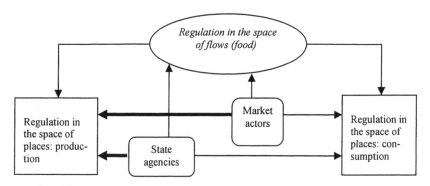

*Figure 8.6    Global regulation of fish in the space of flows and the space of places*

Although such a fair trade approach to the global governance of fish production and trade would be developed in a way comparable to the fair trade coffee label, it still would need to pay comparatively more attention to governing the space of place of production. The large diversity in fishing circumstances and practices, as well as the obligation to include all actors concerned, require labelling organisations to focus especially on translating general principles into local practice.

## CONCLUSION

Private labels and certification schemes represent a new and particularly interesting approach to the problem of regulating global food trade while responding to local environmental and social consequences at the same time. The conceptual model developed in Chapter 3 proved quite helpful to identify the particular role that voluntary labels can play in global food trade. Currently, WTO-guided perspectives dominate approaches to the regulation of international food trade and they essentially aim at governance in the space of flows alone. These approaches are limited to the extent to which they can include social and environmental consequences. In reaction, several NGOs and private companies are developing other regulatory instruments to overcome these limitations. Instruments such as food labels and certification schemes intend to respond more directly with the place-bounded social and environmental impacts of global flows of food without necessarily ending up in some form of de-globalisation. The examples of fair trade coffee and MSC-labelled fish, presented in this chapter, have made clear that privately-initiated food labels and certification schemes can include care for the social and environmental effects of global food production and trade. These NGO-initiated food labels seem more qualified to create the necessary consumer trust in food in contemporary society than governmental or company-controlled labels can. Nevertheless, these NGO-initiated food labels are forced to function in a regulatory context dominated by the WTO-guided approach oriented towards food governance in the space of flows. Although some convergence in codes and monitoring regimes, blurring the conventional regulatory categories, may be underway, there are still critical distinctions between different arrangements (O'Rourke, 2003). Different views exist on issues such as the involvement of different social actors and NGOs, transparency in the results, legitimacy and democracy in decision-making, and strategies for rectifying certain problems. Creating coherence between NGO-initiated and official governmental arrangements is also a challenge. For the moment, it remains unclear how both approaches will interact in the future, but it is unlikely that over time the different NGO-initiated food labels will be incorporated simply into official governmental regulations as suggested by Wessells (1998). As it is also improbable that consumer concerns about the environmental and food safety impact of food will diminish in the near future, it is more likely that various forms of collaboration between governments, private firms and NGOs will remain.

The future role of voluntary food labelling and certification initiatives is not yet fully clear. Some NGOs advocate the expansion of social and environmental standards into one or more open, public standard, yet most corporate actors seem to prefer the privatisation of environmental and social accountability in 'sustainable contracts' that protect retailer power (Mutersbaugh, 2005). O'Rourke (2003) identified the following issues that make the use of voluntary labels and certification schemes in governing global food provision extremely challenging:

- it may be difficult to apply and monitor them consistently because of the long and mobile nature of global food supply chains;
- they may primarily create 'enclaves of sustainability' in the global economy rather than being applied universally;
- they may just provide public relations cover to corporate brands ('green washing');
- they may confuse consumers through a proliferation of labels and certifications;
- they may have unintended negative consequences particularly in developing countries.

Despite the presence of these difficult challenges, non-governmental global food governance arrangements using labels and certification schemes point to promising innovative ways of linking the local social and environmental impact with global food trade. Due to the absence of a global government and due to the presence of strong free trade-promoting institutions like the WTO, it is unlikely that concerns about the local social and environmental impact of producing food will be dealt with adequately in any other way for the near future.

## NOTES

1. See Cashore et al. (2003) for a debate on the certification of timber.
2. SASA (Social Accountability in Sustainable Agriculture) is an initiative from four main social and environmental movements: Fairtrade Labeling Organisation (FLO), Social Accountability International (SAI), Sustainable Agriculture Network (SAN) and the International Federation of Organic Agriculture Movements (IFOAM). See: http://www.isealalliance.org/sasa/
3. Large retailers are necessarily rather sensitive to the demands from NGOs, especially those that attract media attention (Freidberg, 2003).
4. ISO 14001 is one in a larger group of environmental management standards developed by ISO: the ISO 14000 family (1996). ISO 14001: environmental management systems; ISO 14004: general guidelines for environmental management systems; ISO 14010: guidelines for environmental auditing; ISO 14011: procedures for environmental auditing, and ISO 14012: qualification criteria for environmental auditors (ISO, 1998).
5. The general objectives of ISO 14001 are (Boudouropoulos and Arvanitoyannis, 1999):
   - support environmental protection in balance with socio-economic needs;
   - integrate the environmental management system with other management requirements, for example as found in the ISO 9000 series;
   - encourage organisations to consider the implementation of the best available technology for environmental management systems where appropriate and where commercially viable.
   The standard does not state specific environmental performance criteria.
6. The first initiatives were taken by private firms producing branded products, because they wanted an easy way to trace food-borne illnesses to a particular source (Unnevehr and Jensen, 1999).

7.   The direct costs involved in the HACCP certification process vary between €1,600 and €16,000 per firm, depending on the scale of the company and the type of activities (URL: http://www.voedselveiligheid.nl).

8.   For example: since 1995, HACCP is obligatory for producers of meat and fish, and for retailers and restaurants in the Netherlands. The animal fodder industry is applying HACCP only through private initiatives. Currently the Dutch Ministry of Agriculture, Nature and Food Quality intends to introduce HACCP for primary food producers and for slaughterhouses (LNV, 2002).

9.   In the context of globalised food trade there seems to be greater potential for voluntary (or market-based) approaches of food safety than for those oriented to environmental protection where the possible damage is not borne by the users of the final products. 'The efficiency of both the output and the safety decisions of the firm hinges on the information available to both consumers and producers and the likelihood that firms would actually be held liable for damages resulting from a contamination episode' (Segerson, 1999: 67).

10.  Despite the growing popularity of HACCP as the principal instrument for guaranteeing food safety, originally this was never intended, because even if the scheme is introduced following the best guidelines it is still prone to human error and failed execution. Therefore, for food manufacturers additional controls must always be in place (Adams, 2002). Many elements in HACCP are based on the systematic application of the traditional parameters of good management practices and the national regulatory hygiene requirements rather than on an assessment of food-borne risks to the consumer (Hathaway, 1995).

11.  This may be the case for small firms in developed countries as well: a Dutch potato firm has obliged all its suppliers to become HACCP-certified and those without a certificate will receive €0.20 less per kilogram. The firm will cover the costs, €240, during the first year, but after that the suppliers will have to pay themselves. In this case, the amounts are not very high, but it may have further financial consequences when on-farm practices have to be adapted and farmers have to change the ways they are organising their production process (*Oogst*, 2001).

12.  The legitimacy of private company-based forms of governance is a contested issue as well and although this can be established pragmatically through public acceptance of the result, it remains unlikely this solution will satisfy all concerned (Papadopoulos, 2003).

13.  This comment is confirmed by the observation that there seems to be 'an inherent conflict between two necessary conditions for effectiveness in voluntary, market-driven instruments: the need for strong environmental standards and the need for widespread participation of producers' (Gulbrandsen, 2004: 95).

14.  The first International Coffee Agreement was signed in 1962 by most coffee producing and consuming countries. Under the ICA regulatory system (1962–89) a target price (or a price band) for coffee was set and export quotas were allocated to each producing country. When the indicator price calculated by the International Coffee Organisation (ICO) rose over the set price, quotas were relaxed; when it fell below the set price, quotas were tightened. Over the years, the ICA system became increasingly undermined by free-riding and endless discussions about the distribution of quota while the volume of the coffee traded continued to grow, the market became increasingly fragmented and the number of non-member coffee importing countries rose (Ponte, 2001, 2002).

15.  Organisations like the umbrella organisation of coffee producing countries, the Association of Coffee Producing Countries (1993) and the ICO have not been very successful in developing new forms of global regulation. The recent (September 2004) adherence by the US to the International Coffee Organisation might change the situation although much uncertainty remains (ICO; letter from the executive director, September 2004).

16.  Three international trading firms – Neumann, Volcafé and Cargill – control around one-third of the world market in coffee. Four large roasters are dominating the world market for coffee processing: Kraft Foods/Philip Morris, Nestlé, Sara Lee and Procter & Gamble. Recently retailers have also gained a more prominent role in the organisation of the coffee markets in developed countries.

17.  The rapid increase in coffee production in Vietnam has been an important driver for the growth of global coffee production. The country's coffee exports rose by 400 per cent

during the 1990s and today Vietnam has become the world's second-largest coffee exporting nation.

18. Ponte (2002) distinguishes seven environmental and socio-economic standards, both voluntary (NGO-based) and private (enterprise initiatives). UNCTAD and IISD (2003) identify two additional private eco-labels for coffee. In general, product standards are likely to have re-distributive effects because larger estates are often better able (through their financial resources and their managerial and technical skills) than smaller farmers to respond to the specific requirements. In addition, it is easier for buyers to have to deal with firms offering large quantities of coffee produced according to the requested standards than being forced to contact many farmers each producing only small quantities.

19. The coffee-hulling process, which largely takes place in the production areas, has also considerable negative environmental impacts. 'Wet processing techniques, which are used for approximately 40 per cent of the global production, generate large quantities of polluted waste water' (with a BOD of 150 g/l) (UNCTAD and IISD, 2003: 5). Drying the coffee beans after hulling requires large quantities of timber and thereby contributes to deforestation. See also Dünckmann and Mayer (2002).

20. The total production capacity of the co-operatives in the fair trade register is estimated at 363,000 tonnes.

21. The national members of FLO in several western European countries manage and promote the fair trade label on a daily base while FLO is co-ordinating and monitoring this in order to assure global uniformity and reliability in the label (Oxfam, 2002a).

22. Since 1988 more than €26 million has been transferred to coffee farmers above the world market prices from sales in the Netherlands alone (Roozen and Van der Hoff, 2001).

23. Max Havelaar guarantees the following minimum prices for coffee: Arabica coffee 126 dollar cents per pound (456 grams) and Robusta coffee 112 dollar cents per pound (Roozen and Van der Hoff, 2001).

24. Most consumers assume that ethically produced goods have a positive human as well as ecological impact (Blowfield, 1999).

25. The European Commission (1999) demands that EU member states follow their obligations within the WTO considering the introduction of regulatory mechanisms based on fair trade principles. Only when fair trade initiatives remain private and operate through voluntary participation can they be considered consistent with a non-discriminatory multilateral trading system.

26. Fair trade labels strive to re-establish consumer trust in the origin and content of their food, attesting that items have been produced outside of the conventional agro-industrial system that is considered responsible for recent food scares and widespread environmental degradation. Consumers buy fair trade products for reasons of health, environment and animal welfare and to support people in developing countries (Browne et al., 2000).

27. Although producer groups are involved in setting the certification standards, the use of these quality standards and the certification process itself may reflect existing North/South power relations.

28. For example the export co-operative La Central in Honduras is exporting 9,200 tons of coffee of which only 7 per cent is fair traded because market demand is limited. (Interview with Tatiana Lara, consultant at La Central.)

29. Raynolds (2002) claims that the market success of fair trade-labelled products is also tied to the deployment of industrial conventions rooted in formal standards, inspections, certifications and public conventions based on the increasing recognition of fair trade labels. Fair trade shortens the social distance between Southern producers and Northern consumers and this is realised in a continued tension and with recurrent conflicts between: (1) traditional commercial and industrial conventions, rooted in price competition, bureaucratic efficiency, product standardisation and formal certification, and (2) alternative domestic and civic conventions, rooted in trust, equality, global social and environmental responsibility, collective effort and society wide benefits. Raynolds also underlines the difference between fair trade and other voluntary certification schemes that attempt to regulate ecological and production conditions internationally because these schemes fail to engage in creating alternative patterns of economic co-ordination and instead rely on

commercial conventions. Hughes (2005), in his study on ethical trade, points to the continued embeddedness of such standards and codes within the existing corporate strategies and management systems. The multiplicity of corporate strategies and management systems is therefore generating a highly uneven geography of governance practices in the context of global commodity chains.

30. See, for example, the sustainable commodity initiative launched by UNCTAD and IISD to improve the social, environmental and economic sustainability of commodity production and trade by developing global multi-stakeholder strategies on a sector-by-sector basis. Identification of strategies for the coffee sector is part of the first phase of this initiative (UNCTAD and IISD, 2003).

31. However, if such a form of regulation is to become reality in the future, the WTO should accept, contrary to its current approach, the inclusion of environmental and social concerns as an integrated aspect of global trade regulation deserving particular attention by market partners, governments and civil society organisations.

32. The concept of 'fisheries' refers to a combination of the stock of a certain fish species in a specific area with the fishermen trying to catch (part of) this stock.

33. Technological innovations have a radical impact on the human fishing capacities. For example: 'in an hour, one factory ship could haul in as much cod (around a hundred tonnes) as a typical boat of the sixteenth century could land in a season' (MSC: Fish Facts).

34. Registration of fishing vessels under the jurisdiction of certain countries (flags) that do not or cannot comply with international regulations is an example of this globalisation process. In the past this practice already existed to evade taxes and labour requirements, but now evasion of environmental regulations is becoming an additional motivation (Garcia and Willmann, 1999).

35. Before 1977, countries had jurisdiction over just a narrow band of water outside their coast, usually three nautical miles wide.

36. The centrepiece in the (voluntary) FAO code of conduct for responsible fisheries (1995) is the creation of exclusive use rights combined with political institutions and economic instruments to protect the resource base (Garcia et al., 1999).

37. Scientific advice is playing a central role in policy initiatives and this may lead to fundamental changes in the policy guidelines; see the shift from measures based on 'maximum sustainable yield', via 'optimal yield' to 'multispecies management' (Peterson, 1993).

38. For example, within the WTO, fish was excluded explicitly in the Uruguay Round and therefore no specific WTO regulations exist for fish as they do for agriculture.

39. Governments present at the Earth Summit in Johannesburg, 2002, reached an agreement, although not legally binding, to restore fish stocks to a sustainable level by 2015 (Reuters, 30 August, 2002).

40. The FAO estimated the economic loss resulting from these subsidies at US$54 billion (Stone, 2002: 293).

41. See, for example a submission on 24 April, 2003 by Japan to the WTO Committee on Trade and Environment (WT/CTE/W/226) protesting against automatic prohibition of certain fisheries' subsidies. Japan claims that the possible effects of subsidies on resources depend on the specific resource status of the fisheries concerned and on the present fishery management regimes.

42. The following operational principles have been identified by a panel of experts to integrate trade, development and environmental policies (WWF, 1999):
   • Efficiency;
   • Equity;
   • Ecosystem Integrity;
   • Good Governance;
   • Stakeholder Participation and Responsibility;
   • International Co-operation.

43. Other labels used in fisheries are: 'mark of origin', 'dolphin safe', 'organic seafood', 'marine aquarium council (MAC)' and ISO 14000 (Deere, 1999).

44. The definition developed for *sustainable fishing* is: a fishery conducted in such a way, that:

- it can be continued indefinitely at a reasonable level;
- it maintains, and seeks to maximise, ecological health and abundance;
- it maintains the diversity, structure and function of the ecosystem on which it depends as well as the quality of its habitat, minimising the adverse effects that it causes;
- it is managed and operated in a responsible manner, in conformity with local, national and international laws and regulations;
- it maintains present and future economic and social options and benefits;
- it is conducted in a socially and economically fair and responsible manner.

45. See also Greenpeace Germany's (2000) statement that the MSC criteria are much too weak to contribute really to sustainable fisheries, and in particular that no fisheries should be certified when endangered species are caught as well like in the case of the New Zealand Hoki.
46. The participation of WWF is used by the MSC-labelling organisation as an argument against the criticism that their standards are too low or that the certificate is granted too easily.
47. WWF is elaborating a methodology for community based fisheries certification. Community based fisheries certification maximises the use of local knowledge and is based on partnership with the local fishing communities. (See the WWF Endangered Seas Campaign 2000.)

# 9. Conclusions

Erst kommt das Fressen dann kommt die Moral.
Erst muss es möglich sein auch armen Leuten,
Vom grossen Brotlaib sich ihr Teil zu schneiden.
(Bertold Brecht (1928) in 'Denn wovon lebt der Mensch' from *Die Dreigro-schenoper*)

Taking action: voting with forks.
Our overabundant food system, a result as well as a cause of our flourishing economy, gives most of us the opportunity to make a political statement every time we eat – and to make a difference.
(Nestle, 2002: 372)

## INTRODUCTION

This book began by observing that, in the context of global modernity, the organisation of food production and consumption is changing as well. A consequence of these changes is that previously unknown risks and concerns are emerging while conventional nation-state-based regulatory practices can no longer satisfactorily deal with food-related risks and concerns, either old or new. Therefore, innovative governance arrangements are needed to achieve more environmental effectiveness and social justice in global food provisioning. Identifying such innovative global food governance arrangements and reviewing them were the main objectives of this book. The theoretical basis for this study was provided by Castells' concept of the global network society, as this framework facilitated our understanding of the dynamics in food production and consumption in contemporary global modern society. The central question that guided the empirical research was therefore to identify innovative governance arrangements that deal more adequately with contemporary food-related concerns than the conventional nation-state-based regulations do. Through different case studies, the ways in which such innovative global food governance arrangements aimed at combining the regulation of global food supply and local environmental and social impacts were reviewed. Effective contemporary governance arrangements have to involve different social actors in multiple roles and therefore particular attention has been paid in this study to the changing role of the nation-state, market parties and civil society organisations. The case studies also facilitated our insight into the ways in which these emerging global food governance arrangements deal with multiple definitions of food quality, allow consumers to choose food produced with the inclusion of particular social, environmental and health concerns and (re-)establish consumer trust in contemporary food provision.

The four case studies presented here offer clear indications for the emergence of innovative global food governance arrangements, exemplified in the initiatives taken by different private and non-governmental social agencies that supplement but also compete with conventional nation-state-based food regulations. This final chapter is intended to reflect on the main conclusions of these case studies. The chapter starts by summarising the outcomes of the different empirical chapters. The following section builds on these outcomes to improve our understanding of these phenomena by making use of the sociology of flows. After discussing the changing roles of several social agents in innovative global governance arrangements, the chapter concludes with an epilogue providing some suggestions for future research.

## KEY CHANGES IN FOOD GOVERNANCE: CONCLUSIONS FROM THE CASE STUDIES

Chapters 5–8 presented the results of the four case studies that clearly illustrated the fundamental changes taking place in food provision within global modernity. Moreover, these case studies also indicated the difficult challenges facing contemporary global food governance and provided examples of different initiatives taken to respond to these challenges.

Globalisation has become a driving force in changing food production and processing practices in many parts of the world. Despite the fact that the international food trade still represents only a limited part of global food production, the impacts of this globalisation process are nevertheless nearly universal and radical. As demonstrated in Chapter 7, for example, Thai shrimp farming may continue to be organised within the local system of land ownership, regulated by local and national politics, and applying the locally available technology. At the same time, however, the actual shrimp production practices in Thailand cannot be understood without referring to the dynamics in the global shrimp market, the involvement of international NGOs and the international politics on food safety. For example, changes in Thai shrimp farming practices today are linked closely to the drop in shrimp production in Ecuador, to the growing worries among shrimp processing and trading firms in Europe about their consumer image, to consumer actions in the Netherlands protesting the destruction of mangrove forests and to other developments in different parts of the world.[1]

Because of the process of globalisation, contemporary food production and consumption practices are changing, while the risks and concerns associated with these evolving practices are displaying novel characteristics as well. During the BSE crisis, analysed in Chapter 5, governments in Western Europe were surprised by the unexpected side effects of the modernisation process in beef production and processing. Another example is the scientific uncertainty about the possible longer-term effects of producing and consuming GM food, which made the public debates on the international regulation of GM food rather complex (see Chapter 6).

While the potential effects of contemporary food risks seem to increase, the capacities of national governments to respond effectively to them only seem to diminish. Science is no longer able to produce final and undisputed solutions to these newly emerging kinds of food problems or to provide unambiguous guidance to governmental regulations. The search for alternative solutions to certain contemporary food problems has even undermined the previously existing certainties that were contained in the conventional nation-state- and science-based food risk policy. In the case of BSE, a complex and dynamic process of interaction between scientific, political and social agencies in different countries and between various conventional and innovative national and EU-level food safety regulations emerged, leading to new regulatory responses. One striking result was the introduction of the precautionary principle in EU food regulation, which fundamentally changed the role of scientific evidence and allowed the use of non-scientific considerations in deciding on regulatory arrangements. It was in particular this precautionary principle that later on led to intense debates with the US authorities on how to regulate GM food. US food safety authorities, private companies and several scientific experts accused the EU of obscuring the previously clear relationship between science and politics because using the precautionary principle opens the possibility for using non-scientific arguments in the regulation of food.

The problem of balancing economic interests, food safety worries and environmental concerns raises difficult challenges for contemporary food politics. Moreover, besides the absence of clear scientific guidance in defining political measures regarding food, national governments no longer have the capacity to control contemporary food provisioning fully. Today, food risks may be the result of particular food production and processing practices occurring at large distances in space and time from the places of consumption. Moreover, governmental regulations in one country may lead to unexpected consequences in other parts of the world. For example, the public and political discussions between the US and the EU authorities on GM food regulation resulted in intense conflicts about the presence of genetically modified maize in the food aid delivered for the starving populations of countries in Southern Africa.

All case studies clearly showed the growing involvement of non-state actors in the debates on food governance arrangements in global modernity. However, the solutions to the problems facing contemporary food provision suggested by these non-state actors showed an enormous diversity. Some commentators, for example, considered the BSE crisis an indication of the presence of fundamental flaws in the modern industrial way of producing food in Western European countries, and only radical de-modernisation of agriculture could provide an adequate solution for this problem. Others suggested that further modernisation through adaptations in production and processing practices, the use of innovative technologies and more intensive governmental control through labelling and through monitoring and tracing of beef could offer the necessary environmental and food safety assurances required. Guided by such divergent suggestions, increasingly non-state social actors became involved in contemporary food governance arrangements in different ways. Food labelling schemes initiated by NGOs (see Chapter 8) are a clear example of the development of innovative global food governance arrangements. Such food labels facilitate the inclusion of particular requirements for food production and trade practices going beyond the labelling of product characteristics only, as is done in most governmental regulations because they are restricted by the WTO framework.

The globalisation of food production and consumption, the emergence of new food risks, the limits to conventional nation-state-based regulation and the growing involvement of non-state actors in food policy debates and regulatory practices form a complex challenge to food governance in global modernity. This situation has evoked a confusingly large variety of different responses to regulate global food provision. A clear example of this confusion is the diversity in attempts to govern aquaculture (see Chapter 7). Future marine fisheries are endangered by the worldwide declining fish stocks, but if and under what conditions aquaculture will be able to fill the gap between the increasing consumer demand for fish and the diminishing supply remains unclear. While some NGOs are protesting against modern aquaculture in general because they consider this a principally unsafe and unsustainable activity, other NGOs are trying to encourage the consumption of fish from more sustainable sources by introducing guides to orient consumer behaviour. At the same time, aquaculture producer organisations are promoting different codes of conduct to contribute to more sustainable fish production, while several national governments use the instrument of spatial planning to ensure more sustainability in aquaculture. The situation becomes even more confusing because although, for producers, fish from aquaculture may be clearly distinguishable from fish produced through capture fisheries, they merge into one different category of globally traded fish for most consumers.

The case of aquaculture makes perfectly clear how the already existing confusion about contemporary food governance arrangements is complicated further by the engagement of different social actors. Past certainties about food regulation seem to have disappeared as well as most consistency in the resulting regulatory arrangements. How can we make sense of this confusion where various levels, actors and responsibilities overlap and a growing variety of food governance arrangements is being introduced? How can the pressing and diversified demands for global food governance be responded to against the background of diminishing state power? How can innovative governance arrangements adequately cover multiple qualities and risks related to more diverging food flows distantiated in time and space and thereby include more actors from more different backgrounds (North–South, consumers, producers, private companies, NGOs, governments, and so on)?

## GOVERNING FOOD IN GLOBAL MODERNITY: THEORETICAL REFLECTIONS

One clearly identifiable reaction to this confusion about global food governance, and to the potentially negative consequences of globalising food provision in general, is to redirect the modernisation process towards local provisioning of food. This way, the specificity and certainty of locally or regionally organised food production and consumption will replace the fluidity and risks of a globalised food supply. Creating short food supply chains would re-establish direct contacts between producers and consumers and thereby reduce the environmental, health and social impacts of globalised food production and consumption. In addition, such a process of localisation (or regionalisation) would encourage (regional and seasonal) diversity in food products and even reduce the need for using most modern conservation technologies.

However, regionalisation does not necessarily provide the only adequate response to the negative impacts of globalising food provision. First, because large quantities of food are already traded globally, re-creating short food supply chains does not seem a realistic option for the immediate future. It remains quite unlikely that consumers in richer countries will be prepared to forego many of the food items coming from all over the globe that they are able to consume today. Second, many propositions for the creation of short food supply chains seem biased towards the food producers and are intended to counter the trend towards declining farmers' incomes, while a genuine inclusion of the consumers' interests remains questionable. Shortening the physical distance between the food producer and consumer, and building personalised trust between both social actors, requires intensive face-to-face interaction and it seems rather unrealistic to expect consumers to spend the time needed for such interaction routinely with all the different regional producers involved in providing their food. Most likely, this remains an option for a few selected food products only. Finally, a fundamental problem in designating short food supply chains as the only adequate response to the complex problems resulting from the globalising supply of food is the conflation of rather diverse concerns (environmental, food safety, socio-economic, ethical, animal welfare) into the single and conventional dimension of physical distance.[2] The distance between man and nature is growing through the process of industrialisation and the formation of increasingly complex food supply chains in global modernity. Therefore, distance should be seen here as social distance covering different dimensions. For example, the socio-economic concerns promoting fair trade cannot be understood without paying attention to the growth of NGOs and different mass media, which facilitate communication between people living at large distances. In addition, even food supply, which is organised locally, is influenced by worldwide dynamics of price, quality and taste. However, in many suggestions for localization in food provision, this social distance is equated with the physical distance between the producer and consumer.[3] Therefore, the intuitively attractive identification of localisation and de-modernisation as the most adequate response to the problems of globalising food provisioning can be questioned seriously.

If regionalisation is not necessarily the only or the best response to the challenges offered by global food supply, alternative solutions have to be identified; solutions that are capable of effectively contributing to more sustainable and socially just global food provisioning. Governing globalised food supply, or global food circuits (Van der Meulen, 2000), necessitates more than simply adding a new global-level governance arrangement to the existing local and national ones. Although the nation-state is not becoming redundant, state agencies alone, be it at the national or international level, cannot sufficiently fulfil the task of regulating global food supply by themselves (Held et al., 1999; Held, 2004). As the discussion in Chapter 4 on the regulations for global food trade developed within the WTO framework has made clear, nation-state-based food governance arrangements are severely restricted in the kind of concerns that they can include, while these arrangements are also limited in the possibilities they allow for public participation. Nation-state-based responses are not able to deal adequately with the complex interactions taking place between practices organised at the global level in the space of flows and the different and particular production, trade and consumption practices structured in the local space of places. Thus, if a process of de-modernisation or localisation is insufficient and hardly realistic, and if global governmental arrangements in the space of flows alone are too restricted, alternative global food governance arrangements become necessary in responding adequately to the challenges facing modern food supply.

During the 1980s and the 1990s, the diminishing regulatory capabilities of the nation-state were generally explained by pointing at the increasing strength of market actors *vis-à-vis* state actors and this trend was considered the consequence of globalisation. As discussed in Chapters 2 and 3, however, to conceptualise the contemporary practices of global actors like TNCs and NGOs and the incapacity of nation-states to balance their power more accurately, innovative concepts and research methods are necessary, a sociology of global flows going beyond society (Urry, 2000b). In order to offer adequate responses to the present challenges, global food governance arrangements have to acknowledge that in the global space of flows, food provisioning has become increasingly disembedded from the place- and time-boundedness of local space and more and more re-embedded in global flows without direct references to concrete co-ordinates in space and time (Castells, 1996, 1997, 1998; Urry, 2003). At the same time, promising approaches to identify global food governance arrangements will have to recognise that most food-production practices, as well as certain food consumption practices, remain structured within the space of place. Therefore, governing the particular material and local impacts of food production and consumption cannot be structured in the space of flows alone. Dynamics within both spheres of structuring space and time should not be disconnected because there is ongoing interdependence, exchange and interrelationship in terms of the material flows themselves as well as in the networks involved in governing these material flows. In addition, global food flows should not be reified because they meander via interventions from (although are not necessarily fully controlled by) purposeful social actors (Gille, 2006). Therefore, adequate global food governance arrangements have to manage the material and informational flows of food at the global level and, at the same time, relate the functioning of these global food flows to the specific local environmental and social impacts of producing, processing, retailing and consuming food whereby different social actors are involved. Governing food in the global network society is therefore necessarily more complicated than in the sovereign nation-states of the past because it involves a wider variety of social actors and deals with more and more different issues (Buttel et al., 2006). (See Figure 9.1.)

Consequently, food governance arrangements in global modernity have to combine the two distinctive ways in which time and space are structured in order to contribute to more sustainable and socially just food provisioning. In order to achieve this objective, global food governance arrangements have to manage the material and non-material flows of food within the different dynamics of time and space simultaneously and involve all relevant social actors.

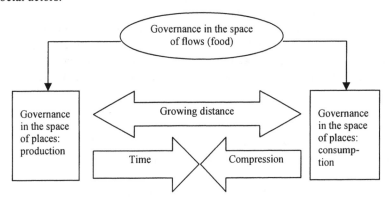

*Figure 9.1  Combining food governance in the global space of flows and the space of places*

An interesting category of the currently emerging innovative global food governance arrangements aims at offering standardised information to the consumers about the practices involved in producing, processing and trading the food they buy. These arrangements try to combine governance in the space of flows with governance in the space of places with the help of certification and labelling schemes. The information about production practices offered this way is not necessarily limited to product-related characteristics but can also address other producer and consumer concerns. These global food governance arrangements, such as food labels, offer transparency about the production process, traceability of the food product throughout the supply chain and verifiability of the standards and criteria applied.[4] Food labels create previously non-existing connections between different (producer and consumer) concerns and different (governmental and non-governmental) social actors. Diversified (varying in terms of priorities and specific choices) consumer concerns are dealt with through these (subpolitical) arrangements. This way, food labels link the space of flows with the space of places and define different scapes. The examples of fair trade coffee and MSC-labelled fish, analysed in the previous chapter, underline the growing influence of these food-labelling arrangements. Authority and power in such approaches are distributed in an indistinguishable way among food producers, processors, traders and consumers along the supply chain. In particular, large private companies, such as supermarket chains and transnational food processing firms, take up more and more prominent roles in these initiatives.[5] Besides private companies, international NGOs claiming to represent food producers and/or consumers are also becoming driving forces behind different certification and labelling schemes. This way, these innovative global food governance arrangements contribute to a situation in which nation-states no longer have the conventional full authority over international food trade (Schaeffer, 1995; Dicken et al., 2001).[6] The rapid spread of food labelling practices over the last ten years suggests a further proliferation of such global food governance arrangements in the coming years.

## CHANGING ROLES OF SOCIAL ACTORS IN INNOVATIVE GOVERNANCE ARRANGEMENTS

The growth in the number of innovative arrangements, attempting to contribute to increased sustainability in global food provision, points at the changing roles of the different social actors involved in global food governance. In particular, the roles of the nation-state, consumers and scientists in the governance of the global food supply are being transformed.

Despite the recent institutional reforms in the regulation of food (Lang and Heasman, 2004), individual nation-states can no longer adequately respond to contemporary food problems. Although sovereign nation-states remain essential, at least in providing legal security for private initiatives, they are often unable to implement measures effectively. It is no longer realistic for sovereign nation-states to deal with the regulation of food independently from other states and different social actors. Increasingly, problems do cross borders and, even when they seem to have only a domestic character at first, they may ultimately prove insoluble within the national borders (Wapner, 1998). The case study of BSE demonstrated how national authorities in the UK initially tried to solve the problem internally by introducing a national regulation based on unequivocal scientific advice. However, when the crisis spread to other countries in Western Europe, these governments were force to solve the problem jointly within the European Union. Moreover, developing national solutions independently from neighbouring countries was excluded because of the legal requirements to guarantee the functioning of the common market within the EU. Increasingly therefore, nation-states are forced to refrain from independent decision-making in the case of contemporary food concerns and to refer to roles such as mediator and facilitator to help the development and effective implementation of adequate common EU food governance arrangements. As shown in Chapter 6, the EU did replace its initial strictly science-based approach to the common regulation of GM food by a much more open approach making it possible to introduce wider public concerns. In the Netherlands, as well as in several other European countries, the government initiated a public debate on GM food to address widespread popular concerns about the potential risks involved. Through the organised exchange of opinions between different social actors, the government hoped to increase support for the regulatory approach chosen. In the case of MSC labelling, nation-states might facilitate the certification process itself, but they are treated as one of the many stakeholders during the actual implementation of the certification process. The importance of the roles of mediator and facilitator taken up by nation-states becomes even clearer in the growing need to operate through international networks in order to create effective global food governance arrangements. The density of such networks may be strong, as in the case of the EU, or less so, as in the case of the WTO or the CBD.

Adequate innovative global food governance necessarily involves non-state actors, resulting in various non-exclusive, non-hierarchical, post-territorial, adaptive and flexible arrangements (Goverde and Nelissen, 2002; Karkkainen, 2004). Civil society organisations constitute an interesting category among these non-state agencies.[7] NGOs are capable of building trust between different actors in the food chain over long distances in time and space. In doing so, NGOs are complementing, and sometimes even replacing, nation-state agencies in legitimising certain food supply chains and food policies. NGOs initiated the public debates in the EU on the import of GM food from the US, and international environmental NGOs, such as Greenpeace and Friends of the Earth, incited consumer boycotts and public protests against these products. These protests fitted in with the already existing consumer concerns about food safety and resounded broadly in the media, so these NGOs exercised a clear influence, resulting in essential changes in the regulatory arrangements for GM food within the EU. The involvement of civil society organisations in global governance arrangements for food will probably become more important in the future as the restricted global governmental institutions will increasingly be less able to fill the growing gap between the global flows of food and the nation-state-based regulatory mechanisms. Civil society engagement may take different forms and does not necessarily have to be institutionalised in the dense and formal approach characteristic for nation-state-based regulations.

Another interesting category of non-state actors engaged in innovative global food governance arrangements is the consumers. Their involvement shows that citizenship and consumerism can no longer be considered opposing practices and discourses (Spaargaren and Martens, 2005).[8] Today no clear boundaries can be drawn easily around what should be called 'public' citizenship and what 'private' consumerism. In their consumer role, critical citizens practice new forms of action, outside the formal political arena within the 'sub-political' sphere (Beck, 1992). As the case of fair trade coffee made clear, critical food consumers use their shopping-bag power to make conscious choices in their everyday lives, thereby directly addressing the organisation of the market and combining public and private aspects of altruism. A particular category of coffee is offered to the consumers with the inclusion of specific meanings (regarding ecology, solidarity, fairness, and so on) that go beyond the objectively verifiable characteristics of the coffee itself. By using such a label, new social relationships are being built between the coffee producers and consumers that go beyond the economic relationship of buyer and seller.[9] Consumer engagement in governing the global supply of food is therefore not necessarily only based on product prices or 'objective' information about the composition of food products, but may also comprise much more intangible issues such as 'trust', 'social justice' and 'quality'. However, different groups of consumers may deal with these dimensions in different ways, making one homogeneous and universal global food governance arrangement based on consumer concerns rather elusive.

Finally, contemporary global food governance arrangements are characterised by ambivalence and ambiguity in the ways in which they deal with the (potential) risks involved (Grove-White et al., 1997; Halkier, 2001). This ambivalence is, at least in part, a consequence of the changing role of science in global modernity. Today, the complexity and 'invisibility' of certain food risks require the use of scientific instruments to guide regulatory arrangements and orient consumer behaviour.[10] However, modern science cannot offer the clear guidance for governmental regulations and consumer behaviour that is traditionally expected from it. Even when a widely accepted scientific agreement about a particular food risk exists, as was the case in the early stage of the BSE crisis, tragically reality may prove otherwise. The absence of general agreement between scientists about the presence of potential, sometimes long-term, risks involved in producing or consuming certain food products makes science-based governance arrangements even more problematic. Scientists may differ in their views on the existence and eventual consequences of certain food-related risks, but also in their opinion on whether socio-economic or ethical considerations should be included in food policy making as well. Interestingly, the GM food case also showed how the impact of science on food policy making depends not necessarily only on the results of scientific research but also on the relative influence of the discursive and regulatory networks of which different scientists form part. Through these networks, scientists engage with other state and non-state actors to influence food governance arrangements effectively.

## EPILOGUE

Globalisation in food production and consumption is not simply the upscaling of food provision practices from the past. The process of globalisation in general is not just adding another layer to social reality, but is fundamentally transforming a wide range of social practices at different layers at the same time. Simply adding another level of governance will therefore not adequately solve the problems related to food production and consumption in global modernity. The different layers in the social reality of global modernity are mutually connected and, next to their internal dynamics, interaction between them takes place. This study has shown the usefulness of the 'flows' concept in understanding these interactions in the case of food. However, more empirical research and further conceptual clarification is needed to better comprehend and analyse current and future dynamics in global food governance arrangements.

An empirical challenge is to identify and study different innovations in global food governance arrangements dealing with the impacts of global flows of food. This way our understanding of varying ways to balance the interests of state and non-state actors, and of market and non-market actors, operating at different levels, can be improved. Furthermore, the ways in which global food governance arrangements can deal with the wide diversity and variability in food-related concerns among consumers should be better examined. In doing so, it is important to realize that convergence between the different consumer concerns should not be considered evident or even necessary. How are hierarchies among different consumer concerns established? In addition, how is the co-ordination between these concerns organised within the global food supply chains? Particular attention should be paid to identify ways in which consumer concerns, which cannot be expressed through the market mechanism because of a lack of buying power, are dealt with. There is a real danger that only the concerns of the richer consumers are dealt with, while the poor may suffer dramatic consequences.

Another challenging future task is to elaborate the actor-orientedness in the sociology of flows further. Arrangements intended to govern global flows of food are infused constantly with the interests and cultures of the affected actors at various levels. Different flows of food exhibit different dynamics, enabling the facilitation and/or blockage of flows by social actors in different ways. Better understanding of the differences between the dynamics in various flows of food and how different (networks of) social actors deal with them would facilitate the analysis of power relations in the sociology of flows.

Finally, a last but very important future task is to improve our understanding of the relationships between the changes in social (food-related) practices occurring simultaneously at the global, regional, national and local levels. The concept of 'global attractor' (Urry, 2003) might offer a helpful tool to this end. A global attractor would operate as a sort of centre of gravity within the range of different social practices. A particularly interesting research question would then be to study to what extent 'the virtual European green consumer' is becoming a global attractor influencing food production practices and governance arrangements in many parts of the world at the same time.

## NOTES

1.  In November 2004, Milieudefensie (Friends of the Earth, The Netherlands) and Novib (Oxfam, the Netherlands) launched a public campaign called 'Het tragische verhaal achter de tropische garnaal' ('the tragic story behind tropical shrimp'). Through this campaign these organisations asked consumers to put pressure on their supermarkets, fishmongers and restaurants to assure that the shrimp they sell are produced with respect for 'man and the environment'.
2.  Even in the case of short food supply chains, distance may be problematic, as the research done by Teng et al. (2004) made clear. The distance between farmers' markets and their home may impede consumers from buying cheese at these markets.
3.  Moreover, even justifying short food supply chains by pointing at the reduction of energy use, because less transport is required (less 'food miles'), may not be as straightforward as initially thought. The way in which consumers transport their food from the shopping location to their home may drastically change the overall environmental impact of food production and consumption as only a full lifecycle analysis will show. As Pretty et al. conclude, 'proximity alone may not be a good measure of sustainability, as a journey on water has a lower impact than a shorter one by road' (2005: 16).
4.  In order to be successful, certification schemes should be objective, based on measurable crop-specific standards, developed on the basis of a consultative process with considerable transparency and room for public comment and discussion and furthermore be driven by major actors in the market chain (governments, retailers and manufacturers) (Clay, 2004; Gulbrandsen, 2004). The absence of global harmonisation and co-ordination agencies may lead to competition between different schemes.
5.  This concentration of power over the food system in private companies is becoming remarkable whether one looks nationally, regionally or globally (Lang, 2003). However, the importance of these large private corporations should not cause us to lose sight of the limits to their power in global modernity. The absence of formal and legal structures at the global level, for example, complicates the operation of large multinational corporations because, despite their power, they are never sure they cannot be criticised/commented upon by other social actors. For example, their image can be damaged very rapidly by effective NGO campaigns (Beck and Willms, 2004; Lang, 2003).
6.  Alternative approaches try to establish trust within the space of flows through direct information exchange between consumers and producers with the help of modern means of communication. See, for example, information provided by webcams such as seen on

URL: http://www.petersfarm.com/NL/. Other examples are coffee that can be traced back to the producers based on the (end of sale) date: URL: http://www.ah.nl/perla/herkomst.jsp?id=209786&trg=perla/herkomst and the tool developed to trace the complete supply chain for clothing produced under sustainable and fair trade conditions: URL: http://www.ontmoetdemakers.nl/start_flash.html.

7.  The formation of a global civil society is not restricted to the citizens of the developed Western societies, but today includes many individuals and organisations from the South as well (Dwivedi, 2002; Dalton et al., 2003; Sassen, 2004). Although *the* global civil society remains a fuzzy and contested concept, it can be comprehended as a sphere of ideas, values, institutions, organisations, networks and individuals located between the family, the state and the market and operating beyond the confines of national societies, polities and economies (Diamond, 1996; Anheier et al., 2001a, 2001b, 2002; Lipschutz and Fogel, 2002; Tews et al. 2003).

8.  Conventional national citizenship may become undermined by the emerging global network society but it is not being replaced simply and fully by global citizenship. It seems that a wide variety of different citizenships is coming about (c.f. citizenships of flows, Urry, 2000b). Citizenship is thus no longer restricted to the domain of formal politics alone and may involve other practices as well, representing an enlargement of the modern political repertoire (Held, 1987, 2004). The rights and duties of citizenship in the space of flows can be instantiated through global arrangements, but also in many everyday decisions from consumers, such as the ones about what food to buy today (Halkier, 1999; Held, 2004).

9.  Consumer behaviour is not determined by factual knowledge alone, or by changes in (relative) prices. Many socio-cultural elements other than economic considerations play a role in everyday decision-making by consumers.

10.  This problem is particularly aggravating in attempts to establish national regulations because there seems to be a gap between the narrowly reductionist, one-product-at-a-time focus of most of the national regulatory frameworks and the broader, more analytically elusive concerns of the wider public (Grove-White, 1999).

# References

Abbott, J., S. Roberts and N. Robins (1999), *Who Benefits?* London: IIED.

Accion Ecologica et al. (1996a), *NGO statement concerning unsustainable aquaculture to the UN Commission on sustainable development,* URL: http://www.earthsummitwatch.org/shrimp/positions/pov2a.html.

Accion Ecologica et al. (1996b), *The Choluteca Declaration,* A statement by Non-Governmental Organizations from Latin America, Europe and Asia at a Forum on 'Aquaculture and its Impacts', in Choluteca, Honduras, 16 October, 1996. URL: http://www.earthsummitwatch.org/shrimp/positions/pov3a.html.

Adam, Barbara (1999), 'Industrial food for thought: timescapes of risk', *Environmental Values,* **8**: 219–38.

Adam, Barbara (2000), 'The temporal gaze: the challenge for social theory in the context of GM food', *British Journal of Sociology,* **51** (1): 125–42.

Adams, W.M. (1990), *Green Development. Environment and Sustainability in the Third World,* London and New York: Routledge.

Adams, John (1995), *Risk,* London: UCL Press.

Adams, Catherine E. (2002), 'Hazard analysis and critical control point – original "spin"', *Food Control,* **13**: 355–58

Aerni, Philip (2001), 'Aquatic resources and technology: evolutionary, environmental, legal and developmental aspects', Science, Technology and Innovation Discussion Paper No. 13, Cambridge, MA, USA: Center for International Development.

Agriculture and Environment Biotechnology Commission (AEBC) (2003), *GM crops? Coexistence and Liability,* London: UK government, URL: http://www.aebc.gov.uk/.

Allen, Patricia and Martin Kovach (2000), 'The capitalist composition of organic: the potential of markets in fulfilling the promise of organic agriculture', *Agriculture and Human Values,* **17**: 221–32.

Allison, Edward (2001), 'Big laws, small catches: global ocean governance and the fisheries crisis', *Journal of International Development,* **13**: 933–50.

Ammenberg, Jonas, Gunnar Wik and Olof Hjelm (2001), 'Auditing external environmental auditors – investigating how ISO 14001 is interpreted and applied in reality', *Eco-Management and Auditing,* **8**: 183–92.

Anderson, Troy (2002), 'The Cartagena Protocol on Biosafety to the Convention on Biological Diversity: trade liberalisation, the WTO, and the environment', *Asia Pacific Journal of Environmental Law*, **7** (1): 1–38.

Anderson, James L. (2003a), 'Introduction', in James L. Anderson (ed.), *The International Seafood Trade*, Boca Raton, US and Cambridge, UK: CRC Press and WoodHead Publishing Ltd., pp. 1–13.

Anderson, James L. (2003b), 'Aquaculture, fisheries and evolution of the market', in James L. Anderson (ed.), *The International Seafood Trade*, Boca Raton, US and Cambridge, UK: CRC Press and WoodHead Publishing Ltd., pp. 151–66.

Anderson, James L. and Josué Martínez-Garmendia (2003), 'Trends in international seafood trade', in James L. Anderson (ed.), *The International Seafood Trade*, Boca Raton, US and Cambridge, UK: CRC Press and WoodHead Publishing Ltd., pp. 39–54.

Anderson, James L., Jonathan R. King and Josué Martínez-Garmendia (2003a), 'Trends in capture and aquaculture production', in James L. Anderson (ed.), *The International Seafood Trade*, Boca Raton, US: CRC Press and Cambridge, UK: WoodHead Publishing Ltd., pp. 14–38.

Anderson, James L., Josué Martínez-Garmendia and Jonathan R. King (2003b), 'Trade by major seafood group', in James L. Anderson (ed.), *The International Seafood Trade*, Boca Raton, US and Cambridge, UK: CRC Press and WoodHead Publishing Ltd., pp. 55–92.

Anheier, Helmut, Marlies Glasius and Mary Kaldor (eds) (2001a), *Global Civil Society 2001*, Oxford: Oxford University Press.

Anheier, Helmut, Marlies Glasius and Mary Kaldor (2001b), 'Introducing global civil society', in Helmut Anheier, Marlies Glasius and Mary Kaldor (eds), *Global Civil Society 2001*, Oxford: Oxford University Press, pp. 3–22.

Anheier, Helmut, Marlies Glasius and Mary Kaldor (eds) (2002), *Global Civil Society Handbook, 2002*, Oxford: Oxford University Press.

Appadurai, Arjun (ed.) (1986), *The Social Life of Things. Commodities in Cultural Perspective*, Cambridge: Cambridge University Press.

Appleton, Arthur E. (1999), 'Environmental labelling schemes: WTO law and developing countries implications', in Gary P. Sampson and W. Bradnee Chambers (eds), *Trade, Environment, and the Millennium*, Tokyo: United Nations University Press, pp. 195–222.

Arce, A. and T.K. Marsden (1993), 'The social construction of international food: a new research agenda', *Economic Geography*, **69** (3): 293–311.

Arnoldi, Jakob (2001), 'Niklas Luhmann. An Introduction', *Theory, Culture & Society*, **18** (1): 1–13.

Atkins, Peter and Ian Bowler (2001), *Food in Society. Economy, Culture, Geography*, London: Arnold Publishers.

Atkinson, A. (1983), *Principles of Political Economy*, London: Belhaven.

Bailly, Denis and Rolf Willmann (2001), 'Promoting sustainable aquaculture through economic and other incentives', in R.P. Subasinghe et al. (eds), *Aquaculture in the Third Millennium. Technical Proceedings of the Conference on Aquaculture in the Third Millennium, Bangkok, Thailand, 20–25 February, 2000*, Bangkok and Rome: NACA and FAO, pp. 95–101.

Barbier, B. Edward, Ivar Strand and Suthawan Sathirathai (2002), 'Do open access conditions affect the valuation of an externality? Estimating the welfare effects of mangrove-fishery linkages in Thailand', *Environmental and Resource Economics*, **21**: 343–67.

Barbier, Marc and Pierre-Benoit Joly (2000), 'La sécurité alimentaire à l'épreuve de la crise de l'ESB. Obsession du risque ou émergence d'une démocratie des risques?', *Renc. Rech. Ruminants*, **7** (suppl.): 39–44.

Barling, David (2000), 'Regulating GM foods in the 1980s and 1990s', in David F. Smith and Jim Phillips (eds), *Food, Science, Policy and Regulation in the Twentieth Century. International and Comparative Perspectives*, London: Routledge, pp. 239–55.

Barnhizer, David (ed.) (2001), *Effective Strategies for Protecting Human Rights*, Aldershot: Ashgate Publications.

Barrett, Christopher B., Edward B. Barbier and Thomas Reardon (2001), 'Agroindustrialization, globalization, and international development: the environmental implications', *Environment and Development Economics*, **6**: 419–33.

Bartley, Devin M. and Eric M. Hallerman (1995), 'A global perspective on the utilization of genetically modified organisms in aquaculture and fisheries', *Aquaculture*, **137**: 1–7.

Batie, Sandra S. and David E. Ervin (2001), 'Transgenic crops and the environment: missing markets and public roles', *Environment and Development Economics*, **6**: 435–57.

Bauman, Zygmunt (1987), *Legislators and Interpreters*, Cambridge: Polity Press.

Bauman, Zygmunt (1993), *Postmodern Ethics*, Oxford: Blackwell Publishers.

Bauman, Zygmunt (2000), *Liquid Modernity*, Cambridge: Polity Press.

Baumüller, Heike (2003), *Domestic Import Regulations for Genetically Modified Organisms and their Compatibility with WTO Rules. Some Key Issues*, Winnipeg: International Institute for Sustainable Development (IISD).

Beardsworth, Alan and Teresa Keil (1997), *Sociology on the Menu. An Invitation to the Study of Food and Society*, London and New York: Routledge.

Beck, Ulrich (1986), *Risikogesellschaft. Auf dem Weg in eine andere Moderne*, Frankfurt a. M: Suhrkamp.

Beck, Ulrich (1992), *Risk Society: Towards a New Modernity*, London: Sage.

Beck, Ulrich (1996), 'World risk society as cosmopolitan society? Ecological questions in a framework of manufactured uncertainties', *Theory, Culture and Society,* **13**: 1–32.

Beck, Ulrich (1997), *The Reinvention of Politics. Rethinking Modernity in the Global Order*, Cambridge: Polity Press.

Beck, Ulrich (1999), *World Risk Society*, Cambridge: Polity Press.

Beck, Ulrich and Johannes Willms (2004), *Conversations with Ulrich Beck*, Cambridge: Polity Press.

Beck, Ulrich, Anthony Giddens and Scott Lash (1994), *Reflexive Modernization. Politics, Tradition and Aesthetics in the Modern Social Order*, Polity Press: Cambridge.

Beckers, T., G. Spaargaren and P. Bargeman (2000), *Van Gedragspraktijk naar Beleidspraktijk; Een Analytisch Instrument voor een Consument-Georienteerd Milieubeleid*, The Hague: Netherlands Ministry of the Environment.

Belton, Ben et al. (2004), *Open Ocean Aquaculture*, Minneapolis: Institute for Agriculture and Trade Policy (IATP), URL: http://www.iatp.org/fish (accessed 30 March, 2004).

Benbrook, Charles M. (2002), *Antibiotic Drug Use in U.S. Aquaculture*, Minneapolis: Institute for Agriculture and Trade Policy (IATP).

Bernstein, Peter L. (1996), *Against the Gods. The Remarkable Story of Risk*, New York: John Wiley & Sons.

Bhatia, J. and D.A. Powell (2000), 'The labelling of genetically engineered foods', *Agri-food Risk Management and Communications Technical Report*, **13**. URL: http://www.foodsafetynetwork.ca/gmo/GMO-lbl-mar23-00.htm (accessed 2 May, 2003).

Blowfield, Mick (1999), 'Ethical trade: a review of developments and issues', *Third World Quarterly*, **20** (4): 753–70.

Bock, Anne-Katrin et al. (2002), *Scenarios for Co-existence of Genetically Modified, Conventional and Organic Crops in European Agriculture*, Seville: Institute for Prospective Technology Studies/Joint Research Centre European Commission.

Bonanno, Alessandro et al. (eds) (1994), *From Columbus to ConAgra. The Globalization of Agriculture and Food*, Lawrence: University Press of Kansas.

Boselie, Dave and Jan Buurma (2003), 'Grades and standards in the Thai horticultural sector', in Sietze Vellema and Dave Boselie (eds), *Coopera-*

*tion and Competence in Global Food Chains; Perspectives on Food Quality and Safety*, Maastricht: Shaker Publishing, pp. 123–55.

Boudouropoulos, Ioannis D. and Ioannis S. Arvanitoyannis (1999), 'Current state and advances in the implementation of ISO 14000 by the food industry. Comparison of ISO 14000 to ISO 9000 to other environmental programs', *Trends in Food Science & Technology*, **9**: 395–408.

Bourdieu, Pierre (1979), *Distinction. A Social Critique of the Judgement of Taste*, New York and London: Routledge.

Boutrif Ezzeddine (2003), 'The new role of Codex Alimentarius in the context of WTO/SPS agreement', *Food Control*, **14**: 81–8.

Boyd, W. and M. Watts (1997), 'Agro-industrial just-in-time: the chicken industry and post-war American capitalism', in David Goodman and Michael Watts (eds), *Globalizing Food. Agrarian Questions and Global Restructuring*, New York and London: Routledge, pp. 192–225.

Braithwaite, John and Peter Drahos (2000), *Global Business Regulation*, Cambridge: Cambridge University Press.

BRIDGES (different updates), *Trade BioRes*, Geneva: The International Centre for Trade and Sustainable Development (ICTSD), URL: http://www.ictsd.org.

Brown, Lester R., Janet Larsen and Bernie Fischlowitz-Roberts (2003), *The Earth Policy Reader*, London: Earthscan Publications.

Browne, A.W. et al. (2000), 'Organic production and ethical trade: definition, practice and links', *Food Policy*, **25**: 69–89.

Brownstein, Carrie, Mercédès Lee and Carl Safina (2003), 'Harnessing consumer power for ocean conservation', *Conservation in Practice – Online*, **4** (3), URL: http://conbio.net/InPractice/article44HCP.cfm (accessed 29 April, 2004).

Buonanno, Laurie, Sharon Zablotney and Richard Keefer (2001), 'Politics versus science in the making of a new regulatory regime for food in Europe', *European Integration online Papers (EIoP)*, **5** (12), URL: http://eiop.or.at/eiop/texte/2001-012a.htm.

Busch, Lawrence (1997), 'Grades and standards in the social construction of safe food', in Reider Almas (ed.), *Social Construction of Safe Food. Health, Ethics and Safety in Late Modernity*, Workshop report 5/79, Trondheim: Center for Rural Research.

Busch, Lawrence et al. (2000), *Markets, Rights and Equity: Food and Agricultural Standards in a Shrinking World. Recommendations from an International Workshop*, East Lansing: Institute for Food and Agricultural Standards MSU.

Buttel, Fred, Gert Spaargaren and Arthur P.J. Mol (2006), 'Epilogue: environmental flows and early twenty-first century environmental social sciences', in Fred Buttel, Arthur P.J. Mol and Gert Spaargaren (eds), *Gov-*

*erning Environmental Flows in Global Modernity*, Cambridge, MA: The MIT Press, pp. 351–69.

Buuren, H. van, W. de Wit and B. ter Kuile (2004), 'Voedselkeuring door de eeuwen heen', *Justitiële Verkenningen*, **30** (2): 54–64.

Byrne, David (EU Commissioner for Health and Consumer Protection) (2001), *The Commission Policy on the Health Aspects of BSE – Address to COPA, 9 February, 2001*, Brussels: European Union, URL: http://europa.eu.int/comm/dgs/health_consumer/library/speeches/speech8 1_en.html.

Cameron, James (1999), 'The precautionary principle', in Gary P. Sampson and W. Bradnee Chambers (eds), *Trade, Environment, and the Millennium*, Tokyo: United Nations University Press, pp. 239–70.

Camilleri, Joseph A. (2002), 'Major structural reform', in Esref Aksu and Joseph A. Camilleri (eds), *Democratizing Global Governance*, Houndmills: Palgrave MacMillan, pp. 255–71.

Cardello, A.V. (1995), 'Food quality: relativity, context and consumer expectations', *Food Quality and Preference*, **6** (3): 163–70.

Carter, Neil (2001), *The Politics of the Environment. Ideas, Activism, Policy*, Cambridge: Cambridge University Press.

Cashore, Benjamin, Graeme Auld and Deanna Newsom (2003), 'Forest certification (eco-labelling programs and their policy-making authority: explaining divergence among North American and European case studies', *Forest Policy and Economics*, **5**: 225–47.

Castells, Manuel (1996), *The Information Age. Economy, Society and Culture. Volume I. The Rise of the Network Society*, Malden US: Blackwell Publishers.

Castells, Manuel (1997), *The Information Age. Economy, Society and Culture. Volume II. The Power of Identity*, Malden, US: Blackwell Publishers.

Castells, Manuel (1998), *The Information Age. Economy, Society and Culture. Volume III. End of Millennium*, Malden, US: Blackwell Publishers.

Castells, Manuel (2000), 'Materials for an exploratory theory of the network society', *British Journal of Sociology*, **51** (1): 5–24.

Castells, Manuel (ed.) (2004), *The Network Society. A Cross-cultural Perspective*, Cheltenham, UK and Northampton, MA, USA: Edward Elgar Publishing Limited.

Caswell, Julie A. (2000), 'An evaluation of risk analysis as applied to agricultural biotechnology (with a case study of GM labelling)', *Agribusiness*, **16** (1): 115–23.

Cerny, Philip G. (1999), 'Globalization, governance and complexity', in Aseem Prakash and Jeffrey A. Hart (eds), *Globalization and Governance*, London and New York: Routledge, pp. 188–212.

Charnovitz, Steve (2002a), 'Solving the production and processing methods (PPMs) puzzle', in Kevin P. Gallagher and Jacob Werksman (eds), *The Earthscan Reader on International Trade and Sustainable Development*, London: Earthscan, pp. 227–62.

Charnovitz, Steve (2002b), 'The supervision of health and biodiversity regulation by world trade rules', in Kevin P. Gallagher and Jacob Werksman (eds), *The Earthscan Reader on International Trade and Sustainable Development*, London: Earthscan, pp. 263–87.

CIEL (The Center for International Environmental Law) (2006), *EC-Biotech: Overview and Analysis of the Panel's Interim Report*, Washington and Geneva: CIEL.

Clark, E. Ann and Hugh Lehman (2001), 'Assessment of GM crops in commercial agriculture', *Journal of Agricultural and Environmental Ethics*, **14**: 3–28.

Clay, Jason (2004), *World Agriculture and the Environment. A Commodity-by-Commodity Guide to Impacts and Practices*, Washington: Island Press.

*Communicatie* (Dutch magazine for communication professionals), 31 May, 2001.

Constance, Douglas H. and Alessandro Bonanno (2000), 'Regulating the global fisheries: the World Wildlife Fund, Unilever, and the Marine Stewardship Council', *Agriculture and Human Values*, **17**: 125–39.

Constanza, Robert et al. (1999), 'Commentary: ecological economics and sustainable governance of the oceans', *Ecological Economics*, **31**: 171–87.

Consumer Union (1998), *The Role of Science and 'Other Factors' in Codex Decisions. A Discussion Paper by Consumers International*, Washington: Consumers Union. URL: www.consumersunion.org/food/olfw6ny8 98.htm (accessed 17 May, 2001).

CTA (2003), *Study of the Consequences of the Application of Sanitary and Phytosanitary (SPS) Measures on ACP Countries*, Wageningen: CTA.

Cummins, Ronnie and Ben Lilliston (2000), *Genetically Engineered Food. A Self-Defense Guide for Consumers*, New York: Marlowe & Company.

Cutler, A. Claire (2002), 'Private regimes and interfirm cooperation', in Rodney Bruce Hall and Thomas J. Biersteker (eds), *The Emergence of Private Authority in Global Governance*, Cambridge: Cambridge University Press, pp. 23–40.

Dagevos, Hans (2002), *Panorama Voedingsland. Traditie en Transitie in Discussies over Voedsel*, Rathenau werkdocument 88, Den Haag: Rathenau Instituut.

Dagevos, Hans (2004), 'Consumentenkijk op voedselveiligheid in Nederland', *Justitiële Verkenningen*, **30** (2): 30–41.

Dalton, Russell J., Steve Recchia and Robert Rohrschneider (2003), 'The environmental movement and the modes of political action', *Comparative Political Studies*, **36** (7): 743–71.

Davidson, Alan (1999), *The Oxford Companion to Food*, Oxford: Oxford University Press.

Deere, Carolyn (1999), *Eco-labelling and Sustainable Fisheries*, Cambridge: IUCN and Rome: FAO.

Denton, W. (2003), 'Tracefish: the development of a traceability scheme for the fish industry', in J.B. Luten, J. Oehlenschläger and G. Ólafsdóttir (eds), *Quality of Fish from Catch to Consumer. Labelling, Monitoring and Traceability*, Wageningen: Wageningen Academic Publishers, pp. 75–91.

Diamond, Larry (1996), 'Toward democratic consolidation', in Larry Diamond and Marc Platter (eds.), *The Global Resurgence of Democracy*, Baltimore: Johns Hopkins University Press, pp. 227–40.

Dicken, Peter et al. (2001), 'Chains and networks, territories and scales: towards a relational framework for analysing the global economy', *Global Networks*, **1** (2): 89–112.

Dickens, Peter (1992), *Society and Nature. Towards a Green Social Theory*, Harvester: Wheatsheaf.

Dixon, Jane (2002), *The Changing Chicken. Chooks, Cooks and Culinary Culture*, Sydney: UNSW Press.

Dommen, Caroline (1999), *Fish for Thought. Fisheries, International Trade and Sustainable Development. Initial Issues for Consideration by a Multi-Stakeholder Policy Dialogue. Natural Resources, International Trade, and Sustainable Development Series. No. 1*, Geneva: ICSTD and Cambridge: IUCN.

Douglas, Mary and Aaron Wildavsky (1983), *Risk and Culture. An Essay on the Selection of Technological and Environmental Dangers*, London: University of California Press.

Dragun, Andrew K. and Clem Tisdell (eds) (1999), *Sustainable Agriculture and Environment. Globalisation and the Impact of Trade Liberalisation*, Cheltenham: Edward Elgar.

Drahos, Peter and John Braithwaite (2001), 'The globalisation of regulation', *The Journal of Political Philosophy*, **9** (1): 103–28.

Dratwa, Jim (2002), 'Taking risks with the precautionary principle: food (and the environment) for thought at the European Commission', *Journal of Environmental Policy & Planning*, **4** (3): 197–214.

Dryzek, John S. (1987), *Rational Ecology. Environment and Political Economy*, Oxford: Basil Blackwell.

Dünckmann, Florian and Claudia Mayer (2002), 'Den Markt eine nachhaltige Exportlandwirtschaft nutzen. Umweltstandards im Kaffeesektor', in Dietrich Soyez and Christian Schulz (eds), *Wirstschaftgeographie und Umweltpolitik,* Heft 76, Cologne: Geographical Institute University Cologne.

Duraiappah, Anantha Kumar et al. (2000), *Sustainable Shrimp Farming in Thailand,* CREED policy brief, Amsterdam: IVM/VU and Bangkok: TDRI.

Dwivedi, Ranjit (2001), 'Environmental movements in the global south. Issues of livelihood and beyond', *International Sociology,* **16** (1): 11–31.

Eberle, U. et al. (2004), *Umwelt-Ernährung-Gesundheit. Beschreibung der Dynamiken eines gesellschaftlichen Handlungsfeldes,* Freiburg: Öko-Institut.

Echols, Marsha A. (2001), *Food Safety and the WTO. The Interplay of Culture, Science and Technology,* The Hague: Kluwer Law International.

*Economist, The* (2003), *The Promise of a Blue Revolution. Special Report: Fish Farming,* 9 August, 2003.

Edwards, Steven (2003), 'Analysis: property rights to multi-attribute fishery resources', *Ecological Economics,* **44**: 309–23.

Eijk W.H.B.J. van (2001), *Beleidsnota Viskweek,* Rijswijk: Productschap Vis.

Einarsson, Peter (2000), *Agricultural Trade Policy; as if Food Security and Ecological Sustainability Mattered. Review and Analysis of Alternative Proposals for the Renegotiation of the WTO Agreement on Agriculture,* Stockholm: Forum Syd.

EJF (Environmental Justice Foundation) (2003a), *Smash & Grab: Conflict, Corruption and Human Rights Abuses in the Shrimp Farming Industry,* London: Environmental Justice Foundation.

EJF (Environmental Justice Foundation) (2003b), *Squandering the Seas: How Shrimp Trawling is Threatening Ecological Integrity and Food Security around the World,* London: Environmental Justice Foundation.

Esty, Daniel C. and Maria H. Ivanova (eds) (2002), *Global Environmental Governance. Options and Opportunities,* New Haven: Yale School of Forestry and Environmental Studies.

European Commission (1999), *Communication on 'Fair Trade' from the European Commission to the Council,* COM (1999) 619, Brussels: European Union.

European Commission (EC) (2000a), *White Paper on Food Safety,* COM (1999)/719, Brussels: Commission of the European Communities.

European Commission (EC) (2000b), *Economic Impacts of Genetically Modified Crops on the Agri-food Sector,* Working document rev. 2, Brussels: Directorate-General for Agriculture, European Union.

European Commission (EC) (2000c), *Internal EU Press Statement: DN: IP/00/1289,* Brussels: European Union.

European Commission (EC) (2001), *Public Health and Animal Health – BSE. The Situation and Outlook*, Brussels: European Union, URL: http://europa.eu.int/scadplus/leg/en/lvb/112043.htm (accessed 15 March, 2002).

European Commission (EC) (2003a), *European Commission regrets US Decision to File WTO Case on GMOs as Misguided and Unnecessary*, Press release, 13 May 2003, Brussels: European Union.

European Commission (EC) (2003b), 'Commission Recommendation of 23 July 2003 on guidelines for the development of national strategies and best practices to ensure the coexistence of genetically modified crops with conventional and organic farming' (2003/556/EC), *Official Journal of the European Union L 189/36*, Brussels: European Union.

European Commission, Directorate-General Health and Consumer Protection, Scientific Steering Committee (2003), *Opinion on: The Feeding of Wild Fishmeal to Farmed Fish and Recycling of Fish with regard to the Risk of TSE*, Brussels: European Union.

Evans, Nick, Carol Morris and Michael Winter (2002), 'Conceptualizing agriculture: a critique of post-productivism as the new orthodoxy', *Progress in Human Geography,* **26** (3): 313–32.

Eyerman, Ron and Andrew Jamison (1991), *Social Movements: a Cognitive Approach*, Cambridge: Polity Press.

Falk, Michael C. et al. (2002), 'Food biotechnology: benefits and concerns', *Journal of Nutrition,* **132**, 1384–90.

FAO (Food and Agricultural Organisation of the United Nations) (1999), *Understanding the Codex Alimentarius,* Rome: FAO/WHO, URL: http://www.fao.org/docrep/w9114e/W9114e0.htm (accessed: 24 April, 2002).

FAO (Food and Agriculture Organisation of the United Nations) (2000), *Yearbook of Fisheries Statistics*, Rome: FAO.

FAO (Food and Agriculture Organisation of the United Nations) (2002), *The State of World Fisheries and Aquaculture; 2002*, Rome: FAO.

FAO, Committee on Fisheries, sub-committee on fish trade (2004a), *Status and Important Recent Events concerning International Trade in Fishery Products (including World Trade Organisation)*, COFI:FT/IX/2004/2, Rome: FAO.

FAO, Committee on Fisheries, sub-committee on fish trade (2004b), *Safety and Quality, with Particular Emphasis on Fishmeal and BSE*, COFI:FT/IX/2004/4, Rome: FAO.

FAO/WHO (Food and Agriculture Organisation of the United Nations/World Health Organisation) (1997), *Risk Management and Food Safety – FAO Food and Nutrition Paper 65*, Rome: FAO.

FAZ (*Frankfurter Algemeine Zeitung*), several issues.

FEAP (Federation of European Aquaculture Producers) (undated), *Code of Conduct,* Brussels, FEAP. URL: www.feap.info (accessed 11 April, 2002).

Feenstra, Gail (2002), 'Creating space for sustainable food systems: lessons from the field', *Agriculture and Human Values,* **19**: 99–106.

Fernández-Armesto, Felipe (2001), *Food. A History,* London: Macmillan.

*Financiële Dagblad, Het,* several issues.

Fine, Ben (1998), *The Political Economy of Diet, Health and Food Policy,* New York and London: Routledge.

Fischler, Claude (2000), At a meeting of the Office Parlementaire d'Evaluation des Choix Scientifiques et Technologiques, 21/11/2000, URL: http://www.assemblee.nationale.fr/2/oecst/c-rendus/esb.htm (accessed 12 March, 2001).

Fitter, Robert and Raphael Kaplinsky (2001), 'Who gains from product rents as the coffee market becomes more differentiated? A value-chain analysis', *IDS Bulletin,* **32** (3): 69–82.

Flaherty, Mark and Peter Vandergeest (1998), '"Low-Salt" shrimp aquaculture in Thailand: goodbye coastline, hello Khon Kaen!', *Environmental Management,* **22** (6): 817–30.

Flaherty, Mark, Peter Vandergeest and Paul Miller (1999), 'Rice paddy or shrimp pond: tough decisions in rural Thailand', *World Development,* **27** (12): 2045–60.

FLO (Fairtrade Labelling Organizations International) (2003), *Fairtrade Standards for Coffee,* Version January 2003.

Folke, Carl et al. (1998), 'The ecological footprint concept for sustainable seafood production: a review', *Ecological Applications,* **8** (1, supplement: ecosystem management for sustainable marine fisheries): S63–S71.

Fox, John A. and Hikaru Hanawa Peterson (2004), 'Risks and implications of bovine spongiform encephalopathy for the United States: insights from other countries', *Food Policy,* **29**: 45–60.

Frankic, Anamarija and Carl Hershner (2003), 'Sustainable aquaculture: developing the promise of aquaculture', *Aquaculture International,* **11**: 517–30.

Franklin, Sarah, Celia Lury and Jackie Stacey (2000), *Global Nature, Global Culture,* London: Sage Press.

Freidberg, Susanne (2003), *The Contradictions of Clean: Supermarket Ethical Trade and African Horticulture,* IIED Gatekeeper series no. 109, London: IIED.

Freidberg, Susanne (2004), 'The ethical complex of corporate food power', *Environment and Planning D: Society and Space,* **22**: 513–31.

French, Duncan A. (2002), 'The role of the state and international organizations in reconciling sustainable development and globalization', *International Environmental Agreements: Politics, Law and Economics*, **2**: 135–50.

Frewer, Lynn (2004), *Consumers, Food, Trust and Safety. Inaugural Address*, Wageningen: Wageningen University

Friedland, William (1994), 'The new globalization: the case of fresh produce', in Alessandro Bonanno et al. (eds), *From Columbus to ConAgra. The Globalization of Agriculture and Food*, Lawrence: University Press of Kansas, pp. 210–31.

Friedland, William, A. Barton and R. Thomas (1981), *Manufacturing Green Gold*, New York: Cambridge University Press.

Friedmann, Harriet and Philip McMichael (1989), 'Agriculture and the state system. The rise and decline of national agricultures, 1870 to the present', *Sociologia Ruralis*, **29** (2): 93–117.

Friends of the Earth (2003), *GMOs co-existence or contamination? Conference Report*, Brussels: Friends of the Earth.

FSA (Food Standards Agency) (2000), *Review of BSE controls. December 2000*, London: Food Standards Agency, URL: www.bsereview.org.uk (accessed 25 September, 2001).

FSIS (Food Safety and Inspection Services) (2004), *Preliminary Analysis of Interim Final Rules and an Interpretive Rule to prevent the BSE agent from entering the U.S. food supply*, Washington: FSIS. URL: http://www.fsis.usda.gov/OPPDE/rdad/FRPubs/03-025N/BSE_analysis.pdf (accessed 16 December, 2005).

GAA (Global Aquaculture Alliance) (2001), *Codes of Practice for Responsible Shrimp Farming*, URL: http://www.gaalliance.org/revi1.html (accessed 11 April, 2002).

Gabriel Y. and T. Lang (1995), *The Unmanageable Consumer*, London: Sage.

Gallastegui, Ibon Galarraga (2002), 'The use of eco-labels: a review of the literature', *European Environment,* **12**: 316–31.

Garcia, Serge M. and Rolf Willmann (1999), *Status and Issues in Marine Capture Fisheries: A Global Perspective*, Rome: FAO Fisheries Department.

Garcia, S.M. et al. (1999), 'Towards sustainable fisheries: a strategy for FAO and the World Bank', *Ocean & Coastal Management*, **42**: 369–98.

Gardiner, Rosalie (2002), *Oceans and Seas: Harnessing the Marine Environment for Sustainable Development*, Towards Earth Summit 2002, Environmental briefing no. 3.

Giampietro, Mario (2002), 'The precautionary principle and ecological hazards of genetically modified organisms', *Ambio*, **31** (6): 466–70.

Gibbon, Peter (2001), 'Agro-commodity chains. An introduction', *IDS Bulletin*, **32** (3): 60–8.

Giddens, Anthony (1976), *New Rules of Sociological Method*, London: Hutchinson.

Giddens, Anthony (1979), *Central Problems in Social Theory. Action, Structure and Contradiction in Social Analysis*, Berkeley: University of California Press.

Giddens, Anthony (1984*)*, *The Constitution of Society. Outline of the Theory of Structuration*, Cambridge: Polity Press.

Giddens, Anthony (1987), *Social Theory and Modern Sociology*, Cambridge: Polity Press.

Giddens, Anthony (1990), *The Consequences of Modernity*, Stanford: Stanford University Press.

Giddens, Anthony (1991), *Modernity and Self-Identity: Self and Society in Late Modern Age*, Cambridge: Polity Press.

Giddens, Anthony (1994), 'Replies and critiques. Risk, trust, reflexivity', in Ulrich Beck, Anthony Giddens and Scott Lash, *Reflexive Modernisation. Politics, Tradition and Aesthetics in the Modern Social order*, Cambridge: Polity Press, pp. 174–215.

Gilbertsen, Neal (2003), 'The global salmon industry and its impacts in Alaska', *Alaska Economic Trends*, **23** (10): 3–11.

Gille, Zsuzsa (2006), 'Detached Flows or Grounded Place-making Projects?', in Fred Buttel, Arthur P.J. Mol and Gert Spaargaren (eds), *Governing Environmental flows in global modernity*, Cambridge, MA: The MIT Press, pp. 137–56.

Gilmore, James H. and B. Joseph Pine II (1999), *The Experience Economy*, Boston: Harvard Business School Press.

GMO-Compass (2006), *Commercial GM Crop Production in Five EU Member States*. URL: http://www.gmo-compass.org (accessed 1 June, 2006).

Goldberg, Rebecca J., Matthew S. Elliott and Rosamund L. Naylor (2001), *Marine Aquaculture in the United States: Environmental Problems and Policy Options*, Arlington: PEW-Oceans Commission.

Goode, A. and F. Whoriskey (2003), 'Finding resolution to farmed salmon issues in Eastern North America', in Derek Mills (ed.), *Salmon at the Edge*, Oxford: Blackwell Publishers, pp. 144–58.

Goodland, Robert (2002), *Ecolabelling: Opportunities for Progress toward Sustainability*, Washington: Consumer Choice Council.

Goodman, David (1999), 'Agro-food studies in the "age of ecology": nature, corporeality, bio-politics', *Sociologia Ruralis*, **39** (1): 17–38.

Goodman, David (2001), 'Ontology matters: the relational materiality of nature and agro-food studies', *Sociologia Ruralis*, **41** (2): 182–200.

Goodman, David (2004), 'Rural Europe Redux? Reflections on alternative agro-food networks and paradigm change', *Sociologia Ruralis*, **44** (1): 3–16.

Goodman, David and E. Melanie DuPuis (2002), 'Knowing food and growing food: beyond the production–consumption debate in the sociology of agriculture', *Sociologia Ruralis*, **42** (1): 5–22.

Goss, Jasper, David Burch and Roy E. Rickson (2000), 'Agri-food restructuring and Third World transnationals: Thailand, the CP Group and the global shrimp industry', *World Development*, **28** (3): 513–30.

Goverde, Henri J.M. and Nico Nelissen (2002), 'Networks as a new concept for governance', in P.P.J. Driessen and P. Glasbergen (eds), *Greening Society*, Dordrecht: Kluwer Academic Publishers, pp. 27–45.

Gowdy, John M. and Marsha L. Walton (2003), 'Consumer sovereignty, economic efficiency and the trade liberalisation debate', *International Journal of Global Environmental Issues*, **3** (1): 1–13.

Grader, Zeke et al. (2003), 'Going beyond fish eco-labelling: is it time for fair trade certification too?', *Fishermen's News of March 2003*, URL: http://www.pcffa.org/fn-mar03.htm (accessed 5 November, 2003).

Gräslund, Sara and Bengt-Erik Bengtsson (2001), 'Chemicals and biological products used in south-east Asian shrimp farming, and their potential impact on the environment – a review', *The Science of the Total Environment*, **280**: 93–131.

Green, Ken, Mark Harvey and Andrew McMeekin (2003), 'Transformations in food consumption and production systems', *Journal of Environmental Policy & Planning,* **5** (2): 145–63.

Greenpeace (1997), *Shrimp – the Devastating Delicacy: the Explosion of Shrimp Farming and the Negative Impacts on People and the Environment*. URL: http://www.greenpeaceusa.org/reports/biodiversity/shrimp/ (accessed 5 November, 2003).

Greenpeace Germany (2000), *Das MSC-Siegel ist derzeit kein glaubwürdiges 'Ökosiegel' für Fischprodukte*, URL: http://archiv.greenpeace. de/GP_DOK_3P/HINTERGR/C10HI100.HTM (accessed 17 December, 2004).

Griffin, Keith (2003), 'Economic globalization and institutions of global governance', *Development and Change*, **34** (5): 789–807.

Griswold, Wendy and Nathan Wright (2004), 'Cowbirds, locals and the dynamic endurance of regionalism', *American Journal of Sociology*, **109** (6), 1411–51.

Gross, T. (2003), 'Consumer attitudes towards health and food safety', in J.B. Luten, J. Oehlenschläger and G. Ólafsdóttir (eds), *Quality of Fish from Catch to Consumer. Labelling, Monitoring and Traceability*, Wageningen: Wageningen Academic Publishers, pp. 401–11.

Grove-White, Robin et al. (1997), *Uncertain World. Genetically Modified organisms, Food and Public Attitudes in Britain*, Lancaster: Centre for the Study of Environmental Change (CSEC) at Lancaster University.

Grove-White, Robin (1999), Afterword: On 'Sound Science', the Environment, and Political Authority, *Environmental Values*, **8**: 277-282

Guivant, Julia Silvia (2002), 'Heterogeneous and unconventional coalitions around global food risks: integrating Brazil into the debates', *Journal of Environmental Policy & Planning*, **4** (3): 231–46.

Gulbrandsen, Lars H. (2004), 'Overlapping public and private governance: can forest certification fill the gaps in the global forest regime?', *Global Environmental Politics*, **4** (2): 75–99.

Gupta, Joyeeta (2004), 'Global sustainable food governance and hunger; traps and tragedies', *British Food Journal*, **106** (5): 406–16.

Haas, Peter M. (1999), 'Social constructivism and the evolution of multilateral environmental governance', in Aseem Prakash and Jeffrey A. Hart (eds), *Globalization and Governance*, London and New York: Routledge, pp. 103–33.

Haas, Peter and Ernst Haas (1995), 'Learning to Learn: International governance', *Global Governance*, **1**: 255–84.

Haas, Peter M., Robert O. Keohane and Marc A. Levy (1993), *Institutions for the Earth. Sources of Effective International Environmental Protection*, Cambridge, MA: The MIT Press.

Hagendijk, Rob (1996), *Wetenschap, Constructivisme en Cultuur* (PhD thesis), Amsterdam: University of Amsterdam.

Hajer, Maarten (1995), *The Politics of Environmental Discourse: Ecological Modernization and the Policy Process*, Oxford: Clarendon Press.

Hajer, M.A., J.P.M. van Tatenhove and C. Laurent (2004), *Nieuwe Vormen van Governance*, RIVM report 500013004/2004, Bilthoven: RIVM.

Halkier, Bente (1999), 'Consequences of the politicization of consumption: the example of environmentally friendly consumption practices', *Journal of Environmental Policy & Planning*, **1**: 25–41.

Halkier, Bente (2001), 'Risk and food: environmental concerns and consumer practices', *International Journal of Food Science and Technology*, **36**: 801–12.

Hall, Rodney Bruce and Thomas J. Biersteker (2002), 'The emergence of private authority in global governance', in Rodney Bruce Hall and Thomas J. Biersteker (eds), *The Emergence of Private Authority in Global Governance*, Cambridge: Cambridge University Press, pp. 3–22.

Halweil, Brian (2002), *Home Grown. The Case for Local Food in a Global Market*, Worldwatch paper 163, Washington: Worldwatch Institute.

Hammond, Bruce et al. (2002), *Business Guide to Sustainable Seafood*, New York: Alliance for Environmental Innovation.

Hanna, Susan S. (1999), 'Strengthening governance of ocean fishery resources', *Ecological Economics*, **31**: 275–86.

Hannigan, John A. (1995), *Environmental Sociology. A Social Constructivist Perspective*, London: Routledge.

Harvey, David J. (2003), *Aquaculture Outlook; Aquaculture Production Forecast to Grow, but many Uncertainties Loom*, Electronic outlook report from the economic research service, Washington: USDA, URL: http://www.ers.usda.gov (accessed 11 November, 2003).

Hathaway, Steve (1995), 'Harmonization of international requirements under HACCP-based food control systems', *Food Control*, **6** (5): 267–76.

Held, David (1987), *Models of Democracy*, Cambridge: Polity Press.

Held, David (1995), *Democracy and the Global Order. From the Modern State to Cosmopolitan Governance*, Cambridge: Polity Press.

Held, David (2004), *Global Covenant. The Social Democratic Alternative to the Washington Consensus*, Cambridge: Polity Press.

Held, David et al. (1999), *Global Transformations. Politics, Economics and Culture*, Cambridge: Polity Press.

Henson, Spencer and Julie Caswell (1999), 'Food safety regulation: an overview of contemporary issues', *Food Policy*, **24**: 589–603.

Henson, Spencer, Ann-Marie Brouder and Winnie Mitullah (2000), 'Food safety requirements and food exports from developing countries: the case of fish exports from Kenya to the European Union', *American Journal of Agricultural Economics*, **85** (5): 1159–69.

Hertz, Noreena (2001), *The Silent Takeover – Global Capitalism and the Death of Democracy*, New York: Harper Collins.

Hines, Colin (2003), 'Time to replace globalization with localization', *Global Environmental Politics*, **3** (3): 1–7.

Hinrichs, C. Claire (2000), 'Embeddedness and local food systems: notes on two types of direct agricultural market', *Journal of Rural Studies*, **16**: 295–303.

Hites, Ronald A. et al. (2004), 'Global assessment of organic contaminants in farmed salmon', *Science*, **303**: 226–9.

HM Government in consultation with the devolved administrations (2001), *Response to the Report of the BSE Inquiry*, London, 28 September, 2001.

Hogenboom, Joris, Arthur P.J. Mol and Gert Spaargaren (2000), 'Dealing with environmental risks in reflexive modernity', in Maurie Cohen (ed.), *Risk in the Modern Age. Social Theory, Science and Environmental Decision-Making*, Houndmills: Macmillan Press, pp. 83–106.

Hoogvelt, Ankie (2001), *Globalisation and the Postcolonial World. The New Political Economy of Development*, Houndmills, Basingstoke: Palgrave.

Hooker, Neal H. (2000), 'Food safety regulation and trade in food products', *Food Policy*, **25**: 653–68.

Horrigan, Leo, Robert S. Lawrence and Polly Walker (2002), 'How sustainable agriculture can address the environmental and human health harms of industrial agriculture', *Environmental Health Perspectives*, **110** (5): 445–56.

Howarth, David (2000), *Discourse. (Concepts in the Social Sciences)*, Buckingham: Open University Press.

Hughes, Alex (2005), 'Corporate strategy and the management of ethical trade: the case of the UK food and clothing retailers', *Environment and Planning A*, **37**: 1145–63.

Huitric, Miriam, Carl Folke and Nils Kautsky (2002), 'Development and government policies of shrimp farming industry in Thailand in relation to mangrove ecosystems', *Ecological Economics*, **40**: 441–55.

Hutchings, Jeffrey A. and John D. Reynolds (2004), 'Marine fish population collapses: consequences of recovery and extinction risk', *BioScience*, **54** (4): 297–309.

ICFFA (The International Commission on the Future of Food and Agriculture) (2003), *Manifesto on the Future of Food*, San Rossore.

IFPRI (International Food Policy Research Institute) (2002), *Reaching Sustainable Food Security for All by 2020. Getting the Priorities and Responsibilities Right*, Washington: International Food Policy Research Institute.

IFPRI (2003), *Outlook for Fish to 2020. Meeting Global Demand*, Washington: International Food Policy Research Institute and Penang: Worldfish Center.

Ilbery, Brian (2001), 'Changing geographies of global food production', in Peter Daniels et al. (eds), *Human Geography. Issues for the 21st Century*, Harlow: Prentice Hall, pp. 253–73.

Infante, Rodrigo (2003), 'Correcting myths: facts about salmon farming', *Global Aquaculture Advocate* (April 2003): 11–3.

INNI (International NGO Network on ISO) (2002), *International Standards*, Pacific Institute for Studies in Development, Environment, and Security, URL: www.pacinst.org (accessed 1 October, 2003).

Institut de l'élevage (2000), 'ESB: impact de la crise actuelle sur le marché de la viande bovine', *Tendences: la Lettre de Conjoncture GEB Supplement*.

Interfaith Network (2003), *Portland's Bounty. A Guide to Eating Locally and Seasonally in the Greater Portland and Vancouver Areas*, Portland: Ecumenical Ministries of Oregon, URL: http://www.emoregon.org/inec_food.htm (accessed 15 December, 2003).

Irwin, Alan (2001*), Sociology and the Environment. A Critical Introduction to Society, Nature and Knowledge*, Cambridge: Polity Press.

ISA Net (Industrial Shrimp Action Network (1998), *The Guayaquil Declaration. A Statement made by ISA Net Members at the Second ISA Net International Conference*, Guayaquil: ISA NET.

ISO (1998), *ISO 14000 – Meet the Whole Family!*, Geneva: ISO Central Secretariat.

Jackson, P. and N. Thrift (1995), 'Geographies of consumption', in D. Miller (ed.), *Acknowledging Consumption. A Review of New Studies*, London: Routledge, pp. 204–37.

Jackson, Jeremy B.C. et al. (2001), 'Historical overfishing and the recent collapse of coastal ecosystems', *Science*, **293**: 629–38.

James, Clive (2005), *Global Status of Commercialized Biotech/GM Crops: 2005*, ISAAA Briefs No. 34-2005, Manila: International Service for the Acquisition of Agri-Biotech Applications (ISAAA).

Jänicke, Martin and Jacob Klauw (2004), 'Lead markets for environmental innovations: a new role for the nation state', *Global Environmental Politics*, **4** (1): 29–45.

Janvry, Alain de (1981), *The Agrarian Question and Reformism in Latin America*, Baltimore: Johns Hopkins University Press.

Jasanoff, Sheila (1997), 'Civilization and madness: the great BSE scare of 1996', *Public Understanding of Science: An International Journal of Research in the Public Dimension of Science and Technology*, **6**: 221–32.

Jenkins, David (2003), 'Atlantic salmon, endangered species, and the failure of environmental policies', *Comparative Studies in Society and History*, **45** (4): 843–72.

Joly, Pierre-Benoît (2000), 'Contested innovation: what lessons may be drawn from public controversies on GMOs?', *Acta Horticulturae*, **539**: 33–8.

Josling, Tim, Donna Roberts and David Orden (2004), *Food Regulation and Trade. Toward a Safe and Open Global System*, Washington: Institute for International Economics.

JRC (Joint Research Centre) European Commission (2003), *Review of GMOs under Research and Development and in the Pipeline in Europe*, Seville: Institute for Prospective Technological Studies.

Kalaitzandonakes, Nicholas and Peter Phillips (2000), 'GM food labelling and the role of the Codex', *AgBioForum*, **3** (4): 188–91.

Kaosa-ard, Mingsarn and Pornpen Wijukprasert (2000), *The State of Environment in Thailand: A Decade of Change*, Bangkok: Thailand Development Research Institute.

Karkkainen, Bradley C. (2004), 'Post-sovereign environmental governance', *Global Environmental Politics*, **4** (1): 72–96.

Kastner, Justin J. and Rosa Pawsey (2002), 'Harmonising sanitary measures and resolving trade disputes through the WTO–SPS framework. Part I: a case study of the US–EU hormone-treated beef dispute', *Food Control*, **13**: 49–55.

Kastner, Justin and Douglas Powell (2002), 'The SPS Agreement: addressing historical factors in trade dispute resolution', *Agriculture and Human Values*, **19**: 283–92.

Keeley, James and Ian Scoones (2003), *Understanding Environmental Policy Processes. Cases from Africa*, London: Earthscan Publications.

Keil, Alan and Teresa Beardsworth (1996), *Sociology on the Menu: An Invitation to the Study of Food and Society*, London: Routledge.

Keohane, Robert O. (2002), *Power and Governance in a Partially Globalized World*, London and New York: Routledge.

Keohane, Robert O. and Joseph S. Nye Jr. (2002), 'Governance in a globalizing world', in Robert O. Keohane (ed.), *Power and Governance in a Partially Globalized World*, London and New York: Routledge, pp. 191–218.

Keuringsdienst van Waren (2005), *Report of Nitrate Monitoring Results Concerning Regulation EU 194/97*, The Hague: Food and Consumer Product Safety Authority (VWA).

Kirchmann, Holger and Gudni Thorvaldsson (2000), 'Challenging targets for future agriculture', *European Journal of Agronomy*, **12**: 145–61.

Kirwan, James (2004), 'Alternative strategies in the UK agro-food system: interrogating the alterity of farmers' markets', *Sociologia Ruralis,* **44** (4): 395–415.

Klein, Naomi (2000), *No Logo*, London: Flamingo.

Kleinwächter, Wolfgang (2003), 'Global governance in the information age', *Development*, **46** (1): 17–25.

Klintman, Mikael (2002), 'The genetically modified (GM) food labelling controversy: ideological and epistemic crossovers', *Social Studies of Science*, **32** (1): 71–91.

Klintman, Mikael and Magnus Boström (2004), 'Framings of science and ideology: organic food labelling in the US and Sweden', *Environmental Politics*, **13**, (3): 612–34.

Konefal, Jason, Michael Mascarenhas and Maki Hatanaka (2003), *Governance in the Global Agro-food System: Backlighting the Role of Transnational Supermarket Chains*, paper presented at the Agriculture, Food, and Human Values Society and the Association for the Study of Food and Society Joint Annual Meetings, Austin, TX.

Krimsky, Sheldon and Alonzo Plough (1988), *Environmental Hazards. Communicating Risks as a Social Process*, Dover: Auburn House Publishing Company.

Krut, Riva and Harris Gleckman (1998), *ISO 14001. A Missed Opportunity for Sustainable Global Industrial Development*, London: Earthscan Publications.

Kura, Yumiko et al. (2004), *Fishing for Answers: Making Sense of the Global Fish Crisis*, Washington: World Resources Institute.

Lake, David A. (1999), 'Global governance. A relational contracting approach', in Aseem Prakash and Jeffrey A. Hart (eds), *Globalization and Governance*, London and New York: Routledge, pp. 31–53.

Lang, Tim (2003), 'Food industrialisation and food power: implications for food governance', *Development Policy Review*, 21 (5/6): 555–68.

Lang, Tim and Michael Heasman (2004), *Food Wars. The Global Battle for Mouths, Minds and Markets*, London: Earthscan Publications.

Lash, Scott and John Urry (1987), *The End of Organized Capitalism*, Oxford: Polity Press.

Lash, Scott and John Urry (1994), *Economies of Signs & Space*, London: Sage Publications.

Lash, Scott, Bronislaw Szerszynski and Brian Wynne (eds) (1996), *Risk, Environment and Modernity. Towards a New Ecology*, London: Sage Publications.

Le Heron, Richard (1993), *Globalized Agriculture. Political Choice*, Oxford: Pergamon Press.

Lebel, Louis et al. (2002), 'Industrial transformation and shrimp aquaculture in Thailand and Vietnam: pathways to ecological, social, and economic sustainability?', *Ambio*, 31 (4): 311–23.

Lehmann, Volker (2002), *From Rio to Johannesburg and Beyond: Globalizing Precaution for Genetically Modified Organisms*, Washington: Heinrich Böll Foundation.

Leslie, Deborah and Suzanne Reimer (1999), 'Spatializing commodity chains', *Progress in Human Geography*, 23 (3): 401–20.

Leuck, Dale, Mildred Haley and David Harvey (2004), *U.S. 2003 and 2004 Livestock and Poultry Trade Influenced by Animal Disease and Trade Restrictions*, Electronic outlook report from the economic research service, Washington: USDA.

Leydesdorff, Loet (2002), 'May there be a "Socionomy" beyond "Sociology"?', *SCIPOLICY – The Journal of Science and Health Policy*, 2 (1): 11 pages. URL: http://scipolicy.net/scipolicy_journal/index4.htm#2003-2002 (accessed 11 January, 2003).

Lind, David and Elizabeth Barham (2004), 'The social life of the tortilla: food, cultural politics and contested commodification', *Agriculture and Human Values*, 21: 47–60.

Lipschutz, Ronnie D. (2005), 'Regulation for the rest of us? Global social activism, corporate citizenship, and the disappearance of the political', *eScholarship Repository, 2005*, URL: http://repositories.cdlib.org/cgirs/ CGIRS-2003-1 (accessed 23 April, 2006).

Lipschutz, Ronnie D. and Cathleen Fogel (2002), '"Regulation for the rest of us?" Global civil society and the privatization of transnational regulation', in Rodney Bruce Hall and Thomas J. Biersteker (eds), *The Emergence of Private Authority in Global Governance*, Cambridge: Cambridge University Press, pp. 115–40.

Litfin, K. (ed.) (1998), *The Greening of Sovereignty in World Politics*, Cambridge, MA: The MIT Press.

LNV (Netherlands Ministry of Agriculture, Nature Conservation and Food Safety), (2002), Dossier Traceerbaarheid, The Hague, LNV. URL: http:// www.vwa.nl (accessed 14 October, 2003).

Lockie, Stewart and Simon Kitto (2000), 'Beyond the farm gate: production–consumption networks and agri–food research', *Sociologia Ruralis*, **40** (1): 3–19.

Löfstedt, Ragnar E., Baruch Fischhoff and Ilya R. Fischhoff (2002), 'Precautionary principles: general definitions and specific applications to genetically modified organisms', *Journal of Policy Analysis and Management*, **21** (3): 381–407.

Luhmann, Niklas (1991), *Soziologie des Risikos*, Berlin: Walter de Gruyter.

Luhmann, Niklas (1997), 'Limits of Steering', *Theory, Culture & Society*, **14** (1): 41–57.

Luiten, Esther (undated), *Controverse rond Kweek van Vis in Nederland?*, Den Haag: Stichting Toekomstbeeld der Techniek.

Lunel, Jean (1995), 'Biotechnology regulations and guidelines in Europe', *Current Opinion in Biotechnology*, **6**: 267–72.

Mackenzie, Ruth (2003), *Globalisation and the International Governance of Modern Biotechnology. The International Regulation of Modern Biotechnology*, Paper prepared for the globalisation and poverty programme, Brighton: IDS. URL: http://www.gapresearch.org (accessed 19 June, 2004).

Maclean, Norman and Richard James Laight (2000), 'Transgenic fish: an evaluation of benefits and risks', *Fish and Fisheries*, **1**: 146–72.

Macnaghten, Phil and John Urry (1998), *Contested Natures*, London: Sage.

MAFF (1996), *Leaflet – 'Eradicating BSE in Britain'*, London: Ministry of Agriculture, Fisheries and Food.

Maher, Imelda (2002), 'Competition law in the international domain: network as a new form of governance', *Journal of Law and Society*, **29** (1): 111–36.

Mansfield, Becky (2003a), 'From catfish to organic fish: making distinctions about nature as cultural economic practice', *Geoforum*, **34**: 329–42.

Mansfield, Becky (2003b), 'Fish, factory trawlers, and imitation crab: the nature of quality in the seafood industry', *Journal of Rural Studies*, **19**: 9–21.

Mansfield, Becky (2004), 'Organic Views of Nature: the Debate over Organic Certification for Aquatic Animals', *Sociologia Ruralis*, **44** (2): 216–32.

Margaronis, Maria (1999), 'As bio tech frankenfood are stuffed down their throats, consumers rebel', *The Nation*,27 December, 1999.

Marks, G., L. Hooghe and K. Blank (1996), 'European integration from the 1980s: state-centric versus multi-level governance', *The Journal of Common Market Studies*, **34** (3): 341–78.

Marsden, Terry (1997), 'Creating space for food. The distinctiveness of recent agrarian development', in David Goodman and Michael Watts (eds), *Globalising Food: Agrarian Questions and Global Restructuring*, London: Routledge, pp. 169–91.

Marsden, Terry (2000), 'Food matters and the matter of food: towards a new food governance?', *Sociologia Ruralis*, **40** (1): 20–9.

Marsden, Terry (2004), 'The quest for ecological modernisation: re-spacing rural development and agri-food studies', *Sociologia Ruralis*, **44** (2): 129–46.

Matthews, Ralph, Nathan Young and Brian Elliott (2002), *Contested Science and the Social Construction of Environmental Risk: The Case of Aquaculture*, Paper presented at the International Sociological Association, XV World Congress of Sociology, Sociology of Environment Section, Brisbane Australia.

Max Havelaar, URL: http://www.maxhavelaar.nl (accessed 22 December, 2002).

Maxwell, Simon and Rachel Slater (2003), 'Food policy old and new', *Development Policy Review*, **21** (5/6): 531–53.

Maybin, Eileen and Kevan Bundell (1996), *After the Prawn Rush. The Human and Environmental Costs of Commercial Prawn Farming*, London: Christian Aid. URL: http://www.christian-aid.org.uk/indepth/9605praw/prawn.htm (accessed 23 August, 2004).

Mayer, Sue and Andy Stirling (2002), 'Finding a precautionary approach to technological development – lessons for the evaluation of GM crops', *Journal of Agricultural and Environmental Ethics*, **15**: 57–71.

McGarity, Thomas O. and Patricia I. Hansen (2001), *Breeding Distrust: An Assessment and Recommendations for Improving the Regulation of Plant Derived Genetically Modified Foods*, Austin: University of Texas Law School, URL: www.biotech-info.net/Breeding_Distrust.html (accessed 19 June, 2004).

McGinnis, Michael D. (1999), 'Rent-seeking, redistribution, and reform in the governance of global markets', in Aseem Prakash and Jeffrey A. Hart (eds), *Globalization and Governance*, London and New York: Routledge, pp. 54–76.

McHughen, Alan (2000), *A Consumer's Guide to GM Food. From Green Genes to Red Herrings*, Oxford: Oxford University Press.

McKenna, Megan, Richard Le Heron and Michael Roche (2001), 'Living local, growing global: renegotiating the export production regime in New Zealand's pipfruit sector', *Geoforum*, **32**: 157–66.

McMichael, Philip (1994), 'Global restructuring: some lines of inquiry', in Philip McMichael (ed.), *The Global Restructuring of Agro-Food Systems*, Ithaca and London: Cornell University Press, pp. 277–300.

McMichael, Philip (1996), 'Globalization: myths and realities', *Rural Sociology*, **61** (1): 25–55.

McMichael, Philip (2000), 'The power of food', *Agriculture and Human Values*, **17**: 21–33.

McMichael, Philip (2001), 'Revisiting the question of the transnational state: a comment on William Robinson's "Social Theory and Globalization"', *Theory and Society*, **30**: 201–10.

Meere, dr. F.B.J. de and C. Sepers (2000), *Een Verwrongen Beeld? Kranten- en Persberichten tijdens de BSE-crisis*, LEI report 5.00.03, Den Haag: LEI.

Mennell, Stephen (1996), *All Manners of Food. Eating and Taste in England and France from the Middle Ages to the Present*, Urbana and Chicago: University of Illinois Press.

Micheletti, Michele (2003), *Political Virtue and Shopping. Individuals, Consumerism, and Collective Action*, New York: Palgrave Macmillan.

Miget, Russell (2004), *The HACCP Seafood Program and Aquaculture*, SRAC Publication No. 4900, Stoneville: Southern Regional Aquacultural Center.

Miller, Max (1994), 'Intersystemic discourse and co-ordinated dissent: a critique of Luhmann's concept of ecological communication', *Theory, Culture & Society*, **11**: 101–21.

Millstone, Erik and Tim Lang (2003), *The Atlas of Food. Who Eats What, Where and Why*, London: Earthscan.

Minister of Research (2000), 'At a Meeting of the Office Parlementaire d'Evaluation des Choix Scientifiques et Technologiques, 21/11/2000', Paris: Assemblée Nationale. URL: http://www.assemblee.nationale.fr/2/oecst/c-rendus/esb.htm (accessed 29 April, 2001).

Mintz, Sidney (1995), 'Food and its relationship to concepts of power', in Philip McMichael (ed.), *Food and Agrarian Orders in the World-Economy*, Westport and London: Praeger, pp. 3–13.

Mintz, Sidney W. (2002), 'Food and eating: some persisting questions', in Warren Belasco and Philip Scranton (eds), *Food Nations. Selling Taste in Consumer Societies*, New York: Routledge, pp. 24–32.

Mol, Arthur P.J. (1995), *The Refinement of Production. Ecological Modernization Theory and the Chemical Industry*, Utrecht: Van Arkel.

Mol, Arthur P.J. (2001), *Globalization and Environmental Reform. The Ecological Modernization of the Global Economy*, Cambridge, MA: The MIT Press.

Mol, Arthur P.J. (2003), 'Global institutional clashes: economic versus environmental regimes', *International Journal of Sustainable Development and World Ecology*, **10**: 303–18.

Mongelard, Michaela and Kitty Warnock (2002), *Genetically Modified Crops in Africa: Promises, Problems and Threats*, Special Background briefing, London: Panos.

Moonen, Ilse (2004), *The Aflatoxin Case. Process and Impact of the EU Regulation on Aflatoxin*, The Hague: Netherlands Ministry of Foreign Affairs.

Morgan, D. (1980), *Merchants of Grain*, Harmondsworth: Penguin.

Motaal Doaa Abdel (1999), 'The Agreement on Technical Barriers to Trade, the Committee on Trade and Environment and eco-labelling', in Gary P. Sampson and W. Bradnee Chambers (eds), *Trade, Environment, and the Millennium*, Tokyo: United Nations University Press, pp. 223–38.

Motarjemi, Y., M. van Schothorst and F. Käferstein (2001), 'Future challenges in global harmonization of food safety legislation', *Food Control*, **12** (6): 339–46.

MSC (Marine Stewardship Council) (2002), *Fish 4 Thought. The MSC Quarterly Newsletter*, Issue 2, January 2002, London: MSC.

MSC (Marine Stewardship Council) (2002), *Fish Facts*, URL: http://eng.msc.org/html/content_528.htm, London: MSC.

Murdoch, Jonathan (2000), 'Networks – a new paradigm of rural development?', *Journal of Rural Studies*, **20**: 407–19.

Murphy, Craig N. (2000), 'Global governance: poorly done and poorly understood', *International Affairs*, **76** (4): 789–803.

Mutersbaugh, Tad (2005), 'Fighting standards with standards: harmonization, rents, and social accountability in certified agrofood networks', *Environment and Planning A*, **37**: 2033–51.

Myers, Ransom A. and Boris Worm (2003), 'Rapid worldwide depletion of predatory fish communities', *Nature*, **423**: 280–3.

Myhr, Anne Ingeborg and Terje Traavik (2002), 'The precautionary principle: scientific uncertainty and omitted research in the context of GMO use and release', *Journal of Agricultural and Environmental Ethics*, **15**: 73–86.

NASCO (North Atlantic Salmon Conservation Organization), (1994), *Resolution by the Parties to the Convention for the Conservation of Salmon in the North Atlantic Ocean to Minimise Impacts from Salmon Aquaculture on the Wild Salmon Stocks*, CNL (94) 53, 1994.

Naylor, Rosamund L. et al. (2000), 'Effect of aquaculture on world fish supplies', *Nature*, **405**: 1017–24.

Nestle, Marion (2002), *Food Politics. How the Food Industry Influences Nutrition and Health*, Berkeley: University of California Press.

Nestle, Marion (2003), *Safe Food. Bacteria, Biotechnology, and Bioterrorism*, Berkeley: University of California Press.

Neumayer, Erich (2001), *Greening Trade and Investment. Environmental Protection without Protectionism*, London: Earthscan Publications.

New, Michael B. and Ulf N. Wijkström (2002), *Use of Fishmeal and Fish Oil in Aquafeeds: Thoughts on the Fishmeal Trap*, FAO Fisheries Circular No. 975 FIPP/C975, Rome: FAO.

Newell, Peter (2001), *Biotechnology and the Politics of Regulation*, Brighton: Institute for Development Studies, University of Sussex.

Newell, Peter (2003), *Domesticating Global Policy on GMOs: Comparing India and China*, IDS working paper 206, Brighton: Institute for Development Studies, University of Sussex.

NFTC (National Foreign Trade Council, Inc) (2003), *Looking Behind the Curtain: The Growth of Trade Barriers that Ignore Sound Science*, Washington, DC: National Foreign Trade Council, Inc. URL: www.nftc.org (accessed 15 June 2004).

Nierenberg, Danielle (2005), *Happier Meals. Rethinking the Global Meat Industry*, World Watch Paper 171, Washington: Worldwatch Institute.

Nyangito, Hezron (2002), *Post-Doha African Challenges in the Sanitary and Phytosanitary and Trade Related Intellectual Property Rights Agreement*, KIPPRA Occasional paper, no. 4, Nairobi: Kenya Institute for Public Policy Research and Analysis.

O'Hara, Sabine U. and Sigrid Stagl (2001), 'Global food markets and their local alternatives: a socio-ecological economic perspective', *Population and Environment*, **22** (6): 533–54.

O'Rourke, Dara (2003), 'Outsourcing regulation: analyzing nongovernmental systems of labor standards and monitoring', *The Policy Studies Journal*, **31** (1): 1–29.

OECD (Organisation for Economic Co-operation and Development) (1993), *Safety Evaluation of Foods Derived by Modern Biotechnology – Concepts and Principles*, Paris: OECD.

OECD (2001), *Sustainable Consumption; Sector Case Study Series, House-hold Food Consumption: Trends, Environmental Impacts and Policy Re-sponses*, Report by the Working Party on National Environmental Policy from the Environment Policy Committee, ENV/EPOC/WPNEP (2001)13/FINAL, Paris: OECD.

OECD (2002), *Policies to Promote Sustainable Consumption: An Overview*, Report (unclassified) by the Working Party on National Environmental Policy from the Environment Policy Committee, ENV/EPOC/WPNEP (2001)18/FINAL, Paris: OECD.

*Oogst* (2001), Dutch farmers' magazine.

Oosterveer, Peter (2002), 'Reinventing risk politics: reflexive modernity and the European BSE crisis', *Journal of Environmental Policy & Planning*, **4** (3): 215–29.

Oosterveer, Peter (2004), 'Greening small and medium-sized food process-ing enterprises in Northern Thailand', *International Journal of Business and Society*, **5** (1): 58–77.

Oosterveer, Peter (2006), 'Labelling: a new arrangement in regulating global flows of food?', in Fred Buttel, Arthur P.J. Mol and Gert Spaarga-ren (eds), *Governing Environmental Flows in Global Modernity*, Cam-bridge, MA: The MIT Press, pp. 267–302.

Oostindie, Henk, Jan Douwe van der Ploeg and Henk Renting (2000), 'Farmers' experiences with and views on rural development practices and processes: outcomes of a transnational European survey', in Jan Douwe van der Ploeg, Ann Long and Jo Banks (eds), *Living Country-sides. Rural Development Processes in Europe: the State of the Art*, Doetinchem: Elsevier, pp. 213–30.

Osorio, Néstor (2002), *The Global Coffee Crisis: A Threat to Sustainable Development*, Submission to the World Summit on Sustainable Devel-opment, Johannesburg, 2002, London: International Coffee Organisation.

Ostrom, Elinor (1990), *Governing the Commons. The Evolution of Institu-tions for Collective Action*, Cambridge: Cambridge University Press.

Otsuki, Tsunehiro, John S. Wilson and Mirvat Sewadeh (2001), 'Saving two in a billion: quantifying the trade effect of European food safety stan-dards on African exports', *Food Policy*, **26**, 495–514.

Oxfam (2002a), *Mugged. Poverty in your Coffee Cup*, Oxford: Oxfam.

Oxfam (2002b), *Rigged Rules and Double Standards. Trade, Globalisation and the Fight against Poverty*, Oxford: Oxfam International.

Papadakis, Elim (2002), 'Social theory and the environment: a systems-theoretical perspective', in Riley Dunlap et al. (eds), *Sociological Theory and the Environment. Classical Foundations, Contemporary Insights*, Lanham: Rowman and Littlefield, pp. 119–43.

Papadopoulos, Yannis (2003), 'Cooperative forms of governance: problems of democratic accountability in complex environments', *European Journal of Political Research*, **42**: 473–501.

Paterson, Matthew (1999), 'Overview: interpreting trends in global environmental governance', *International Affairs*, **75** (4): 793–802.

Peoples Earth Decade (2003), *Declaration of the Regional Workshop on GM Food Aid held at Malawi Institute*, Lilongwe, URL: http://www.peoplesearthdecade.org/articles/article.php?id=86 (accessed 28 February, 2003).

Pérez-Villarreal B. and X. Aboitiz (2003), 'Characteristics of European fishery chain, GMP and needs for quality information', in J.B. Luten, J. Oehlenschläger and G. Ólafsdóttir (eds), *Quality of Fish from Catch to Consumer. Labelling, Monitoring and Traceability*, Wageningen: Wageningen Academic Publishers, pp. 43–56.

Perrow, Charles (1984), *Normal Accidents. Living with High-risk Technologies*, New York: Basic Books Inc. Publishers.

Peters, Guy and John Pierre (1998), 'Governance without government? Rethinking public administration', *Journal of Public Administration Research and Theory*, **8**: 223–43.

Peterson, M. J. (1993), 'International fisheries management', in Peter M. Haas, Robert O. Keohane and Marc A. Levy (eds), *Institutions for the Earth. Sources of Effective International Environmental Protection*, Cambridge, MA: The MIT Press, pp. 249–305.

Phillips (2000), *The BSE Inquiry: The Report. The Inquiry into BSE and variant CJD in the United Kingdom*, London: UK government, URL: http://www.bseinquiry.gov.uk (accessed 28 November, 2001).

Phillips, Peter W.B. and Heather Foster (2000), *Labelling for GM Foods: Theory and Practice*, Managing Knowledge-based Agri-food Development; Working Paper 3, Saskatoon: University of Saskatchewan.

Phyne, John and Jorge Mansilla (2003), 'Forging linkages in the commodity chain: the case of the Chilean salmon farming industry, 1987–2001', *Sociologia Ruralis*, **43** (2): 108–27.

Picciotto, Sol (2002), 'Introduction: reconceptualizing regulation in the era of globalization', *Journal of Law and Society*, **29** (1): 1–11.

Pillay, T.V.R. (1992), *Aquaculture and the Environment*, Oxford: Fishing News Books.

Pillay, T.V.R. (2001), 'Aquaculture Development: from Kyoto 1976 to Bangkok 2000, Keynote Address', in R.P. Subasinge et al. (eds), *Aquaculture in the Third Millennium. Technical Proceedings of the Conference on Aquaculture in the Third Millennium*, Bangkok, Thailand, 20–25 February, 2000, Bangkok: NACA and Rome: FAO, pp. 3–7.

Polanyi, Karl (1944), *The Great Transformation*, Boston: Beacon Press.

Ponte, Stefano (2001), *Coffee Markets in East Africa: Local Responses to Global Challenges or Global Responses to Local Challenges?*, CDR Working paper 01.5, Copenhagen: Centre for Development Research.

Ponte, Stefano (2002), *Standards, Trade and Equity: Lessons from the Specialty Coffee Industry*, CDR Working paper 02.13, Copenhagen: Centre for Development Research.

Poppe, Christian and Unni Kjaernes (2003), *Trust in Food in Europe – A Comparative Analysis*, Oslo: National Institute for Consumer Research.

Potter, Clive and Jonathan Burney (2002), 'Agricultural multifunctionality in the WTO: legitimate non-trade concern or disguised protectionism?', *Journal of Rural Studies*, **18**: 35–47.

Pretty, J.N. et al. (2005), 'Farm costs and food miles: an assessment of the full costs of the UK weekly food basket', *Food Policy*, **30**: 1–19.

Princen, Thomas (1997), 'The shading and distancing of commerce: when internationalization is not enough', *Ecological Economics*, **20**: 235–53.

Princen, Sebastiaan (2002), *EU Regulation and Transatlantic Trade*, The Hague: Kluwer International.

Public Citizen (2001), 'USDA's Mad Cow Disease Surveillance Program: a comparison of State Cattle-Testing Rates', Public Citizen, URL: http://www.citizen.org (accessed 15 March, 2005).

Raikes, Philip et al. (2000), 'Global commodity chain analysis and the French filière approach: comparisons and critique', *Economy and Society*, **29** (3): 390–417.

Raynolds, Laura T. (2000), 'Re-embedding global agriculture: the international organic and fair trade movements', *Agriculture and Human Values*, **17**: 297–309.

Raynolds, Laura T. (2002), 'Consumer/producer links in fair trade coffee networks', *Sociologia Ruralis*, **42** (4): 404–24.

Read, Paul and Teresa Fernandes (2003), 'Management of environmental impacts of marine aquaculture in Europe', *Aquaculture*, **226**: 139–63.

Reardon, T. et al. (1999), 'Global change in agrifood grades and standards: agribusiness strategic responses in developing countries', *International Food and Agribusiness Management Review*, **2** (3/4): 421–35.

Renard, Marie-Christine (1999), 'The interstices of globalization: the example of fair coffee', *Sociologia Ruralis*, **39** (4): 484–500

Renn, Ortwin (1992), 'Concepts of risk: a classification', in Sheldon Krimsky and Dominic Golding (eds), *Social Theories of Risk*, Westport: Praeger, pp. 53–79.

Renting, Henk, Tony Marsden and Jo Banks (2003), 'Understanding alternative food networks: exploring the role of short food supply chains in rural development', *Environment and Planning A*, **35** (3): 393–411.

Ritzer, G. (1996), *The McDonaldization of Society*, New York: Pine Forge Press.

Ritzer, G. (2001), *Explorations in the Sociology of Consumption. Fast Food, Credit Cards and Casinos*, London: Sage Publications.

River, Luis et al. (1998), 'Evaluation of clean technology processes in marine products processing industry', *Journal of Chemical Technology and Biotechnology*, **73**: 217–26.

Robelin, M. (2000), *At a Meeting of the Office Parlementaire d'Evaluation des Choix Scientifiques et Technologiques, 21/11/2000*, Paris: Assemblée Nationale, URL: http://www.assemblee.nationale.fr/2/oecst/c-rendus/esb.htm (accessed 17 April, 2001).

Roberts, Donna, Timothy E. Josling and David Orden (1999), *A Framework for Analyzing Technical Trade Barriers in Agricultural Markets*, US Department of Agriculture, Technical Bulletin no. 1876, Washington: USDA.

Roberts, Sarah and Nick Robins (eds) (2000), *The Reality of Sustainable Trade*, London: IIED.

Robins, Nick and Sarah Roberts (1998), *The Workbook. Environmental Responsibility in World Trade. A British Council International Conference 6–9 September 1998, London*, London: IIED.

Robinson, William I. (2001), 'Social theory and globalization: the rise of a transnational state', *Theory and Society*, **30**: 157–200.

Roheim, Cathy (2003), 'The seafood consumer; trade and the environment', in James L. Anderson (ed.), *The International Seafood Trade*, Boca Raton: CRC Press and Cambridge: WoodHead Publishing Ltd., pp. 193–204.

Roheim, Cathy A. and Holger Donath (2003), *The Battle of Taste Buds and Environmental Convictions: Which one Wins?* Unpublished.

Roozen, Nico and Frans van der Hoff (2001*)*, *Fair Trade. Het Verhaal achter Max Havelaar-koffie, Oké-bananen en Kuyichi-jeans*, Amsterdam: Van Gennep.

Rosenberry, Bob (ed.) (1997), *World Shrimp Farming 1997*, Annual Report Shrimp News International, San Diego: Shrimp News International.

Rosenberry, Bob (ed.) (2003), *The New Shrimp Farming Technology*, San Diego: Shrimp News International.

Rosso Grossman, Margaret and A. Bryan Endres (2000), 'Regulation of genetically modified organisms in the European Union', *American Behavioral Scientist (ABS)*, **44** (3): 378–434.

Roth, Dik and Ernst-Paul Zambon (2001), *Dutch Co-financing Agencies and Their Support Activities in the Field of Standardization, Certification, and Labelling*, Study commissioned by the Steering Committee for the Evaluation of the Netherlands' Co-financing Programme, The Hague: DGIS.

Rothstein, Henry (2005), 'Escaping the regulatory net: why regulatory reform can fail consumers', *Law and Policy*, **27** (4): 520–48.

Roughgarden, Jonathan (1998), 'How to manage fisheries', *Ecological Applications,* **8** (1), supplement: ecosystem management for sustainable marine fisheries, S160–64.

Rowe, Gene and Lynn Frewer (2000), 'Public participation methods: a framework for evaluation', *Science, Technology and Human Values*, **25** (1): 3–29.

Rowe, Gene, Roy Marsh and Lynn Frewer (2004), 'Evaluation of a deliberative conference', *Science, Technology and Human Values,* **29** (1): 88–121.

Rowell, Andrew (2003), *Don't Worry. It's Safe to Eat. The True Story of GM food, BSE and Foot and Mouth*, London: Earthscan Publications.

Sand, Inger-Johanne (2001), 'The legal regulation of the environment and new technologies – in view of changing relations between law, politics and science', *Zeitschrift für Rechtssoziologie*, **22** (2): 169–206.

Sandholz, Wayne (1999), 'Globalization and the evolution of rules', in Aseem Prakash and Jeffrey Hart (eds), *Globalization and Governance*, London and New York: Routledge, pp. 77–102.

Sassen, Saskia (2002), 'The state and globalization', in Rodney Bruce Hall and Thomas J. Biersteker (eds), *The Emergence of Private Authority in Global Governance*, Cambridge: Cambridge University Press, pp. 91–112.

Sassen, Saskia (2004), 'Local actors in global politics', *Current Sociology*, **52** (4): 649–70.

Schaeffer, Robert (1995), 'Free trade agreements: their impact on agriculture and the environment', in Philip McMichael (ed.), *Food and Agrarian Orders in the World Economy*, Westport: Praeger Publishers, pp. 255–75.

Schierow, Linda-Jo (2001), *IB94036: The Role of Risk Analysis and Risk Management in Environmental Protection*, Congressional Research Service (CRS) Issue Brief for Congress, Washington: The National Council for Science and the Environment (NCSE), URL: http://www.cnie.org/nle/rsk-1.html (accessed 17 April, 2004).

Schram Stokke, Olav (1997), 'Regimes as governance systems', in Oran R. Young (ed.), *Global governance. Drawing Insights from the Environmental Experience*, Cambridge, MA and London: The MIT Press, pp. 27–63.

Schram Stokke, Olav (2000), 'Managing straddling stocks: the interplay of global and regional regimes', *Ocean and Coastal Management*, **43**: 205–34.

Scoones, Ian (2001), *Science, Policy and Regulation: Challenges for Agricultural Biotechnology in Developing Countries*, Brighton: Institute for Development Studies, University of Sussex.

Scoones, Ian and Camilla Toulmin (1999), *Policies for Soil Fertility Management in Africa*, Edinburgh: IIED, Brighton: IDS and London: DFID.

Scott, James C. (1998), *Seeing like a State; How Certain Schemes to Improve the Human Condition have Failed*, New Haven and London: Yale University Press.

Seaweb (2001), 'Controversy surrounds fishery certification', *Seaweb Ocean Update*, June 2001, URL: http://www.seaweb.org (accessed 7 November, 2003).

Segerson, Kathleen (1999), 'Mandatory versus voluntary approaches to food safety', *Agribusiness*, **15** (1): 53–70.

Sénat (2001), Rapport de la Commission d'Enquète (1) sur les Conditions d'Utilisation des Farines Animales dans l'Alimentation des Animaux d'Élevage et les Conséquences qui en Résultent pour la Santé des Consommateurs, Créée en vertu d'une Résolution adoptée par le Sénat le 21 Novembre 2000, Paris: Sénat.

Shahin, Magda (1999), 'Trade and the environment: how real is the debate?', in Gary P. Sampson and W. Bradnee Chambers (eds), *Trade, Environment and the Millennium*, Tokyo: United Nations University Press, pp. 35–64.

Shaw, Martin (2000), *Theory of the Global State. Globality as an Unfinished Revolution*, Cambridge: Cambridge University Press.

Shaw, Alison (2003), 'Public understanding of food risks: expert and lay views', *FoodInfo Online Features*, 27 February, 2003, URL: http://www.foodsciencecentral.com/library.html#ifis/11831 (accessed 2 March, 2003).

Sheldon, Ian M. (2002), 'Regulation of biotechnology: will we ever "freely" trade GMOs?', *European Review of Agricultural Economics*, **29** (1): 155–76.

Silverglade, Bruce (2000), 'The WTO agreement on sanitary and phytosanitary measures: weakening food safety regulations to facilitate trade?', *Food and Drug Law Journal*, **55** (4): 517–24.

Skjaerseth, Jon Birger and Jorgen Wettestod (2002), 'Understanding the effectiveness of EU policy: how can regime analysis contribute?', *Environmental Politics*, **11** (3): 99–121.

Skladany, Mike and Craig K. Harris (1995), 'On global pond: international development and commodity chains in the shrimp industry', in Philip

McMichael (ed.), *Food and Agrarian Orders in the World Economy*, Westport: Praeger Press, pp. 169–91.

Sklair, Leslie (1999), 'Globalization', in Steve Taylor (ed.), *Sociology. Issues and Debates*, London: Macmillan, pp. 321–45.

Slovic, Paul (2000), *The Perception of Risk*, London: Earthscan Publications.

Spaargaren, Gert (1997), *The Ecological Modernization of Production and Consumption. Essays in Environmental Sociology*, PhD thesis, Wageningen: Wageningen University.

Spaargaren, Gert (2000), 'Milieurisico's, voedselketen en de consument', *Tijdschrift voor Sociaalwetenschappelijk onderzoek in de Landbouw (TSL)*, **15** (2/3): 88–97.

Spaargaren, Gert and Susan Martens (2005), 'Globalisation and the role of citizen-consumers in environmental politics', in Frank Wijen, Kees Zoeteman and Jan Pieters (eds), *A Handbook of Globalisation and Environmental Policy*, Cheltenham, UK and Northampton, MA, USA: Edward Elgar, pp. 211–45.

Speth, James Gustave (2002), 'The global environmental agenda: origins and prospects', in Daniel Esty and Maria H. Ivanova (eds), *Global Environmental Governance. Options and Opportunities*, New Haven: Yale School of Forestry and Environmental Studies, pp. 11–30.

Stone, Christopher D. (2002), 'Too many fishing boats, too few fish: can trade laws trim subsidies and restore the balance in global fisheries?', in Kevin P. Gallagher and Jacob Werksman (eds), *The Earthscan Reader on International Trade and Sustainable Development*, London: Earthscan Publications, pp. 288–323.

Stonehouse, John M. and John D. Mumford (1994), *Science, Risk Analysis and Environmental Policy Decisions*, Environment and Trade 5, Geneva: UNEP.

STT (Stichting Toekomstbeeld der Techniek) (2003), *Ocean Farming – Sustainable Exploitation of the Sea. International Case Studies*, The Hague: STT, URL: http://www.stt.nl/stt2/projecten/ocean/oceaninterna tional.htm (accessed 31 March, 2004).

Szerszynski, Bronislaw (1999), 'Risk and trust: the performative dimension', *Environmental Values*, **8**: 239–52.

Tacke, Veronika (2001), 'BSE as an organizational construction: a case study on the globalization of risk', *British Journal of Sociology*, **52** (2): 293–312.

Tacon, Albert G.J. and Ian P. Forster (2003), 'Aquafeeds and the environment: policy implications', *Aquaculture*, **226**, 181–9.

Tansey, Geoff and Tony Worsley (1995), *The Food System. A Guide*, London: Earthscan Publications.

Taylor, Eunice (2001), 'HACCP in small companies: benefit or burden?', *Food Control*, **12**: 217–22.

TAZ, *Die Tageszeitung*, several issues.

Tehranian, Majid (2002), 'Globalization and governance: an overview', in Esref Aksu and Joseph A. Camilleri (eds), *Democratizing Global Governance*, Houndmills: Palgrave Macmillan, pp. 3–27

Teng, Diana, Anne Wilcock and May Aung (2004), 'Cheese quality at farmers markets: observation of vendor practices and survey of consumer perceptions', *Food Control*, **15**: 579–87.

Tews, Kerstin, Per-Olof Busch and Helge Jörgens (2003), 'The diffusion of new environmental policy instruments', *European Journal of Political Research*, **42**: 569–600.

Thompson, Graham F. (2005), 'Is the future "regional" for global standards?', *Environment and Planning A*, **37**: 2053–71.

Tickell, Adam and Jamie A. Peck (1995), 'Social regulation after Fordism: regulation theory, neo-liberalism and the global-local nexus', *Economy and Society*, **24** (3): 357–86.

Toke, Dave (2002), 'Ecological modernisation and GM food', *Environmental Politics*, **11** (3): 145–63.

Toke, David and David Marsh (2003), 'Policy networks and the GM crops issue: assessing the utility of a dialectical model of policy networks', *Public Administration*, **81** (2): 229–51.

Tolstrup, Karl et al. (2003), *Report from the Working Group on the Coexistence of Genetically Modified Crops with Conventional and Organic Crops*, Copenhagen: Ministry of Agriculture.

Trondsen, T. et al. (2004), 'Consumption of seafood – the influence of overweight and health beliefs', *Food Quality and Preference*, **15**: 361–74.

Tsamenyi, Martin and Alistair McIlgorm (1999), *International Environmental Instruments: their Effects on the Fishing Industry*, Canberra: Fisheries Research and Development Corporation (FRDC).

UNCTAD (United Nations Conference on Trade and Development) (2004), *The Least Developed Countries Report 2004. Overview by the Secretary-General of UNCTAD*, New York and Geneva: United Nations.

UNCTAD and IISD (2003), *Sustainability in the Coffee Sector: Exploring Opportunities for International Cooperation. A. Background Document for Brainstorming Mechanisms for Sustainability in the Coffee Sector*, Geneva: UNCTAD and Winnipeg: IISD, URL: http://www.iisd.org/pdf/2003/sci_coffee_background.pdf (accessed 17 April, 2004).

United States Trade Representative (USTR) (2003), *U.S. and Cooperating Countries File WTO Case against EU Moratorium on Biotech Foods and Crops. EU's Illegal, Non-Science Based Moratorium Harmful to Agri-*

*culture and the Developing World*, Press release, May 13, 2003, Washington: US Government.

Unnevehr, Laurian J. (2001), *Shaping Globalization for Poverty Alleviation and Food Security. Food Safety and Food Quality*, IFPRI, 2020 Focus 8, brief 7, Washington: IFPRI.

Unnevehr, Laurian J. and Helen H. Jensen (1999), 'The economic implications of using HACCP as a food safety regulatory standard', *Food Policy*, **24**: 625–35.

Urry, John (2000a), 'Mobile sociology', *British Journal of Sociology*, **51** (1): 185–203.

Urry, John (2000b), *Sociology Beyond Societies. Mobilities for the Twenty-First Century*, London: Routledge.

Urry, John (2002a), *Global Complexities*, Paper presented at the World Congress of Sociology, Brisbane 2002.

Urry, John (2002b), *Mobilities, Networks and Communities*, Paper presented at the World Congress of Sociology, Brisbane 2002.

Urry, John (2003), *Global Complexity*, Cambridge: Polity Press.

Van der Belt, Henk (2003a), *Biotechnology, the US–EU Dispute and the Precautionary Principle*, Paper presented at FRONTIS Workshop 'Environmental Costs and Benefits of Transgenic Crops', Wageningen 2–4 June, 2003, Wageningen: Wageningen University.

Van der Belt, Henk (2003b), 'Debating the precautionary principle: "guilty until proven innocent" or "innocent until proven guilty"?', *Plant Physiology*, **132**: 1122–6.

Van der Meulen, Hielke S. (2000), *Circuits in de Landbouwvoedselketen. Verscheidenheid en Samenhang in de Productie en Vermarkting van Rundvlees in Midden-Italië*, Wageningen: Circle for Rural European Studies, Wageningen University.

Van der Ploeg, Jan Douwe et al. (2000a), 'Rural development: from practices and policies towards theory', *Sociologia Ruralis*, **40** (4): 391–408.

Van der Ploeg, Jan Douwe et al. (2000b), 'The socio-economic impact of rural development processes within Europe', in Jan Douwe van der Ploeg, Ann Long and Jo Banks (eds), *Living Countrysides. Rural Development Processes in Europe: the State of the Art*, Doetinchem: Elsevier, pp. 179–91.

Van Houtte, Annick (2001), 'Establishing legal, institutional and regulatory frameworks for aquaculture development and management', in R.P. Subasinge et al. (eds), *Aquaculture in the Third Millennium. Technical Proceedings of the Conference on Aquaculture in the Third Millennium, Bangkok, Thailand, 20–25 February, 2000*, Bangkok: NACA and Rome: FAO, pp. 103–20.

Van Tatenhove, Jan, Bas Arts and Pieter Leroy (eds) (2000), *Political Modernisation and the Environment: The Renewal of Environmental Policy Arrangements*, Dordrecht, Boston and London: Kluwer Academic Publishers.

Van Zwanenberg, Patrick and Erik Millstone (2003), 'BSE: a paradigm of policy failure', *The Political Quarterly*, **7** (1): 27–37.

Vidal, John (2001), 'Supermarket giants pave way for "GM-free" Britain', *The Guardian*, 26 January, 2001.

Vincent, Keith (2004), '"Mad cows" and Eurocrats – community responses to the BSE crisis', *European Law Journal*, **10** (5): 499–517.

Visser, A.J.C et al. (2000), *Crops of Uncertain Nature? Controversies and Knowledge Gaps Concerning Genetically Modified Crops*, PRI Report 12, Wageningen: Plant Research International of Wageningen University and Research.

Vogel, David (1995), *Trading Up. Consumer and Environmental Regulation in a Global Economy*, Cambridge, MA: Harvard University Press.

*Volkskrant, De* (Dutch daily newspaper) several issues.

Von Moltke, Konrad (1997), 'Institutional interactions: the structure of regimes for trade and the environment', in Oran R. Young (ed.), *Global Governance. Drawing Insights from the Environmental Experience*, Cambridge, MA and London: The MIT Press, pp. 247–72.

Vos, Timothy (2000), 'Visions of the middle landscape: organic farming and the politics of nature', *Agriculture and Human Values*, **17**: 245–56.

Wackernagel, Mathis and William Rees (1996), *Our Ecological Footprint. Reducing Human Impact on the Earth*, Gabriola Islands: New Society Publishers.

Wales, Corinne and Gabe Mythen (2002), 'Risky discourses: the politics of GM food', *Environmental Politics*, **11** (2): 121–44.

Walker, Elizabeth, Catherine Pritchard and Stephen Forsythe (2003), 'Hazard analysis critical control point and prerequisite programme implementation in small and medium size food business', *Food Control*, **14**: 169–74.

Wall, Ellen, Alfons Weersink and Clarence Swanton (2001), 'Agriculture and ISO 14000', *Food Policy*, **26**: 35–48.

Wapner, Paul (1997), 'Governance in global civil society', in Oran R. Young (ed.), *Global Governance. Drawing Insights from the Environmental Experience*, Cambridge, MA and London: The MIT Press, pp. 65–84.

Wapner, Paul (1998), 'Reorienting state sovereignty: rights and responsibilities in the environmental age', in Karen T. Litfin (ed.), *The Greening of Sovereignty in World Politics*, Cambridge, MA: The MIT Press, pp. 275–97.

Ward, Neil, Andrew Donaldson and Philip Low (2004), 'Policy framing and learning lessons from the UK's foot and mouth disease crisis', *Environment and Planning C: Government and Policy*, **22**: 291–306.

Ward, Ruby, DeeVon Bailey and Robert Jensen (2005), 'An American BSE crisis: has it affected the value of traceability and country-of-origin certifications for US and Canadian beef?, *International Food and Agribusiness Management Review*, **8** (2): 92–114.

Warde, Alan (1997), *Consumption, Food and Taste. Culinary Antinomies and the Commodity Culture*, London: Sage Publications.

Watkins, Kevin (2002), 'Is Oxfam Right to Insist that Increased Access to Northern Markets is a Solution to the Third World's Problems?', The Ecologist-website, published 22 June 2002. URL: http://www.theecologist.org/archive_article.html?article=323&category=78 (accessed 17 December, 2003).

Watson, James L. (ed.) (1997), *Golden Arches East: McDonald's in East Asia*, Stanford: Stanford University Press.

Watts, D.C.H., B. Ilbery and D. Maye (2005), 'Making reconnections in agro-food geography: alternative systems of food provision', *Progress in Human Geography*, **29** (1): 22–40.

WCED (World Commission on Environment and Development) (1987), *Our Common Future*, Oxford: Oxford University Press.

Weale, Albert (1992), *The New Politics of Pollution*, Manchester: Manchester University Press.

Weaver, Robert D. (2003), *Ex Poste Evidence on Adoption of Transgenic Crops: US Soybeans*, Paper presented at FRONTIS Workshop 'Environmental Costs and Benefits of Transgenic Crops', Wageningen, 2–4 June, 2003, Wageningen: Wageningen University.

Weber, Michael L. (2003), *What Price Farmed Fish: A Review of the Environmental and Social Costs of Farming Carnivorous Fish*, Providence: Seaweb Aquaculture Clearinghouse.

*Welt, Die* (German daily newspaper), several issues.

Wessells, Cathy R. (1998), *Barriers to International Trade in Fisheries*, Discussion paper prepared for the first FAO e-mail Conference on Fish Trade and Food Security, October–November 1998, Rome: FAO.

WFP (World Food Programme) (2002), *WFP Policy on Donations of Foods Derived from Biotechnology (GM/biotech foods)*, WFP/EB.3/2002/4-c, Rome: WFP.

Whatmore, Sarah and Lorraine Thorne (1997), 'Nourishing networks. Alternative geographies of food', in David Goodman and Michael J. Watts (eds), *Globalizing Food. Agrarian Questions and Global Restructuring*, London: Routledge, pp. 287–304.

Wijkstrom, U.N. (2003), 'Short and long-term prospects for consumption of fish', *Veterinary Research Communications*, **27** (Suppl. 1): 461–8.

World Bank (2002), *Globalization, Growth and Poverty: Building an Inclusive World Economy*, New York: World Bank and Oxford: Oxford University Press.

Woteki, Catherine E., Sandra L. Facinoli and Danielle Schor (2001), 'Keep food safe to eat: healthful food must be safe as well as nutritious', *Journal of Nutrition*, **131**: 502S–509S.

WSSD (World Summit on Sustainable Development) (2002), *Plan of Implementation*, URL: http://www.johannesburgsummit.org/html/documents/summit_docs/2309_planfinal.htm (accessed 12 December, 2003).

WTO (World Trade Organisation) (2001), *International Trade Statistics*, Geneva: WTO, URL: http://www.wto.org.

WTO (World Trade Organisation) (2002), *International Trade Statistics*, Geneva: WTO, URL: http://www.wto.org.

WTO (World Trade Organisation) (2003), *Understanding the WTO*, Geneva: WTO, URL: http://www.wto.org/english/thewto_e/whatis_e/whatis_e.htm (accessed 18 December, 2003).

WWF (World Wide Fund for Nature) (1999), *Towards Sustainable Trade: For People and the Environment*, Gland: WWF.

WWF (World Wide Fund for Nature) (2003), *Position Paper on Intensive Marine Fish Aquaculture*, Gland: WWF.

WWF Endangered Seas Campaign and WWF Australia (2000), *Community Fisheries Workshop Report. Using the MSC in Traditional, Community-Based Fisheries and Identifying Candidate Fisheries in the South Pacific*, Workshop 4 and 5 July, 2000, Sidney: WWF, Australia.

Wynne, Brian (1996), 'May the sheep safely graze', in S. Lash, B. Szerszynski and B. Wynne (eds), *Risks, Environment and Modernity: Towards a New Ecology*, London: Sage Publications, pp. 44–83.

Wynne, Brian and Kerstin Dressel (2001), 'Cultures of uncertainty – transboundary risks and BSE in Europe', in G. Sjöstedt, J. Linnerooth-Bayer and R. Löfstedt (eds), *Transboundary Risk Management*, London: Earthscan Publications, pp. 121–54.

York, Richard and Marcia Hill Gossard (2004), 'Cross-national meat and fish consumption: exploring the effects of modernization and ecological context', *Ecological Economics*, **48**: 293–302.

Young, E.M. (2004), 'Globalization and food security: novel questions in a novel context?', *Progress in Development Studies*, **4** (1): 1–21.

Young, Oran R. (1994), *International Governance: Protecting the Environment in a Stateless Society*, Ithaca: Cornell University Press.

Young, Oran R. (1997), 'Rights, rules, and resources in world affairs', in Oran R. Young (ed.), *Global Governance. Drawing Insights from the*

*Environmental Experience*, Cambridge, MA and London: The MIT Press, pp. 1–23.

Zhen, Lin and Jayant K. Routray (2003), 'Operational indicators for measuring agricultural sustainability in developing countries', *Environmental Management*, **31** (1): 34–46.

# Appendix 1: The most important arguments used by proponents and opponents of GM foods

The following considerations are used in the public debate on GMOs and indicative for the breadth of issues involved.

Several potential benefits of GMOs are identified by proponents (Batie and Ervin, 2001):

1. Yields will grow through improvements in plant efficiencies.
2. Costs of labour and agriculture inputs (including irrigation water) will reduce.
3. Food quality will be higher and value-added products can be produced.
4. The environment will benefit because more friendly methods of managing weeds and insect pests, and/or increasing yields will be applied
5. Hunger will be reduced because of the higher yields, improved storage and reduced costs of food. This is important for the middle term (2020) as the demand for food will increase substantially.
6. Pressure on the remaining limited resources of natural habitats will reduce because of the increasing yields on existing croplands.
7. Better adaptation to consumer/processor requirements (pharmaceutical crops): protein, starch and oil composition and content as well as micronutrients (such as vitamins and minerals) can be improved (Falk et al., 2002).
8. GM foods can be stored for longer periods.
9. GM crops may fit better into specific circumstances protecting crops from either biotic or abiotic stress.

Opponents on the contrary argue that the following risks exist:

A. Potential human health effects:

1. New combinations of genes may have unintended effects on the human body, such as producing unexpected toxins (McGarity and Hansen, 2001).
2. New allergenic proteins may be created (McGarity and Hansen, 2001).
3. The use of antibiotic marker genes might increase antibiotic resistance in disease-causing organisms (Millstone and Lang, 2003: 43).

B. Potential environmental effects:

4. Gene flow from GM crops into adjacent crops of the same or related species, creating unwanted pollution; it seems difficult to determine the appropriate distance needed (Myhr and Traavik, 2002).
5. Reduction of biodiversity, via limitation in the genetic variety within a certain crop and via damage to insects and to soil organisms (Myhr and Traavik, 2002).
6. Superweeds: hybridization may occur between GM crops and wild plants and, as a result, weedy relatives of commercial plants can acquire the transferred traits, making them more competitive (Löfstedt et al., 2002: 388).
7. Resistance making certain pesticides and alternative practices impossible (that is, the Bt technique is used by organic farming, but when resistance is growing because of GM crops using Bt, organic agriculture may be severely handicapped (Batie and Ervin, 2001; Cummins and Lilliston, 2000)).

C. Potential socio-economic effects:

8. Organic food producers may run into problems because they can no longer guarantee their food free from GMOs.
9. Farmers may become more dependent on a limited number of large agro-companies that provide the GM seed and the pesticide or fungicide matching with it.
10. The inventors (discoverers) of specific GM traits can apply for patenting, but the existing crop produced by generations of farmers is considered a public resource freely accessible.

Finally, ethical concerns also play an important role in public debates on GMOs, notably the question whether humans are allowed to interfere with nature ('playing God').

# Appendix 2: The international environmental instruments influencing fisheries[*]

## A. BINDING INSTRUMENTS DIRECTLY INFLUENCING FISHERIES

1.  Law of the Sea Convention (LOSC), 1982. (Imposing obligations on parties to adopt management measures to achieve a sustainable use of fisheries resources.)
2.  Agreement to Promote Compliance with International Conservation and Management Measures by Fishing Vessels on the High Seas, 1993. (Empowering parties to impose stringent conservation requirements on national fishing vessels fishing on the high seas, such as gear and by catch restrictions.)
3.  Agreement for the implementation of the Provisions of the United Nations Convention on the Law of 10 December, 1982 relating to the Conservation and Management of Straddling Fish Stocks and Highly Migratory Fish Stocks, 1995. (Provides for the conservation and management of straddling fish stocks and highly migratory fish stocks on the high sea; and in limited circumstances, it also applies to fisheries management in the EEZ.)

## B. BINDING INSTRUMENTS INDIRECTLY INFLUENCING FISHERIES

1.  Convention on Wetlands of International Importance. Especially as Waterfowl Habitat (RAMSAR Convention), 1971. (Preventing the loss of habitats through encouraging the wise use of all wetlands.)
2.  Convention Concerning the Protection of the World Cultural and Natural Heritage (World Heritage Convention), 1972. (The conservation of natural and cultural areas of outstanding universal value through their

inclusion on a World Heritage List and a List of World Heritage in Danger.)

3. Convention on International Trade in Endangered Species of Wild Fauna and Flora (CITES), 1973. (Prevent the over-exploitation of endangered species of flora and fauna by means of import and export permits identified in the appendices to the Convention.)

4. Convention for the Conservation of Migratory Species of Wild Animals (Bonn Convention), 1979. (Protect species of wild animals that migrate across national boundaries.)

5. Convention on Biodiversity (CBD), 1992. (The conservation of biological diversity and the promotion of the sustainable use of its components. In 1995, the Jakarta Mandate specifically addressed the relationships between conservation and fishing activities and established coastal and marine biodiversity as one of the first substantive sectors to be considered.)

## C. NON-BINDING INSTRUMENTS INFLUENCING FISHERIES

1. Agenda 21 (UNCED), 1992. (Chapter 17 requires the international community to address environmental issues that affect the marine environment in a comprehensive manner.)

2. FAO Code of Conduct for Responsible Fishing, 1994. (Giving guidelines for responsible approaches to fishing.)

3. Kyoto Declaration, 1995. (Identifying the critical link between food security and the sustainability of fisheries, which contributes to the income, wealth and food security of all people.)

## NOTE

\* Based on Tsamenyi and McIlgorm, 1999, pp. 8-9.

# Index